Old England, New England,
and the Civil War

Old England, New England, and the Civil War

How a Clash of Cultures Ignited a Global Campaign for Racial Equality and Civil Rights

LEN GOUGEON

Cover credit: "They can't fight" by Frederick Opper, published by Keppler & Schwarzman (1896). Courtesy of the Library of Congress.

Published by State University of New York Press, Albany

© 2025 State University of New York

All rights reserved

Printed in the United States of America

No part of this book may be used or reproduced in any manner whatsoever without written permission. No part of this book may be stored in a retrieval system or transmitted in any form or by any means including electronic, electrostatic, magnetic tape, mechanical, photocopying, recording, or otherwise without the prior permission in writing of the publisher.

Links to third-party websites are provided as a convenience and for informational purposes only. They do not constitute an endorsement or an approval of any of the products, services, or opinions of the organization, companies, or individuals. SUNY Press bears no responsibility for the accuracy, legality, or content of a URL, the external website, or for that of subsequent websites.

EU GPSR Authorised Representative:
Logos Europe, 9 rue Nicolas Poussin, 17000, La Rochelle, France
contact@logoseurope.eu

For information, contact State University of New York Press, Albany, NY
www.sunypress.edu

Library of Congress Cataloging-in-Publication Data

Name: Gougeon, Len, author.
Title: Old England, New England, and the Civil War : how a clash of
   cultures ignited a global campaign for racial equality and civil
   rights / Len Gougeon.
Description: Albany : State University of New York Press, [2025] | Includes
   bibliographical references and index.
Identifiers: LCCN 2024042800 | ISBN 9798855802122 (hardcover : alk. paper) |
   ISBN 9798855802139 (ebook) | ISBN 9798855802115 (pbk. : alk. paper)
Subjects: LCSH: United States—History—Civil War, 1861-1865—Foreign public
   opinion, British. | New England—Intellectual life—19th century. | Great Britain—
   Intellectual life—19th century. | Great Britain—Politics and government—
   1837-1901. | United States—Foreign relations—Great Britain. | Great Britain—
   Foreign relations—United States.
Classification: LCC E469.8 .G68 2025 | DDC 973.7/2—dc23/eng/20250203
LC record available at https://lccn.loc.gov/2024042800

For Deborah,

my North Star

Contents

Acknowledgments		ix
Abbreviations		xi
Introduction		1
Chapter 1	1860: Slavery, Race, and the Seeds of Cultural Conflict	11
Chapter 2	1861: As Civil War Approaches, the Debate over Slavery Intensifies at Home and Abroad	25
Chapter 3	War Against Slavery at Home Brings Conflict Abroad	37
Chapter 4	The North Suffers a Humiliating Defeat: British Critics Gloat	53
Chapter 5	The Old World and the New Collide: The *Trent* Affair Brings the Threat of War	75
Chapter 6	1862: Talk of Emancipation Fuels British Fears of a Global Race War	85
Chapter 7	Union Victories Temper British Critics	99
Chapter 8	The North Suffers Military Reversals: British Consider Intervention	119

Chapter 9	Lincoln Proclaims Emancipation as Race Takes Center Stage	137
Chapter 10	Midterm Elections Focus on Race	153
Chapter 11	1863: As the Civil War Becomes a Second Revolution, Conflict with Great Britain Looms	165
Chapter 12	British Conservatives React with Alarm as Race and Class Become Central Issues	179
Chapter 13	New England Liberals Herald the Rise of the "African American": British Critics Scoff	197
Chapter 14	Union Victories and Colored Soldiers Change the Course and Complexion of the War	209
Chapter 15	Lincoln Affirms Commitment to Emancipation: Animosity Toward Great Britain Deepens	227
Chapter 16	Lincoln Speaks for Equality: The Anglo-American Divide Widens	241
Chapter 17	1864: The "Negro Question" Spurs Intense International Debate	253
Chapter 18	Republican Radicals Declare Slavery Must Go: British Call for "Regulated Coercion"	269
Chapter 19	Atlanta Falls and Lincoln Rises: British Criticism Intensifies	279
Chapter 20	1865: The Civil War Ends, but the Battle for Human Rights Continues	291
Epilogue		309
Notes		315
Bibliography		361
Index		381

Acknowledgments

Over the many years that mark the gestation of this study, I accumulated a mountain of debt owed to the many institutions and individuals that contributed to its making. Among the former are the administrations and staffs of the several libraries and archives that provided invaluable help in locating and accessing the multitude of magazines, newspapers, pamphlets, personal journals and correspondence, miscellaneous documents, and other primary materials that provide the foundation upon which this study rests. These institutions include the Houghton Library, Harvard University; the Rare Books and Manuscripts Department of the Boston Public Library; the Library of Congress, Serials Collection; the Concord Free Public Library; the Eisenhower Library, Birney Antislavery Collection, Johns Hopkins University; the Massachusetts Historical Society, Boston; the Newberry Library, Chicago; the New York Public Library, Serials Collection; the Thomas Cooper Library and the South Caroliniana Library, University of South Carolina, Columbia; the Wilson Library, Southern History Collection, University of North Carolina at Chapel Hill; the Arthur & Elizabeth Schlesinger Library, Radcliffe Institute for Advanced Study, Harvard; and the Interlibrary Loan and Research Departments, Weinberg Memorial Library, the University of Scranton.

Additionally, throughout my long scholarly career I have had the good fortune to enjoy the friendship of many gifted scholars who have contributed, both directly and indirectly, to my work. To name all of these individuals would require more space than is available here. And so I will limit myself to those who were kind enough to read and comment on various parts of this study as it evolved and who provided much advice and encouragement along the way. Foremost among these are the late Joel Myerson and Robert Richardson. Their vast knowledge of the period and its major figures, as well as their kind friendship, were invaluable to me and something for which I will be forever grateful. Others include Philip Gura, Lawrence Buell, Robert Gross, Henry Louis Gates Jr., Jay Parini, Wesley Mott, Kenneth Sacks, David M. Robinson, Albert von Frank, Sandra Petrulionis, Robert Habich, Daniel Malachuk, Phyllis Cole, Helen Deese, and my colleague historian Adam Pratt. I am especially indebted to another colleague, dear friend, and gifted writer, Carl Schaffer, who, in a remarkable instance of enduring friendship and intellectual stamina, read through the many iterations of this study as it went through a multitude of drafts of interminable length. His comments, suggestions, and corrections were invaluable in improving both the content and style of the final product.

I wish also to thank the legions of student research assistants who are, literally, too numerous to mention individually. This study would not have been possible without their able assistance. The same could be said for my departmental secretary, Melissa Eckenrode, whose generous help in preparing my manuscript went well beyond her job description, the National Endowment for the Humanities for support that came in a variety of forms over the years, and the Faculty Research Committee of the University of Scranton for innumerable travel and research grants.

Finally, closer to home, I would like to thank my daughter, Nadia Lynn Dunn, who spent many hours by my side in various archives reeling through what must have seemed like endless miles of microfilm. And last, my wife, Deborah, whose unflagging support and irrepressible optimism reassured me throughout this very long process that I was, indeed, writing a book.

Abbreviations

Works

AL   *A Cycle of Adams Letters, 1861–1865* Edited by Worthington Chauncey Ford. 2 vols. Boston: Houghton Mifflin, 1920.

ArL   *The Letters of Matthew Arnold*. Edited by Cecil Y. Lang. 2 vols. Charlottesville: University Press of Virginia, 1997.

CCD   *The Correspondence of Charles Darwin*. Edited by Frederick Burkhardt et al. 30 vols. Cambridge: Cambridge University Press, 1985–2023.

CEC   *The Correspondence of Emerson and Carlyle* by Ralph Waldo Emerson and Thomas Carlyle. Edited Joseph Slater. New York: Columbia University Press, 1964.

CWL   *The Collected Works of Abraham Lincoln*. Edited by Roy P. Basler. 10 vols. New Brunswick, NJ: Rutgers University Press, 1953.

DL   *The Letters of Charles Dickens*. Edited by Graham Storey et al. 10 vols. Oxford: Clarendon Press, 1998.

EAW   *Emerson's Antislavery Writings*. Edited by Len Gougeon and Joel Myerson. New Haven, CT: Yale University Press, 1995.

E-CL   *Emerson-Clough Letters* by Ralph Waldo Emerson and Arthur Hugh Clough. Edited by Howard Lowry and Ralph Rusk. 1934. Reprint, Hamden, CT: Archon Books, 1968.

ECW   *The Collected Works of Ralph Waldo Emerson*. Edited by Alfred R. Ferguson et al. 10 vols. Cambridge, MA: Harvard University Press, 1971–2013.

EEL   *The Letters of Ellen Tucker Emerson.* Edited by Edith E. Gregg. 2 vols. Kent, OH: Kent State University Press, 1982.

EJ   *The Journals and Miscellaneous Notebooks of Ralph Waldo Emerson.* Edited by William H. Gilman et al. 16 vols. Cambridge, MA: Harvard University Press, 1960–82.

EL   *The Letters of Ralph Waldo Emerson.* Edited by Ralph L. Rusk and Eleanor M. Tilton. 10 vols. New York: Columbia University Press, 1939, 1990–95.

ELL   *The Later Lectures of Ralph Waldo Emerson: 1843–1871.* Edited by Ronald Bosco and Joel Myerson. 2 vols. Athens: University of Georgia Press, 2001.

EUL   *Uncollected Lectures by Ralph Waldo Emerson.* Edited by Clarence Gohdes Jr. New York: William Edwin Rudge, 1932.

EW   *The Complete Works of Ralph Waldo Emerson.* Edited by Edward Waldo Emerson. 12 vols. Boston: Houghton, Mifflin, 1903–4.

GL   *The Letters of Mrs. Gaskell* by Elizabeth Gaskell. Edited by J. A. V. Chapple and Arthur Pollard. Cambridge, MA: Harvard University Press, 1967.

HLL   *Life and Letters of Oliver Wendell Holmes.* Edited by John T. Morse Jr. 2 vols. Cambridge, MA: Riverside, 1896.

HW   *The Centenary Edition of the Works of Nathaniel Hawthorne.* Edited by William Charvat et al. 23 vols. Columbus: Ohio State University Press, 1963–75.

LL   *The Letters of James Russell Lowell.* Edited by Charles Eliot Norton. 2 vols. New York: Harper & Brothers, 1894.

LongL *The Letters of Henry Wadsworth Longfellow.* Edited by Andrew Hilen. 6 vols. Cambridge, MA: Belknap Press of Harvard University Press, 1972.

MCW   *Collected Works of John Stuart Mill.* Edited by Francis Mineka et al. 33 vols. Toronto: University of Toronto Press, 1963–91.

ML   *The Correspondence of John Lothrop Motley.* Edited by George William Curtis. 2 vols. New York: Harper & Brothers, 1889.

NL *Letters of Charles Eliot Norton, with Biographical Comment.* Edited by Sara Norton and M. A. DeWolfe Howe. 2 vols. Boston: Houghton Mifflin, 1913.

R-NC *The Correspondence of John Ruskin and Charles Eliot Norton.* Edited by John Lewis Bradley and Ian Ousby. Cambridge: Cambridge University Press, 1987.

TL *The Letters of Anthony Trollope.* Edited by John Hall. 2 vols. Stanford, CA: Stanford University Press, 1993.

Archives

BPL   Rare Books and Manuscripts Department, Boston Public Library

CPL   Concord Free Public Library

EL   Birney Antislavery Collection, Eisenhower Library, Johns Hopkins University

HL   Houghton Library, Harvard University

LC   Library of Congress, Serials Collection

MHS   Massachusetts Historical Society

NL   Newberry Library, Civil War Manuscripts

NYP   New York Public Library, Serials Collection

TCL   Thomas Cooper Library, Joel Myerson Collection, University of South Carolina

SCL   South Caroliniana Library, Newspaper Collection, University of South Carolina

SL   Arthur & Elizabeth Schlesinger Library, Radcliffe Institute for Advanced Study

WL   Wilson Library, University of North Carolina, Chapel Hill

Introduction

This study tells for the first time the story of a bitter cultural and political conflict that arose between Great Britain and the North during the Civil War. While it involved many issues early on, the conflict eventually focused on one: the viability of a liberal democracy based on the idea that "all men are created equal." Ultimately, it precipitated a reevaluation of each nation's differing beliefs regarding racial equality in particular and human rights in general. These ideas, controversial then, remain a source of controversy today.

The question in contention was this: What type of social, political, and cultural paradigm was best suited to ensure the advancement of civilization—one in which all have equal rights, regardless of race or class, or one where a small number of privileged white elites exercise a controlling power? New England liberals, and eventually most of the North, embraced the former, while the South and the conservative governing class of Great Britain were wedded to the latter. The British believed that social hierarchies were dictated by natural law and that equality was a pernicious democratic myth. While theoretically opposed to slavery, they saw it as an unfortunate, but ultimately tolerable, by-product of a social system where everyone knew their place. They denied that slavery was the cause of the war and insisted that the North's desire to dominate the South was the real culprit. The result was a bitter alienation that grew more intense as the war progressed. The combatants included many of each nation's foremost writers and intellectuals. In America, these were almost all New Englanders.

Despite the claims of British conservatives, it was clear from the start that the South went to war to preserve slavery. Alexander Stephens, the Confederacy's vice president, proclaimed at the outset that the new nation's "foundations are laid, its corner-stone rests upon the great truth that the negro is not equal to the white man; that slavery—subordination to the superior race—is his natural and normal condition. This, our new government," he declared, "is the first, in the history of the world, based upon this great physical, philosophical, and moral truth."[1] The cause in the North, initially, was to preserve the Union, a Union that included slavery. As the war went on, however, most Northerners came to recognize that slavery had caused the war and that a lasting reunion was impossible with slavery still in place. Abraham Lincoln's dramatic Emancipation Proclamation, coming at the war's midpoint, was not only a major step leading to the abolition of slavery but also an affirmation of the president's belief that the Founding Fathers intended to establish a nation "dedicated to the proposition that all men are created equal."[2]

Early on in the war, the New England intelligentsia, motivated by a tradition of idealism, began to promote the liberal values of racial equality and universal human rights. New England at the time was home to the most highly regarded writers and thinkers in America. Foremost among them was Ralph Waldo Emerson. The group also included other luminaries such as James Russell Lowell, Henry Wadsworth Longfellow, John Greenleaf Whittier, Oliver Wendell Holmes, Lydia Maria Child, Harriet Beecher Stowe, Charles Eliot Norton, George W. Curtis, and Richard Henry Dana Jr. Several were members of Boston's prestigious Saturday Club. Even before Lincoln's proclamation, these writers were vigorously promoting freedom and equal rights for all. In an address at the Smithsonian Institute in January 1862, Emerson declared, "Emancipation is the demand of civilization." In a lecture that fall he went even further, stating that the laws should ensure that "every man shall . . . have an equal vote in the state, and a fair chance in society," regardless of race.[3] Other New England idealists were equally emphatic.

The New England intelligentsia's commitment to the principle of equal rights for all caused a deep alienation between them and the intelligentsia of Old England. At the height of the war, Holmes wrote in the April 1864 *Atlantic Monthly* that the North's renewed commitment to equal rights had revived the animosity of 1776. The New Englanders saw the Civil War as America's "second Revolution." In England it was no more welcome than the first. At that time, Holmes argued, "the true-born Briton read as far as the first sentence of the second paragraph of the Declaration of Independence ["We hold these truths to be self-evident, that all men are created equal . . ."]. There he stopped, and there he has stuck ever since. That sentence has been called a 'glittering generality,'—as if there were some shallow insincerity about it. . . . [But] 'glittering generality' or not," he insisted, "the voice which proclaimed that the birthright of equality belonged to all mankind was the *fiat lux* of the new-born political universe, . . . threatening all the dynasties, menacing all the hierarchies, undermining the seemingly solid foundations of all Old-World abuses."[4]

The British governing class took this threat very seriously. At the time, England ruled a vast global empire, one populated largely by dark-skinned "others" who were subject to the rule of what Stephens referred to as "the superior race." Before the war, Great Britain had been widely admired by Northern reformers as a model for liberal progress, having abolished slavery in the British West Indies, its last remnant in the empire, in 1833. The British also embraced a tradition of individual rights dating back to the Magna Carta in the thirteenth century, but freedom had its limits in Victorian England. British society, like the British Empire, divided power in accordance with a well-defined hierarchy based on the Victorian notions of class, caste, and race. The latter two were most important in the far reaches of the empire, where the principle of white supremacy was fundamental to British rule. In England itself, class was the determining factor. The bête noire of this social, political, and cultural paradigm was American democracy, not the oligarchy of the South where white supremacy was a given but the growing liberal democracy of the North.

A bitter war of words between New and Old England ensued. This cultural conflict brought into relief the dominant ideological characteristics of each sphere. The North became more liberal, while the essentially conservative nature of British governance became more prominent. The role played by the British in what came to be a dramatic redefining of American identity was an important one. Their opposition to liberal democracy elicited increasing support for it in the North, especially among New Englanders. Emerson described this phenomenon succinctly. "The men in the street by no means think Emancipation a primary duty," he observed, "but the moment they meet the Englishman or the Frenchman and would reproach him with the virtual aid he gives to slavery, they are prepared to show that the North is for liberty, that this is substantially a war for freedom, and that all the honest and civil portions of mankind ought to be with us."[5]

By the end of the war, the principles of liberal democracy were clearly to the fore and gaining. Attitudes toward race in America had changed dramatically. The courage and heroism displayed by the Union army's nearly 200,000 Black soldiers had a great deal to do with it. This service, as David Blight notes, was absolutely critical for "the irrevocable recognition of [their] manhood and citizenship."[6] The activities of these United States Colored Troops were followed closely by the Northern press, especially *Harper's Weekly* and the *Atlantic Monthly*. Throughout the war, New England's leading liberals were at the forefront of what became an international crusade for the rights of man. By the war's end, most Northern Americans, people whom the British frequently disparaged as the "mottled masses," considered universal human rights as the sine qua non of a civilized society. They also saw American diversity as a strength rather than a weakness, as the British and the Confederates consistently claimed.

This process of liberalization emerged steadily over the course of the war. As it evolved, emancipation came to be seen by many as just the first step in a global movement toward the recognition of universal human rights. The British governing class saw this development as a threat to the stability of the British Empire, at home as well as abroad. Their concern was well founded. The Sepoy Mutiny in India, the crown jewel of the British Empire, had been put down with great violence and bitterness just two years before the firing on Fort Sumter.[7] It was a costly and painful object lesson for the British of what can happen when indigenous people are aroused.

Conservative MP and future prime minister Robert Cecil was one of the most vociferous British critics. He argued with intense conviction in the *Quarterly Review* of July 1861 that "the rights of man were a beautiful subject for theory-drawing in the study, but no one had dreamed of applying them to the actual wants of life." This liberal theory, he insisted, was politically implausible and culturally corrosive. An article in *Fraser's Magazine* from April 1861 offered an example. The author declared that the literature of America was inferior to the British model because of the leveling effect of democracy, especially the notion of racial equality. He took specific aim at New England. Race was at the center of his argument. In New England, he noted, "slavery has been proclaimed a crime by the preacher, the poet, and novelist," and "they are, as it were, maddened to do good, and to destroy evil." Such fanaticism, the writer insisted, was not conducive to the creation of a great culture because it blinded one to the facts. "The poets of the Northern United States have judged slavery from their own mental and moral standpoint," he observed. As a result, "the care-free, hog-and-hominy, and possum-eating Negro is elevated, in the mind and heart of the poet, to his own plane," a perversion of reality that, presumably, would never happen among England's literary sages.[8]

In England, the common workingman was seen by many in the governing class as the equivalent of America's "possum-eating Negro." In the face of a growing demand for social reform that would extend political rights to workingmen, British conservatives defended the status quo. For them, the American Civil War provided a timely and telling example of the dangers of liberal democracy, especially the pitfalls of equal rights and universal male suffrage.

British workers, however, had a different view. The liberal movement in the North energized a similar movement in England in a way that had not been seen since the agitation of the Chartists a decade earlier. As the antislavery aspect of the war became more prominent, these workers aligned with the North as the defenders of free labor and the rights of common people everywhere. The Emancipation Proclamation confirmed this alignment in a dramatic way. Young Henry Adams (whose father, Charles Francis Adams, served as the American minister to Great Britain throughout the war) witnessed its impact.

Adams wrote to his brother Charles from London just weeks after the Emancipation Proclamation went into effect. It "is creating an almost convulsive reaction in our favor all over this country," Adams said. "The *London Times* [is] furious and scolds like a drunken drab," while the "vast mass of the lower orders" showed enthusiastic support for the Union cause. The previous evening, young Adams had attended "a democratic and socialist meeting" that quickly assumed "a tone and proportions that are quite novel and alarming in this capital. . . . They met to notify Government that 'they would not tolerate' interference against us. I can assure you," he told Charles, "this sort of movement is as alarming here as a slave insurrection would be in the South." British workers, he noted, were now "making common cause with us."[9]

As British workers expressed strong support, British liberals criticized their country's growing hostility toward the North. Writing in the *Westminster Review* in October 1862, John Stuart Mill, one of the relatively few British intellectuals to support the Union cause, asked rhetorically why "the general voice of our press, the general sentiment of our people, [is] bitterly reproachful to the North, while for the South, the aggressors in the war, we have either mild apologies or direct and downright encouragement?" The primary reason for this, he believed, was the North's increasingly liberal attitude toward race. "It must be remembered," Mill wrote, "that though the English public are averse to slavery, several of the political and literary organs which have most influence over the public are decidedly not so. For many years," he asserted, "the [London] *Times* has taken every opportunity of throwing cold water . . . on the cause of the negro," as had other conservative publications.[10] This practice intensified considerably during the war.

The British governing class obviously had a vested interest in preserving a social hierarchy based on class, caste, and race, and most major journals and newspapers reflected this. The benefit of such a system for them was clear. What was not clear was why so many of England's finest writers and intellectuals, people who considered themselves enlightened progressives, would align with a feudalistic, slaveholding oligarchy rather than a liberal democracy. With the benefit of historical perspective, the answer, in part at least, lies in the fact that they were major shareholders in what Edward Said calls an "imperial culture."

According to Said, "culture is a concept that includes a refining and elevating element, each society's reservoir of the best that has been known and thought, as Matthew Arnold put it in the 1860s."[11] For most Victorian authors, that "refining and elevating element" had a distinctly imperial hue. By the mid-nineteenth century, Great Britain was at the top of its game. The British Empire was a powerful, massive, and complex organization of territories and colonies that spread around the globe. Despite the fact that England exercised an absolute and, at times, extremely oppressive imperial authority over all these entities, most British intellectuals—even those who, like Arnold, considered themselves liberals—believed that Great Britain was the freest, most enlightened and progressive nation on earth. There was much to support this view. The abolition of slavery throughout the empire and England's concerted effort to suppress the international slave trade placed them in a position of moral superiority over the United States, where slavery was not only tolerated but actually considered by its defenders to be a necessary good.

Great Britain's abolition of slavery, however, did not mean the abolition of racism. Britain's vast empire was populated by a variety of indigenous peoples who were seen as inferior "others." They were distinguished by caste and class and, most importantly, by race. The last of these was especially significant because the concept of natural racial inferiority provided moral cover for Great Britain's occupation and exploitation of vast territories that were wrested from native populations. Victorians believed their empire was a source of benefit to these "benighted" masses. The imposition of this "benefit," they felt, required forceful leadership and discipline, especially where there was resistance, as in the case of the Sepoys. They insisted that the imposition of a clearly defined social hierarchy was a major element in establishing and maintaining a proper, civilized society, both at home and abroad.

These stark cultural and political differences between conservative Old England and liberal New England (and, eventually, the rest of the North) made conflict all but inevitable. As Said notes, "culture is a sort of theater where various political and ideological causes engage one another. Far from being a placid realm of Apollonian gentility, culture can even be a battleground on which causes expose themselves to the light of day and contend with one another."[12] Such was the case throughout the Civil War as the forces of American liberalism and British conservatism clashed in a transatlantic arena.

The vast majority of England's creative class of writers, poets, and intellectuals supported the conservative position. They not only favored the Confederacy, overtly or covertly, but they frequently offered bitter criticisms of the North and its democratic "common man" culture in Great Britain's most popular and influential magazines, journals, and newspapers.[13] Among them were Thomas Carlyle; Matthew Arnold; John Ruskin; Charles Dickens; poet laureate Alfred, Lord Tennyson; William Makepeace Thackeray; Charles Kingsley; and several others. As the war went on, the New England intelligentsia vigorously promoted the liberal values of racial equality and universal human rights, while most of England's intelligentsia defended with equal vigor the conservative notion of a social hierarchy based on class, caste, and race. The bitter war of words that ensued would have lasting consequences in both countries.

This study presents the Civil War and the struggle for human rights that it ignited from the perspective of those who experienced it, day by day. These include not only notable intellectuals, artists, and political figures but also common soldiers and their families, members of the working class, slaves and freedmen, journalists, correspondents, professional commentators, and religious leaders. It is based on an examination of several thousand primary documents, both public and private, including newspapers, weekly journals, magazines, addresses, lectures, pamphlets, diaries, personal journals, and private correspondence from both sides of the Atlantic. Most of this material is drawn from archives. The focus on the American side is largely on New England, but material from other parts of the country is also included.

British materials include a broad selection of Great Britain's most influential magazines and newspapers. All of these had a strong interest in American affairs, and many were published in American editions. The content of the London *Times* and the *Saturday Review* was widely reported and frequently reprinted in newspapers and magazines throughout the country. The *Living Age*, published in Boston by Littell and Co., for example, specialized in reprinting the content of British magazines and newspapers, filling sixty double-column pages per month with articles and items, primarily those dealing with the United States.[14] It attracted many readers, including Emerson. This study also draws extensively from the private correspondence, published and unpublished, of major Victorians, including artists, intellectuals, and members of the British government. There is also the private correspondence of less well-known British figures, drawn from archival files.

The organization here is chronological. Significant developments and reactions to them are presented as they occurred, "in real time," as journals, newspapers, and personal correspondence crossed from shore to shore. What emerges is a lively and often acerbic transatlantic colloquy between formidable ideological combatants concerning the future of liberal democracy and the struggle for human rights. All of this transpired as the most important conflict of the century played out on American battlefields.

The result is an account of the war as seen through the eyes of the participants. The story is told in large part using their own words. These words often have a tone and meaning different from those inflected by an historical perspective. Thus, at several critical points in the conflict, many were convinced that an Anglo-American war was not only possible but inevitable. That "fact" had a huge and lasting impact on the way each side viewed the other. Furthermore, reading their commentaries in the immediate context of an ongoing horrible and bloody conflict that touched virtually every citizen personally reveals a depth of emotion that an objective historical account, written many years after the fact, cannot communicate.

Additionally, throughout the war, reports and editorials published in newspapers and journals were often wrong, many purposely so. "Fake news" was common in British journals, which often relied on materials provided by Southern propagandists. The prestigious London *Times* frequently published reports based on rumors and half-truths that were rife with errors and deliberate misrepresentations and omissions. Often, developments favorable to the North were simply ignored. All of this served only to fuel the growing animosities, suspicions, and mistrust on both sides.

Historical accounts rarely report on such matters, since they proved to be inaccurate, products of the fog of war. At the time, however, these reports were a continuing source of fear, anxiety, and anger. The effects were lasting. While before the war many Americans, especially New Englanders, were pleased to think of themselves as "Anglo Americans," after the war most saw themselves as different from, and superior to, their elite English cousins. As Samuel Huntington points out in *The Clash of Civilizations*, "people define their identity by what they are not."[15] By the war's end, American culture had acquired a new and unique identity. Americans were no longer "Englishmen in their shirt-sleeves," as a British commentator once described them.[16] They were now simply Americans.

Chapter 1

1860

Slavery, Race, and the Seeds of Cultural Conflict

One of the leading causes of conflict between New and Old England during the Civil War was the initial failure of the British to acknowledge that the North was fighting against slavery. Transcendentalism was a widely influential force among a broad and diverse swath of the Northern population, especially in New England. The movement was strongly antislavery. Emerson was a major force in this movement. Black Transcendentalists like William C. Nell, Henry Highland Garnet, and Alexander Crummell organized Transcendental clubs that promoted Black activism. As one scholar notes, these Black reformers helped shape the "political unconscious of Boston radicalism" at the time.[1] Beginning in the 1840s, Transcendental idealists like Emerson, Henry David Thoreau, Samuel Joseph May, Bronson Alcott, and others formed a de facto alliance with established antislavery organizations like William Lloyd Garrison's American Anti-Slavery Society. Eventually, nearly every Transcendentalist became a vigorous supporter of the antislavery cause.[2]

During this same period, the British intellectual class grew increasingly reactionary. Their response to the revolutionary spirit sweeping through Europe in the late 1840s was largely conservative, as was their response to the Chartists, the world's first independent movement for the rights of the working class. New England liberals, however, applauded what they saw in Europe as evidence of a broad movement toward democratization.[3] These pronounced differences were a sign of things to come.

Europe was in a state of revolutionary upheaval in 1848. Emerson was on a lecture tour of England at the time. He was well known in Great Britain and was considered the most influential American author among British intellectuals.[4] During his visit, Emerson witnessed demonstrations by the Chartists in London and the revolutionaries in Paris. These experiences had a profound effect on his thinking about England, social reform, and the future of American democracy. The Chartists were agitating for greater working-class representation in government. There were Chartist demonstrations in London almost every day. Emerson attended a gathering on March 9, 1848, called to celebrate recent events in France. Although he was at first disturbed by what seemed to be the random violence and lack of leadership evidenced in these demonstrations, eventually he came to sympathize with the cause.

As a result of his experience in England, Emerson became increasingly critical of British culture, especially as represented by the British literary class. For the most part, these elite intellectuals refused to support the lowly Chartists, despite the fact that they thought of themselves as progressive, liberal thinkers. Chief among these was Matthew Arnold. Although a self-declared "Liberal," Arnold thought of himself as "a Liberal tempered by experience, reflection, and renouncement."[5] He met Emerson in England and attended a Chartist rally just a month after Emerson did, but he had a very different reaction. While he was "much struck with the ability of the speakers," Arnold told his mother that he "should be very sorry to live under their government" and added "nor do I intend to." He reported in the same letter that Emerson told him that "he gives our institutions, . . . aristocracy, Church, etc., five years" before they succumb and that "a European revolution was inevitable."[6]

Like other Transcendentalists, Emerson had a deep respect for the dignity of labor and felt that English scholars and poets like Arnold should support the Chartists.[7] In his journal he wrote, "I fancied, when I heard that the times were anxious & political, that there is to be a Chartist revolution on Monday next, and an Irish revolution in the following week, that the right scholar would feel now was the hour to test his genius. . . . Let him produce its Charter now, & try whether it cannot win a hearing."[8] But the Victorian sages remained silent.

This fault line was indicative of a fundamental difference between the volatility of America's liberal democracy and the inherent conservatism of the Victorian worldview. Emerson and Arnold were on opposite wavelengths.[9] Arnold felt the intellectual's role was to offer stability in the face of chaos. His goal was to find in literature things "to know," "to learn," and "to propagate," while Emerson's goal was "to unsettle all things."[10] In this regard, Arnold and Emerson could hardly be more different, operating as they were from opposite ends of a Norman-Saxon cultural tradition, one a Cavalier Royalist, the other a Puritan revolutionary.[11] Arnold's strong aversion to liberal democracy underlies his criticism of the North during the war. It also explains his failure to criticize the conservative, hierarchical South or even the institution of slavery, a trait he shared with most other Victorian elites. These profound differences were the seeds of the cultural conflict that erupted during the war.[12]

Tensions in America over the issue of slavery grew throughout the tumultuous 1850s. Open warfare broke out in Kansas in 1856 as Free-Soil farmers, many from Massachusetts, defended themselves against repeated attacks by Border Ruffians from Missouri. The conflict in "Bleeding Kansas" soon gave rise to a charismatic militant hero who emerged as the leader of the Free-Soil partisans, John Brown. It was in the midst of this turmoil that the *Atlantic Monthly* was born.

From the beginning, the *Atlantic* was the voice of Northern liberalism. The list of its core contributors was a veritable who's who of New England's literati. Included were Emerson, John Greenleaf Whittier, James Russell Lowell, Oliver Wendell Holmes, Henry Wadsworth Longfellow, John Lothrop Motley, Richard Henry Dana Jr., Thomas Wentworth Higginson, and others.[13] While the prospectus promised that the *Atlantic* would be the "organ of no party or clique," it was clear from the start that the magazine was passionately antislavery.[14] Lowell was the first editor. Under him and his successor, publisher James T. Fields, the *Atlantic* projected what one critic calls "an aggressive liberalism" and a "politics of moral principle."[15] Throughout the war years, the *Atlantic*'s political commentary "was generally cast in terms of an Emersonian moral evolution."[16]

Emerson's Transcendental idealism would be a strong liberalizing force in New England throughout the war years, as it was earlier.[17] The *Atlantic* reflected his influence. Fields's biographer testifies that "the Transcendental movement in its many ramifications" had a great effect upon the magazine.[18] From its very inception, the goal of the *Atlantic* was to "unite the strongest forces of expression in the joined cause of letters and reform."[19] It was to be a "high-class antislavery magazine" and not a mere vehicle for propaganda."[20] True to its name (which Holmes suggested), the magazine sought an international audience. The publisher, Ticknor and Fields, employed a London agent, Nicholas Trubner, to distribute the *Atlantic* in England.[21]

The *Atlantic* was "nearly coeval in birth" with the Saturday Club, many of whose members were frequent contributors.[22] This club included some of the finest minds in America as well as the country's most esteemed literary figures. During the war, the Saturday Club became an important meeting place for them. At the time, Boston was the hub of America's cultural universe and the Saturday Club was the center of that hub. Established in 1855, this group of gentlemen met on the last Saturday of every month at the Parker House in Boston to enjoy good food, good cigars, and good conversation.[23] It was a gathering of the gifted. Membership included poets, philosophers, college professors, scientists, doctors, politicians, artists, lawyers, and businessmen. Several were dedicated liberal reformers, like Emerson and Richard Henry Dana Jr. Others were more conservative, like Oliver Wendell Holmes and Nathaniel Hawthorne. With the advent of the war, however, the group soon became decidedly liberal.[24]

The New England literati also had an important connection with New York publishers through George W. Curtis. Curtis was a New Englander, born in Rhode Island. As a young man he experienced an early immersion in Transcendentalism while living in the utopian community known as Brook Farm in West Roxbury, Massachusetts. This was followed by an extended residence in Concord, home to Emerson and Thoreau. After his stay in Concord, where he developed enduring friendships with Emerson, Thoreau, and other Transcendentalists, Curtis set out on a grand tour of Europe and Egypt that lasted four years. During this trip he met and became fast friends with another New England traveler and intellectual, Charles Eliot Norton.[25] Upon his return to America in 1850, Curtis took a job as a reporter for Horace Greeley's liberal *New York Tribune*, the same paper that employed Margaret Fuller.

Later, Curtis joined the editorial staff at *Harper's New Monthly Magazine*, where he wrote a regular column, The Editor's Easy Chair. He was also a very popular and influential lecturer and lyceum speaker.[26] Eventually, his role at *Harper's* expanded to include a regular column called The Lounger for the magazine's sister publication, *Harper's Illustrated Weekly*, one of the nation's most popular and highly regarded newspapers. He became its political editor at the height of the Civil War in December 1863. In that position, Curtis was able to turn *Harper's Weekly*, with its circulation of more than 125,000, into a veritable platform for his New

England liberalism.[27] Though residing in New York, he was a frequent guest in Boston and Concord. Throughout the war, Curtis was a key player in the extensive network of prominent New England intellectuals, publishers, poets, educators, and political figures who promoted emancipation and equal rights.

In addition to this New York connection, the Saturday Club had an equally important European connection. American historian John Lothrop Motley was the author of the widely acclaimed *History of the United Netherlands*. Because of his international reputation and deep knowledge of Europe and European affairs, Motley was appointed by Lincoln to serve as the American minister to Austria. Massachusetts senator Charles Sumner helped secure the appointment. Motley was well connected with many influential individuals in Great Britain. From his vantage point, he was able to keep members of the club informed of European, especially British, affairs throughout the war.[28]

Just before the outbreak of the war, Holmes wrote to Motley, who was in London. "In the midst of so much that renders the very existence of a civilization amongst us problematical to the scholars of the Old World," he stated, it was a great benefit to have such a capable representative there. He reminded Motley of his special role as a cultural ambassador in these critical times and noted that his New England friends now regarded him "as the plenipotentiary of the true Republic, accredited to every Court in Europe."[29]

The "problematical" issue that Holmes referred to most likely concerned the British view of American democracy, reflected in articles like "The United States through English Eyes," which had recently appeared in *Fraser's Magazine* in February. *Fraser's*, a Tory journal established in 1830, was noted for its political commentaries. Many important British writers were published in its pages; Thomas Carlyle's *Sartor Resartus* first appeared there in 1833–34.[30] In 1860, *Fraser's* was edited by James Anthony Froude, who, in the words of his biographer, was known to be "more radical in religion and more Carlyean in politics" than his predecessor. Carlyle was a major influence on Froude, and not surprisingly, under his editorship *Fraser's* became more politically conservative.[31]

In this article, the author argued that American democracy was inferior to the British model of governance. It was clear that his interest was as much in British politics as American, which was almost always the case for conservative commentators. He noted a growing demand for reform in England at the moment and that American democracy, "with its franchise and the representative system," provided the model of government favored by British reformers, even though "there are many who question its immediate advisability."

The writer observed that at the time of the Declaration of Independence, "the franchise was restricted more or less in every State." The men who held the foremost positions were "British subjects born under a monarchial constitutional government." It was under their elite leadership that the young republic prospered. Things subsequently changed, however. Now, "the franchise has been extended to every male of twenty-one years of age, except of course Sambo, who never comes of age." As a result of this liberalization, which resembled that presently sought by British reformers, "petty lawyers and village schoolmasters" dominated the ballot, and "the more highly educated and competent of the wealthier classes are scared away from becoming representatives."

For this conservative Englishman, what Americans proudly considered the age of the common man was also an age of decline. "The tyrannical power of mobular opinion" now ruled in America. "Is it not painfully ludicrous," he wrote, "to contrast the 'White House' in the days of Washington with the same place in 1859?—the dignity and decorum of the former with the unwashed confusion of the latter."[32] This "unwashed" quality of American democracy would soon become even more significant for English critics with the election of the backwoods rail-splitter, Abraham Lincoln.

The growing unrest and violence in America's "model Republic" had a chilling effect on reform efforts in Great Britain. *Fraser's* July issue included an article by Thomas Collett Sandars, a conservative scholar and expert on English constitutional law and history. In his monthly column, "Chronicle of Current History," Sandars made note of "the furious intestine dissensions that threaten to break up the [American] union . . . and the growing excitement of the Presidential election." He suggested that these developments had a large share in the extinction of the Reform Bill in England. Recent events in America, he noted, had "inspired a general dread of Democratic constitutions." As a result, while in the beginning of the year "it was taken as a certainty that a moderate Reform Bill would be passed," that bill was now effectively dead. Sandars went on to conclude that the burning desire for political change that Radical Liberal MP John Bright recently described as "lurking everywhere" no longer existed and that "the general feeling of the nation is essentially Conservative."[33]

In addition to journal articles, some New Englanders learned about the political climate in Great Britain from personal correspondence. Around this time, fugitive slave William Craft, who escaped from Boston shortly after the passage of the Fugitive Slave Law, wrote to Samuel May from England. May, brother-in-law of Bronson Alcott, was a committed Transcendentalist and an active reformer. Craft told him there are "many pro-slavery Americans in the country" who influence public opinion and many "books & newspaper articles" that "poison & mislead the public." He went on to indicate his desire to work for the antislavery movement in England because he felt "that laborers are very much needed to counteract this evil & wicked influence."[34]

That task was especially challenging at the moment because of the turmoil in America. English reformer and author Harriet Martineau wrote to a friend that "British eyes & consciences" were now focused on "the dissolution of the Union."[35] Martineau was well known in antislavery circles on both sides of the Atlantic. She published a twice-weekly column in the London *Daily News*, an antislavery workingman's newspaper, as well as the Boston-based *National Anti-Slavery Standard*, edited by Lydia Maria and David Child.[36] Her essays also frequently appeared the *Edinburgh Review*.[37]

Tensions in America over the issue of slavery grew throughout the tumultuous 1850s, culminating with John Brown's famous raid on the Federal arsenal at Harpers Ferry in the fall of 1859. The raid failed and Brown was captured, tried for treason, and executed on December 2, 1859, before a crowd of some two thousand spectators. His execution added considerably to the deep social unrest threatening the stability of the American body politic. Very soon, that unrest would lead to open warfare.

The *Economist*, England's premier business journal, offered its views in an essay titled "The Political Crisis in America" by the editor, Walter Bagehot, one of the most influential political commentators of his day. Bagehot was something of an anomaly, at least by modern standards. Although he was a self-proclaimed, career-long liberal, Bagehot had no love for democracy. While he more or less accepted the inevitability of democratic reform in England, like many other Victorian elites he wished to slow down the process.[38] They preferred a more limited democracy where the voice of the people was expressed through enlightened leaders who were selected by an element of the general population educated to the task. For these conservatives, the English Constitution was superior to the American, which provided for universal white male suffrage, and parliamentary governance was preferable to strong presidential power.[39] Racism, pervasive in the nineteenth century, was also a major factor in their resistance to liberal democracy. They believed in a natural racial hierarchy that placed Caucasians at the top and all other races below in a descending order, with Blacks usually at the bottom. The notion of equality was, literally, foreign to them.

Despite these reservations about democracy and race, however, Bagehot was an implacable foe of the institution of slavery, which he saw as a relic of the barbaric past that had no place in the modern world. "In no other quarter of the world are good and evil so distinctly in conflict as is just now the case in America," he wrote. "The question is whether or not the permanent existence of a servile class is to be incorporated with the essence of a modern civilization in one of the greatest nations on earth." In Bagehot's view, radical "ultra-Southerners" were leading a crusade to defend the institution of slavery. He condemned them as "violent, desperate, united men" who had no place in a civilized society.[40] Eventually, Bagehot and the *Economist* would take a very different position regarding the South and its leadership, but at this early point in the crisis, it was clear to Bagehot that Southern extremism was at the center of the brewing storm.

The tug of war between the free states and slave states came to a climax in the presidential election in November 1860. Observers, both in America and abroad, recognized that the election would be a defining event in the short history of the American republic. Norton (Curtis's friend) wrote to a British friend, poet Arthur Hugh Clough, in late September. He told him to look for Lowell's article in October's *Atlantic* on " 'The Election in November,' which gives as fair a view as I have seen of our political conditions and prospects."[41]

Like Martineau, Lowell saw the upcoming election as defining. "We are approaching, . . . a crisis in our domestic policy more momentous than any that has arisen since we became a nation," he wrote. This election would be a turning point in the nation's history because, "although there are four candidates, there are really . . . but two parties, and a single question that divides them."[42] That question concerned slavery. Lowell maintained that the strength of the nation was its idealism and the moral principles that gave it original life. New England idealist that he was, Lowell couched his argument in the language of Transcendental philosophy. The principles articulated in the Declaration of Independence, he explained, were a "living emanation of the Eternal Mind." Unfortunately, they had been eroded by compromise to the point where they were now merely "dead formula on men's lips and the dry topic of the annalist."

The crisis of the present hour, however, offered an opportunity for a political rebirth because it "has forced us to reconsider the primal principles of government . . . by bringing the theories of the Declaration of Independence to the test of experience in our thought and life and action." This was no time for compromise, Lowell insisted. It came down to a "question of Right and Wrong." He held that party platforms were like just laws. "Those are strong which appeal to reason, but those are impregnable which compel the assent both of reason and the common affections of mankind," as was the case with the party of Lincoln.[43]

Apologists for Southern slavery on both sides of the Atlantic were always annoyed by the kind of abstract moral argument Lowell offered. While they were more than capable of justifying slavery through biblical reference in the convention of religious polemics and, later, through the strategy of scientific racism, intuitional morality (a key element of Transcendental philosophy) was a moving target.[44] For thirty years prior to 1860, Southern dominance of all three branches of government had given them numerous legislative and legal victories, such as the Fugitive Slave Law (1850), the repeal of the Missouri Compromise (1854), and the Dred Scott decision (1857). Despite these Southern victories, Northern abolitionists, especially the New Englanders, insisted there was a "Higher Law" than the Constitution that abrogated such patently immoral measures. This universal law, which could be intuitively perceived even by the unlettered, had greater authority than the Constitution, and its moral effects were inexorable.[45] Thus, Emerson could say with confidence in 1854 that "the inconsistency of slavery with the principles on which the world is built guarantees its downfall."[46]

Emerson often referred to this abstract spiritual force as "moral sentiment," which equated with Lowell's "common affections of mankind." In his "Address to the Citizens of Concord on the Fugitive Slave Law" (1851), he explained that all just laws "are merely declaratory of the natural sentiments of mankind."[47] The Fugitive Slave Law contradicted these sentiments and, therefore, could not be obeyed. Emerson also asserted, presciently, that "as soon as the Constitution ordains an immoral law, it ordains disunion."[48]

Conservatives were flummoxed by such idealism, especially since it was not based on any objective authority. The Declaration itself, they insisted, was merely a collection of "glittering generalities," which, they pointed out, had no authority in law.⁴⁹ In the eyes of conservatives, it was this naive sentimentalism that was now pushing the nation to the brink of war.⁵⁰ Throughout the turmoil of that war, New England idealists would repeatedly appeal to the "moral sentiments" articulated in the Declaration in their effort to reinvent American democracy. British liberals supported them in this effort because they believed the cause of democracy in America was the cause of democracy everywhere. Their conservative opponents, more numerous and more powerful, believed the same thing, and they were adamant in their resistance.

Conservative British commentators, like Walter Bagehot, Robert Cecil, Alexander Beresford-Hope, and the proprietors of the London *Times*, saw idealism as a dangerous form of sentimental stargazing that had no place in the real world of commerce and polity. They resisted the movement toward liberal democracy in America because their cultural and social experience led in the opposite direction. They embraced a pragmatic philosophy that acknowledged realistic limitations rather than a dreamy idealism that imagined a broad equality of races and classes, an equality contrary to nature and the facts of life as they knew them. These conservatives often pointed to compelling examples of the disastrous effects of such addled thinking: the French Revolution and its Reign of Terror in the eighteenth century, followed by another revolution and dictatorship in the nineteenth for one.

Lowell, in his October *Atlantic* article, attempted to assuage conservative fears regarding the possibility of radical change by offering assurance that "the administration of Mr. Lincoln will be conservative" and adhere to the Constitution. At the same time, however, he threw down an ideological gauntlet by asserting that Republicans would seek "the utter extirpation of dogmas which are the logical sequence of the attempts to establish [slavery's] righteousness and wisdom, and which would serve equally well to justify the enslavement of every white man unable to protect himself."⁵¹ Lowell's stance would likely do little to assure Southerners of the future security of their "peculiar institution."

The major political parties reflected the divisiveness of the times. A badly divided Democratic Party nominated Stephen Douglas for president. The Southern Democrats nominated John C. Breckenridge of Kentucky. The Republicans, meeting in Chicago, nominated Abraham Lincoln. The central issue in the campaign was, of course, slavery. The Republican platform denied the authority of Congress, or a territorial legislature, to legalize slavery in the territories, while it reaffirmed the Wilmot Proviso, which excluded slavery from all territories acquired as a result of the Mexican-American War. The object was to contain, not abolish, slavery.

In the end, Lincoln carried the election without a single Southern electoral vote, a sign of how deeply divided the nation had become. Emerson was delighted with the results. They confirmed his faith in democracy. In his journal, he commented, "The news of last Wednesday morning (7th) was sublime, the pronunciation of the masses of America against slavery."[52] He was undoubtedly expressing what many other New Englanders felt. Motley wrote to his mother that, initially, he was "intensely anxious for the success of the Republican cause," but now "I rejoice in the triumph at last of freedom over slavery more than I can express."[53]

Many British readers would be introduced to America's new president through Robert Black's *A Memoir of Abraham Lincoln, President Elect of the United States of America*. This brief biography (123 pages) was published in London in early 1861. In it, Black presented Lincoln as a thoroughly democratic representative man. It was "by untiring energy, by unswerving integrity, by uncompromising courage, by kindness of heart, by genial humour, by strong common sense," he wrote, that Lincoln was elected by the popular suffrage of a free people. As would often be the case throughout the war, this example of the success of the democratic process was attributed to the influence of the nation's New England Puritan past. Through "a spirit not unworthy of the stern Old Pilgrim Fathers," Black declared, "America has chosen for her ruler a simple, honest working-man."[54]

Not only was Lincoln's background dramatically different from all of his predecessors, but so was his striking physiology. Lincoln's physical appearance would be a subject of endless fascination, and often derision, for English commentators, especially those from the elite governing class. From the beginning, this rustic backwoodsman did not possess the visual or personal demeanor of what Victorians considered a proper statesman. Additionally, Black depicted the new president as something of a racial hybrid, another democratic marker. "He stands six feet four . . . in his stockings. His head is well set upon his shoulders, and would be a pleasing study for a phrenologist. . . . His complexion is that of an octoroon;[55] his face is cut into innumerable angles, and in each there seems to lurk the genius of humour. . . . His frame is gaunt, his arms long, and his lower limbs proportioned to his gigantic height."[56] All of these qualities served to make Lincoln an oddity to many Englishmen who were raised in a culture that placed great emphasis on proper appearance, proper manners, and, above all, proper speech.[57]

Regarding the political tensions brought about by Lincoln's election, Black was very clear and, as it would turn out, predictive. "Let the hot-blooded Southerns bluster as they will," he declared. If secession should occur, it will be "an evil day," not only for the United States but for the mother country herself. Secession would certainly be followed by war, and "the cotton trade shall languish and the southern ports be blockaded. . . . Then the wailing which is heard from the cotton-fields will find a sad response in the factories of Lancashire; the coloured bondsman and the white freeman will be whelmed in a common ruin."[58]

Initially, the reaction in England to Lincoln's election was generally positive, in part because of the widespread antislavery sentiment there. The London *Times* declared that his election was "the protest of the freest and best educated part of the American people against the acts of high-handed violence and oppression which preceded the advent of Mr. Buchanan to power." Another article opined, "Let there be no mistake on this subject. If we have paid a sincere homage to the rising greatness of America, it has not been to that which the Southerners are so anxious to conserve." At the end of November, the *Times* declared that Mr. Lincoln could do anything he sets his mind to, "partly from natural pliability, partly from an impressive power of fixing his attention on whatever is before him."[59] Unfortunately for the North, this positive attitude would soon change dramatically.

In the month following the election, *Fraser's* also published a very positive commentary on the Republican victory based largely on the party's antislavery platform. The anonymous writer observed that Lincoln's election "marks a new era in American politics," one where the North would no longer "submit to the dictation of the South." Moreover, the writer claimed, excluding slavery from the territories would be "a gain not only to America but to the world."[60] He went on to note that the South, predictably, had "begun to murmur loudly that it will never stoop to obey the Government of a Republican President." *Fraser's* noted that this type of obtuse arrogance was to be expected from Southerners because Southern society was dominated by men "who are without education and who live in an atmosphere of dogmatic assertion in which the slightest approach to free discussion is never tolerated."[61]

On December 20, the South Carolina legislature made good on its earlier threats and passed an Ordinance of Secession. Soon, ten other Southern states followed in what became known as the "Secession Winter." In only three states were the ordinances submitted to the voters for ratification. Delegates from the seceding states gathered in Montgomery, Alabama, in February 1861. They wrote a Constitution that protected slavery in every state and any new territories acquired by the Confederacy. The rebels also chose a provisional president, Jefferson Davis of Mississippi, and vice president, Alexander Stephens of Georgia. Both assumed office immediately. They would not be officially "elected" until the following November.[62] The "Confederate States of America" was now a reality, at least on paper, its leaders, in effect, chosen by the few rather than elected by the many, something English conservatives would later speak of approvingly.

Northern abolitionists generally welcomed this development. For almost three decades they had witnessed with great anxiety the effects of the dominance of slave power in the federal government. The departure of the slave states would bring an end to this distress and such compromise measures as the widely reviled Fugitive Slave Law. Samuel May wrote to his British friend and liberal reformer Richard Davis Webb that "the abolitionists are not at all disconcerted at the secession of South Carolina and her sister states. . . . We would not put a straw in the way of their leaving the Union but only repent that the North had not virtue and self-respect enough to leave their fellowship long since." May then added a telling caveat. "We would speed their parting," he wrote, "but would demand to have it done decently, with a certain courtesy, and decidedly that they should not dishonestly lay a hand upon U.S. property as they go."[63]

Conservative New Englanders, however, were shocked at these developments. They held the radical abolitionists chiefly responsible for the apparent rending of the Union.[64] Several measures were considered to appease the South, including, in Massachusetts, "a petition to the General Court for the repeal of the Personal Liberty Bill" that protected fugitive slaves.[65] Prominent businessmen met and developed other proposals for compromise that they hoped would bring an end to the secession movement. Among them was a Thirteenth Amendment that would explicitly protect slavery forever wherever it existed. By February 1861, the conservatives had collected 22,313 signatures in Massachusetts for a petition favoring a compromise with slavery.[66]

Emerson and his liberal New England cohorts realized that the times were critical. There was a strong desire among many to preserve the Union at all costs, even if that meant further concessions to the slave power. While various compromise proposals were introduced and debated in Congress, Emerson felt certain that any compromise would be a moral catastrophe. The only way to end slavery would be to contain it, and secession was clearly a major step in that direction. He was prepared to do what he could to prevent the train from being derailed. In his journal he wrote, "Do the duty of the day. Just now the supreme duty of all thinking men is to assert freedom. Go where it is threatened, & say, 'I am for it, & do not wish to live in the world a moment longer than it exists.' "[67]

As the drama continued to unfold, Norton wrote again to Arthur Clough about the increasingly chaotic situation in America. "Confusion and alarm are the order of the day with us," he reported. "The movement for the breaking-up of the Union has acquired a most unexpected force. No one could have supposed beforehand that the South would be so blind to its own interests." It now looked like the split would become permanent, and Norton had "little hope that the Union can be preserved." While in some ways regrettable, this development was inevitable, he believed, because this conflict was "not one of parties but of principles."

Norton was not willing to see those principles compromised out of existence as they had been in the past. He felt confident that "all we have to do at the North is to stand firm, . . . to have faith that though the heavens fall, liberty and right shall not fail," because there is "no chance and no anarchy in the universe." This position reflected an Emersonian idealism that Norton fully embraced. He told Clough that "the only new book of interest" was Emerson's *Conduct of Life*. It "could not have appeared at a fitter time," he wrote, "for it is full of counsels to rebuke cowardice, to confirm the moral principles of men, and to base them firmly on the unshaken foundations of eternal laws."[68] Very soon, though, Norton's faith in Emersonian idealism would be put to the test.

Chapter 2

1861

As Civil War Approaches, the Debate over Slavery Intensifies at Home and Abroad

Throughout the tumultuous period from the election of Lincoln in November 1860 to the firing on Fort Sumter in April 1861, Northerners felt confident of Great Britain's sympathy and good will. During the "Secession Winter," the British government and the British press offered repeated expressions of sympathy coupled with the hope that the quarrel would be settled amicably. Both liberal and conservative journals basically agreed that slavery was at the center of the dispute. England, they professed, was no friend of this dehumanizing institution, which they had abolished more than two decades earlier. Additionally, conservatives concerned with England's need for a continuing supply of raw cotton felt that open warfare would jeopardize their supply. England's interests would be best served by peace, not war.

With secession now gaining momentum, *Fraser's* in January insisted that "no compromise will do; . . . peace can only be obtained if the South . . . tacitly acknowledges itself unequal to the conquest." The writer was confident that "when the bulk of Southerners are impressed with this conviction," the movement would end. This, he insisted, "must be the wish of every Englishman."[1] Alexander Beresford-Hope's conservative *Saturday Review* ran several articles during this period highly critical of the South, its leaders, and the institution of slavery they sought to preserve.[2] In "A Slave-Holding Republic" published November 17, the writer observed that the disturbances now menacing the American republic derived from "one or two Southern States, peopled by bigots of more than ordinarily furious temper." When considering the idea of a separate federation of slave-owning states, the author could only "wonder at the folly of the undertaking."[3] Later, the *Review* opined that it was "the duty of the President to treat secession as treason." That author also noted that the rebels had never been strongly attached to the principles of American democracy, which had disappointed them so in the recent election. He pointed out that letters extolling the British system were not uncommon in Southern newspapers, with several writers insisting "that they have always preferred a Monarchical Government to their own."[4]

The following week, the *Review* voiced a growing concern that an American civil war would put at risk Great Britain's supply of cotton, essential to an industry that "feeds four or five millions of our population." This writer laid the blame for this situation squarely on the backs of Southern agitators who are "carrying into action the policy which their bragging political leaders intended to confine to words." The result of this lamentable and unexpected situation was that "the fate of the American Union" was in the hands of a class of men who were "the most ignorant, the most unscrupulous, and the most lawless in the world." These were the "poor or 'mean' whites of the Slave States," who now exercised "mastery of the South."[5]

Walter Bagehot, writing in the *Economist* on January 12, furthered this criticism. He described the South as a crude and backward place. The volatile voices of rebellion in South Carolina, he observed, revealed "an almost insane degree of virulent excitement" that stood in contrast to the "temperate, conciliating, and rational" rhetoric of the North. Three-fourths of Southern whites, he contended, were "sunk into a state of social and moral degradation," which would only worsen with secession.[6]

Like the *Saturday Review* and the *Economist*, the London *Times*, which was also concerned about Great Britain's economic interests, initially placed responsibility for the current crisis on Southern rabble-rousers, declaring on January 9 that "the Southern people [are] a proud, lazy, excitable and violent class, ever ready with the knife and revolver." They were dangerous and unreasonable. "We cannot disguise from ourselves that there is a right and wrong in this question," the *Times* observed, and "the right belongs to the States of the North. . . . South Carolina has as much right to secede from the nation called the United States as Lancashire from England," the writer declared. "The Southern States expected sympathy for their undertaking from the public opinion of this country. The tone of the press has already done much to undeceive them."[7]

Regardless of such commentaries, some English journals were coming around to the opinion that if Southerners persisted in their effort at secession, there was no way to force them back. The London *Examiner* of January 5 noted that the Federal forces were clearly superior and "if by mere trial of physical strength the issue is to be determined, the unequal odds admit of no serious doubt as to the result." At the same time, however, the writer observed that "the subjugation of the South by the armed levies of the North and West" would be "a fatal triumph for the principle of Federalism."[8] These were ominous signs for the North.

The following month, the *Saturday Review* published another harsh criticism of Southern society and culture. In "Pleas for Slavery," the writer denounced the Southerners' efforts to proclaim the social advantages and moral acceptability of the institution of slavery. "Their main principle," he noted, "is that nature has drawn a broad line between the negro and the white man, and has not endowed the former with those qualities which alone can fit men for freedom." In refutation, the author pointed out that "many negro nations possess an organized form of society [and] are engaged in agriculture and trade." In these societies, "justice is fairly administered . . . and a high degree of happiness [is] enjoyed. Even Hayti," he maintained, "seems not unlikely before long to furnish a satisfying example of self government." The overall effect of slavery, on the other hand, "is not to elevate, but to degrade both the slave and the master."[9] Despite this strong condemnation, the *Saturday Review* and most other major British journals would soon articulate a diametrically opposite view.

At this early stage of the crisis, however, the sentiments of the conservative *Saturday Review* resembled those expressed in the liberal *British Quarterly Review*. In April the latter offered a searing condemnation of slavery and the slave-owning oligarchy that had dominated national politics in America for the "last half century."[10] The essay presented a detailed overview of the economic devastation and stagnation of a slave-based economy. "In the South," the writer noted, "there is squalid poverty of the whites, utter wretchedness of the blacks, and a dreary absence of commerce, shipping, and manufactures." He wondered aloud why the free states "submit to be overborne by the slave-breeding, slave-enamored South."[11]

In the same month, the *Edinburgh Review* expressed the view that the breakup of the American Union was inevitable and that race played a central role in the conflict. In the North, the writer observed, "negroes are regarded as belonging to an inferior race" but still share in "a common humanity," while Southerners "regard slaves as property." Moreover, instead of treating slavery "as a necessary evil," Southerners "represent it as preferable to the freedom of the working classes, and as the Utopia of the African race."[12] Given these facts, a permanent division was the only way to defuse the present crisis.

Despite its initial criticisms, the *Economist* also began to warm to the notion of an independent Confederacy. Bagehot now sought to neutralize the issue of slavery, which previously placed the North in a morally superior position. If the war really was about slavery, he maintained, it would certainly be worth fighting, but it was not. The recent compromises offered by the North showed this. Bagehot now argued that the conflict was caused by the protectionist North attempting, by coercion, to dominate the free-trade South. Therefore, he declared, Englishmen should not sympathize with those Northerners who wished to maintain the old Union by force on the erroneous impression that they are about to fight "on the ground of confining Slavery for ever within its present area. . . . Alas, it is not so."[13] With the moral issue thus neutralized, British interests now resided with a free-trade partner rather than a protectionist one.

A week later, the *Economist* observed that the new Confederate constitution was an improvement over the federal Constitution on which it was based because it was "more English." The writer noted also that the Confederates "have adopted a moderate tariff," a measure that would please British manufacturers.[14] What went unmentioned was that this "improved" constitution also guaranteed, in perpetuity, the right to own slaves. Once it became apparent that Southerners were determined to go forward with secession, the trend toward accepting both Confederate independence and slavery accelerated.

The generally sympathetic and supportive tone of the early commentaries in the British press were deeply appreciated, even if expected, by the North. Some in the North hoped that Great Britain would take the lead in an international effort to defuse the crisis. In early February, America's former minister to Great Britain, Edward Everett, presented the British minister in Washington, Lord Lyons, with a "long petition from Boston calling for a joint mediation by England, France, and Russia."[15] At the same time, politicians in Washington continued to work toward a compromise, but New England liberals resisted any effort at compromise on the issue of slavery. In a letter to Arthur Clough, Charles Eliot Norton stated that he was sure "we are seeing now the beginning of the death struggles of Slavery, and there is no ground for wonder at the violence of its convulsions." Norton would play a central role in the transatlantic dialogue that developed during the war between liberal factions in New and Old England.[16]

Clough reported to Norton that British opinion was evolving and just now was split between those who thought the South would be starved into submission and those who believed it would succeed. He also noted a substantial concern that, if the latter should be the case, the resulting two nations would be naturally "hostile in principle and sure to fall into war with each other." Conservatives feared this would have a disastrous effect on British trade and, most importantly, on the cotton supply. Clough indicated that England also had its liberal idealists "who deprecate above all things pro-slavery concessions on the part of the North."[17] Idealism, however, was not characteristic of the majority of English thinkers, as he later made clear.

After receiving Norton's letter, wherein he had praised Emerson's new book, *Conduct of Life*, Clough agreed that the work was "quite as good, if not better than any former Volume." In noting some rather harsh British reviews of the work, he explained that, unlike New England, the English mind was pragmatic and reflected a strong "anti-mysticism." As a result, "a dense, supercilious narrow-minded common sense" often "speaks pretty loudly."[18]

This pragmatism was evident in the *Saturday Review*'s critique of Emerson's work. Rather than seeing it as the invaluable moral guide Norton believed it to be, the *Review* declared, "The essays themselves have nothing in them, with the exception of occasional jets of nonsense." Indeed, "the whole book, from end to end, is a continuous stream of twaddle, relieved by nonsense."[19] These contrasting cultural characteristics would become increasingly significant throughout the war years as New England's idealism, deployed in defense of liberal democracy, repeatedly clashed with the pragmatism of British conservatives.

At this point, most Transcendentalists and abolitionists were, like Emerson, generally pleased with national developments. Poet and painter Christopher Pearce Cranch, then in Paris, wrote in January to his friend John Sullivan Dwight, composer and music critic, about the possibility of secession. Dwight, a former Transcendental Brook Farmer like George Curtis, welcomed that possibility. Cranch expressed his hope that "the North will make no miserable compromises." He then added, "Let S[outh] C[arolina] cut her own throat, if she is bent on it.—I can't help thinking that North & South had better be divorced, if the South is so rabid."[20]

While abolitionists saw a breakup of the Union as the first step in eradicating slavery, some of the New England intelligentsia took a less radical position. Norton, Lowell, and Holmes initially desired only to hold slavery within the boundaries of the slave states and within constitutional limits. This, they believed, could be done through the political process. In his *Atlantic Monthly* article of October 1860, Lowell insisted that the goals of the Republican Party were not revolutionary. "No man pretends that under the Constitution there is any possibility of interference with the domestic relations of the individual states," he wrote. "What the Republicans affirm is, that in every contingency where the Constitution can be construed in favor of freedom, it ought to be and shall be so construed." At the same time, Lowell emphasized that "the object of the Republican party is not the abolition of African slavery."[21] Future events, however, would change this policy dramatically.

At this early point in the growing crisis, Holmes also held a conservative position. In his letter to Motley, he was critical of "the impracticable Abolitionist" who was "bent on total separation from the South as Carolina is on secession from the North."[22] Some years earlier, Holmes had referred to abolitionists as "men of extreme party" who could be seen as traitors because in "flippant and playful language" they spoke of the inevitable dissolution of the Union, a position for which Emerson criticized Holmes at the time.[23]

While not as severe as Holmes, Norton also agreed fully with the Republican platform that the government should "let slavery alone in each state," while preventing its spread into the territories.[24] Norton's friend William James Stillman, who, at the moment, was improving his painting skills in Europe under the tutelage of John Ruskin and others, also felt the Union should be preserved. He wrote from Paris that he "would have seen the states of servitude go on their miserable way with little feeling," but such a development should be resisted since the United States would suffer "disgrace and shame before the world to be divided."[25] At this point, it seemed to many New Englanders that a Union with slavery was preferable to no Union at all.

Abolitionists were disappointed and even angered at times by the conservative views of some of New England's intelligentsia. For a radical abolitionist like Samuel Joseph May, it was as much a matter of class as it was politics. In a letter to Richard Webb in March, he complained at length about Lowell's recent article in the *Atlantic Monthly*. May wrote, in part, "I believe [Lowell] has wanted, for years, to 'cut' the Abolitionists, having got into the smooth, dignified, self-complacent, and change-hating society of the college [Harvard] & its Boston circles. No man can possibly be identified with antislavery without losing caste & submitting to much slight and indignity."[26] Emerson was a conspicuous exception. Eventually, the war would exert a strong liberalizing influence on New England's intellectuals, and abolitionism would be embraced at practically all levels of society as a necessary step in the reinvention of American democracy. But this would take time.

Virtually all of New England's intellectual class assumed the British would recognize that the North, in its effort to at least contain the growth of slavery, occupied the high moral ground. In the initial stages of the crisis, this assumption was correct. However, things were now changing as British positions continued to lean toward support of the South in its struggle for independence. Eventually, New Englanders would come to realize there was a vast difference between America's democratic culture and the imperial culture of Great Britain. This realization would have a distinct liberalizing effect on the group as a whole. In their defense of the Union cause, they would eventually find themselves in a de facto coalition with the radical abolitionists they once criticized.

Emerson had been there for some time. His increasingly radical antislavery position throughout the 1840s and 1850s was, in part, the logical consequence of his Transcendental philosophy, which insisted on the unity and divinity of the human family.[27] The alliance that abolitionists, Transcendentalists, and Brahmin intellectuals eventually formed provided a critical boost to the development of liberal democracy in America. It did not come without a struggle. As George Fredrickson notes in his classic study *The Inner Civil War*, "although the intellectuals conveyed their opposition to the South on the eve of the war, it was certain that once the war had begun they would fight not only against the South but among themselves for possession of the ideological meaning of the conflict and, more than this, to determine the meaning of America and the dominant style of American thought."[28]

The new American identity that Fredrickson points to would result not only from the cultural and political clash between the North and the South, of which he writes, but also from a similar contest between the cultural icons of New and Old England. The New Englanders would be led, finally, to unqualified support for the principles of universal liberty and equal rights—essential liberal values—in part by the Victorians' denegation of these principles. As New England's intellectual class moved to increasingly liberal positions, it became clear that England could no longer serve as a cultural, social, or political role model.

Attitudes toward slavery and race were central in this division. Initially, for cultural conservatives like Norton, Motley, and Holmes, slavery was a political issue with moral connotations. For Transcendental liberals and radical abolitionists like Samuel Joseph May, Theodore Parker, and Emerson, slavery was a moral issue with political connotations. The problem for the conservatives at first was how to bend the moral principle of antislavery to make it compatible with a Constitution that accommodated such immorality. Was a war to preserve a Union founded upon an immoral compromise worth it? For the Transcendentalists, this problem did not exist. They appealed to a "higher law" and universal moral principles. For them, it was possible to change the Constitution to bring it into alignment with this higher law. To do the reverse was simply impossible.

For their part, many of the Victorian sages at the outset of the war were skeptical that the situation in America would lead to the moral improvement of the place. Around this time, Matthew Arnold wrote to his sister Jane, the wife of Liberal MP William Forster, a strong supporter of the North. In his letter, Arnold indicated that, unlike his brother-in-law, he did not have "much faith in the nobility . . . of the Northern Americans." He believed "they would consent to any compromise sooner than let the Southern States go," a concern Emerson and other New England liberals shared.

It was Arnold's personal belief that the Northerners would do better if they allowed the Southerners to secede, because then "the baseness of the North" would not be amplified by that of the South. He also believed that if the American Union broke up, several widely different nations would develop in America because of regional differences in "climate and mixture of race." For Arnold, this would not be a bad thing; it would increase the chances "of one nation developing itself with grandeur and richness." Nowhere in his letter did he mention slavery.[29] Throughout the war, the balkanization of the United States was an attractive proposition to many conservative Englishmen, not because they thought a nation of "grandeur and richness" would emerge from the mix but rather because a global competitor would be diminished.

Even at this early stage, some in the North were becoming suspicious of British intentions. Samuel May wrote to Richard Webb that "it is reported that the British Consul at Charleston, S.C. has been making himself and his government a party to the rebellious and treasonable acts of South Carolina by granting clearance papers to British vessels in the name of the new government there." While May did not believe this action was sanctioned by the British government, others were not so sure. "Some of our journals," he reported, "are already exciting themselves with the idea that the British government is a new Slaveholding Empire."[30]

In the meantime, the first signs of a domestic fault line within the Union ranks themselves began to appear. The issue was race. Many New Englanders, especially the radical abolitionists and their Transcendental allies, saw open warfare as preferable to an immoral compromise with slavery. Conservative Democrats throughout the North condemned what they saw as an addled idealism that proclaimed a false and pernicious notion of racial equality while also promoting acts of violence and insurrection, like those of John Brown, as a means of achieving it. The *Daily Democratic Union* (of Peoria, Illinois) noted, "The Republic is threatened to be torn asunder. The millions of people who inhabit this once happy and prosperous land are in consternation and confusion." Unfortunately, in the midst of this crisis there are those "whose love for the poor negro is greater than that for their own brother, father or mother, [and they] pile the fuel on the fire daily" and seek to "plunge us into civil war."[31]

Three months later, on the eve of the firing on Fort Sumter, the paper returned to the topic of racial equality in a report on the "Speech of Hon. J. R. Barrett of Missouri, Delivered in the House of Representatives, February 21, 1861." According to Barrett, "The stump orators in slave and free States all advocate the claims of Mr. Lincoln upon this doctrine of negro equality," which, they insisted, was supported by the Declaration of Independence. Barrett argued that the "Declaration did not mean to place the negro upon an equality with the white man," and he objected vehemently to what he saw as the Republicans' effort "to abolish slavery in the States."

Among the heroes of this radical faction, Barrett insisted, was John Brown because he "considered the negro equal to a white man." Like other conservatives, he associated this radical agenda with both the Republican Party and the Transcendentalists, who declared Brown a modern martyr. Barrett noted, "Theodore Parker says: 'John Brown sought by force what the Republican party works for with other weapons; the two agree in the end, and differ only in the means.'"[32] The perceived philosophical and political coalition between New England Transcendentalists and the Republican Party would garner increasing attention, and criticism, from conservative Democrats following the actual outbreak of war.[33]

These heated exchanges from both sides of the cultural conflict would culminate on March 4, 1861, when Lincoln delivered his long-awaited Inaugural Address. In it, he attempted to assuage conservatives' fears by making his position on the slavery issue absolutely clear. "I have no purpose, directly or indirectly," he declared, "to interfere with the institution of slavery in the States where it exists. I believe I have no lawful right to do so, and I have no inclination to do so." His desire, he emphasized, was to preserve the Union as it was.[34] Lincoln's declaration on the slavery question came as a surprise to many in England who believed that the American crisis was centered on this issue. The Inaugural Address, however, suggested something different, that the conflict was actually about the preservation of the Union and, with it, all the constitutional protections afforded slavery. The consequences would be significant. The antislavery faction in England were strong supporters of the antislavery movement in America. For them, Lincoln's pronouncement had the effect of depriving the North of the high moral ground in the contest, thus relieving many liberals and most conservatives in Great Britain of the need to choose sides on the basis of morality.[35] As a result, commercial concerns soon came to dominate.

In 1860, Great Britain was the most industrialized nation in the world. The United States was a major trading partner, especially the South. Britain depended on the Southern states to provide nearly 80 percent of the raw cotton needed for their booming textile trade. In turn, because its economy was based largely on agriculture, the South was a lucrative market for English manufactured goods. In March 1861, in the midst of the secession crisis, the US Congress passed the Morrill Tariff. Signed into law by President James Buchanan just two days before Lincoln was sworn into office, the law nearly doubled the duties on imported manufactured goods. The timing of its passage could not have been worse. It was seen in the South as providing protection to Northern manufacturers while placing a significant burden on Southerners. It was also widely disparaged in England, where it was seen as blatantly protectionist.[36]

John Lothrop Motley, in England at the time, reported in a letter to his mother on a disturbing shift in British attitudes. "There has been a change, a very great change, in English sympathy since the passing of the Morrill Tariff bill," he wrote. Motley indicated that the measure had done "more than any commissioner from the Southern Republic could do to alienate the feelings of the English public towards the United States." The fallout from this act, Motley feared, could have catastrophic consequences since the English were now "much more likely" to recognize the Southern Confederacy.[37]

The benefit to the South of British disaffection over the Morrill Tariff was soon apparent. The *Saturday Review* of March 16 now spoke of "the Southern Confederation of American States" and noted that they are ready to admit British commodities "at a low and reasonable duty." In the rest of the country, however, the Morrill Tariff "all but closes . . . the Northern and Western markets."[38] The *Review* also began to dramatically reverse its opinion of the new Confederacy. Previously, like the *Economist* and the London *Times*, the *Saturday Review* had described Southern secessionists as ignorant and lawless hotheads. However, the journal now reported that Southern gentlemen had assumed leadership and, as a result, "the affairs of the secessionists" are "excellently managed," while "confusion still reigns at Washington." With this, the *Saturday Review* completely reversed direction regarding affairs in America. The Confederacy was now an admirable and dignified state run by capable statesmen and "natural leaders" who were "selected" by their elite peers. The North, on the other hand, was rife with rowdiness and incompetence, the inevitable by-products of liberal democracy. From this point forward, Beresford-Hope's *Saturday Review* would be a powerful and unwavering ally of the aristocratic South and an unrelenting critic of the democratic North. Several of Great Britain's most distinguished journals, as well as the mighty London *Times*, would soon follow suit.

Meanwhile, the rending of the Union continued apace. The focal point became a Federal installation at the mouth of the port of Charleston, South Carolina, one of the South's wealthiest cities and ground zero for the secession movement. After final negotiations broke down, on April 12, 1861, at 4:30 a.m., the Confederates began bombarding Fort Sumter. Thirty-four hours later, the bombing achieved its goal: Major Robert Anderson surrendered the fort.[39] The war that would ultimately determine the future of democracy in America, Great Britain, and the world had begun.

Chapter 3

War Against Slavery at Home Brings Conflict Abroad

Although many believed war was all but inevitable, news of the firing on Fort Sumter shocked the nation. James Russell Lowell's biographer remarks that Northerners generally had grown so accustomed to the political dominance of Southerners in national affairs that they were unaware of a counter force in the rising tide of antislavery and Union sentiment. As a result, the feeling of outrage that swept over the North after the attack on Sumter "came with almost as much surprise to them as to the South."[1] The *Boston Weekly Transcript* (April 17) expressed the intense feeling of patriotism that resulted. "The war has begun," the paper declared, and "the first incident has been "the lowering of the flag of the United States to an armed force of traitors and rebels." Despite this humiliation, "the blood of the people is up," and those few Northerners who, in the past, "fawned on the traitors of the slave States like spaniels, will find that their miserable occupation is gone." The entire city, the *Transcript* reported, was experiencing "unparalleled excitement."

The same dramatic turnaround was also apparent on a personal level. Whereas previously abolitionists had welcomed secession as a positive step that would effectively insulate the free states from the further contamination of slavery, a military campaign would provide an opportunity now to destroy the heinous institution with one mighty blow. For Transcendental idealists like Emerson, however, the war would not be just an antislavery crusade. Their ultimate goal was to establish equal rights throughout the land, regardless of class or race. Many others saw it as a war of the common man of the North against the "rebellious aristocracy" of the South.² From the outset, the New England literati understood that British support would be critical for the North. Lowell felt that as an internationally known author his particular mission was "to convince his doubtful English cousins that this was a righteous war."³

The *Atlantic Monthly* very soon altered its title page, replacing the image of the venerable John Winthrop, first governor of Massachusetts Bay Colony, with the American flag. Throughout the war, its patriotic articles, poems, and political essays would lend invaluable support to the Union cause both at home and abroad. The Saturday Club—which included many, if not most, of New England's notable intellectuals, writers, educators, and political figures—would become an important center for Union activists. Its members, with few exceptions, were liberals and idealists whose Unitarian roots often bore Transcendental fruit.⁴ Ultimately, they would play a key role in the reinvention of American democracy that the war would bring.

As Union troops gathered in Washington, leaders of public opinion scrambled to define the purpose of the war and its ultimate goal. Emerson's Concord neighbor and Thoreau's friend, William Robinson, a Free-Soiler and a strong ally of Massachusetts's liberal governor, John A. Andrew, was quick to express what he saw as the war's purpose in the columns of the *Springfield Republican* on April 25. For him, this war was not just to preserve the Union. Like many New Englanders, Robinson believed this would be a "holy war," one that would, at last, wash the sin of slavery from the nation's soul and prompt a rebirth of American democracy.⁵

Not all New Englanders were prepared to embrace such a grand vision. Initially most saw it as an effort to preserve the Union and to prevent the spread of slavery, not destroy it.⁶ Some conservative Northerners expressed a strong contempt for those "radicals" who saw the war as anything more than an effort to suppress rebellion. Lydia Maria Child wrote to a friend about a Union meeting her husband attended in Wayland, Massachusetts. When he suggested that the government should shelter fugitive slaves and offer them an opportunity to fight for the Union, "he was very violently treated, and almost mobbed. . . . He was told the war had 'nothing to do with the damned niggers': the war was to preserve the *Union*."⁷

Emerson, however, was convinced from the start that the time had come to bring an end to slavery. Not long after the attack on Fort Sumter, on April 23, in a Boston lecture aptly titled "Civilization at a Pinch," he declared that "civilization depends on morality" and that morality meant equal justice for all.[8] The destruction of slavery would be the first step in the moral elevation of American civilization. As reported in the Boston *Evening Traveller* the following day, Emerson declared that "without slavery and for the first time the United States would be a nation of free men, and for the first time it would stand among the nations for freedom." The report observed that "the expression of these sentiments was greeted with loud applause." Clearly, these New Englanders were girding themselves for a holy war.

Emerson's words were not lost on those free Blacks in the North, who, from the beginning, saw the war as an opportunity to demonstrate their courage, dignity, and integrity. The Boston *Investigator* reported that "the colored people of this city are in a high state of excitement, and express their readiness to volunteer whenever allowed to do so. A leading man in them, in a conversation at the State House to-day, expressed the belief that a few companies of colored troops, placed in the Slave States would soon have an army of thousands of slaves at their backs."[9]

The Boston *Advertiser* reported the same day on a meeting of Black Bostonians that included some famous figures. The paper noted that "the Baptist Church in South Street . . . was filled to overflowing with our colored citizens. Remarks were made by Robert Morris, ESQ., William Wells Brown, and others. *A series of patriotic resolutions was passed.* Among other sentiments contained in the resolution, are warm *expressions of the patriotism of the free colored people,* and a hope that the embarrassment placed upon them by the laws of the state may be removed, *so that they can take up arms upon an equal footing with the whites,* and do their share towards defending and maintaining the government under which they have enjoyed a great prosperity."[10]

The Boston *Herald* reported on the same gathering, indicating that at the meeting "a committee was appointed to wait on the Governor and tender to him the services of the colored men as a Home Guard to protect the families and property of those who have gone to fight the country's battles. Over two hundred men were enrolled for the purpose of forming a drill company."[11] Despite their obvious eagerness to serve, it would not be until the midpoint in the war that the nation they so wished to defend would finally be moved to accept their offer. Clearly, racism did not stop at the Mason-Dixon Line.[12]

Unlike Emerson, some prominent New England intellectuals were still uncertain whether the war should be defined as an antislavery crusade.

If the Union was to be preserved, it was necessary to avoid alienating the slaveholding border states that, so far, had remained loyal. Lowell, in keeping with his earlier *Atlantic* articles, declared in a political essay titled "E Pluribus Unum" that slavery is not "the matter in the debate, and we must beware of being led off upon that side issue. The matter now in hand is the reestablishment of order, the reaffirmation of national unity."[13] The generally cautious *Advertiser* agreed, declaring simply and forcefully that "*The Union and the Constitution Must Be Preserved*," and it was "the duty of the citizen" to support this effort.[14]

British correspondents frequently expressed their concerns about the American crisis in letters to their American friends. These personal relationships would become increasingly important to the North as the war escalated. Aubrey de Vere, Anglo-Irish poet and Northern sympathizer, wrote to Norton before news of Sumter reached Great Britain: "The [London] *Times* yesterday alarmed us with rumors of war between North & South in America." Like most British observers, de Vere felt that compelling the South to remain in the Union "would prove a source of disquiet from the first." It was far preferable for them "to part as good friends as may be."[15]

Northerners and Southerners both expected that Great Britain would support their cause. Northern abolitionists believed that the British, as the liberal vanguards of progressive civilization, would support the North in its effort to bring an end to slavery, which they did initially. The New England intelligentsia were also confident that close cultural ties between New and Old England would assure British support. As George Curtis wrote in *Harper's Weekly*, we are "of the same blood, of the same sympathy, of the same hope. . . . Carlyle and Macaulay, Wordsworth and Tennyson, Dickens and Thackeray, they were ours as they were England's."[16] This shared cultural identity did not extend to the Southern slave states. New England authors saw themselves as part and parcel of an Anglo-American literary culture reaching back to Chaucer and beyond. In 1860, Boston was the hub of America's literary universe, and the substantial and ongoing literary trade between New and Old England served to affirm this transcultural relationship.[17] There was nothing comparable in the South, which was seen by many Northerners as something of a cultural wasteland.

Southerners, on the other hand, were confident that commercial ties would be strong enough to bind the British to them, despite the dangers of offending the North. The Morrill Tariff was a major irritant to the

British from its inception, but an even bigger issue came to the fore just now. Cotton was a commodity crucial to England's economy. More than four million operatives depended for their livelihoods on employment in Britain's textile industry. Lincoln's blockade of Southern ports, declared on April 19, threatened to cut off that supply. Southerners were confident, or at least hopeful, that this action would prompt Great Britain to intercede. They also felt that their pseudo-aristocratic culture and hierarchical form of governance would find favor with British conservatives. In this, they were correct.[18]

Regardless of England's long-standing antipathy toward the institution of slavery and those who supported it, there were some early signs of a growing Southern influence among British conservatives. On May 3 and 9, Lord John Russell, Prime Minister Lord Palmerston's foreign secretary, met privately with William Yancey and Pierre Rost, Confederate commissioners to Great Britain.[19] Fears that the British were considering formal recognition of the Confederacy were amplified when, as reported in the *Saturday Review*, "Lord John Russell . . . announced that the English government has recognized the Southern Confederation as a belligerent Power."[20] The *Review* supported this action. Two days later, Queen Victoria issued a formal "Proclamation of Neutrality" that granted "the Confederate States of America" belligerent rights. While most Englishmen saw the proclamation as utterly reasonable, Northerners were shocked and disappointed. Many were outraged.[21]

A bitter commentary in the *Cincinnati Daily Commercial* on May 31 noted that the Queen's Proclamation "is so extra ordinarily 'neutral' that . . . it proceeds on the presumption, from the start, that the government of the United States and the Confederate usurpation are on equal terms in the eyes of British law. It views them both with equal favor, and with equal indifference." The writer felt this position was especially outrageous since England was presumably antislavery and the Confederacy was led by degenerate slaveholders, who composed "an upstart oligarchy of beggarly traitors." As a result, "the moral power of England," he declared, is now "a collapsed bubble."[22]

Meanwhile, on May 28, the London *Times*, in a complete reversal of its earlier view, spoke in very positive terms of Southern society, making special note of the fact that it was led by "gentlemen, well-bred, courteous and hospitable," who constituted "a genuine aristocracy." These Southern aristocrats were men "who have time to cultivate their minds, to apply themselves to politics and the guidance of public affairs . . . who travel and read, love field sports, racing, shooting, hunting and fishing, are bold horsemen and good shots," a vivid contrast to the self-educated rail-splitter and the degenerate "wire-pullers" who were in charge in the North.[23]

In England, the political defects that conservative Englishmen saw in American democracy continued to carry over in their intensifying criticism of democratic culture. In his study *The Popular Education of France*, published in May 1861, Matthew Arnold observed that "what is now passing in the United States of America is full of instruction for us." Unlike the Americans, "we in England have had, in our great aristocratical and ecclesiastical institutions, a principle of cohesion and unity." These institutions, together with a well-defined social hierarchy, ensured the continuing stability and progress of the British Empire. "Self-government here," he noted, is "quite a different thing from self-government there." In a passage that must have been especially hurtful to Northern idealists, Arnold also asserted that "the capital misfortune of the American people [is] that it is a people which has had to grow up without ideals."[24]

Not surprisingly, the New England intelligentsia were deeply offended by Arnold's harsh critique of American culture. A commentary on Arnold's work in the *North American Review* declared that "the book, otherwise worthy of the highest praise, is disfigured by gratuitous sneers at American civilization, which betray more ignorance than ill nature, and which on that very account are the more unworthy of a volume professing to give the results of actual research and inquiry, and of a scholar whose cosmopolitan culture ought to have raised him above vulgar national prejudice."[25]

As the crisis deepened, Americans, in both the North and the South, became increasingly sensitive to European opinions. New Englanders played a significant role in influencing those opinions. Their voices traveled far and relatively fast.[26] The *North American*'s review of Arnold's *Popular Education*, for example, reached him before the end of the month. In a letter to his mother at that time, he noted, "There is a notice of my French Report in the *North American Review*—it says the Report is of the highest value, but disfigured by sneers at American institutions—which however, it obligingly goes on to say, shew more ignorance than ill nature!"[27] Such criticism would not deter Arnold from making similar disparaging comments as the war progressed.

In the midst of this growing acrimony, New Englanders sought to defend their country. In addition to personal appeals to British friends,

John Lothrop Motley published "Causes of the American Civil War" in two lengthy installments in the London *Times* (May 23 and 24, 1861). In his essay, Motley denied that the North had ever threatened to abolish slavery, a major casus belli for the rebels. "It was no question," he insisted, "that slavery within a state was sacred from all interference by the general government or by the free states."[28] Unfortunately, in the eyes of many British readers, Motley's defense undercut the argument that the North held the moral high ground in the crisis. Moreover, his tone seemed cold and legalistic. One British commentator writing in the *National Review* observed that the arguments made by Motley and others like him "are arguments befitting lawyers, not arguments befitting statesmen. . . . An argument from the mere letter of a written Constitution," the writer declared, "will hardly convince any Englishmen."[29]

The slavery question continued to be a sticking point for Northern supporters in England. On the one hand, it appeared obvious to them that the sentiment of the North was antislavery. On the other hand, the North was also committed to preserving a Union where the right to own slaves was guaranteed by the Constitution. Despite such ambiguity, many antislavery Englishmen remained supportive of the Union. Charles Darwin was one of them. Around this time, he wrote to his Harvard friend botanist Asa Gray, a future member of the Saturday Club. "I have not seen or heard of a soul who is not with the North," Darwin told him. "Some few, and I am one, even wish to God, though at the loss of millions of lives, that the North would proclaim a crusade against Slavery. . . . What wonderful times we live in. Massachusetts seems to show noble enthusiasm."[30]

Samuel Joseph May was among the most enthusiastic. He was confident at this point that Great Britain would not interfere and that the liberal spirit in England would ultimately prevail, the Queen's Proclamation notwithstanding. He wrote Richard Webb that "much anxiety is felt in some quarters at the course which England will take, and by some of our papers the Queen's Proclamation is criticized sharply." But May liked the proclamation. "I understood it as prohibiting any participation in the war here," he wrote, "but all our people do not so interpret it." May's positive view was reinforced by his abolitionist beliefs. "I feel great confidence in the sympathy of the *British People* with our position, as against the seceding slave holders & slave traders," he said. Should the British government "give the least encouragement, or show the least favor to the Confederate states, it will be dishonored & disgraced before all people; for nothing could go so far to convict it of hypocrisy in its professed desire to put down the slave trade, and slavery." Ultimately, May felt certain that "the British people will not suffer their govt to betray them."[31]

As the implications of British neutrality became clear, the early optimism of New Englanders like May gave way to alarm. *Harper's Weekly*, which had been so confident of British support for the North a week earlier, on June 8 wondered aloud "how a friendly power can justify this conduct."[32] On a more personal level, abolitionist Sarah Shaw, whose son, Robert Gould Shaw, would eventually give his life to the cause while leading the Union army's first all-Black regiment in battle, declaimed in a letter to Lowell against "wicked old pro-slavery England!" The British declaration is "the cruelest blow to me," she told him, especially because "I was one of her lovers."[33]

Around the same time, Longfellow noted in his journal the "angry articles in the papers about England. John Bull is not behaving well about this rebellion of ours," he wrote. "He chooses to put Civilization and Barbarism on an equality, and to take sides with neither, which is virtually taking sides with barbarians." A week later, Longfellow had dinner with a group of his Saturday Club friends that included Richard Henry Dana Jr. and Massachusetts senator Charles Sumner. These distinguished gentlemen "sat from five till ten, discussing mostly the War, and the tone of England and her newspapers."[34]

Throughout the North, attitudes toward England continued to sour as news of the Queen's Proclamation spread. American correspondent Bancroft Davis reported in the London *Times* of June 12 on the growing American reaction to the neutrality declaration. "The public mind," he observed, "however unjustly, [is] rapidly becoming possessed of the idea that England sympathizes with Southern Slavery. . . . I fear that it will be long before the hearty admiration—one might almost say affection—for England that existed throughout the North two months since will be restored."[35]

New Englanders especially were distressed by what they saw as the perfidy of their English cousins. Harriet Beecher Stowe published an "Open Letter" in the New York *Independent* indicating her shock and disappointment with the position taken by the British government on the war and the general lack of sympathy from the British people.[36] *Uncle Tom's Cabin*, the book that had brought her international renown, was immensely popular in England.[37] Shortly after its publication in 1853, Stowe received a public letter of support from the antislavery women of

England titled "An Affectionate Address of Many Thousands of Women of Great Britain and Ireland to Their Sisters, the Women of the United States of America."[38] That affection, it seemed, had now cooled considerably.

The growing disappointment and anger with Britain's declaration of neutrality became clear to Motley as soon as he stepped off the boat in Boston. In contrast to the positive feelings he experienced while in England, Motley now reported to his wife (who had remained there) the "intense feeling of bitterness and resentment towards England just now in Boston." He went on to note that "the most warm-hearted, English-loving men in this England-loving part of the country are full of sorrow at the attitude taken up by England." Much of this was the result not only of the policies of the British government but also of the tone of the British press. "It would be difficult to exaggerate," Motley reported, "the poisonous effects produced by the long-continued, stinging, hostile articles in the [London] *Times*."[39] At least some in England shared Motley's concern regarding the effect of the *Times*'s invectives. Charles Dickens told one correspondent, "I am sore afraid that *The Times*, by playing fast and loose with the American question, has very seriously compromised this country."[40]

Many in England, even those inclined to support the North, remained confused as to the actual cause of the conflict and the Union's objectives. Novelist Elizabeth Gaskell, who would eventually emerge as a strong supporter of the Union, explained to her close New England friend Charles Eliot Norton that she was "thoroughly *puzzled* by what is now going on in America." The primary cause of her puzzlement, and that of many British, was the legal status of secession, which she believed was lawful. "I (average English) cannot understand how you (American) did not look forward to 'secession' at some time not very far distant," she told him.

The second part of the "great puzzle" was "What are you going to do when you have conquered the South, as no one doubts you will? . . . *Conquering* the South won't turn them into friends, or pre-dispose them to listen to reason or argument, or to yield to influence instead of force." Like many in England, Gaskell also questioned how the North could possibly occupy the entire South, a massive area of land and people, twenty times the size of England. She concluded, "Now I have said out the very worst I have ever heard said, & you know I live in S. Lancashire where all personal & commercial intimacies are with the South. Every one looks & feels sad—oh *so* sad, about this war."[41]

The issues raised by Gaskell became common fodder in the British press as well as in private correspondence. Such "puzzlement" on the part of the British, however, must have seemed odd to her New England friends who were committed, heart and soul, to what they saw as a war to defend the very existence of their country. Motley had explained it all to an English audience at the outset, and for many this was deemed sufficient to settle the matter. Unfortunately, while Motley's defense of the Union provided a detailed legal argument against secession, it left unanswered the central question for many in England, namely, is this a war against slavery, or is it not?

The angry response in the Northern press to Britain's neutrality policy came as a surprise to some. The *Economist* expressed astonishment at "the virulent and utterly unwarranted and unexplained irritation against England manifested by the United States (or, as we now call them, the Federalists)."[42] Even the liberal *Spectator* expressed dismay that "the feeling towards England in the Northern States seems to increase in bitterness." The problem, according to the *Spectator*, was that the Lincoln administration had not made it clear that this was a war against slavery. "They look on our luke warmness as treachery, not only to them but to humanity." It was especially disturbing that it was "from the very best and calmest Americans, from Boston rather than New York, that the most earnest denunciation comes."[43] The cultural and social bridges that once linked New England and the North to Old England were now on fire. The situation would only grow worse. While the governments of the two countries pursued policies that sought to maintain a peaceful if not amicable relation, the popular press in both places continued to fuel the flames of animosity.

Now more than ever, New England abolitionists realized that enlisting Blacks in the Union army would do much to convince skeptics in both countries that this truly was an antislavery war. To encourage this idea, the *Atlantic Monthly*'s June issue included Thomas Wentworth Higginson's article on the Black insurrectionist Denmark Vesey. This was one of several articles he would publish on militant Black heroes.[44] Higginson was himself a militant Transcendental idealist. Inspired by Emerson at an early age, he was one of the "Secret Six" who were intimate supporters of John Brown. When the Civil War erupted, Higginson was quick to join the fight.[45]

One of the arguments against Blacks serving in the Union army was that they lacked the courage and fortitude required for military service, especially where the enemy was white. In an effort to refute this widespread view, in this article and a companion piece on Nat Turner published in August, Higginson depicted both men as heroic leaders of slave rebellions. He described Turner, who led a bloody revolt in the summer of 1831, as a Black avenger who was "a symbol of retribution triumphant."[46] Slave rebellion was always a possibility, Higginson insisted, because Black people, like all people, were willing to fight for their freedom.

Higginson's articles would help convince Northerners that African Americans would make good soldiers. Higginson would eventually lead a regiment of Black "contrabands," fighting men who were former slaves.[47] Because of these efforts and other early developments in the war, resistance to the notion of emancipation slowly began to lessen in the North. Around this time, a Massachusetts Union army captain wrote to his wife that he was "fast growing to believe that the upshot of this war will be the pretty rapid emancipation of slaves in the border states & the loosening of the hold that slavery has upon the country." He added, "If this had been the object of the war" at the outset, he would not have volunteered, but "as a result of treachery on the part of the South I am content to see it so."[48]

As the movement for emancipation began to take shape, *Fraser's Magazine* became more critical of the North, a pattern that would be followed by several other prestigious British publications. In July, the journal reported a large increase in slaves escaping "to the quarters of the Northern army." In response, General Benjamin Butler, "who at the opening of the contest was one of the loudest to proclaim that property . . . must be protected, now adopts the doctrine that fugitive slaves are contraband of war, and must be kept in the service of the State as long as the war lasts," in effect freeing them. This practice, the writer observed, has "made the Northern army abolitionist, and the further south it marches the more completely this character will be imposed on it."

Rather than applauding this development, the author complained that such "lawlessness" was yet another attempt to subvert the nation's Constitution, which guaranteed the rights of slaveholders to their "property." These acts, he insisted, should not be tolerated in a society founded upon laws.[49] Despite these qualms, which American conservatives shared, General Butler's practice of freeing and employing "contrabands" would soon become official Federal policy, bringing about the very result that *Fraser's* predicted, much to the dismay of slaveholders and a growing chorus of their British supporters.[50]

The use of contrabands proved to be an important first step toward emancipation. Butler employed these men in various ways and paid them for their work. As news spread, more and more slaves were emboldened to escape to the Union lines, in effect freeing themselves and, ultimately, forcing a permanent change in government policy.[51] British critics recognized the implications of this policy. The liberal but often skeptical antislavery *Spectator* commented that, if the war were of long duration, it would mean "the root and origin of all this strife [will] be plucked away" because "as each state in succession [is] occupied by the [Union] troops," slaves would be freed. They could then be settled on land abandoned by fleeing rebels.[52] New England liberals were quick to see both the political and the practical benefits of such a contraband policy.

The November *Atlantic Monthly* applauded the de facto biracial alliance that was emerging. In "The Contrabands at Fortress Monroe," the journal reported that "breastworks have been built by their common toil" as "they stood side by side in the din of cannonade." Additionally, the writer noted, in a recent attack "fourteen negroes, lately Virginia slaves, faithfully and without panic worked the after-gun of the upper deck of the *Minnesota*, and hailed with a victor's pride the Stars and Stripes as they again waved on the soil of the Carolinas."[53] It was a sign of things to come.

Blackwood's Edinburgh Magazine responded to these developments by attacking the idea of a biracial alliance. *Blackwood's* was popular, prestigious, and ultra-conservative. Walter Houghton notes that "'Maga' [as it was known] championed a semi-feudal society, supporting a privileged, usually landowning class with certain self-imposed duties and responsibilities to the lower orders," which helps explain *Blackwood's* popularity in the American South even before the war.[54] In keeping with its conservative ideology, it would offer constant and often bitter criticism of the North and its liberal (and now liberating) democracy from this point forward.[55]

In a lengthy article in July, *Blackwood's* denied that slavery was at issue in the war, and even if it were, the writer opined, "remembering the condition of the African tribes in their own country . . . we cannot believe that even slavery is a bad exchange for such a life of unmitigated savagery." Henceforth, *Blackwood's* would "consider slavery as a matter to be left out of the question of Secession," a position that effectively denied the North any claim to moral superiority. The writer also predicted that Northern democracy, under the pressure of war, would give way to a de facto dictatorship, as suggested by the recent example of the French. Such was always "the fate of a republic whose principle is equality," the article declared. For *Blackwood's* the American Civil War was the death knell of a foolish and now failing concept.[56]

The *Quarterly Review* also used the American crisis to launch a full-scale attack on the principle of democratic equality as a latent British hostility became viral. An especially strident piece, "Democracy on Its Trial," appeared in the July issue. The author, future prime minister Robert Cecil, was at this time a Conservative Member of the House of Commons and an implacable foe of reform in England.[57] Cecil detested democracy, especially liberal democracy. One biographer reports that American democracy was "the peril across the Atlantic that terrified him . . . [and] gave him nightmares."[58]

When the Civil War broke out, it unnerved Cecil to think that, should the North prevail, liberal democracy would likely be extended over the whole North American continent and from there spread by example to Europe. Throughout the war, Cecil's unwavering support of the South was due in part to the belief that a Southern victory would diminish considerably the influence of American democracy. He also found Southern "aristocratic" values to be more consonant with his own, especially where slavery and race were concerned. He once remarked that American slavery "produces a very effective . . . form of aristocracy."[59]

In the July 1861 essay, Cecil observed that "the Americans have . . . told us that the old machinery of graduated conditions and balanced power is but useless and costly gear, working only for the benefit of the few, humiliating and impoverishing the many."[60] Therefore, the Americans "patented a cheap and ingenious mechanism of [popular] government, never tried before for anything like an extensive territory," and "for a time the experiment succeeded." This great experiment, however, was doomed to fail because it was based on a false premise and an impossible ideal. As Cecil explained, "the rights of man were a beautiful subject for theory-drawing in the study, but no one had dreamed of applying them to the actual wants of life" (250).

Unfortunately, Cecil noted, the American experiment had had a pernicious influence in Europe. "The idea of entrusting political supremacy to the rude and destitute, was not . . . an opinion which was looked upon as a mark of advanced views and liberality of thought." But "the weak mind of Lafayette" fell prey to the contagion, and he "brought back to France the poison from which thenceforth no state in Europe was destined to be secure." In England, the example of America "kept alive . . . the party of so-called progress" (250). These reformers "looked upon the Reform Bill as only one stride in a career of which no human eye could descry the ultimate goal, but of which the light of America, far away ahead, at once indicated the direction and guaranteed the safety." Now, however, "'the great Republican bubble has burst,' . . . . It has collapsed, as its predecessors have done, into a chaos of anarchy and bloodshed" (256). Clearly, the support of English conservatives like Cecil for the aristocratic South was based as much on their fear of the North's liberal democracy and its growing emphasis on equal rights as it was on geopolitics and economic concerns.

Meanwhile, the Northern animus toward Great Britain grew. Henry James Sr., who would soon be inducted into the Saturday Club, delivered a Fourth of July oration to the citizens of Newport, Rhode Island, that offered sharp criticisms of British cultural snobbery and a stirring defense of American democracy. It was a harbinger of things to come. James described America as "the country of all mankind," open to "the exile of every land." Unfortunately, "the ordinary European mind inevitably fails to do any justice" to this idea. England was a major offender. "The purblind piddling mercenaries of literature, like Dickens, and the ominous scribes and Pharisees of the *Saturday Review*," he declared, "have just enough cheap wit to see and caricature" American ideals.

Despite such vile ridicule, James asserted, "an education of the heart which all the studies of Oxford never yield" will reveal "the rich human soul" of this country. American idealism was "laughable only to literary louts and flunkies who live by pandering to the prejudices of the average human understanding." These prejudices were evident in the "artificial structure of society in England." One cannot live there long before getting a sense of its "acute and stifling . . . class-distinctions" and "the consequent abject snobbery or inbred and ineradicable servility of its lower classes." For James, "a log-cabin in Oregon" was preferable because at least it offered "the charm of comparative dignity and peace." In a final jab at British elites, he declared, "we are not fighting for our own country only" but for "universal man, for the ineradicable rights of human nature itself." Therefore, while "the mutton-headed hereditary legislators of England raise a shout of insult and exultation over our anticipated downfall, the honest unsophisticated masses everywhere will do us justice," a proposition that would soon be put to the test.[61]

On the same day that James spoke to the people of Newport, Lincoln delivered his July 4 "Message to Congress." In his address, the president cast the war as a struggle to preserve the principles of democracy, something that would only confirm the worst fears of British conservatives. "This is essentially a People's contest," the president insisted. "On the side of the Union, it is a struggle . . . to elevate the condition of men—to lift artificial weights from all shoulders—to clear the paths of laudable pursuit for all—to afford all, an unfettered start, and a fair chance, in the race of life."⁶² The democratic values that both James and Lincoln identified were precisely those that British conservatives were vigorously attacking at every opportunity.

Not surprisingly, liberals in New England readily ratified Lincoln's notion that this was a "people's war," one where the welfare of the common people was pitted against a culture in which only the privileged elite prospered. Writing in his Lounger column in *Harper's Weekly* on June 20, George Curtis declared that of all the presidential messages of late years, Lincoln's was "the most thoroughly democratic." He agreed emphatically that the Union cause "is a movement of the people." Curtis reminded his many readers that the nation "was founded upon the rights of man," and for the first time in years it had a "President [who] recognizes that fact." Lincoln, he declared, "is a people's President."

While liberal reformers welcomed that part of his message, Lincoln also stated, once again, that he had "no purpose, directly or indirectly, to interfere with slavery in the States where it exists." Later in the month, Congress would pass the Crittenden-Johnson Resolution, which affirmed that the purpose of the war was "to defend and maintain the supremacy of the Constitution and to preserve the Union."⁶³ But as long as slavery was sanctioned by the Constitution, the Union cause remained morally ambiguous for liberal reformers on both sides of the Atlantic.

In England, conservative journals like the *Saturday Review* ridiculed both the president and his message, which it described as "the oddest document which was ever issued by the Government of a great nation." Lincoln's common-man diction, they said, was simply appalling. "In style and rhetoric," it was on a level with a "bargeman on the Thames," the *Review* declared. The writer objected especially to Lincoln's use of the term "sugar-coated" when referring to the idea that Southern leaders were "drugging the mind of their section" by suggesting that rebellion would be both peaceful and legal if they simply called it secession. Lincoln's crude expression, the author asserted, showed only that "the honest President . . . in his process of self-education, learned to write imperfectly, and it is strange that an educated country should be governed by an utterly illiterate ruler."⁶⁴

The *Review*, in concert with other conservative British publications, frequently made invidious comparisons between the "vulgar" democratic Lincoln and the aristocratic president of the Confederacy. "Mr. Jefferson

Davis's Message" was typical. As before, the *Review* objected to Lincoln's "bad grammar" and insisted that, overall, his "Message to Congress" presented "a fair picture of the man—illiterate, narrow-minded, technical, without any definite aim or policy." In comparison, "Mr. Davis's recent message . . . reads rather like a European State-paper than the appeals to the Bunkhum which ordinarily serve the turn in America." The contrast between the two messages and the two men was indicative of the culture that each represented, one purely American and democratic, the other "European" and aristocratic. At present, the author concluded, "mobs and cheap newspapers rule at Washington [while] statesmen rule at Richmond."[65]

British liberals did not share this view of Lincoln. The London *Daily News*, a workingman's paper, was unambiguously positive about his "Message." The "plain, unvarnished speech of the Republican President," the *News* declared, will "sink deep into the hearts and consciences of a people possessed of any moral sense. . . . The 'plain people' know well 'that this is essentially a people's contest.'" While in the South, "the secessional oligarchy deliberately 'press out of view the rights of men and the authority of the people,'" the writer was certain that "any people aspiring to freedom throughout the world" will appreciate what "the President of the United States describes in the simplest words, as 'a great lesson of peace,'" teaching such men that "what they cannot take by an election, neither can they take by war.'"[66] As the conflict went on, the British working class would continue to warm toward this American president who spoke their language both literally and figuratively.

New England critics were well aware of the damage the *Times* and other prominent British newspapers and magazines were doing to relations between Great Britain and the North. Motley told his wife in a letter written three days after Lincoln's "Message," "The *Times* has played the very devil with our international relations." He was determined to do all he could to improve those relations and to persuade his many English friends and acquaintances to support the Union cause. Despite such efforts, Motley acknowledged that great damage had already been done, and "there will never in our generation be the cordial, warm-hearted, expansive sentiment towards England which existed a year ago."[67] Very soon, dramatic events on the battlefield would strain Anglo-American relations nearly to the breaking point.

Chapter 4

The North Suffers a Humiliating Defeat

British Critics Gloat

The first major battle of the war took place on July 21, 1861, near a small creek known as Bull Run in Manassas, Virginia. It resulted in a humiliating defeat for the Union army. Neither side had forces adequately trained for a major engagement. The commander of the Union force, General Irvin McDowell, advised against the effort, pointing out that his troops were still green. But Lincoln overruled his commander, saying that both sides were "green alike" and there was no need to delay. So McDowell marched his force of thirty-five thousand men to Manassas, a vital rail junction, and encamped.

When fighting erupted on the morning of July 21, the Union forces nearly carried the day as the battle waxed and waned. Eventually, however, Confederate reinforcements that had been rushed to the site overnight arrived, and the tide quickly turned. The Union line broke as the rebels rushed forward with renewed strength. A disorderly retreat soon turned into a rout when frantic Union soldiers dropped their weapons and tangled with spectators who had come out from Washington to witness what they believed would most certainly be a proper trouncing of the upstart rebels. Confusion reigned as ragged remnants of Union army units scurried back to the safety of the capital. It was a decisive victory for the South and a humiliating defeat for the North. Union forces suffered almost three thousand causalities and the Confederates nearly eighteen hundred. Although small compared to battle losses that would follow, the carnage of this first major clash was shocking to many both at home and abroad.[1]

Motley was devastated by the news. The following day he wrote to his wife. "We are for the moment overwhelmed with gloom. . . . There is no doubt that we have sustained a great defeat," he told her. "The measure of our dishonor, which I thought last night so great as to make me hang my head forever, I cannot now thoroughly estimate." He indicated that he would write again shortly, but unlike his previous missives, he added in closing, "Don't show this letter to any one."[2] In a few days Motley would share his dismay with fellow members of the Saturday Club.[3] Other New Englanders, though clearly depressed, were not as devastated as Motley. In fact, some saw the defeat as a necessary step in defining the true nature of the war and preparing the people for what now promised to be a long and costly struggle. Moncure Conway, a second-generation Transcendentalist, author, and abolitionist who was visiting Concord at the time, reported that Henry Thoreau was "in a state of exaltation," believing the defeat would help bring about the moral regeneration of the nation.[4]

Norton felt the same way. He wrote to George Curtis just four days after the event, saying that he looked on the defeat in Virginia as "a hard lesson, not as a disaster to be greatly regretted. It has taught us much. . . . Had we marched to easy victory we might have had but half a triumph; now the triumph of our cause is likely to be complete."[5] That "cause" was the abolition of slavery. Curtis agreed with Norton. The loss was "very bitter," he wrote, "but we had made a false start, and we should have suffered more dreadfully in the end had we succeeded now."[6] Curtis's positive attitude was reflected in a subsequent Lounger essay in *Harper's Weekly* (Aug. 10), where he observed that "the action at Bull Run" has only fortified the North and made it more united for the struggle ahead. This view aligned with that of the radical wing of the Republican Party.[7]

Emerson believed the conflict had awakened the nation. Some weeks after Bull Run, he wrote to James Elliot Cabot that the war "has assumed such huge proportions that it threatens to engulf us all—no pre-occupation can exclude it, & no hermitage hides us." The moment had come for the New England intelligentsia to lend their voices and their pens to the cause of freedom. "'Scholar' & 'hermit' will no longer be exempts," he insisted, "neither by the country's permission nor their own, from the public duty. . . . The good heart & mind, out of all private corners, should speak." He undoubtedly had in mind the friends and fellows he conversed with every month at the Saturday Club. "We must all go to the next Club," he told Cabot, where the great struggle ahead would undoubtedly be the main topic of discussion.[8]

News of Bull Run reached England on August 4, and the first reports appeared in the *Times* the next day. Those reports and others like them helped confirm the belief of many Englishmen that the Confederate states could not be brought back into the Union by force of arms.[9] The separation appeared to be a fait accompli. Indeed, the *Times* declared bluntly on September 4 that "the United States of North America have ceased to be."[10] Like other conservative publications, the *Times* used the Northern loss to attack liberal British reformers.[11] In "The Defeat at Manassas" (August 6), the paper commented that certain American journals, "conducted avowedly by men of disgraceful personal character," have moved Englishmen to laughter by their "impotently malignant attacks on 'our rotten old monarchy,' while the stones of their bran new [sic] republic are tumbling about their ears." This comment was clearly aimed at Radical Liberal MPs like John Bright and Richard Cobden, who frequently praised the United States as a "model republic" whose example Great Britain should follow.[12]

The coupling of the crisis in America with British political concerns at home became a regular practice among conservative English newspapers, journals, and magazines. Echoing Robert Cecil's recent essay in the *Quarterly Review*, the *Times* noted in an editorial on August 12 that "we are contemplating the results of [democratic] principles which it was sought to force upon ourselves. Such a lesson we cannot afford to lose. . . . We see, in short, Democracy in a crisis which brings all its various pretensions to trial."[13] The *Times*'s criticisms reflected a long-simmering resentment toward American influence and actions. In a letter to correspondent William Howard Russell in December, John Delane, the *Times*'s editor, described the motivation behind the paper's animus toward the Union and its sympathy with the rebels. "It is real, downright, honest desire to avenge old scores," he told Russell, "not the paltry disasters of Baltimore and New Orleans [in the war of 1812], but the foul and incessant abuse of the Americans, statesmen, orators, and press."[14] According to the *Times*'s biographers, the paper's manager, Mowbray Morris, whom they describe as "a convinced conservative," also sympathized with the South. He had been born in the West Indies and "had the background of a not dissimilar society." Additionally, Morris was said to be "in the closest sympathy and communication with Palmerston," who bore a strong animus toward American democracy.[15]

Many British correspondents found the carnage of Bull Run horrifying. Depressed by the news, Norton's English friend John Ruskin was, in the words of Norton's biographer, "profoundly alienated from Americans by the horrors of their fratricidal war."[16] Dickens, while not quite as negative as Ruskin, felt that in the wake of the defeat at Bull Run, "the people of the North will neither raise the money nor the men required by the govt.; and that an ignoble and contemptible compromise will be made soon."[17] Other British correspondents were more sympathetic and supportive than Ruskin and Dickens. John Stuart Mill, who would soon emerge as a major Union supporter, felt that if the war continued it would eventually lead to a rebirth of democracy in America.[18]

Some British supporters had already received hopeful responses to the crisis from American friends concerned with the potential impact of the defeat on the British public. Elizabeth Gaskell reported to Norton that she had received three American letters. "One from you, one from Mrs. [Sarah] Shaw, and one purely political from her son-in-law Mr. [George W.] Curtis, whom I have never seen." She went on to ask for additional information about Bull Run that could be used to counter the propaganda appearing in the pages of the *Times* and other conservative publications. "You will see we gain—'we' the English generally, our information from *The Times*; and I know that Russell's writing is Panorama painting," she wrote. Curtis's letter, which she described as "just and admirable," would help blunt the *Times*'s unflattering reports. Therefore, Gaskell took "some pains to have it printed & published in a county paper," a practice she followed throughout the war.[19]

A number of Americans living in Europe were deeply depressed by the negative newspaper accounts of the battle. Sculptor William Wetmore Story wrote to Norton from Vaudois, Switzerland. Story likely learned about Bull Run from William Russell's graphic account of the chaotic retreat published in the London *Times*. "I cannot tell you how very bad an impression the defeat at Bulls run [sic] has made in Europe," he wrote. "The disgraceful cowardice, the utter want of manliness exhibited by the 'Grand Army of the Potomac' has made us a laughing stock; after all our boasting and bragging & threatening, one would have thought that shame at least would have kept men in their ranks—but if half of what is told is true, there never was so disgraceful a battle."[20]

While in Europe, Story had developed a close friendship with Robert and Elizabeth Browning. In his letter to Norton, he communicated the sad news that Elizabeth Barrett Browning had recently died and been buried in the same Roman cemetery as Boston Transcendental reformer and preacher Theodore Parker. Story and his wife had spent three years with the Brownings in Italy, a popular destination for many Englishmen. He complained that the English do not understand the American situation. "The English mind is not a philosophic one," he wrote, an observation many New Englanders would be inclined to agree with. However, he added, Browning "is by nature not an Englishman."[21] Throughout the war, unlike most of his Victorian cohorts, Browning was consistently supportive of the Union cause.

As Story indicates, the *Times* account and others like it were very damaging.[22] Minister Adams wrote to his son Charles that the "feeling here, which at one time was leaning our way, has been very much changed by the disaster at Bull's run [sic], and by the steady operation of the press against us."[23] It was clear that British government officials took some pleasure in this early and dramatic Union defeat. Lord Palmerston referred to it sneeringly as "Bull's Run Races" and "Yankee's Run" and seemed convinced that the Confederacy had now plainly established its separation.[24]

Not surprisingly, the *Economist* saw the defeat at Manassas as confirmation of its earlier declaration that secession was a fait accompli. The journal surmised that the South's confidence has been "restored by a victory which has certainly surpassed in completeness the expectations even of the most sanguine." On the other hand, the North, after suffering deep humiliation, was "burning to avenge their losses and to redeem their military reputation." Given that neither side showed any sign of compromise, the war promised to be "a somewhat long business." This was most unfortunate because the permanent "disruption of the Union must be the inevitable result." The writer believed the North should simply accept that "the project of subduing the South . . . [is] simply insane, and must ere long be tacitly abandoned or avowedly renounced."[25] The *Economist*, from this point forward, would place all responsibility for the carnage, bloodshed, and economic disruption that warfare inevitably entails at the feet of the Northern "aggressor."

Union sympathizers in England did what they could to mitigate the damage from the Bull Run fiasco. Thomas Hughes published his "Opinion on American Affairs" in the August issue of *Macmillan's*.[26] He noted that following "the defeat of the Northern army at Manassas Junction . . . the tone of all our leading journals . . . has, with the single exception of the *Spectator*, been ungenerous and unfair, and has not represented the better mind of England." Hughes went on to note that the defeat at Manassas, "had it been ten times as disastrous as it has been, has not altered in the least, and cannot alter the rights and wrongs of the great question at issue.... If the North were right before," Hughes argued, "they are right now, though defeated." He reminded his readers that "it is the battle of human freedom which the North are fighting, and which should draw to them the sympathy of every Englishman."[27]

This admonition would be repeated by British and American liberals throughout the war. In her "Letter to Lord Shaftesbury," referenced earlier, Harriet Beecher Stowe made essentially the same argument. She expressed her deep disappointment with the failure of British abolitionists to support the Union cause because they believed the war was not about slavery. Stowe explained that "the war has not been proclaimed a war for the emancipation of the negro specifically [because] the extent and the magnitude of the issue transcended the wants of any particular race and had to do with the very existence of a free society." In supporting this broad moral and philosophical interpretation of the war's purpose, Stowe pointed out that Emerson, whom she described as "a deep thinker and popular lecturer," had "well embodied" this view in "a lecture delivered at the time ... entitled 'Civilization at a Pinch.'"[28]

Despite the hesitation of abolitionists there, many Union supporters in England agreed with Thomas Hughes that the Union cause was ultimately defined by its de facto opposition to slavery, formal declaration or not. Among the most important of these was the liberal philosopher and economist John Stuart Mill. As one scholar points out, the Civil War in America provided Mill with "a thermometer with which to take the moral temperature of English society as a whole."[29] He found it wanting. "The tone of the English press and English opinion," Mill told a friend, "has caused me more disgust than anything has done for a long time."[30] He felt that leading newspapers and journals, the *Times* and the *Saturday Review* in particular, by siding with the Confederacy, had revealed a partiality for, and a willingness to tolerate, slavery. Another liberal Union supporter who agreed with Hughes was John Elliott Cairnes, an economist and reformer who taught at the University of Dublin. Cairnes had recently delivered a series of lectures there showing that, because cotton crops eventually exhausted the soil, American slavery was doomed to extinction if it could not expand. This being the case, Lincoln's policy of preventing that expansion was, by definition, an antislavery policy, one which English abolitionists should support.

Cairnes sent copies of his lectures to Mill, who was himself being slowly but steadily drawn into the controversy surrounding the American war. On August 18 he wrote to Cairnes, thanking him for those copies.

In the letter, Mill observed that the "English organs of opinion cry out for a recognition of the secession, and for letting slavery alone," but the reality was that "slavery will not let freedom alone." He went on to note that he believed Cairnes had shown in his lectures, "more powerfully than had been done before, [that] American slavery depends upon a perpetual extension of its field; it must go on barbarizing the world more and more."

Given this, Mill contended, the Southern states will never consent to a peace unless they have access to the territories, which would give them the power of "unlimited conquest towards the South" into Mexico, Central America, and Cuba. Consequently, "instead of calling on the North to subscribe to this," Mill stated, "it would be a case for a crusade of all civilized humanity to oppose it." He then suggested that Cairnes recast his lectures to "connect them expressly and openly with the present crisis" and publish them in that form.[31] Cairnes accepted this suggestion. In the following year he published, in a book titled *The Slave Power*, a powerful indictment of both American slavery and the newly born Confederacy.

Around this same time, on the other side of the Atlantic, Norton composed a long essay titled "Emancipation and the Constitution," in which he attempted to reconcile the apparent contradiction that plagued the North and its British supporters and fueled the argument that the war was not about slavery. The question was: How could the North be fighting against slavery while defending the very Constitution that sanctions it? After completing his text, Norton put it aside. The headnote on the proof-page copy in his private papers reads, "Written in Sept. 1861; but not published because I was doubtful as to the correctness of the 'general welfare' argument. I did not wish to publish anything which, not being incontrovertible, might hurt the cause of liberty."[32]

The difficulty Norton had with his argument reveals the stubborn complexity of the situation facing Northern intellectuals at this early stage in the war. How could they make a compelling case for the North's moral superiority while staying within the four corners of the Constitution? Norton began with the assertion that "no person of intelligence will be inclined to dispute the assertion, that the origin of the existing civil war is to be traced immediately to the influence and results of the institution of slavery," and that "a continuance of political union between the North and the South [is] impossible on the old basis." While the president did not have the express power "to interfere with slavery," he could take action "if the general welfare be threatened by any circumstance whatever," including "the growth of institutions irreconcilable to its continuance or its increase." Therefore, "if slavery becomes dangerous to the general welfare, Congress has the power to make laws such as are required by the occasion."[33]

The problem with Norton's argument was this: If the institution of slavery existed in America legally for more than two hundred years, what had caused it to become a "danger to the general welfare" now? The answer for defenders of the institution was obvious: the violent opposition of fanatical abolitionists in the North. The North could be seen, therefore, as the true aggressor in this war, a position that both British critics and Southern apologists vigorously argued. This problem would not be resolved until Norton and his liberal New England cohorts accepted the fact that the Constitution "as it is" simply could not be sustained. American democracy would need to reinvent itself in the crucible of war. Emerson, who had anticipated this situation early on, would help lead the way as the war finally became what he always hoped it would be—America's second revolution.

British supporters like Mill and Cairnes were undoubtedly pleased when the North appeared to take at least a small step toward emancipation. On August 6, 1861, Lincoln signed the Confiscation Act, which provided for the seizure of "slaves used in aiding Insurrection."[34] The number of "contrabands" serving in Union army camps began to grow. The passage of the act undoubtedly had some positive effect in England, where antislavery reformers had felt only bewilderment regarding the position of the Union on the slavery question and, specifically, the treatment of runaway slaves who managed to reach Union lines. Writing in his *Harper's Weekly* Lounger column on August 24, Curtis reported receiving a "private letter" from an English supporter stating, "Anti-slavery people in England were sadly daunted in their sympathies by an account . . . of the way in which fugitive slaves were being sent back by the Northern free states to their masters." This, the correspondent noted, has "to a certain degree in England, taken off the character of the war being an anti-slavery war."

Now that was beginning to change. Heretofore, in the absence of a fixed policy, Union generals had made their own decisions regarding the disposition of fugitive slaves who reached Union lines. As noted earlier, Massachusetts general Benjamin Butler was the first to take the controversial position that they were "enemy contraband," and he refused to return them. Other generals saw the fugitive slaves as stolen property and, following federal law, returned them to their "owners." Now the Confiscation

Act offered at least some clarification. The measure was controversial, however, since it seemed to provide not only a federal mechanism for the seizure of private property but also a clear route to freedom for the contrabands. Conservative Democratic border-state congressmen objected and all but three of them voted against it. This, according to James McPherson, was "a signal that if the conflict became an antislavery war, it would thereby become a Republican war." This political controversy would grow with the passage of time, as slaves in ever-growing numbers became "contraband" by coming into Union lines.[35]

As might be expected, the Confiscation Act prompted outrage in the South. Virginian Rebecca Meade wrote to her son, who was serving in the Confederate army, just weeks after the law was passed. Apparently aware of Northern conservative opposition to the measure, she noted, "Did you ever read of a more Satanic body than the last Federal Congress? I do believe it will be the last. We are expecting a demonstration throughout the North against the [Lincoln] administration that will surpass anything that has ever occurred!" Meanwhile, the mischief prompted by the act was already manifest. Meade recounted "a public whipping at P[rince]. Georges County" of a Black person "associated with a gang up there bent upon insurrection as soon as the Yankees landed at City Point." She also reported that "we are in full expectation of our recognition by England and France, after which the North will be obliged to come to definite terms."[36]

Some of the positive impact of the Confiscation Act on Northern supporters abroad was lost due to an incident at the end of August, when Union general John C. Fremont issued a rather dramatic proclamation. As the commanding Union general in the border state of Missouri, he declared martial law and confiscated the property of all active Confederates in the state, freeing their slaves in the process. The proclamation caused a sensation, and Lincoln called upon Fremont to modify his emancipation edict, confiscating only the property, including slaves, employed as part of the war effort. When Fremont failed to comply, Lincoln removed him from command and revoked the proclamation.[37]

This proved to be controversial since, after Bull Run, many felt that the destruction of slavery must be part of the Union agenda if victory was to be achieved. Such a policy would be both morally and pragmatically correct. As Frederick Douglass declared, "Fire must be met with water—darkness with light, and war for the destruction of liberty must be met with war for the destruction of slavery."[38] Emerson agreed and encouraged his Saturday Club fellows to take a similarly liberal and liberating view of the matter. Progress on this front, however, would take time.

These were new and dangerous waters for intellectuals like Norton who were, at this early stage, still dedicated to preserving the Union *and* the Constitution. An essay, "Slavery and the War," appearing in *Harper's Weekly* on August 24 took a similar position. It argued that if the Constitution is to be followed, "neither the Congress nor the Administration has any more power to free the slaves in Virginia than to confiscate cattle in New England." This fact continued to complicate relations with Great Britain. An article in Charles Dickens's magazine, *All the Year Round*, observed that "in the political heart of the North itself a separate secession threatens by the Abolitionists. The standard they have raised . . . is Emancipation of the Slave."[39] Such dissension, the writer opined, was the inevitable consequence of unfettered freedom, yet another timely lesson for would-be English reformers.

Despite such widespread criticism, the Union was never without British supporters. Among the staunchest and most effective were MPs Richard Cobden and John Bright. Before the war, Cobden had visited the United States twice. These visits confirmed his admiration for American democracy. Cobden was highly regarded by many of the New England intelligentsia, especially Ralph Waldo Emerson. The two had met in Manchester when Emerson was lecturing there in 1847. Anthony Trollope noted the importance of Cobden and Bright as advocates of the Union cause. He told Kate Field that the two could be depended upon to "re-echo American ideas and American desires" in Parliament and elsewhere, which they did consistently and effectively.[40] Bright also enjoyed a personal friendship with Massachusetts senator and Saturday Club member Charles Sumner.

Others in the business and literary class in England were also supportive. Henry Bright, a Liverpool shipping executive and sometime literary critic, was one. Bright had visited Concord in 1852 where he met and befriended Nathaniel Hawthorne. Their friendship grew when Hawthorne later served as American consul to Liverpool. Bright had other friends among the New Englanders, including Charles Eliot Norton. He wrote to Norton to offer his support at this critical time. "You have many English friends," he assured him. "Most of us . . . have only one strong feeling—hope that peace may soon be restored. Few people attempt to justify the South," he reported, but at the same time, few "believe that the South can be subjugated & we all long to see some peace or compromises before more blood is spilt." Bright concluded by noting that his "dearest American friends are all Boston men, & even their opinions cannot make me think Civil War is anything but a monstrous, terrible evil out of which no good can come."[41]

As word of the British reaction to Bull Run spread throughout the North, there was a predictable backlash. The London *Times* was the target of much of the vitriol, most of it directed against its American correspondent, William Russell. *Harper's Weekly* expressed outrage that he described the Union defeat as "a cowardly rout, a miserable, causeless panic, and disgraceful to men in uniform," and that "the Union Army lost all, even their military honor," at Manassas. Another article in the same issue offered caustic criticism of all Englishmen, describing them as "Ishmaels and pariahs. . . . At home and abroad they hate every body and are hated in return," the writer declared. "Out of England, there is not a town in the world where Englishmen are not avoided by the educated classes and hated by masses of people."[42] Long gone were the fond notions of the "mother country" and the idea of an Anglo-American culture that *Harper's* had taken such comfort in just weeks earlier.

Meanwhile, friends of the North in England did their best to tamp down the fires. The London *Daily News* took a hopeful view on August 6 of the defeat at Manassas. "The Union is bound to conquer now," the writer insisted. "The spirit of New England and the North-west will rise to the occasion, and . . . never rest until they have turned defeat into victory." Liberal reformer Harriet Martineau, writing in the *National Anti-Slavery Standard* on September 7, insisted now was the time for the North to declare that "the abolition of slavery [is] an aim . . . no less essential than the maintenance of the Union. Whenever you do that," she declared, "our people will be with the North to a man." Soon this promise would be tested.

Even as the alienation between Great Britain and the North deepened, the British government continued its effort to maintain lines of communication with the Confederacy, in violation of international law. Not long before Bull Run, the British consul in Charleston, Robert Bunch, sent a letter to his friend William Porcher Miles requesting copies of official Confederate government documents relating to the tariff and other matters. Miles, after resigning from the US Congress in 1860, served as chair of the committee on foreign relations in the South Carolina secession convention. He was now serving in the Confederate Congress, where his special area of expertise was foreign affairs.[43]

Bunch informed Miles that he had "received a pressing instruction from Lord John Russell to furnish the Foreign Office with quadruplicate copies . . . of all authentic Documents which may emanate from authorities in the Southern States." These included "the various proclamations issued by Mr. Davis, together with all material State Papers." He closed on a personal note. "We have always looked anxiously for news from you and have been glad to hear from your brother that you are well."[44]

Miles also occasionally received British visitors, despite the difficulties of wartime travel. In his papers is a letter from William Gregory introducing two English gentlemen. Gregory, a Conservative MP, had recently presented the first bill in the House of Commons calling for the recognition of the Confederacy.[45] During a visit to the United States in 1859, he made the acquaintance of several Southern congressmen, including Miles. In the letter, dated July 20, he told Miles, "I send you two of my friends, Sir James Fergusson and Robert Bourke, with the full confidence that you will appreciate one another—you will find them very good fellows in every respect and withal of considerable ability. Sir James was a soldier all though the Crimean War, and is now a rising member of Parliament; and Robert Bourke is a lawyer making his way rapidly."[46]

The purpose of their journey, Gregory explained, was to gather information that could be used to support the Confederate cause in England. Gregory made it plain that the support of English conservatives, like himself, was due in large part to a shared opposition to liberal democracy. "I look forward to the establishment of a really well governed Republic," he wrote, "not as the United States were, the prey to universal suffrage and to the prejudices of the ignorance [of the] many—but a Republic governed by highly educated honorable men. . . . I am confident of your ultimate success—and judging from what has already been done, of the wise and temperate course that your government once established will follow."[47]

Miles was apparently able to respond to Gregory's letter, using Bunch as a conduit. In a letter to Miles that followed, Bunch stated, "I have to thank you so much for your interesting letter of the 5th. . . . I am . . . indebted for the supply of Public Documents. . . . L[ord]. Russell is now supplied with everything up to the proceedings of the last session." He then assured Miles that his "letter for Mr. Gregory shall go by the first opportunity, but it is really not easy to say when that will be—the gov't of the U.S. has, as you know, cut off all communication with the 'rebels,' and no provision seems to have been made for the correspondence of Foreign Agents with their gov'ts," he explained. "It is impossible that this can continue, as some means must be found." If this did not happen, Bunch assured Miles that he would "dispatch one myself, and let the U.S. turn him back, as they probably will. But your letter shall go whenever I send anything myself."

Bunch ended his letter on a cautionary note about placing too much emphasis on the *Times*'s reporting on the recent battle at Bull Run and English reaction. "I think that [*Times* reporter] Russell has jumped at a good many conclusions about the part of the battle which he did *not* see—you will have observed that throughout all his letters there runs the same somewhat supercilious style. . . . We, at home, are used to it and have quite made up our minds that no one knows anything except the *Times*. . . . We are looking anxiously for news from the Potomac."[48]

Bunch's role as a conduit for communications from officials of the Confederate government was eventually discovered, much to the embarrassment of the British. A dispatch from Lord Lyons to Lord Russell at this time indicates that Seward accused Bunch of using his office "for facilitating the transmission of treasonable correspondence." Lyons reported that he "went immediately to the State Department and spoke to Mr. Seward on the subject." He told Seward that "not only was Mr. Bunch remarkably correct in the observance of his official duties, but that his political sentiments were by no means such as to render it likely that he would have any desire to engage in the practices attributed to him."[49] In light of the letters referenced here, Lyons's statement appears either disingenuous or simply uninformed, but it was apparently effective. Seward had instructed Adams to request Bunch be removed, but Russell insisted (based on his correspondence from Lyons, apparently) that Bunch was only doing his job and could not be fired for that. Seward and the State Department let the matter drop for the time.[50]

When Bunch finally completed his service in Charleston, in February 1863, the Charleston *Mercury* spoke of him as a true friend of the Confederacy.[51] The two men whom Gregory introduced to Miles, MP James Fergusson and political activist Robert Bourke, eventually completed their tours of the South. Upon their return, they would both publish accounts of their experiences in *Blackwood's Edinburgh Magazine*. In these travelogues, they praised the nascent Confederacy and its leaders lavishly, applauded Southern culture and values, and generally disparaged the North, just as Gregory had virtually assured they would.[52]

Meanwhile, the New England intelligentsia continued their efforts to counter the demoralizing effects of the disaster at Manassas. In a pamphlet titled "The Soldier of the Good Cause," Norton stressed the moral aspects of the struggle while invoking the spirit of Puritanism. Southerners disparaged such expressions of New England's Puritan-inspired idealism. They saw it as yet another example of Yankee fanaticism. Just a week after the publication of Norton's pamphlet, Southern clergyman Moses Ashley Curtis wrote to a friend that he found it annoying that Northern commentators like Norton could actually take inspiration from defeat. "Providence favors our cause," he wrote. "Why can not the pious Puritans of the North argue the same way?" The Reverend Curtis was convinced that "Puritanism is at the bottom of all our troubles" and "Puritanism is especially cruel and intolerant. . . . Thank Heaven," he declared, "that there was a world outside of New England."[53] Confederate sympathizers in Great Britain felt the same way.

Several articles appearing in various British journals throughout the fall reflected an emerging pattern. Liberal-leaning journals were generally supportive of the Union cause, which they insisted was antislavery, despite the lack of a formal proclamation. *Macmillan's Magazine* argued that "the real cause of revolt [was] the manifest weakening of the power of the slaveholders to subordinate the legislation and administration of the country to the promotion of slavery" and that "the moral forces are on the side of the North."[54] The liberal *British Quarterly Review* also berated the rebels and condemned "the establishment of a vast slaveholding empire in America, unchecked by any restraint from the North, with slavery as the principle of its being, and the basis of its property and institutions."[55]

Conservative journals, on the other hand, were increasingly critical of the North and its "corrupt" and "vulgar" culture, which was seen as the inevitable by-product of its liberal democratic values. While denying any sympathy with slavery, they now openly supported the Confederacy, which they saw as properly conservative in its limited interpretation of human rights. They argued that, like themselves, Southerners wished to maintain a proper social order based on traditional distinctions of class, caste, and race.

In October, *Blackwood's*, the foremost among those journals in both prestige and bitter antipathy toward the North, celebrated the Union's humiliation at Bull Run. This fiasco, the writer contended, exposed "the empty pretensions of a bully, and . . . the exploits of the Grand Army of the Potomac are filling all Europe with inextinguishable laughter." The whole thing was "a screaming farce, and, moreover, a farce containing a moral for all mankind." The writer descended to ridicule in describing "that rabble of Bobadils which they called their army, with its 'Fire Zouaves,' and its Irish regiments 'stripped to their pants,' all in desperate career the wrong way. . . . All is farce of the very broadest stamp. . . . The end of the Union," it appeared, "seems more likely to be ridiculous than terrible."[56]

The *Saturday Review* was almost as harsh as *Blackwood's*. The journal was euphoric over the recent rebel victory. "It fills the *Times*. . . . It is the grand theme of conversation. . . . Everybody thinks that it is a 'screamer' and that Bull's Run was the most magnificent whipping ever received upon that Continent." The success of the Confederacy now seemed certain, and the balkanization of the North American continent was sure to follow for "the mutual benefit of different populations." If the Northerners were wise, the writer opined, "they would quietly accept the judgment of Nature."[57]

It was now more important than ever that the North imbue the struggle with a moral purpose in order to win British support or, at the least, ensure its neutrality. Harriet Martineau noted in one of her letters in the *National Anti-Slavery Standard* that there continued to be a great deal of uncertainty among British abolitionists regarding the Union's position on the slavery question. She explained that, despite her own belief that this was a war against slavery, "every mail brings me a bushel of letters from Northern citizens, insisting that the only question is of the Union and that nothing will be done about slavery."[58]

British abolitionist Richard Webb expressed the same concern in a letter to Boston reformer Anne Warren Weston. Webb explained that, from what he could gather, his British friends believed "this is on the part of the North a war for maintenance of the Union" and not "a war for the purpose of abolishing or diminishing slavery." This being the case, "it is, therefore, expecting too much to look for English sympathy" because, while the "the English dislike slavery," they did not especially "care for the Union."[59]

There was a desperate need for clarification on this critical question. An October 3 article in the antislavery *Independent* titled "The Voice of New England, by a New Englander" demanded action. The writer reported,

> Seven-Eighths of the intelligent adult inhabitants of the six Eastern states, whatever their party predilections, if asked individually today "What action of the Federal government would best suit you?" would reason and answer thus. "Slavery is the cause of this rebellion. . . . The sooner the Federal Government strikes at the root of the evil, declares itself unequivocally in favor of universal freedom, the better." Such is the voice of New England—the sentiment for which her fifty thousand volunteers will fight, and if need be die. . . . Why then delay the declaration? Publish it, and God is with us; good men are with us; the right is with us.

Eventually, this plea would be answered, but much suffering would be endured on both sides before that moment arrived.

For their part, Southerners were increasingly bitter about the role New Englanders had played in bringing the war about and now played in their efforts to define its goals as liberal and antislavery. A November 3 article in the New Orleans *Daily Picayune* titled "Massachusetts in This War" condemned the state, especially the citizens of Worcester and Middlesex Counties, home to Transcendentalists like Higginson and Emerson, as the primary source of antagonism that led to the war. "It was from that neighborhood, 'the heart of the Commonwealth,' as they were wont boastingly to call it," that came "the foster fathers of the faction which had succeeded in breaking up the American Union. Thence was wont for years to flow forth that never failing stream of petitions to Congress for the abolition of slavery in the Territories and in the District of Columbia, against the annexation of Texas, and of any other territory in which slavery existed. There were, and still are, held the conventions and conventicles of that pestilent brood of fanatics whose machinations brought about the election of Abraham Lincoln, and the war which has followed . . . was an inevitable consequence."

Mary Chesnut agreed with the *Picayune*. In her diary she declaimed bitterly against the intellectual class from the North that led the charge against Southern culture and Southern values. She was especially irate toward "Mrs. Stowe, [Horace] Greeley, Thoreau, Emerson, [and] Sumner, [who all live] in nice New England homes—clean, clear, sweet-smelling—shut up in libraries, writing books which ease their hearts of their bitterness to us, or editing newspapers—all [of] which pays better than anything else in the world. Even the politician's hobbyhorse—

antislavery, is the beast to carry him highest. What self-denial do they practice? It is the cheapest philanthropy trade in the world—easy. Easy as setting John Brown to come down here and cut our throat in Christ's name." Chesnut's earlier regard for Emerson and the other popular authors of New England, whose works she once read with delight in the *Atlantic Monthly*, had turned to dust.[60]

On the Northern home front, conservative critics continued to resist the effort of New England liberals to turn the war into a revolution that would bring equality among the races. On October 5 the ultra-conservative New York *Weekly Caucasian* began publication. The Democratic and Unionist weekly described itself as "an independent political journal, devoted especially to the explanation of the so-called slavery question." That "explanation" began with the assertion that "this is 'a White Man's Government,' and that the Supreme Court Decision in the Dred Scott case was a true and faithful exposition of the Constitution of the United States in respect to the *status* of the negro race." The *Caucasian*'s intention was to "defend the justice, wisdom and humanity of that decision" and to show that it is "in conformity both to human and divine laws." According to the *Caucasian*, "the supremacy of the white race and the subordination of the negro race are *natural* facts, which cannot be gainsayed or denied." Indeed, "all just civil laws are those, and only those, that embody natural laws." Therefore, "that society, which recognizes and regulates the *differences* between the races, must be fundamentally correct" (all emphasis in original).

While not as extreme as the *Caucasian*, Massachusetts conservatives were also disturbed by the liberal demand for emancipation, perhaps out of economic as much as social concerns. The Boston *Courier* published on November 13 a strident attack on abolitionists and their long-standing "no-Union with slaveholders" policy. The writer referred to abolitionists as "enemies of the Constitution and the Union" and reported that many were now trying to disassociate themselves from that group. He contended, "Northern abolitionism is the original, active element, which first attacked the Union." Northern conservatives, it seemed, were clearly in no mood for a second revolution. It was obvious to them that emancipation would make reunion on the basis of the status quo ante impossible. Their sentiments frequently echoed those expressed by British conservatives and Southerners, especially when it came to matters of race and equality.

In light of the flurry of criticisms that followed the disaster at Bull Run, many New Englanders were concerned that the North was rapidly losing whatever public support it had in Great Britain. Samuel May expressed his anxiety about the situation in a letter to Richard Webb. British newspapers and journals, he noted, "have spoken apologetically, and in some cases even approvingly, of the Southern Movement," while their "spirit and tone . . . towards us of the North has been unjust and ungenerous." Especially irritating to May was Robert Cecil's recent London *Quarterly Review* article, "Democracy on Its Trial." "How transparent & marked is its satisfaction in what it considers as the virtual overthrow of this Republican government and of the failure of this experiment in Democratic Government," he exclaimed.[61]

Many New Englanders continued to believe that a formally stated antislavery policy would help turn British public opinion around, but the Lincoln administration remained silent regarding the issue, perhaps recognizing that the rest of the country might not be as enthusiastic about emancipation as the liberals of New England. It was clear to many that victory on the battlefield would do much to discourage European recognition of the Confederacy, but since Bull Run and a change in command that put George McClellan, the Union's "Young Napoleon," in charge, no major action had been fought. Under pressure to act, the Union army finally engaged the enemy in a significant clash at Ball's Bluff, Virginia, on October 21. The result was another disaster. Over half of the 1,700 Union soldiers engaged were killed, wounded, or captured as the North suffered yet another humiliating defeat.[62]

The clash had a very personal significance for Lowell, Holmes, and others among New England's intelligentsia. Two Massachusetts regiments were mauled at Ball's Bluff. Oliver Wendell Holmes Jr. was severely wounded, shot twice in the chest.[63] James Russell Lowell's nephew James was also wounded.[64] Another nephew, William Lowell Putnam, was killed in the action. All were serving in the Massachusetts 20th, known as the "Harvard Regiment" because so many of its officers were graduates of the school, where antislavery feeling ran high.[65] Before the war was over, Lowell would suffer the loss of two more beloved nephews, young men he considered his adoptive sons.[66] Ultimately, the war would cost the lives of many sons from New England's most prominent families, "the golden youth" as Norton once called them. This added a truly personal element to the conflict, in turn making the sneering criticism of British journals like *Blackwood's* even more deeply alienating (as with its description of the Union's efforts as a "screaming farce"). As more and more lives were lost in the struggle, this personal element contributed considerably to the growing bitterness felt toward all things British.

Such bitterness was reflected in a long article in the November *Atlantic Monthly*. The author, George Ellis, was a prominent Unitarian minister and writer and a highly regarded member of New England's intellectual class.[67] Responding to recent criticism in the *Quarterly Review*, Ellis presented a litany of British "offenses" to date. The first and foremost was that they assumed from the outset that the Union was forever broken and could never be restored. Second, this assumption gave aid and comfort to the enemy, encouraging them in rebellion and disheartening Unionists. Third, the English seemed to assume that this division should occur on the terms demanded by the rebels. Fourth, there was no expression of sympathy at this catastrophe. Fifth, British critics and commentators never had a good thing to say about Lincoln and the reasonableness and restraint he had shown thus far, despite the great burden laid upon him. Sixth, the English press had uniformly, it seemed, taken the breakup of the Union to be the death knell for democracy itself. And last, the English likened the rebels to the revolutionaries of '76, thus giving historical and moral sanction to their effort. Overall, Ellis declared, "the tone and the strain of English opinion and sentiment have been such as to inspirit the South and dispirit the North," an unkindly cut that the New Englanders never expected from the once-beloved mother country.[68]

Ellis's blunt essay, appearing in what was arguably America's most prestigious journal, garnered almost immediate attention from the London *Times*. It was now apparent to some that the alienation and antipathy felt in the North toward England was more than a mere matter of cultural testiness. It was a strong, visceral, and deeply felt anger that could have serious consequences for both nations. The *Times*'s New York correspondent, Bancroft Davis, an American, reported that a "wide-spread feeling of dissatisfaction [toward England] . . . finds expression in different ways. . . . In the 'sensation' journals of New York it blazes forth in language of questionable English, but strong denunciation. In the more dignified pages of the magazines it clothes itself in the more guarded and regretful language which appears in the November number of the *Atlantic Monthly*." Davis explained that he could not "better illustrate the views of the educated classes on this subject than by quoting a few words from the article entitled, 'Why the North felt aggrieved at England.'"

Davis then offered substantial extracts from Ellis's essay, followed by a warning. "These few extracts sufficiently show how this [alienation] is regarded by the educated classes," he wrote, "and goes far to justify all I have ever said either of the depth or the prevalence of the feeling. It is out of such national antipathies as are germinating under our eyes, without an effort to stop them, that national discords grow." Englishmen ignore these antipathies at their peril, Davis warned. "If unchecked, they grow with each passing day, until they are infused through the body politic, and at length break out in violent action."[69] It is somewhat ironic that all of this resulted largely from the acrimony expressed in the British press and not by the British government, which continued to follow an official policy of neutrality. The fear that animosities expressed in the popular press of both countries could trigger a catastrophic war remained a major concern throughout the balance of the conflict and for some time thereafter.

Despite this caution, Davis offered no suggestions for dealing with the growing alienation. He might have been aiming his comments at the *Times* itself, given the pernicious role it had thus far played in the matter. The editor of the *Times*, John Delane, apparently did not share Bancroft's concern. In an editorial appearing just two days later, the paper was both defensive and offensive in what it had to say about the situation. The editorial noted that the *Times* "did not need the information of our own Correspondent in New York to convince us . . . that what is called 'the public mind' in the Northern States of America is very ill disposed towards this country. We might have gathered the fact from Mr. Seward's circular to the Governors of the States advising them . . . to prepare themselves for an attack by Great Britain." The editorial pointed out that American animosity toward the mother country had a long history. "For a great many years," the *Times* noted, England had stood "very low in the good graces of the multitudinous monarch of the United States."[70] As to the current conflict, the *Times* was unapologetic. "We do believe, and shall continue to do so, that the Secession of the South has destroyed the Federal Union, and that, to whichever side victory inclines, its reconstruction on the old basis is impossible." Adding insult to this injury, the *Times* offered the following: "We further think—and every word of the *Atlantic Monthly* confirms us in the opinion—that the contest is really for empire on the side of the North, and for independence on the side of the South." Clearly, the *Times* had little interest in calming the stormy relationship between the British and their Northern American cousins. The breakdown in relations between the two countries that Davis warned of would not be long in coming.

The harsh sentiment of the *Atlantic* article was reinforced by others in the Northern press as animosity toward England grew for all of the reasons stated in that article. Later in the month (November 19), *Harper's Weekly* published a piece by Curtis titled simply "English Hate." The essay contrasted Northern expectations with the surprisingly harsh criticism appearing in the British press. The painful silence of the British literary establishment was also unexpected and deeply disappointing. "The malignity of hatred which the leading papers evince towards us—papers which are known to be the organs of eminent, public men in England," Curtis declared, "reveals a condition of the English mind which few of us could have suspected." "The Laureate of England [Tennyson]," he pointed out, once "dreamed of a 'federation of the world.' So, possibly, did many a dreamer who was no laureate." Now that hope was quickly becoming an empty dream, and yet the laureate remained silent. The British reaction to the Union defeat at Bull Run had laid bare a cultural, social, and political divide that reached a crisis stage when a dramatic confrontation at sea bought the United States and Great Britain to the very brink of war.

Chapter 5

The Old World and the New Collide

The *Trent* Affair Brings the Threat of War

On November 8, 1861, the USS *Jacinto*, commanded by Captain Charles Wilkes, stopped the British steamer *Trent* by firing two shots across her bow and removed James Mason and John Slidell, Confederate commissioners en route to England. This action was a violation of international law, but Wilkes felt otherwise.[1] On November 16, Americans learned of what would soon become known as the *Trent* affair. Given the deep animosity toward England felt by most Northerners at this point in the war, it is not surprising that, as one historian reports, when word of Wilkes's action arrived, "there broke out a widespread rejoicing and glorification in the Northern press."[2] Northerners were delighted and celebrated what they felt was a well-deserved slap in the face of the perfidious mother country. Young Charles Francis Adams reported in a letter to his father that the seizure of Mason and Slidell "created quite a stir and immense delight, though at first everyone thought that it must be a violation of [inter]national law; but Dana crowed with delight and declared that if Lord John made an issue on that, you could blow him out of [the] water."[3]

Richard Henry Dana Jr. was a prominent Boston lawyer and author of the highly regarded adventure narrative *Two Years Before the Mast* (1840). He was also a founding member of the Saturday Club. Dana was known for his strong antislavery views. He served on the team of lawyers who attempted to prevent the rendition of fugitive slave Anthony Burns in that celebrated case in 1854.[4] With the support of influential friends like Charles Sumner, Dana had been appointed by Lincoln as US

Attorney for Massachusetts. A recognized authority on Admiralty Law, Dana's opinion on the *Trent* affair was undoubtedly persuasive with many in Boston. However, despite his early confidence that the seizure of Mason and Slidell was legal under international law, he would later admit that this judgment was wrong.[5]

The mood in the country at the moment, however, was celebratory. The House of Representatives voted Wilkes a gold medal, and a banquet was held in Boston in his honor.[6] Captain Wilkes was also an honored guest at a Saturday Club dinner, where he was hailed as a true hero.[7] The club was clearly becoming more engaged with developments in the war with every day that passed. The growing liberal activism of the group was reflected in the new members welcomed into this exclusive coterie. Samuel Gridley Howe, a noted Boston physician and radical abolitionist (one of the "Secret Six" who supported John Brown), became a member in the first year of the war, as did Estes Howe, another active abolitionist reformer and Free-Soiler.[8] Charles Sumner, one of the most radical and outspoken abolitionists in the United States Senate, became a member the following year.[9]

Sumner was the chair of the Senate's Foreign Relations Committee throughout the war years. He knew the British mind well as a result of his extensive European travels before the war and realized immediately that Wilkes's action would lead to serious difficulties with Great Britain. "They will have to be given up," he told his friends at a dinner party shortly after news of the event arrived.[10] Eventually, Longfellow, as well as Norton, Curtis, and others, would agree with the senator's sober assessment, but not before the crisis that the action gave rise to was resolved.[11] That resolution came only at the end of a long and dangerous process that led the United States and Great Britain to the very threshold of war.

The English reaction to the seizure seemed deliberately provocative to the Americans. Young Charles Adams was apprehensive, not because the act was illegal but because the animosity of the English toward the North was intense. He wrote to his brother Henry on December 3 that everyone was "anxious to hear from England of the reception of Mason and Slidell's capture, and your letter . . . created a good deal of uneasiness." He was concerned that "a popular clamor and feeling of hatred towards us" will make "future difficulty very easy," a possibility that the London *Times*'s American correspondent had warned about earlier.[12]

When news of the event reached London on November 27, it touched off an explosion of British indignation. In the eyes of the British public, Commander Wilkes's act was an intolerable insult. With animosities already simmering, the situation quickly rose to a boil. A major crisis was now at hand. Feelings were intense on both sides. As the crisis quickly escalated, Secretary of State William H. Seward told a guest at an evening gathering, within earshot of *Times* reporter William Russell, that if England wanted a war "we will wrap the whole world in fire." The statement sent shock waves across the Atlantic.[13]

The British prepared to send several thousand troops to Canada to enhance defenses there, and they enlarged the British fleet in the North Atlantic. Some in the English press and Parliament called for war if Mason and Slidell were not released immediately. A longtime American resident of London reported to Secretary Seward on November 29 that "there never was within memory such a burst of feeling as has been created by the news of the boarding [of the *Trent*]. The people are frantic with rage, and were the country polled, I fear 999 men out of a thousand would declare for immediate war."[14] The normally friendly *Spectator* was furious. In an article ominously titled "Peace or War," the journal declared that "Captain Wilkes committed an outrage.... American statesmen must stand convicted of preferring a pique to a principle, the gratification of national spleen to the assertion of human right."[15]

England's hostile mood had significant consequences. Pro-Confederate feelings solidified, especially among the aristocrats.[16] Many were sure the situation would lead to war. Palmerston was advised by Crown law officers that the American action was "a wanton violation by the Captain of the Law & Usage of Nations."[17] The British government made an immediate demand for an explanation of this outrageous act. If the explanation was not satisfactory, Lord Lyons was instructed to break diplomatic relations and "leave Washington with all the members of your Legation."[18] Clearly, London was bracing for war, if it came to that.

John Bright wrote to Sumner expressing his concern about the rapidly deteriorating situation. The removal of the "Southern Commissioners . . . from an English ship," Bright told him, "has made a great sensation here, and the ignorant and passionate and 'Rule Britannia' class are angry and insolent as usual."[19] A week later, Bright wrote again to inform Sumner that the increasingly bitter war of words between the North and Great Britain was now threatening to draw the two countries into a shooting war. "The excitement here is great," he wrote, "and it is fed, as usual, by newspapers whose writers seem to imagine a cause of war discovered to be something like a 'Treasure Trove.'" Bright then added, ominously, "I dread the consequences of war quite as much for your sakes as for our own."[20]

With the temperature rising on both sides, Bright was eager to use his personal friendship with Sumner to avert a catastrophe. This effort at back-channel diplomacy was evident in a third letter, sent just two days later, urging conciliation. "I pray that in your Senate in the Committee over which you preside [Foreign Relations], and in your Cabinet Councils, and in the breast of your President, there may be the calm wisdom which will baffle those seeking to force you into war with England—just now endangered by the power of her oligarchy and her overgrown military services."[21]

Shortly after this, Minister Adams wrote to Dana, who had been so enthusiastic about the prospect of a clash with the British. In the letter, he warned Dana that the British would welcome an opportunity to create havoc for the American Union. "The experience of the past summer might have convinced you that [England] *was not indifferent to the disruption of the Union*. In May she drove in the tip of the wedge, and now you cannot imagine that a few spiders' webs of half a century back will now be strong enough to hold her back from driving it home!"[22]

By December 20 the situation appeared hopeless. It seemed certain that the heated rhetoric on both sides would lead to a catastrophic collision. Charles Dickens told a correspondent, "I fear the North will be utterly mad, and war to be unavoidable."[23] An American businessman working in England lamented the rapidly deteriorating situation in a letter to Boston business magnate Amos A. Lawrence. "The outrage in the English press on the removal of the Southern Commissioners from the 'Trent Steamer' has been *the best possible thing that could happen to the cause of the Rebels*," he wrote. "Before this news came, a much better feeling had become manifest towards us, both in England & France. This has thrown it back again and the times [are] worse than before."[24]

Around the same time, Charles Darwin wrote to his American friend, Harvard botanist Asa Gray. "I fear there is no shadow of doubt we shall fight if the two Southern rogues are not given up," he warned.[25] Writing from England on December 17, Robert Browning warned William Wetmore Story that "our people hold to the bone they have got in their jaws this time" and will not let go without an admission that the act was wrong.[26] Obviously, someone had to blink, and it wouldn't be the British. Matthew Arnold was blunt in his assessment. He instructed his mother to tell his brother-in-law, MP William Forster (who was with her at the time), that "the Americans will not cease to be afflicted until they learn thoroughly that man shall not live by Bunkum alone."[27]

Harper's Weekly reported that British newspapers are "full of fury and menace against this county" and threaten that "our 'little fleet is to be swept from the seas.'" In the gravity of the moment, *Harper's* could not help but observe, once more, the perfidy of a nation that, despite being bound to this country "by every tie of blood, language, religion, commerce, treaties, institutions, and a common freedom, at once bestowed her sympathies upon the institution she had denounced for forty years." This apparent de facto alliance with the slaveholding South represented the abnegation of every principle of civilization for which England claimed to stand. Such an anomaly confirmed to *Harper's* and many others that England harbored a deep antipathy toward Northern democracy that superseded all other concerns.

In spite of all the dire talk about the inevitability of war, cooler heads were at work behind the scenes. Charles Sumner was now in regular contact with America's most reliable supporters in the British Parliament, John Bright and Richard Cobden. They wrote to Sumner at the height of the crisis on December 5 and 6. At one point, Bright had suggested submitting the issue to arbitration, but Cobden argued that Mason and Slidell must be released unconditionally. Like Bright, he made his plea personally. "I write to you, of course, in confidence," he told Sumner, "and I write to you what I would not write to any other American,—nay, what it would be perhaps improper for any other Englishman than myself to utter to any other American but yourself."[28]

Cobden and Bright were both sure Palmerston's government wished to avoid war if the Americans would cooperate in the effort. With this information in hand, Sumner wrote the following to Seward on December 24: "I have letters from Cobden & Bright—at length—marked private & confidential, which I am not to allow to go out of my hands, in which they suggest the grounds on which they & their friends can stand in England. I wish to read them to you & the President. When?"[29] In response, Sumner was invited to attend a special meeting of the cabinet on Christmas morning at the White House, where he read the letters aloud, each pleading for a peaceful resolution.[30] It was decided at this meeting that Mason and Slidell would be released immediately in order to defuse the crisis. Later that night, Sumner wrote to Bright, "The case of the *Trent* is settled."[31]

The next day Lincoln met again for four hours with his cabinet, and the decision to surrender the prisoners was confirmed.[32] Secretary of State

Seward ordered the release of Mason and Slidell, ruling they were "contraband" and should have been taken to a neutral port for adjudication. US Marshal John S. Keyes of Concord released the prisoners on January 2, 1862.[33] The role played by Sumner and his British friends was critical in bringing about this resolution.[34] The news undoubtedly brought great relief to many on both sides of the Atlantic, including Sumner's Boston friends. The following month the senator accepted an invitation to join the Saturday Club, where he had frequently been a guest. Sponsored by Emerson, he was the year's only new member.[35]

In the midst of the *Trent* affair, on December 3, Lincoln delivered his first annual message to Congress. By most accounts, not only was the presentation dull and perfunctory, consisting mostly of reports from various government departments, but it also failed to touch upon the two most pressing issues of the moment. The president never mentioned the disposition of Mason and Slidell and, other than some vague proposals for colonizing freedmen somewhere outside the United States, he said nothing about the slavery question.[36] The latter issue would continue to be of supreme importance to Northern supporters in England, who saw it as the only defining difference between the Northern and Southern causes. They made this clear both privately and publicly.

Eliza Wigham, the secretary of the Edinburgh Ladies Emancipation Society, complained to Samuel May that "your people are carping and caviling because we have not at once sprung up & urged them on to fight for the Union, a Union you have taught us to believe, & which we still believe, to be based on the subjugation of the poor slaves."[37] Similarly, William Robson, a Liberal member of the House of Commons, wrote to Francis Jackson Garrison that "there is a wide difference of opinion entertained between New & Old England. . . . [Some] opinion here I think decidedly recognizes the right of the Southern states to choose their own form of government. I have never yet seen an argument against it worthy of note." Without a clear antislavery policy, he reported, it appears to many Englishmen that "the North is simply fighting for Empire—the basest and most brutal tyranny that exists upon the earth is attempting by force of war to sustain *itself*."[38] Southern agents actively promoted this view.

In a letter to Boston antislavery activist Caroline Weston, British abolitionist Richard Webb warned about the growing influence of Southern propaganda in the English press and what was perceived to be "American proslavery policy." "The very class you know the most of in England," he told her, "are those who having been most exposed to this contamination have suffered worst from it." Among them were "writers from the press, literary men & those classes to which travelled Americans have most wished for and obtained access."[39] Martineau wrote in one of her last columns in the *National Anti-Slavery Standard*, on December 7, that, from a British perspective, "the weight of testimony has hitherto shown that the struggle was, or believed to be, for the Union—for the Constitution," a "Constitution which sanctions slavery." The president's message did nothing to change this view.

In England, the antislavery *Spectator* offered a generally negative view of Lincoln's address. A major disappointment for the *Spectator* was the fact that in the president's message, "the thing slavery is never referred to."[40] In an effort to mitigate British criticisms of Lincoln's policies and the war itself, Story chose this time to publish a long essay on "The American Question" in the London *Daily News*. The publication, on December 25 and 27, was arranged by Robert Browning through the intercession of Edward Dicey, a British journalist sympathetic to the Union cause.[41] Story's essay was soon published in London in pamphlet form, a copy of which he sent to Norton.[42]

Unlike others, Story made a distinction between the British press and the British government, and then proceeded to condemn them both: the press for its harsh criticism of the North and its sympathy for the South, the government for its official policies including the Proclamation of Neutrality and the granting of belligerent status to the rebels. Particularly offensive to Story was the fact that the press contrasted what it saw as "the gentlemen of the Confederate States with the sweaty mechanics and 'mud-sills' of the North." He also objected to the claim by British critics that the "sole object" of the war was the "subjugation [of the South] for the sake of empire."[43] Throughout his essay, Story was especially critical of the *Times*, the *Saturday Review*, and the *Edinburgh Review*. Like Motley before him, Story made a long and detailed argument to show that secession was not legal under the Constitution. While well intended, at this point in British-American relations, Story's treatise was of little help. His technical arguments against the legality of secession could easily be met with equally technical arguments for it, and they were.

Story's constitutional argument had the unfortunate effect of reinforcing the claim of British conservatives that the war was not about slavery, thus denying the North the high moral ground and leaving it in the role of an economic aggressor bent on maintaining an empire, the very position Story claimed to argue against. Story's essay was also, of course, ineffective with British liberals and abolitionists who were distressed that Lincoln had *not* by this point adopted an antislavery policy. The war had created certain expectations among liberals on both sides of the Atlantic, and they were now calling for a more liberal and liberating Federal position.

Reflecting the political conflict, the media war showed no sign of abating. The December issue of *Blackwood's* included two articles on the American divide. The first was "A Month with the Rebels" by Robert Bourke, the Anglo-Irish aristocrat and lawyer who, as noted earlier, was introduced to Confederate congressman William Porcher Miles by Conservative MP William Gregory in July.[44] Throughout his article, Bourke presented what could only be called a cheerful view of Southern slavery. At the outset, he indicated that the article was based on his recent journey through the South. While visiting a plantation in Alabama, he reported, "We found ourselves surrounded by about forty slaves, men, women, and children, engaged in 'picking.' They were all well dressed, and seemed happy and cheerful." He went on to indicate that, "wishing to know what time of day it was, I asked Mr.—the hour, whereupon one of the darkies by my side took out a gold watch and informed me. 'Do your labourers generally wear gold watches, sir?' I inquired. 'A great many of them have. Why, sir, my negroes all have their cotton-plots and gardens, and most of them little orchards.'"

In addition to this remarkable display of slave wealth, Bourke described these people as enjoying a life of plenty, all supported by mild labor. "We found from their own testimony that they are fed well, chiefly upon pork, corn, potatoes, and rice, carefully attended to when sick, and on Sundays dress better than their masters. Many of them had six or seven hundred dollars of their own, which they either lend to the banks or hide in the ground. In the hot weather they begin work at six in the morning, and go on till ten; they then go home till about three, and when the sun declines, return to their work till six or seven. In the cool weather they begin soon after daylight, and rest for two or three hours in the middle of the day."[45]

Such positive reports purporting to show the felicity and comfort of Southern slave life were not uncommon in the writings of conservative British visitors. What Bourke claimed to have found on his sojourn through the Confederacy is indicative of the lengths to which the British establishment was willing to go in defense of an institution that the masses of Great Britain had condemned and abolished almost three decades earlier. Often the slaves' relatively comfortable lifestyle was reported to be better than that of the average British laborer.

Blackwood's second article on the subject, "Some Account of Both Sides of the American War," was authored by Bourke's traveling companion, James Fergusson. After returning from his visit to the American South, Fergusson sent a long report about his travels to the leader of the Conservative Party, Lord Derby. This report was later passed on to Lord Palmerston, who was urged by Derby to read it. Palmerston thought enough of it to have the document copied before returning it. Eventually, the information was also shared with arch-conservative Lord Robert Cecil, who fully agreed with its findings.[46] Like Bourke's, Fergusson's article, which basically reiterated the content of his long report, was published anonymously. Also like Bourke's, the article showed a strong bias toward the South, as Gregory had virtually assured Miles it would.[47]

The end of the year brought the publication of what was arguably the most important and effective English book promoting the cause of the Confederacy, James Spence's *American Union*.[48] Spence, who has been called "the South's most prominent British advocate," was a Liverpool businessman with no previous experience in the realm of political polemics.[49] In essence, his book was a comprehensive, conservative attack on what many British critics saw as the manifest flaws and deficiencies of a republican democracy. Like other conservative Southern advocates in England, Spence incorporated the now familiar notion that the South was largely settled by aristocratic "Cavaliers," while the North, beginning with New England, was settled by Puritan commoners. Spence argued that the North's population was made even more common by the influx of a large number of immigrants, the undesirable offscourings of various European societies.[50] Spence also insisted that slavery was not at issue in the war, and even if it were, the problem could best be dealt with through the permanent separation of the South from the North.

The book was well received not only in England but throughout Europe. Positive reviews appeared in several journals, including Dickens's *All the Year Round*.[51] Four editions were published in six months, with translations in French, German, Spanish, and Italian. Richard Webb called it "one of the ablest, craftiest, and most dishonest books I have ever met with."[52] It would play a prominent role in the coming year in the continuing political and cultural warfare between Great Britain and the United States.

Chapter 6

1862

Talk of Emancipation Fuels British Fears of a Global Race War

At the outset of 1862, articles in the British press amplified tensions and fears. The possibility of war with England remained a real concern for Northerners. On the first day of the new year, Longfellow recorded in his journal, "Uncle Tom comes, rather warm with the war against England, and report of British man-of-war in Boston harbor; which turns out to be false, it being only a gun-boat at Provincetown on the Cape, come for Slidell and Mason, the rebel prisoners at Fort Warren."[1] Despite the resolution of the crisis, the Boston *Daily Advertiser* on January 2 doubted "whether England cares to have a peaceful settlement of all the troubles that may arise, and whether she will not welcome some insoluble difficulty, that shall give her the pretext for a violent interference."

Meanwhile, liberal journals in England sought to pour oil on the troubled waters. In their first issue of the new year, *Macmillan's Magazine* warned that "recent frictions" between Great Britain and the United States "are certain to fret into sores, if real wisdom be not actively employed on both sides."[2] *Fraser's Magazine* also called for improved relations with the North. The journal observed that if forced into a war with the United States, England would be compelled to support the slave states, which would be "an odious position for us, to be defending a system with arms which we have long and loudly condemned." Somewhat surprisingly, the author argued not only for the slaves' freedom but also for the full assimilation of all Blacks, North and South, into American society. As things presently stood, he noted, even if emancipation should occur, "the freed negroes will be no nearer to their rights as human beings. The President already hints at deportation; and others talk insolently of their elimination by 'natural selection.' . . . If the poor African is ever to receive good from the more advanced races," he argued, "he must be permitted to associate with them."[3] This was an early hint of what was to come. Very soon, the American war would become ground zero in an international struggle for human rights.

The *Edinburgh Review* argued in January that assimilation was a pipe dream and that emancipation would be a huge mistake. The journal pointed to what it claimed were the deleterious effects of British emancipation in the West Indies in 1833–34.[4] Negroes there, "when they ceased to be slaves, ceased to be industrious; and when they became free, became insolent and 'uppish' in the drunkenness of unwonted liberty." Granting freedom to American slaves, the author argued, would bring the same disastrous results. Negroes in the American South, he insisted, were barely civilized. They were unacquainted "with anything of refined life. . . . Courteous manners . . . he rarely sees; and his religious exercises are confined to howling, groaning, singing, and screaming." In light of these "facts," "to confer on such a semi-barbarous race full civil liberty seems to the Southerners and to many Northerners a dangerous and Quixotic experiment."[5]

On the other side of the Atlantic, the *North American Review*, reflecting its own conservative roots, seemed to agree. The journal acknowledged that, while "the exigencies of the war may render emancipation inevitable . . . this measure would, in the present posture of affairs, be disastrous equally to the slaves and the now dominant race. Whenever the Africans receive the gift of freedom," the writer argued, "it should be under circumstances in which their industry could be directed and employed for the common good." Unless emancipation was carefully controlled, he warned, "a war of races would be inevitable."[6]

Fear of a possible race war was shared by English conservatives. Millions of indigenous peoples of "inferior" race lived under British rule, where they, like the African slaves in America, enjoyed the presumed "benefits" of enlightened subjugation. The sudden emancipation of American slaves would provide a potentially incendiary example to oppressed peoples everywhere. And the result for the British would be catastrophic. The bloody Indian Rebellion (1857–59), an uprising of the Sepoys put down with great violence and cruelty, was a recent example.[7] Any effort to emancipate and "equalize" slaves in America would undermine the moral authority of British overlords throughout the empire.

These concerns undoubtedly contributed to the steady growth of British support for the Confederacy, which paralleled the growing demand for emancipation in the North. Racial politics would soon become a major focus in the war. The British governing class would go to great lengths in propagandizing against emancipation, despite Britain's long-standing opposition to slavery. This was the unkindest cut of all for liberal New Englanders, who had once admired and celebrated Britain's progressive and humane emancipation policy. It also led to a closer transatlantic bond between British aristocrats and Southern oligarchs.

This bond was apparent on a personal level. On the first day of the new year, Dr. Augustus Evans of North Carolina wrote to his wife from London. He had been sent there to procure drugs and medicine for the Confederacy. Dr. Evans reported that he "was received with much kindness and attention" from "many able men in the profession who were very anxious to hear from the South for which there is universal sympathy. It is quite charming to find such enthusiasm in our cause, which I learn . . . is of recent origin—The success of our army and the *Trent* affair have put our cause all right on this side of the water." The doctor was staying with a family that was "very strongly southern," and he was "very much pleased with the English generally." He found them to be "like our Southern people, honest and confiding, not suspicious or tricky, a noticeable contrast to Yankees."[8]

Blackwood's began the new year as it ended the old, with bitter denunciations of the North and Northern democracy. Empowering the common man through universal male suffrage inevitably resulted in the election of commoners who were not fit to rule, the journal argued. The prime example was Abraham Lincoln. "The great achievement in self-government of this vaunted democracy, which we have been so loudly and arrogantly called on to admire," *Blackwood's* declared, "is to drag from his proper obscurity an ex-rail-splitter and country attorney and to place what it calls its liberties at his august disposal. . . . [W]hat other proof is needed," the author asked, "of the inefficacy of their boasted institutions? An imbecile executive above, a restless, purposeless multitude below, linked together like a kite tied to a balloon, and drifting at the mercy of the air-currents, while respectability, moderation, and sense are pushed aside, or dragged helplessly along,—such is the spectacle presented, in the first storm, by the Model Republic."[9] Throughout this long and strident essay, the author made no mention of slavery.

Religious establishments now joined in the transatlantic war of words. A January article in the *Princeton Review* offered acerbic criticism of the blatant immorality and hypocrisy of those Englishmen who expressed sympathy with the slaveholding rebels. The *Review*, a generally conservative Presbyterian journal that was read on both sides of the Atlantic, excoriated the British who had "in this great struggle taken the side of lawlessness, of slavery, and of violence, from selfish and dishonourable motives."

Particularly upsetting was the gross perfidy indicated by recent British conduct. "No two nations are bound together by so many bonds of sympathy and interest as England and America. England," the writer asserted, "is our mother." She has "transmitted to us her Anglo-Saxon life." This bond included a distinct spiritual and moral element. "We are the two great Protestant powers of the world, doing more than all other nations combined, for what we both regard as the best interest of man and the advancement of the Redeemer's kingdom." And now all of that has been cast aside, the *Review* argued, as "Constitutional, anti-slavery England throws the whole weight of her sympathy in favour of this unrighteous pro-slavery rebellion." This unexpected development had brought about "permanent alienation" and "a loss of confidence in the honour and sincerity of the English people." Indeed, "the last hope of justice or kind feeling died within us, when we found that leading religious papers of Great Britain were equally hostile."

In concluding, the *Review* declaimed against the "slanders," like that found in *Blackwood's*, "directed principally against our President, a man held in respect and affection by this whole nation. He may not be a man of polished manners or dignified presence," the author admitted, but "Englishmen . . . know better than most men, that the body is not the man" and "the blood of kings and nobles may flow through limbs of huge proportions." Mr. Lincoln, he declared, is a man "of unimpeachable integrity, of unbending firmness, of kind and gentle feelings, and of genuine simplicity of character."[10] New Englanders' respect and admiration for Lincoln continued to grow throughout the war, which only amplified the resentment caused by continuing British attacks on his character and appearance.

Curtis used his Lounger column in the January 11 *Harper's Weekly* to berate the *Saturday Review* for its constant stream of attacks on the North and its president. He pointed out caustically, "Thackeray calls it the *Superfine Review*, from its affectation of universal superiority; and John Bright dubs it the *Saturday Reviler*, from its universal scurrility." Curtis also noted Henry James Sr.'s comments in his recent lecture, *The Social Significance of Our Institutions*, which held that the *Review* has "no more genuine mission than to show the rank and festering selfishness which has eaten out the vitals of the old European decency." Curtis shared James's hope that the *Saturday Review* did not represent "the scholarly animus of England" at the present time. Soon, however, events would show that it did.

This deep feeling of resentment added to the lingering bitterness felt throughout the North as a result of the *Trent* crisis. Lydia Maria Child summed up how many New Englanders felt in a letter called "England and America" in the *National Anti-Slavery Standard* of January 18. Child reiterated a now familiar complaint among abolitionists regarding English perfidy, which was evident in its sympathy for the slaveholding South and its growing antipathy toward the antislavery North. But she added a new element, one that would increase in importance as the war went on. She associated the cause of the slave directly with the cause of the British workingman. Because "England was an anti-slavery nation," she declared, it was presumed that they would have "no sympathy" with "states striving to build a new government" founded on the belief that "slavery is the natural and healthy condition of laboring men; without regard to complexion, white or black." This association of slaves and laborers would soon become a prominent meme for American critics in the evolving culture war.

Child also assured readers that, despite recent British criticism and predictions of American democracy self-destructing, the democratic government "instituted by that noble band of Pilgrims in the Mayflower" would ultimately endure and triumph. "Under all our faults," she asserted, "there lies a Puritan groundwork of moral strength and intellectual energy." These ancient qualities, she declared, are manifest in the actions of moral and political leaders like Charles Sumner, whom she described as "the voice of Puritanism in politics" and a leader who always spoke out for "Truth and Justice."

Sumner was arguably the strongest abolitionist voice in the Senate at this time. He was chair of the Senate Committee on Foreign Relations, which, as his biographer notes, was a post "he was to make important than that of any ambassador and more influential than that of most Secretaries of State."[11] Sumner was uniquely positioned to provide fellow members of the Saturday Club with a direct connection not only to the inner workings of Washington politics but also to developments in international relations. As evidenced in his role in defusing the *Trent* crisis, Sumner provided an important link with liberal British allies. Prior to the war, he made two long tours of Europe and England, where he made many friends, including the antislavery Duchess of Argyll. Not surprisingly, Sumner was especially concerned to bring British antislavery activists onto the Northern side.[12]

In the first session of Congress in 1862, Sumner defended the administration's handling of the *Trent* affair. From England, Minister Adams reported to his son that "the first effect of the surrender of Messrs. Mason and Slidell has been extraordinary. The current which ran against us with such extreme violence six weeks ago now seems to be going with equal fury in our favor. The reaction in the city was very great yesterday, and even the most violent of the presses, the *Times* and the *Post*, are for the moment a little tamed."[13] The *Saturday Review* also seemed to be satisfied with the result, noting that it was "impossible that a matter of such great national interest should have been conducted in a way more credible and more satisfactory to England."[14]

While Southerners and their British patrons continued to argue that slavery was not the true issue in the war, Northern liberals were becoming more and more convinced that emancipation was not only a moral imperative but also a political necessity. On January 17, Motley wrote to James Anthony Froude, the liberal-leaning editor of *Fraser's* and a good friend of long standing, that the American republic is "dealing at last with that spirit of evil, slavery, which has blighted and blackened its whole past existence. It is a life and death struggle in which the United States must go down, or slavery." At the outset of the war, Motley noted, he believed "the question might be solved in the legal constitutional way."[15] That time, however, was long past.

This fact was clear to Anthony Trollope, who had recently written to James T. Fields to express his concern about the increasingly militant tone of the *Atlantic Monthly*. Trollope correctly observed that the journal was now "going whole hog for abolition," which he thought was a mistake because it was abolition that "drove the South to Secession, & will make a return to Union impracticable."[16] At the same time, John Ruskin continued to express his indifference to the American struggle. Despite Norton's effort to engage his sympathy for the North, Ruskin declared that he was "too lazy to care anything about it unless I hear there's some chance of you or Lowell or Emerson's being shot, in which case I should remonstrate." Otherwise, "the rest is all one to *me*."[17]

Minister Adams wrote to his son at the end of January that British support for the Confederacy would eventually prove to be "fatal" for the British ruling class, as the dynamics of English politics continued to be impacted by the American war. "It pleases an influential class to think that the demon of democracy may be laid at home if it can be stripped of its American garb," he wrote. "Perhaps they are right, though I do not believe it." In words that would prove prophetic, Adams declared that "no more fatal mistake can be committed by them than that of taking up the cause of a slaveholding oligarchy. . . . Every step in its progress would be a new argument against them. For it would more and more establish the fact of their want of sympathy with free institutions and the progress of the age."[18] For Adams, the British establishment, like their Southern kinsmen, were on the wrong side of history.

It was apparent from commentaries in the British press that the failure of the Lincoln administration to articulate a clear emancipation policy continued to deprive the Union cause of moral justification. Emerson, who was at this time arguably the most highly regarded intellectual in America, traveled from his home in Concord to Washington, DC, at the end of January to deliver an address titled "Nationality" at the Smithsonian Institute on the thirty-first. In it, he presented an eloquent demand for universal emancipation.

While visiting the capital, Sumner arranged for Emerson to meet several of the wartime leaders of the country, including Salmon P. Chase, Secretary of the Treasury; Edward Bates, Attorney General; Edwin M. Stanton, Secretary of War; Gideon Welles, Secretary of the Navy; William Seward, Secretary of State; and Richard Pemell, First Earl of Lyons, the British envoy to Washington.[19] When he and Sumner arrived at Secretary Seward's office, they ran into two other friends from the Saturday Club waiting outside, John Murray Forbes and the liberal wartime governor of Massachusetts, John Albion Andrew (a frequent guest who would soon join the fraternity).[20] Seward greeted the men from Massachusetts warmly, and they sat down for conversation while the secretary of state smoked a cigar. Emerson's journal does not reveal the specific content of their conversation, but he was in town to promote emancipation and, with

Sumner, Forbes, and Andrew, all strong abolitionists along, there can be little doubt the subject was central.

During his visit, Emerson met with Lincoln twice. The renowned philosopher, poet, and essayist was favorably impressed by this uncommon common man. In a lengthy journal account of the visit, Emerson described the president as "a frank, sincere, well-meaning man, with a lawyer's habit of mind, good clear statement of his fact, correct enough, not vulgar, as described; but with a sort of boyish cheerfulness." Emerson also felt that the president's deep engagement with important issues relating to the war "showed a fidelity and conscientiousness very honorable to him." For his part, Lincoln was undoubtedly pleased to meet the famous New Englander. As Robert Richardson points out, by this time Emerson had become "an inescapable part—a fixture—of American public life."[21] The two men shared a great deal, not the least of which was their practical idealism. Lincoln and Emerson both possessed a vision of America that was founded on the principle of universal freedom and equal rights, and both understood that this vision could not be realized overnight.[22]

Emerson's Smithsonian lecture was one in a series of controversial antislavery presentations.[23] The *National Anti-Slavery Standard* reported on February 2 that Emerson's lecture "was delivered to a large and brilliant audience" and was received "with unbounded enthusiasm." The article noted that he "examined very thoroughly . . . the subject of slavery and its connection to the war" and he "seemed inspired through nearly the whole of it." Emerson later published a revised version of his lecture in the *Atlantic Monthly* under the title "American Civilization."[24] The piece was requested by James T. Fields, who, like Governor Andrew, would soon be welcomed into the Saturday Club.

In this important address, Emerson offered a vision of American civilization and culture that was strikingly different from the British model. While attacking slavery, he placed an especially strong emphasis on the dignity of free labor and the essential integrity and self-worth of the working class. In fact, this point was so emphatic throughout that it is not improbable that Emerson had an international audience in mind, specifically the English working class. The address included a virtual paean to the dignity and nobility of free labor.[25] The "labor of each for all, is the health and virtue of all beings," he stated. "ICH DIEN, *I serve*, is a truly royal motto."[26] "And it is the mark of nobleness to volunteer the lowest service. . . . Nay, God is God because he is the servant of all." Regrettably, the slaveholders, like their aristocratic British counterparts, "have endeavored to reverse the natural sentiments of mankind, and to pronounce labor disgraceful," all the while indulging themselves "in eating the fruit of other men's labor." Meanwhile, "all honest men are daily striving to earn their bread by their industry." The "object of all governments," Emerson insisted, should be to "protect and ensure it to the laborer."[27]

Aware that British critics had been denigrating the North's lowbrow democratic, common-man culture for some time while praising the higher, aristocratic culture of the South, Emerson here reversed the equation. America has "attempted to hold together two states of civilization," he asserted, "a higher state," which is democratic, "and a lower state," which is essentially "an oligarchy." The tension between the two "has poisoned politics, public morals, and social intercourse in the Republic, now for many years." It was time for change. "We live in a new and exceptional age," Emerson observed, one in which the nation will no longer tolerate the institution of slavery simply because it has enjoyed the sanction of the Constitution. It was time for bold, decisive action.

In words that would later be echoed by the president, Emerson declared that Americans now hold "the fate of the fairest possession of mankind" in their hands, "to be saved by our firmness or to be lost by hesitation." The key to success in the war, and to America's success as a nation, was to embrace universal human rights. "Emancipation is the demand of civilization," Emerson insisted. Nothing short of this would do because emancipation will at once alter "the atomic social constitution of the Southern people" by freeing the slaves and elevating "the poor whites of the South," aligning "his interest with that of the Northern laborer" and, by extension, all other free laborers of the world.

If Emerson's goal was to influence Federal policies, it appears he succeeded. At the end of his address as published in the *Atlantic*, he appended the following: "Since the above pages were written, President Lincoln has proposed to Congress that the Government shall cooperate with any State that shall enact a gradual abolishment of Slavery. In the recent series of national successes, this Message is the best. It marks the happiest day in the political year." This development was, indeed, momentous because, as Emerson noted, "The American Executive ranges itself for the first time on the side of freedom."[28] The nation had taken a giant step forward and there could be no turning back now.

The sentiments expressed in Emerson's Smithsonian address were echoed the following month in *Fraser's Magazine* in a powerful essay by England's most notable liberal, and arguably her most accomplished intellectual, John Stuart Mill. In "The Contest in America," Mill answered in detail the criticisms of British conservatives while presenting a ringing endorsement of the Union cause. As England's leading liberal and the author of the classic political treatise *On Liberty* (1859), Mill had a strong interest in America and its Civil War. In previous commentary on the American democratic experiment, Mill had indicated very clearly that his comments applied only to the Northern states. Any reference to the South as democratic, he told a correspondent, would be "a mere perversion of terms."[29] In his February 1862 essay, Mill was emphatic that the triumph of the North would be the triumph of civilization over barbarism, a point New England liberals had been making for some time. He also believed the war itself could have a rejuvenating effect on American democracy.

At the outset, Mill expressed his deep sense of relief that the *Trent* affair did not lead to war, which for England "would have been a war in alliance with, and . . . in defence and propagation of slavery." He also acknowledged that Great Britain's "attitude towards the contending parties . . . has not been that which becomes a people who are as sincere enemies of slavery as the English really are."[30] Sympathy for the Confederacy, Mill noted, had been expressed in British journals whose political character had, historically, been favorable toward the institution of slavery.

Undoubtedly, Mill had the London *Times*, *Blackwood's*, and the *Saturday* and *Quarterly Reviews*, among others, in mind. These "powerful journals," he observed, have been "very unfavourable exponents of English feeling on all subjects connected with slavery," some from the influences "of West Indian opinions and interests: others from inbred Toryism, which even when compelled by reason to hold opinions favourable to liberty, is always adverse to it in feeling." Indeed, this Toryism has "no moral repugnance to the thought of human beings born to the penal servitude for life." Instead, it "keeps its indignation to be expended on 'rabid and fanatical abolitionists' across the Atlantic, and on those writers in England" who were opposed to slavery (259).

Mill argued that England should support the North and dismiss the negative feelings "which have been engendered not merely by the *Trent* aggression, but by the previous anti-British effusions of newspaper writers and stump orators." Regarding the issues immediately at hand, Mill noted, while there are those who claim that "on the side of the North, the question is not one of Slavery," the world knows "Slavery alone" is responsible for the strife. He acknowledged that presently "the North are not carrying on war to abolish slavery in the States where it legally exists," but he called for patience (262). Mill was confident the North would eventually embrace universal emancipation; it was just a matter of time.

He reminded his readers how he had "foreseen and foretold from the first, that if the South were not promptly put down, the contest would become distinctly an antislavery one." It was now clearly headed in that direction. Mill noted that "the *Times* correspondent Mr. Russell" held the same opinion. "In one of his recent letters he names the end of next summer as the period by which, if the war was not sooner terminated, it will have assumed a complete anti-slavery character." Mill was convinced that not only would a longer war bring an end to slavery, but it was "quite possible that it will regenerate the American people." In the meantime, he reminded antislavery advocates in England that, while "the purpose of the North may be doubted or misunderstood, there is at least no question as to those of the South. They make no concealment of *their* principles" (263). The preservation of slavery had always been their goal.

Mill also addressed the popular claim that "the North will never succeed in conquering the South." As one of England's foremost economists, he was certain "they can conquer it, if their present determination holds . . . for they are twice as numerous, and ten or twelve times as rich." His prescription for victory was prescient. It would come "by wearing them out, exhausting their resources, depriving them of the comforts of life, encouraging their slaves to desert, and excluding them from communication with foreign countries." All of this "depends on the supposition that the North does not give in first" (266).

Mill was confident that, while the American conflict had not yet "arrived at the stage of being altogether a war for justice, a war of principle," there is "a large infusion of that element in it," and he was certain that "if the war lasts," this element "will in the end predominate" (268). Such a powerful statement of support from one of England's most distinguished intellectuals delighted liberals throughout the North. It was reprinted in its entirety in *Harper's Monthly* in April. From this point on, Mill would be an active advocate of the North, both publicly and privately.

Aware of the significance of one of England's most formidable thinkers emerging as a defender of the Union cause, the *Economist* responded almost immediately. The journal agreed that Mill's essay presented "in a very clear and succinct form" how a Northern victory would affect "the prospects of Negro slavery." However, the writer argued, "we consider that view to be altogether mistaken." Although "Mr. Mill thinks that the surest and most salutary means" to end slavery is "the subjugation of the

South;—we think, on the contrary, these means are to be looked for in independence." Indeed, the writer insisted that "it is because we wish well to the Africans" and look forward to "their ultimate emancipation—that we wish for dissolution of that Union which has hitherto crushed them down by its banded, undivided, and resistless might." According to the *Economist*, following the establishment of an independent Confederacy, the North and Europe would combine forces to contain the Confederacy in order to prevent the "aggrandisement and extension of a Slave Empire." Once thus contained, slavery would, presumably, collapse through the exercise of natural economic forces.[31] What the *Economist* ignored in this argument was the determination of Northerners to preserve the Union, whatever the cost might be.

The support of liberal British intellectuals like John Stuart Mill, John Elliott Cairnes, Thomas Hughes, and Goldwin Smith was of inestimable value to the North in the balance of the war.[32] Their writings, appearing in prestigious venues like the *Edinburgh Review*, *Macmillan's*, and, eventually, *Fraser's*, helped blunt the influence of major publications like the London *Times*, the *Saturday Review*, *Blackwood's*, and the *Economist*. They were also, undoubtedly, instrumental in convincing the Palmerston government to maintain England's neutrality in the struggle, even in the face of strong conservative arguments for intervention.[33] Most of the Victorian literary giants, however, continued to criticize the North while defending the South. Thomas Carlyle, for example, sent a copy of "The Contest in America" to a friend with a note that read, "Mill's American Article is a poor shrieky Piece; in case you have it not, here it is; in case you have, it can be burnt."[34]

While this British liberal support was a bright spot in the generally dark landscape of relations between New and Old England, bitterness toward the English still ran deep. In early February, Holmes wrote to Motley that recent efforts to establish an "entente cordiale between this country and England" were welcome, but he did not believe "that England can ever be to us what she has been. Those beautiful breasts of our 'mother' country, from which it seemed that nothing could wean us, have shriveled into the wolf's dugs, and there is no more milk in them for us henceforth evermore."

The relentless criticisms of the *Times* and other prestigious publications, as well as the shocking and totally unanticipated criticisms of the creative class, had convinced Holmes that the North's growing embrace of liberal democracy rendered it a de facto enemy of the British establishment.

"Not by aggression, but by the naked fact of existence," Holmes stated, "we are an eternal danger and an unsleeping threat to every government that founds itself on anything but the will of the governed." In concluding, Holmes thanked Motley for relaying "the transcripts of . . . your English friends—especially the words of John Bright." He shared these materials with fellow members of the Saturday Club, "who always listen with enthusiasm when your name is mentioned." In return, he promised he would tell Motley "what I see and hear from time to time."[35]

William Wetmore Story wrote to Norton from Rome around this same time to report on his latest effort to promote the Union cause to the British public. He indicated that his recent defense of the Union, first published in "*The Daily News*," had been reprinted as a pamphlet. The effort, legalistic in tone, had done little to influence British opinion, and Story admitted, "I was fool enough to think I could do some good—but I doubt whether the English mind is open to argument on the American question." Story also reported that the celebration of Commander Wilkes following the seizure of Mason and Slidell was a gesture that deeply offended the British public. However, "the current in England" seemed to be now setting toward peace. He added, even though "there is undoubtedly a strong party eager for war & using their utmost efforts to push the government into breaking the blockade—I do not think this will be done."[36] Back at home, developments on the battlefield would soon reinforce Story's optimism.

Chapter 7

Union Victories Temper British Critics

About a week after Story wrote to Norton from Europe, the Union army achieved the kind of success that he and other Unionists had been hoping for. On February 18, 1862, General Ulysses S. Grant accepted the surrender of Fort Donelson in Tennessee, which followed the capture of Fort Henry just days earlier. These were major victories for the North, not only militarily but psychologically. They were the first successful demonstrations of the Union's now formidable war power.[1] The surrender of the forts also had international consequences in that it diminished the possibility of foreign intervention.[2] Nashville fell shortly thereafter. Southern diarist Mary Chesnut, like other Southerners, began to sense a shift in the momentum on the battlefield. In her diary she noted, "Confederate affairs in a blue way. Roanoke taken, Fort Henry on the Tennessee River open to them, and we fear the Mississippi River, too. . . . New armies, new fleets, swarming and threatening everywhere. . . . England's eye is scornful and scoffing as she turns it towards us—and on our miseries."[3]

Chesnut was right about the impact of these Union victories in England. Minister Adams wrote to his son Charles from London that "the change produced in the tone towards the United States is very striking. There will be no overt act tending to recognition whilst there is a doubt of the issue." Adams also indicated that sympathy for the South in England "is not the popular feeling but it is that of the governing classes. . . . The aristocracy entertain it as well as the commercial interest."[4] Just before this, on March 7, the first major debate on the American Civil War took place in Parliament. It concerned the effectiveness of the Union blockade. Southern sympathizer William Gregory contended that it was only a "paper blockade" and should be challenged. There was little support for his motion, which was seen by many as tantamount to recognizing the South, and it was withdrawn.[5]

There was a sense among Unionists that things were finally moving in the right direction. This, in turn, led inevitably to further considerations of what a postwar America would be like. To many, it seemed clear that the institution of slavery, the "corner-stone" of the Confederacy, would not survive. On February 21, Captain Nathaniel Gordon became the first and only American to be executed for the crime of international slave trading, something that would never have happened if the Southerners still dominated Washington politics. For some New Englanders, Gordon's execution established an important principle that should be expanded. In his journal, Longfellow wrote "to-day Capt. Gordon, the slaver, is to be hanged. It seems to me very illogical to hang him, and yet to protect with the Constitution all our internal [slave] traders. If one deserves hanging, the others do."[6]

Clearly, such moral anomalies could be resolved only by the abolition of slavery. Many in the North, New England especially, were now coming to this conclusion. There was even some movement among Northern Democrats regarding the future of slavery. A major figure in that movement was George Bancroft, a prominent New England Democrat and an internationally known historian. Bancroft was also an educational innovator. He founded the Round Hill School in Northampton, Massachusetts, in 1823. As his biographer reports, the focus of the school was on "practical utility, fostering the 'active life' " and the " 'exercise of stronger powers.' Competition and exertion would make the school a microcosm of the larger world in which they would one day live."[7] These lessons were apparently well received, at least by some. Several prominent members of the Saturday Club, including John Murray Forbes, John Lothrop Motley, Samuel G. Ward, and Estes Howe, were all former Round Hill students. Like their teacher, they were putting the "active" lessons they learned there to good use in defending and promoting the Union cause and the destruction of slavery.[8]

Like many New Englanders, Bancroft welcomed the outbreak of the war. He saw the fervor of Northern patriots in the aftermath of Sumter as an "uprising of the irresistible spirit of the people in behalf of law and order and liberty." And, like others in New England, Bancroft believed "the North is the country and will make good the rights and the Constitution."[9] Despite his support for the Union, up to this time Bancroft had never expressed sympathy with antislavery. However, in a rather remarkable speech at the Cooper Institute in New York on February 22, he called upon the American people to live up to the promise of the Revolutionary Fathers by abolishing slavery.[10] His conservative Democratic supporters were shocked.

The *New York Weekly Caucasian* that same day fumed that Bancroft "is ready to use the position he has obtained in the public estimation to strengthen the absurd philosophy of the abolitionists, and forward their revolutionary designs. . . . Mr. Bancroft accepts the negro equality philosophy that all men, whether negroes or Indians, are included under the Constitution of the United States and are equally entitled to its rights and privileges. This revolting doctrine," the *Caucasian* declaimed, "so abhorrent even to the natural instincts, Mr. Bancroft has the presumption to dignify as 'the life of the nation'—the animating spirit of the Constitution!" Despite the efforts of conservatives to stop it, the slavery issue had emerged center stage, and with it questions of fundamental human rights. With major intellectuals on both sides of the Atlantic now proclaiming their liberal, antislavery sentiments, the conservatives' goal to restore the "Union as it was and the Constitution as it is" was in danger of becoming a fading dream.

At the same time, diplomatic relations between Great Britain and the North continued to improve now that the *Trent* affair was settled and the North had achieved significant victories on the battlefield. Samuel May noted in a letter to Richard Webb "the altered tone of many of the English journals towards America." He was especially surprised "that the *London Quarterly Review*, so soon after its article of *Democracy on its Trial*, should have published another" that presented an "estimate of the Southern character" that is "true & just, & it contrasts well with the abominably false and very proslavery articles in *Blackwood's Magazine*. Its rebukes of the London *Times* are severe & I think must have been telling." May then added, "We here are inclined to attribute a good deal of influence to J. S. Mill's article in *Fraser's Magazine* on 'The Contest in America.'" While May acknowledged these positive developments, he also complained of a "lack of moral discrimination in viewing the contest" that was still evident in a good deal of English commentary.[11]

British supporters agreed. May's Scottish friend Eliza Wigham wrote, "*Blackwood's* articles are disgraceful" and do not reflect "the state of matters in England & Scotland." She hoped American readers did not see such writing as "exponents of British feeling."[12] But many did. Even journals that normally avoided political commentary, such as *Harper's Monthly Magazine*, entered the fray.¹³ George Curtis, in an Editor's Easy Chair essay in February, declared that the mother country, which he had described as "our true ally" just months earlier, was no friend. "England has chosen by her conduct during the year, to lose our friendship," Curtis wrote. "The tone and temper of English papers and orators . . . has utterly destroyed the reverent faith with which thoughtful Americans had clung to the English name." What have the British gained, Curtis asked, "by hastening to injure a homogenous people?"¹⁴

While Northerners were heartened by the words of British allies, these feelings were dealt a blow when, on March 1, Charles Dickens published "The Young Man from the Country" in his magazine, *All the Year Round*. The short piece consisted largely of defaming comments about American life drawn from his *American Notes*, which had been published twenty years earlier. In the article, Dickens derided the American Congress and press. He depicted American society as generally crude and immoral, a society where "the love of 'smart' dealing . . . gilds over many a swindle and gross breach of trust . . . and enables many a knave to hold his head up with the best." Dickens republished the scathing piece at this time because he felt the war vindicated his views, which had garnered harsh criticism on both sides of the Atlantic when *American Notes* was first published. At the end of the piece, Dickens commented, "The foregoing was written in the year eighteen hundred and forty-two. It rests with the reader to decide whether it has received any confirmation, or any colour of truth about the year eighteen hundred and sixty-two."¹⁵

Dickens's comments originally applied to all of America. But now they seemed to be aimed specifically at the North. In personal letters he made this apparent, writing to a correspondent at this time that "slavery has in reality nothing on earth to do" with the war. In his view, the South was responding to the economic oppression of the North, as evidenced in the Morrill Tariff. "Every reasonable creature may know . . . that the North hates the Negro, and that until it was convenient to make a pretense that sympathy with him was the cause of the War, it hated the abolitionists and derided them up hill and down dale."¹⁶ To the New England literati, Dickens's bitterness was yet another undeserved blow from a once-respected English cousin.

With the war going relatively well, and with pressures mounting for a stronger pro-emancipation policy, on March 6, Lincoln submitted the first emancipation proposal ever presented by a president to Congress.¹⁷ He had asked Sumner to read it over beforehand. The senator was delighted with the document. Unlike the British critics who often faulted Lincoln for his common-man grammar and diction, the sophisticated New England statesman felt Lincoln's style was "so clearly . . . aboriginal, autochthonous" that it could not be improved upon.[18] Lincoln signed the bill on April 10. In it he asked Congress to appropriate financial compensation for "any state which may adopt a gradual abolishment of slavery."[19]

Lydia Maria Child was thrilled with this development, which she felt pointed the way to full emancipation.[20] Curtis was also pleased. On the day of Lincoln's announcement, he wrote to Norton that he had faith in "the President's common sense and practical wisdom. His policy has been to hold the border States. He has held them; now he makes his next step and invites emancipation."[21] Two days later, Norton responded. He agreed that Lincoln's "message on Emancipation is a most important step" and suggested that they should leverage it and "make out the message to be more than it is." In this way, they might "bring the President up to our view of it," an effective strategy the New Englanders would employ from this point forward to advance their liberal agenda.[22]

Just days later, on March 22, *Harper's Weekly*, in "Abolition in High Places," celebrated Lincoln's emancipation bill while noting that other papers like the *New York Tribune*, the *Evening Post*, and the *Journal of Commerce* did the same. "The friends of freedom rejoice of it," *Harper's* declared, "because it placed the United States Government squarely on the record as preferring freedom to slavery, . . . and as looking forward in some future time, and in some yet undetermined way, to the abolition of slavery and the emancipation of the negro race." The same issue of the *Weekly* praised Lincoln for his steady leadership, saying, "It is fortunate for the country and for the world that of this moment" America has a president who is so "wise and calm," despite the desperate nature of the times.[23]

In the context of these positive developments, the *Philadelphia City Item*, a "Journal of the Fine Arts, Business, Literature, and the Drama," expressed its continuing exasperation with *Blackwood's* and its unrelenting assaults on Lincoln and the Union cause. In a withering attack, the paper responded to *Blackwood's* recent critique, "Convulsions in America." The writer indicated that, although the "selfishness and prejudice" of the English papers was not unexpected, "the mendacity of the leading reviews—periodicals that pretend to a cosmopolitan impartiality"—was a surprise and a disappointment.[24] It was obvious to many Northerners that these prestigious British journals were, in effect, serving as surrogates for the Confederates, defending their cause to an international audience. Their criticisms were demoralizing to the North while providing aid and comfort to the enemy.

Even with the Union blockade, most of the content of British publications did, finally, reach American audiences both North and South.[25] "Convulsions in America," for example, was soon reprinted in the *Richmond Dispatch*. From there it made its way to Southern readers like Rebecca Meade, who found it comforting. In a letter to her son John, who was still serving in the Confederate army, she asked, "Did you read an admirable article in the [Richmond] *Dispatch* of the 8th taken from *Blackwood*? It is the finest, keenest summary of Yankee perfidy and recklessness that has yet appeared. I cannot but think the voice of the English people will yet be heard malgré Lord John Russell's indisposition to assist the South by raising the blockade."[26]

Meanwhile, on the war front General McClellan had begun moving a huge Northern army onto the Virginia peninsula. It was the beginning of a campaign to capture the Confederate capital of Richmond. The ignominious end to this effort in July would have a tremendous impact on European views of the war. Before that, however, a naval battle occurred that changed the nature of warfare at sea forever and further altered the relationship between Great Britain and the United States. On March 9, two ironclad warships collided in combat off the coast of Virginia. The Union vessel, the USS *Monitor*, was a 987-ton armored turret gunboat designed and built by John Ericsson in a New York shipyard. Commissioned on February 25, the ship was dispatched immediately to Hampton Roads, Virginia, where the Confederate ironclad, CSS *Virginia* (formally the USS *Merrimack*), had sunk two wooden-hulled US warships the previous day. Their battle, the first between iron-armored warships, ended in a draw when the *Virginia* was forced to retire. The *Monitor* had effectively prevented the *Virginia* from gaining control of Hampton Roads, which would have broken the Union blockade in the Norfolk area.[27]

The clash between these two vessels had a traumatizing effect on Great Britain's Admiralty. After the *Monitor*'s de facto victory, one American observer noted, "John Bull is sorely frightened at the manifest weakness of his own navy and is very civil at once."[28] The duel between the *Virginia* and the *Monitor* struck the imagination of the British people. Minister Adams observed in a letter to his son Charles that it "has been the main talk of the town ever since the news came, in Parliament, in the clubs, in the city, among the military and naval people. The impression is that it dates the commencement of a new era in warfare, and that Great Britain must consent to begin over again." He wrote that recent victories by the Union army in the field seemed to presage complete victory. For the South, he added, "the worst is yet to come. For emancipation is on its way with slow but certain pace."[29]

In the North, where fear of British intervention always focused on the mighty British navy smashing the blockade and ravaging Northern port cities, there was a sense of relief and pride. An April 16 editorial in the Boston *Daily Advertiser* took some pleasure in the notion that the British navy might now have something to fear from the Americans. "It is quite plain," the paper observed, "that the British public has been thrown with one of its periodic panics by the battle of the ironsides in Hampton Roads. . . . The substitution of iron for wood in naval architecture is now the topic on which the public mind is agitated, on which the press expends its argument and Parliament its eloquence." The report went on to note that the British public is "appalled at the prospect that some *Merrimack* or *Monitor* might enter the Thames and work her will."

The British now had to think more carefully about involvement in the war. On September 2, Richard Cobden wrote to John Bright that there were several reasons for British reluctance to become involved in the American conflict. Among them were the need for supplies of corn imported from the North and "the really formidable strength of the Americans at sea. . . . Every iron battery the Federals are building will be a guarantee against interference. . . . But for these considerations" he wrote, "we should have long ago been in the fray."[30]

Meanwhile, developments in the land war continued. Some of these had a direct impact on the slavery question. Wherever the Union army made inroads into the South, thousands of fugitive slaves, officially "contrabands," flocked to their lines, thus effectively freeing themselves.[31] In November 1861, the Union army had occupied the Sea Islands off the coast of South Carolina and laid the groundwork for what would become known as the Port Royal experiment. It began as an effort to clothe and educate newly emancipated slaves that they might become self-sufficient. As it grew, the experiment gained a great deal of national attention, both North and South.[32] Southerners saw the Port Royal experiment as an outright admission that the Union's goal was to foment widespread servile insurrection and, eventually, total emancipation.

Conservatives, in the North and the South, derided the effort and declared the futility of any project to educate Black people. The *New York Journal of Commerce* opined, "The nonsensical, wild and fanatical plans of irresponsible men and women which are having their trial at Port Royal are a subject of sorrow and disgust to the intelligent world." The *Louisville Democrat* was even more vitriolic about the effort. "The abolitionists propose to elevate the black races," the paper observed. "Nothing but hemp could do the same thing properly for them!"[33] Despite such criticism, the experiment was rapidly going forward and experiencing great success.

New England liberals vigorously promoted the Port Royal project. John Murray Forbes visited the islands in the spring of 1862. He later wrote to Charles Sumner that he "used to think emancipation only another name for murder, fire, and rape, but mature reflection and considerable personal observation have since convinced me that emancipation may, at any time, be declared without disorder."[34] Emerson wrote to Forbes upon his return to say that it was a pity he was not able to make it to the recent Saturday Club gathering, "where there was a great deal of vivacious conversation." To compensate, Emerson planned to make a visit to the Forbeses' summer home on Naushon Island specifically "to hear with ears the results of Port Royal."[35]

Support for the experiment soon became widespread. Emerson's daughter Ellen informed him in March that "there is to be a mass-meeting of sewers here [in Concord] on Thursday to make clothes for the negroes at Port Royal."[36] Emerson wrote in his journal that the Port Royal experiment was just one more proof that "at any time, it only needs the contemporaneous appearance of a few superior & attractive [freed]men to give a new & noble turn to the public mind."[37] As he told one correspondent, "when the odds of ten to one are taken off, that is to say, when New York & Massachusetts are not made by false show to help Carolina & Georgia to keep [the Black man] on the ground, I doubt not that he will be able to get to his feet & insist on wages for his work."[38]

Many in the North welcomed Port Royal as yet another sign that the war was pushing the country steadily toward emancipation. Motley told his mother that "the majority, which elected Lincoln in 1860, is larger now than it was then" and that the "600,000 volunteers who have turned out . . . to fight slavery and nothing else, will all come home determined abolitionists." Preserving the Constitution "as it is" was no longer a concern for Motley. "It is rather late in the day . . . to talk about constitutional guarantees. . . . Compromise," he declared, "was killed at Sumter."[39] Norton felt the same way. He wrote to Curtis to say he was "more than content with our progress" and that "Freedom cannot take backwards steps."[40]

Relations with the mother country were undoubtedly improved, at least a bit, by a very positive account of Northern American life in *Macmillan's* April issue. It was written by the magazine's "special correspondent in America," Edward Dicey. Dicey was a Cambridge graduate and a gifted journalist who specialized in foreign affairs. He was also a political liberal and a regular contributor to the antislavery *Spectator*. Dicey had been sent to the United States by Alexander Macmillan himself to produce a series of articles designed to alleviate "misunderstandings" between the North and Great Britain.[41] His essay, "Three Weeks in New York," was the first of five long articles by Dicey that would be published this year.

For an Englishman like Dicey, New York in 1862 stood in stark contrast to Victorian London. What impressed him immediately was the general absence of social distinctions among New York society. "Out of doors," he reported, "you see evidences of a public equality, or rather absence of inequality, among all classes. . . . In the street, the man in the hat and broadcloth coat, and the man in corduroys and jacket out at elbows, never get out of each other's way, or expect the other to make way for him." The same was true for public transportation, where "ladies and washerwomen, working men and gentlemen, sit huddled together without the slightest sense of incongruity." Dicey also reported that "in the shops, and from servants, you meet with perfect civility, but with civility as to an equal, not to a superior. In the bar rooms, there is no distinction of customers; and, as long as you pay your way, and behave quietly, you are welcome, whatever your dress may be."

Free public education, Dicey reported, was available to most citizens in the North. As a result, literacy was the rule, not the exception. "Reading is so universal an acquirement here that a far lower class reads the newspapers than is the case with us," he reported. Dicey also maintained that "the press of America is the press of a great and free country." He was surprised by the number of newspapers, including "evening ones, bi- and tri-weeklies, and so on—of more or less note." As regards education, Dicey felt that the American people were "probably the best educated, not excepting the Prussian, in the whole world" because a system of free education extended "throughout the whole of the Free States." It was a very different story in the slave states, however, where "no such system exists."

Dicey also wrote that attitudes toward emancipation, and Black people generally, were becoming more positive. Formally, New York's "pro-slavery sympathies were stronger than those of any other Northern town," he noted, but "since the secession began, public feeling has changed." He attended a meeting in aid of the slaves deserted by their masters at Port Royal. "There were probably some three thousand well-dressed people present, who cheered enthusiastically every expression of abolition sentiment." What struck Dicey most "was that, sitting amidst the crowd, were numbers of black men and women—a thing which a few years ago would not have been tolerated at a New York meeting." Additionally, abolition papers were now popular, as were abolition lectures. "The negro [Frederick] Douglas [sic]," Dicey reported, "can lecture in the city to crowded audiences; and modified abolitionism is the fashionable opinion of polite society." The recent execution of Gordon the slave-trader was yet another sign of change, as "any attempt to excite popular sympathy in his behalf failed signally."[42] It was clear to Dicey that Northern attitudes toward slavery and race were changing, and rather dramatically, because of the war.

Southern slaveholders were also experiencing change. Life was becoming very difficult on the home front as slaves continued to self-emancipate wherever the Union line was within reach. On April 3, 1862, a constituent wrote to William Porcher Miles that he was "weary and worried. Just as we thought that the approaching summer would make . . . [us] . . . secure, would at least allow us to plant our crops and gather them in time for what the next fall might bring upon us, there has occurred a fearful stampede. . . . 300 of Walter Blake's negroes moved off in a body, a good many of Daniel Blake's and for all I know other places may be abandoned in the same manner." Such wholesale acts of self-liberation by what English conservatives liked to assert were happy, contented slaves were sure to have catastrophic consequences for their "owners." "I am going up tomorrow to see how things are, but I am pretty nearly at my wits end," this correspondent wrote. "I have no place to go, and I am very much disposed to let things take their course and look to the future as a new life entirely."[43] That "new life" was sure to be dramatically different from the old.

It was around this same time that the Lincoln administration began taking additional steps that were certain to please both English and American abolitionists. On March 13 he signed an article of war passed by Congress that forbade the return of fugitive slaves by the Union army. On April 7, William Seward and Lord Lyons signed a treaty to cooperate in the suppression of the slave trade, and on the tenth Lincoln signed into law his bill providing for gradual, compensated emancipation in the border states. Finally, on April 16, he signed a bill providing for the compensated emancipation of slaves in the District of Columbia, an area over which the Federal government had authority.[44] Six days later, Emerson returned to the lecture platform to promote the new vision of America now unfolding.

The tone of Emerson's lecture "Moral Forces," which he delivered in Boston before the Parker Fraternity on April 13, was optimistic. "Things point in the right way," he observed. "A position is taken by the American Executive" on emancipation, and "it has been supported by the legislature." Additionally, Congress "has destroyed servitude in the District of Columbia." There were other positive developments. "An army of slaves is already escaped from 'the Service to which they were held,' in the lavender phrase of our law," he noted. Their service has proven to be "an eye-opener" because it "is showing military men values of slaves which . . . were never set down in any advertisement of the most sanguine auctioneer." A dynamic "moral force" was clearly at work. This progress, Emerson asserted, "is God's doing and is marvelous in our eyes."[45]

Some New England conservatives found Emerson's liberal views to be wildly idealistic, contrary to common sense, and threatening to the established social order. The Boston *Courier* noted the following day, April 14, that "Mr. Ralph Waldo Emerson delivered a transcendentally transcendental discourse, yesterday morning, at Music Hall." In rebuttal to Emerson's celebration of the recent progress on emancipation, the *Courier* offered a long excerpt from a pamphlet that "shows the entire incompatibility between white men and negroes for living together in a state of equality. One would suppose that reason, observation and experience, all confirming such a view would be sufficient to check impracticable philanthropic projects," the writer opined, "but where those fail, facts conclusively meet the question."

In spite of such conservative pushback, the antislavery movement continued to gain momentum, thanks in part to the unwavering support of the New England intelligentsia. John Greenleaf Whittier, like Emerson, celebrated emancipation in the District of Columbia. He told Sumner he saw it "as the first of the 'peaceable fruits of righteousness' which are to follow the chastening of war."[46] Longfellow was now convinced that "the slave-power must be utterly annihilated. There can be no peace without that is done," he told a friend, "and for that I devoutly pray." He felt strongly that "a pseudo-aristocracy, based on the theory that 'a black man has no rights, which a white man is bound to respect,' [from the Dred Scott decision] cannot any longer be tolerated."[47] By the spring of 1862,

Secretary Seward knew the administration would have to address the slavery issue directly. By midsummer, it seemed most Republicans had reached the conclusion that slavery must go.[48]

Northern conservatives were deeply disturbed by these radical developments in a war that was initially aimed at preserving the Union "as it was." According to the April 18 *Boston Statesmen*, the right to make decisions about slavery and emancipation "by the fundamental constitution of our own political system . . . belongs exclusively to the States." This fact, however, was being ignored by those who wished to impose change on the slave states. The writer complained, "A Republican cannot make a speech in Congress or edit a paper in the non-slaveholding states, without having to do with the emancipation of the negro slaves." Such a move, he argued, would only lead to the extirpation of "four millions of negroes on the ground of benefitting them."

Alienation between New and Old England intensified as Great Britain's conservative governing class became increasingly critical of the accelerating movement toward emancipation. Motley wrote to *Fraser's* publisher, James Anthony Froude, to thank him for his reassurance that the harsh critical voices echoing through the British press "don't represent the best or even the prevalent English sentiment." But he also said, while he once believed that the "trans-Atlantic Anglo-Saxon race held the world in their hands if they work[ed] together," such cooperation was no longer possible. "There was a strong affection on the part of America towards England . . . but that is all over now," Motley declared.[49]

Soon there was more good news for the Union on the military front. The South's wealthiest city, New Orleans, fell to the naval forces of Admiral David G. Farragut on April 26. The event took Great Britain by surprise.[50] As Minister Adams reported to his son, after news of the victory reached London, "people here were quite struck aback. . . . It took them three days to make up their minds to believe it. The division of the United States had become an idea so fixed in their heads that they had shut out all the avenues to the reception of any other. As a consequence they are all adrift. The American problem completely baffles their comprehension."[51]

The London *Times* was growing concerned about the possible consequences of a Union victory, given the animosity between the two nations, an animosity that the *Times* helped foment. Young Henry Adams wrote to his brother Charles, "You can judge of the probable effect of this last victory at New Orleans from the fact that friend [William] Russell of the *Times* . . . gravely warned the English nation yesterday of the magnificent

[Union] army that had better be carefully watched by the English people, since it hated them like the devil and would want to have something to do."[52]

Henry Adams, like others, was beginning to think of the changes a Union victory would bring. Surely a new American identity would emerge from the war, and he believed "the New England element" should be predominant.[53] George Curtis wrote to Norton of his own "plan of reconstruction," which began with "military occupation of the states until they initiate emancipation."[54] While somewhat uncertain at the outset of the war, he and his fellow liberals were now adamant that slavery would have no place in postwar America and that the Constitution must be revised to fit this new vision. Edwin Percy Whipple, one of the founding members of the Saturday Club and a respected author and literary critic, argued this very point in an essay in the May issue of the *Atlantic Monthly*.[55] Whipple maintained that slavery was a pernicious anachronism and "we must . . . devise some method by which the existence of the slavocracy as a political power may be annihilated."[56]

On May 3, Minister Adams told Richard Cobden that the United States would not accept any mediation that left slavery in place and the South out of the Union.[57] A little more than two weeks later, Lincoln made an eloquent appeal for slave owners in the border states to accept compensated emancipation.[58] Lord Russell and others in the British government were increasingly concerned that emancipation might lead to "servile insurrection" and racial violence in America that could spread to the British Empire.[59]

On June 19, Lincoln signed legislation that abolished slavery in the territories, without compensation. The measure passed the House on what was basically a party-line vote, with Republicans for and conservative Democrats against. The liberal, antislavery leaders of the Republican Party were gaining strength, and New England continued to play a prominent role in the process, both directly and indirectly. According to James McPherson, "a unique combination of history and geography had given New England-born radicals extraordinary power in Congress, especially the Senate."[60]

It is not surprising that the Radical Republicans under the leadership of men like Sumner and Thaddeus Stevens were able to accomplish so much. Among other things, they had the public and private support of New England's intellectual class. These were arguably the finest and most prominent thinkers, writers, preachers, and lecturers in America.[61] They also had the support of many, if not most, of the North's most prestigious and influential journals and several important newspapers. With this kind of backing, the Thirty-Seventh Congress (March 4, 1861–March 4, 1862) was able to exert a unique and lasting influence on the evolution of American democracy and the growth of a liberal, democratic culture. Indeed, according to Leonard Curry, the Thirty-Seventh Congress succeeded in drawing what became "the blueprint for a new America."[62]

At this point, none of these New England liberals considered the Constitution absolutely binding. They knew this was a historical opportunity for progressive change, and they were not willing to allow a flawed Constitution to hobble the effort. They believed these were truly revolutionary times and the opportunity to reinvent American democracy must not falter. The liberals' ultimate goal was the total annihilation of America's slaveocracy. They were determined that Blacks would be free and the Declaration's promise of equal rights for all would, finally, be kept.[63] Southerners and their British patrons were equally determined this would not happen.

War Democrats and Peace Democrats, the latter known as "Copperheads," remained united in their resolve to preserve the Constitution "as it is." They opposed emancipation tooth and nail and frequently appealed to racial bigotry in the ensuing war of words. The opposition was led by Samuel S. Cox of Ohio.[64] Alarmed by the rise of emancipationist feeling, Cox and his cohorts held a meeting in the House of Representatives on May 10 to organize their resistance.[65] These political developments frequently had a sectional tinge to them, with New England leading the way on liberal issues and the Midwest in reaction.

This polarization was reflected in an editorial in the *Daily Democratic Union* (Peoria, Illinois). The paper noted, "Two years ago we told the people plainly what would be the result of electing a president upon a sectional platform. . . . We are now reaping the fruits of the folly then indulged in. . . . Fanaticism has become rampant, principles lost sight of, and 'wide awakes' numerous." Radical abolitionists were ruining the country, and "the greatness and glory of the American Republic has been swallowed up . . . by the 'nigger worshippers.' "[66] At the end of the month, Secretary Seward informed Minister Adams that he was now authorized to state that the war was, in part at least, intended for the suppression of slavery.[67]

The British continued to follow developments in America closely. "Washington During the War," the second in the series of articles by

Edward Dicey, appeared in the May issue of *Macmillan's Magazine*. Dicey wrote that in the past year "the people of the United States have passed through" what amounted to "a baptism of fire," and during this time much had been achieved. Unfortunately, the British press had largely ignored these achievements. "Our newspapers at home have been so long telling us what the North could 'not' do—how it could not fight, nor raise money, nor conquer the South—that they seem . . . to have quite forgotten to tell us what the North '*has*' done."

Among other things, Dicey noted, the North had created a modern, well-disciplined, and truly formidable army. Despite this, "a writer in a recent English periodical talks of the 'essentially blackguardly character' of the whole American war and . . . sneers at the whole Northern army." Such crass calumnies did not go unnoticed by loyal Americans and could have grave consequences, Dicey warned. These critics "are sowing the seeds of war," and they would do well to "remember that power, and strength, and will, are never 'essentially blackguardly,' and, that there is something in an army of a million men worth thinking about as well as sneering at."

While in Washington, Dicey had the opportunity to meet President Lincoln. The Englishman was impressed with "the perfect terms of equality on which [the president] appeared to be with everybody." Lincoln "talked little and seemed to prefer others talking to him . . . but, when he spoke, his remarks were always shrewd and sensible." Regarding the president's appearance, the subject of endless negative commentary in most of the British press, Dicey reported, "You would never say he was a gentleman; you would still less say he was not one. . . . There is about him an utter absence of pretension, and an evident desire to be courteous to everybody, which is the essence, if not the outward form of good breeding. There is a softness, too, about his smile, and a sparkle of dry humour about his eye."[68]

The third installment of Dicey's American travelogue, "Notes of a Tour Through the Border States," appeared in *Macmillan's* June issue. In his travels through western Ohio, now in a state of rapid development stimulated in part by the war, Dicey observed areas where it seemed "the new world lay before you, in the process of its creation: new roads were making everywhere; new villages were springing up; teams of rough, sturdy horses were plowing up the old fallow land; the swamps were being cleaned of their dank reedy marsh plants; and the broad shallow streams were being banked and dammed up into deep quiet water-courses." All of this impressed him, even more so when he realized that this transformation was being wrought by immigrants. "It was then that I first understood the poetry of the emigrant world," Dicey declared, "not romantic or spasmodic; but idyllic in its nature." For these immigrants, "the promise [of America] had come true," and "this rich western country was, in very truth, the new and the happy land."

What Dicey saw in the slave states, however, was strikingly different. In Tennessee he found that, while the natural environment was beautiful, the social environment was not. "There is less life," he reported, "less energy . . . about the Slave State, less sign of rapid progress; the fields are worked by negroes; every now and then . . . you see the wretched wood-hovels, telling of actual poverty—things which you do not see in Ohio." Dicey's final impression of the place was that "when you look closely into the Tennessee paradise, the garden of Eden is somewhat of a dirty one."[69]

The Civil War proved to be a boon for Northern publishers of newspapers, magazines, and journals. The continuing Anglo-American war of words was undoubtedly a contributor. There was a voracious appetite for newspapers especially. Dicey's earlier observation on the prevalence of Northern literacy and the popularity of newspapers was confirmed when on June 3, *Harper's Weekly* proudly announced that its circulation was almost 130,000. *Harper's* estimated that, with multiple readers for each issue, "a million and a quarter people derive instruction and amusement from this journal." As the war went on, *Harper's* large and growing audience would be exposed to increasingly liberal views, expressed in both words and images.

The Republican-controlled Thirty-Seventh Congress continued to make progress in matters relating to slavery and emancipation. On June 5 Lincoln signed a bill authorizing the appointment of US commissioners to Haiti and Liberia.[70] On June 19 he signed legislation abolishing slavery in the territories. Southerners were well aware of the leading role that the liberals of New England, especially Massachusetts, played in this liberal movement, much to the consternation of some, both North and South. The *Daily Constitutionalist* (Augusta, Georgia) condemned "the fanatical and atrocious spirit of New England" and its "Abolitionists, who fight for the liberty of the slave, and for making him, politically, the equal of the white man."[71] That fight would only grow more intense.

In the meantime, the number of Northern causalities grew. The army needed fresh recruits to fill out its depleted ranks. The War Department now imposed a levy on each state for both ninety-day militia men and three-year volunteers.[72] Emerson's Concord, like other small towns throughout the North, had already been doing its part. The reality of the war was brought home by the absence of so many sons and brothers, fathers and friends. The Concord Selectman's Report for 1861–62 related that "our Town has . . . furnished about seventy men for three years on the war,—their names should . . . be recorded as a matter of justice to the soldiers who may need such authentication sometimes in the future to secure their pension from a grateful country."[73] Many of these soldiers would not live to receive a pension.

British abolitionism was given a significant boost in May when another friend of the North, John Elliott Cairnes, published *The Slave Power*, the book John Stuart Mill had urged him to write. Cairnes dedicated it to Mill and sent him a copy shortly after publication.[74] Mill told Cairnes how pleased he was with it and added, "The great thing now is to get it read." He wanted "to do something *promptly* that might assist in making it widely known. I cannot doubt," he wrote "that the *Daily News*, *McMillan* [sic], and probably *National Review* will make good use of it."[75]

Not long after this, Anthony Trollope's book on his American experience appeared. *Harper's Monthly* noted in August that "it is the work of a genial, observant Englishman, intensely English and honest, and doing us all the justice that he possibly can."[76] In the book, Trollope was unequivocal that slavery "has been the real cause of this conflict."[77] Following his return to England, in a lecture called "The Present Condition of the Northern States of the American Union," he made it clear that his "sympathies in this contest" were with the North because they "are the people who have hated slavery as we have hated it." It was also a place where "the daily labourer has lived as a man, with a man's privileges and a man's enjoyments, and not as a serf, with rights and enjoyments hardly higher than those of the brute."[78] These sentiments were undoubtedly a source of great satisfaction to Trollope's Saturday Club friends, who had welcomed him as an honored guest.[79]

With these publications the North's effort to win the minds and hearts of the British people was finally gaining steam, and Cairnes's book was an important contribution. On the other side, the Confederacy invested considerable resources in what became a very efficient propaganda operation. In addition to the significant self-serving support they received from the British press, their paid agent, Henry Hotze, was getting his propaganda journal, the *Index*, under way at this time. Describing itself as "A Weekly Journal of Politics, Literature, and News Devoted to the Exposition of the Mutual Interests, Political and Commercial, of Great Britain and the Confederate States of America," the first issue was published on May 1, 1862.[80] Hotze, who has been described as the Confederacy's "most effective propaganda agent," filled the pages of the *Index* with articles enumerating the benefits to Great Britain of a free and independent Confederacy. He also promoted scientific racism in an effort to undermine British abolitionists by purportedly showing that Black people were naturally inferior and that enslavement was their proper condition.[81]

Additionally, Hotze sought to influence British public opinion by arguing that Britons, especially those in the governing class, had much more in common with America's racially pure Anglo-Norman Southerner than the mottled masses of the North. In one of his earliest editorials, he declared that "the South, for generations back, has been proud of its closer affinity of blood to the British parent stock, than the North, with its mongrel compound of the surplus population of all the world."[82] Hotze's operation was extensive in its reach and influence. The majority of his staff were British, including the managing editor, John Baker Hopkins. Hotze also hired several English writers on an ad hoc basis to produce favorable articles that he was then able to place in important British journals.[83]

Several people who wrote for Hotze were connected to prestigious and influential publications like the *Saturday Review*, the London *Times*, and the *Morning Post*. The last was especially important because it was often referred to as "Lord Palmerston's organ."[84] The *Times*, on occasion, would actually use Hotze's words, lifted from the *Index*, verbatim when reporting on the war.[85] Other conservative newspapers volunteered their pages for Hotze's personal use. In a letter to his superiors in Richmond, Hotze reported, "Two more newspapers, the '*Herald*,' Lord Derby's organ, and the '*Standard*' . . . have voluntarily placed themselves at my disposal. The editor-in-chief of both called on me, and offered the use of the columns of both, including the editorial columns, of which offer I have, though guardedly, availed myself."[86]

All of this had a significant effect. In July, Cobden complained to an associate that Hotze "managed so completely to delude the public that it will not be very easy to bring him down."[87] Not only was the public being misled by Hotze's Confederate propaganda, but it also fed the appetites of several conservatives in Parliament who subscribed to the *Index*. Among these were some of the leading Southern sympathizers, like William Gregory and William Lindsay. Several notable conservatives outside of government, such as Alexander Beresford-Hope, also subscribed. Many would become members of the Southern Independence Association, which was supported, in part, by Hotze.[88]

Americans were apprised of the close relationship between Hotze and the *Saturday Review*, the London *Herald*, the *Times*, the *Standard*, and other pro-Southern English journals when the *Mobile Register* published an article on December 6 describing this connection and revealing the names of several British journals that often published propaganda parading as news. This article was later reprinted in several Northern publications, including Boston's *Living Age* under the title "Letting the Cat Out" (Feb. 14). While learning of this broad array of English support may have been gratifying to Southerners, the revelation that some of England's most prestigious and influential newspapers and journals were willing participants in a Southern propaganda campaign only served to deepen the feeling of bitterness and hostility that was already pervasive in the North, especially in New England. The situation was about to grow much worse.

Chapter 8

The North Suffers Military Reversals

British Consider Intervention

McClellan's campaign on the peninsula was not going well. The Battle of Seven Pines (May 31–June 1, 1862) was a near defeat for the Union forces and on June 1, the man who would become the Confederacy's greatest military leader, Robert E. Lee, was given command of the Army of Northern Virginia. Shortly thereafter, a series of battles on the Virginia peninsula changed the complexion of the war dramatically. From June 25 to July 1, the Union army suffered a series of defeats in what came to be known as the Seven Days' Battles. These were followed by the Second Battle of Bull Run (August 28–30), which, like the first, resulted in a Confederate win. This rapid succession of victories rejuvenated the Southern cause both at home and abroad. Morale was restored and the prospect of a long war arose again in the North. For abolitionists at least, there was a positive side to all this. The abrupt reversal of fortune now made emancipation more attractive as a war measure.[1]

The Seven Days' Battles (June 25–July 1) ended at Malvern Hill. McClellan's failure to take Richmond despite his huge advantage in men and material led to a renewed Northern concern regarding the possibility of British intervention. The cotton shortage was now a serious issue. Richard Cobden warned Adams that sympathy for the South was growing—along with the need for cotton. The Union cause in England was suddenly in serious trouble.[2] News of the defeats spread quickly through the North, causing a tidal wave of shock followed by depression.

Emerson wrote to his brother William to tell him the sad news of the death of another of Lowell's nephews. "The war drags on," he observed, "& drags us all into it, in some sort, by ourselves, our children, or our friends."[3] The personal dimension of the struggle for these New Englanders, as for others throughout the North, was inescapable. No one was exempt from the suffering and pain, something the recent Conscription Act helped guarantee.

Viewing the war from a distance, Englishmen could afford to see it in an abstract way, as a complex political and cultural equation that was working itself out with a good deal of sound and fury. Such abstraction, however, was not possible for Americans and their diplomats in London. Even before the shocking news of the failure of McClellan's Peninsula Campaign reached England, Minister Adams wrote to his son Charles about his growing concern that the war was dragging on for too long and at too great a cost. At the same time, he was more convinced than ever that the pestilence that caused this calamity must be eradicated once and for all. "My belief is unshaken," he told him, "that the end of this conflict is to topple down the edifice of slavery." Observing that it was the Fourth of July, Adams told his son that the North should never have compromised on the words of the Declaration when the nation was founded and should not compromise now.[4]

Not long after this, the elder Adams wrote to Secretary Seward to emphasize, again, the need to clarify the higher purposes of the war.[5] Such a clarification was especially important now if the Union was to win the minds and hearts of the masses of Englishmen, especially English factory workers, whose suffering was growing more intense every day due to the lack of cotton. *Harper's Weekly* placed the blame for this regrettable situation squarely on the heads of the British governing class, declaring that "if the British Government had not been so eager to see this country divided and democracy discredited, the rebellion would have been crushed long ago."[6] Concern with British opinion remained high. Ephraim Adams reports that "Motley, at Vienna, was keeping close touch with the situation in England through private correspondence," which he routinely shared with his friends in Boston.[7]

At the same time, New England liberals believed that if the Union declared emancipation as a goal, it would do much to convince British laborers that the American war was being fought to defend the dignity of free labor and the honor of the working class everywhere, regardless of race. Emerson had recently made this point in his Smithsonian address as well as in the pages of the *Atlantic Monthly*. In his July 4 "Message to Congress in Special Session," Lincoln offered something different. He chose to cast the war as a test of the nation's faith in the idea of a "people's government," something conservative British critics now openly scoffed at.

Lincoln stated the proposition bluntly. "This issue embraces more than the fate of these United States," he declared. "It presents to the whole family of man, the question, whether . . . a government of the people, by the same people—can, or cannot, maintain its territorial integrity, against its own domestic foes," and "whether discontented individuals" can "break up their Government, and thus practically put an end to free government upon the earth. It forces us to ask: 'Is there, in all republics, this inherent, and fatal weakness?'"[8] At this point, most Northerners understood that the future of democracy depended on winning the war and restoring the Union.[9] Whether a postwar democracy would tolerate slavery, however, was still uncertain.

More and more Republican congressmen were moving toward a more liberal policy on emancipation. On July 17, Congress passed a second Confiscation Act. It was designed to deprive traitors of their property, including slaves, "who shall be deemed captives of war and shall be forever free." While cast as yet another war measure, this act, James McPherson points out, "was important as a symbol of what the war was becoming—a war to overturn the southern social order as a means of reconstituting the Union."[10] An important feature of the act was that it also allowed the government to employ "persons of African descent" and to use them in any way necessary. On the same day, Congress also passed the Militia Act, which specifically authorized the president to use Black troops. These developments were further signs that the North was moving toward total emancipation.

The employment of Blacks in Northern armies for any purpose was extremely controversial. Many argued that Black people lacked both courage and intelligence and would degrade any armed force in which they served. At just this time, the war provided a spectacular example to the contrary. Robert Smalls, a South Carolina slave, was serving as a pilot on a Confederate steamer, the *Planter*, in Charleston Harbor. One evening, white members of the crew and their officers decided to spend a night ashore. Having planned in advance for such an opportunity, Smalls and his Black shipmates put their plan into action. After quietly bringing their wives and children on board, they boldly fired up the boilers and sailed the ship under cover of darkness past Confederate cannons and out of the harbor. Upon reaching open water, they surrendered the *Planter* and its cargo of munitions to the Union fleet patrolling the area.[11]

This courageous act was widely celebrated in the North by both Blacks and whites. In August, Smalls traveled to Washington, DC, where he told his harrowing tale to a large audience at Israel Church. After hearing this account, future African Methodist Episcopal (AME) bishop Henry McNeal Turner declared Smalls "a living specimen of unquestionable African heroism."[12] During his visit to Washington, Smalls was invited to the White House, where he was received by a grateful president. Smalls was among the first of several African Americans who would be cordially received by Lincoln in the balance of the war. Some, such as Frederick Douglass, Charles Lenox Remond, and Sojourner Truth, were well known. Others came to petition for the rights of the freedmen in areas of the South now under Union control. Many were common people who simply melded into the flow of citizens who streamed through "the people's house" during Executive Mansion receptions, which in the past were open only to whites.[13]

The welcoming of Blacks to the White House was a source of scandal in the eyes of conservatives. A Democratic newspaper in Maine described this new openness as "a hideous travestie" and "an abject and shameful truckling to the shocking and unnatural doctrine of negro equality."[14] For liberals, this was a major step forward in their campaign for emancipation and equal rights. They continued to promote the new view of Blacks spreading through the North. *Harper's Weekly* jumped at the chance to celebrate Smalls's heroic actions. On June 14, the paper published two large pictures side by side: "An engraving of the steamer *Planter*, lately run out of Charleston by her negro crew, and a portrait of her captain, ROBERT SMALLS, both from photographs sent us by our correspondent." *Harper's* described Smalls's feat as "one of the most daring and heroic adventures since the war commenced."

Lincoln's openness to Black visitors was one more sign that America, in the North at least, was undergoing a significant change in attitudes toward race. These visitors were treated as equals by the president. Lincoln was always gracious, sometimes inviting Black guests to join him and Mrs. Lincoln in an afternoon tea. As was his habit with others, he listened carefully to them. These conversations undoubtedly served to encourage Lincoln's increasingly liberal thinking regarding race. After reporting on one such meeting, the editors of the *Anglo-African* commented that this was clear evidence "of great change in high quarters."[15]

Meanwhile, the Confiscation Act resulted in a growing numbers of freed slaves. Their legal status, however, remained unclear. While Congress was busy passing landmark legislation, George Curtis delivered the annual Phi Beta Kappa address at Harvard, where Emerson had made his famous "American Scholar" address a quarter century earlier. Curtis used the occasion to promote not only a more liberal policy on emancipation but also something even more radical: a national commitment to the principle of equal rights for all.

Weeks earlier, Curtis had articulated this idea in *Harper's Weekly*, where he argued that the Declaration's assertion of equality was intended to apply to everyone. "The fathers said what they meant, and meant what they said," Curtis declared. "They meant *all men*." Because of this, he insisted, "our National Government . . . is a government of all men who, living in the country, obey the laws and behave themselves." Curtis was unequivocal that American democracy should draw no lines of distinction based on race. "The yellow Chinese, and the olive Spaniard or West Indian, or the red Turk or Hindoo, or the white Englishman or Irishman, or the African or Creole of any race, may be a citizen of the United States," and with citizenship came all the rights thereunto pertaining. And so, "the ballot of the voter of tawny Spanish descent in *New Orleans*, or of dusky African descent in Boston, counts just as much in this Government as the vote of the Honorable Mr. [Samuel] Cox . . . of Ohio."[16] Such a sweeping assertion of universal rights, including suffrage, without regard to race, must have been a bit breathtaking to a sizable segment of the *Weekly*'s million and a quarter readers. The Honorable Mr. Cox, leader of the conservative Democrats in Congress, would soon offer a response to Curtis and other Transcendental idealists of New England.

In his Phi Beta Kappa address, which he titled "The American Doctrine of Liberty," Curtis laid out a concept of freedom and equal rights under the law that, in effect, anticipated the Thirteenth, Fourteenth, and Fifteenth Amendments to the Constitution. "The very root of the American doctrine of liberty," Curtis declared, "is the equality of human rights based upon our common humanity. The ultimate scope of that doctrine is the absolute personal and political freedom of every man: the right . . . of every man to think and speak and act, subject to the equal rights of other men, protected in their exercise by common consent or law. It declares that men are to be deprived of personal liberty only for crime, and that political liberty is the only sure guarantee of personal freedom. These," Curtis insisted, "are the postulates of our civilization."

Of course, the "civilization" Curtis referred to was not that of America in 1862 but rather the one that he, along with Emerson, Norton, Sumner, Lowell, Longfellow, Whittier, and other New England idealists, envisioned as the future of America and, eventually, the world. It was a civilization where differences of race were deemed utterly and literally superficial. All men, Curtis insisted, would fight for their freedom if given the chance to do so. Among the heroes of the cause he named "the African Toussaint L'Overture dying a thousand deaths for his race among the Jura mountains [in Haiti]." This, he declared, "is the unerring heart of man attesting his equal humanity." For Curtis, the "common humanity of man" demanded an "equality of human rights" that was not bounded by oceans or national borders. Curtis then turned specifically to that nemesis of American democracy, Great Britain.

These rights belonged to all, Curtis insisted, including the oppressed "farm laborers in certain districts of England," who are treated "more like animals than any negro" and who, "although forming the most numerous single class in the country, are not thought of in forming an estimate of national character." He also noted the cruel disparity and manifest injustice of a society where "the Marquis of Breadalbane rides upon his own estate seventy miles from sea to sea, while five millions of factory laborers squeeze through life upon starvation wages."

Such appalling inequity suggested that, despite its claim to be the most advanced civilization on earth, "British society is but a modified feudalism." It was this culture of privilege and oppression that made England the enemy of progress and the natural ally of Southern slaveholders. The vaunted "civilization" of the mother country was merely a veneer of gentility masking an inner decay. "The comely feudalism of England," Curtis said, "a system of class privilege, not of human right—stretches out its hand, muffled in cotton, to the hideous hag of human slavery over the sea, in whom it owns a ghastly kindred with itself."[17]

In his address, Curtis gave voice to what virtually all New England liberals believed at this point. Soon after, Norton wrote to him that praises for the oration "come to me from all sides. Last Saturday at the Club there was a general expression of hearty admiration of it. Everyone agreed that "it was one of the most effective pieces of oratory that had been heard here by this generation," and they wholeheartedly endorsed "its sentiment and doctrine."[18] Curtis would eventually repeat this powerful address some forty times throughout the North.[19]

As British conservatives had feared early on, the growth of antislavery sentiment in the North threatened to dominate the war effort.[20] New England intellectuals like Curtis and his Saturday Club friends used powerful resources like the *Atlantic Monthly* and *Harper's Weekly*, as well as the lecture platform, pulpit, lyceum, and newspapers, to further this effort. The campaign would accelerate as *Harper's Monthly*, the *North American Review*, and the newborn Boston *Commonwealth* were added to the arsenal of liberal democracy.

British conservatives were increasingly concerned with this trend, but they were uncertain how to respond. Lord Russell expressed fear that British recognition of the Confederacy at this point might push the Federals to instigate slave insurrections, which could lead to a global race war that would threaten the stability of the British Empire. Memories of the Haitian rebellion under Toussaint-Louverture in the West Indies, an event that abolitionists like Emerson, Higginson, Curtis, and others celebrated yearly, undoubtedly came to mind, as did the more recent Sepoy rebellion in India, the empire's crown jewel.[21]

The Confiscation and Militia Acts, emancipation in the District of Columbia, and Lincoln's proposal for compensated emancipation in the border states were obvious signs of a continuing trend toward total emancipation. If the Civil War resulted in universal emancipation, the next move would likely be a demand for enfranchisement and full civil rights for freedmen. New England intellectuals and their abolitionist allies had been moving in this direction for some time. As Curtis's Harvard address recently confirmed, these idealists were determined that the Declaration's promise of equality for "all men" should be fulfilled. All of this was distressing to Britain's governing class, despite their previous claims of opposition to slavery. The triumph of liberal democracy in America, they believed, would put Great Britain's colonial empire in jeopardy.[22]

The North's recent military reversals helped lessen that fear. Even before the news of the disasters in Virginia reached Great Britain, friends of the North were skeptical that the nation could be reunited through the use of military force. Richard Cobden wrote Charles Summer that "there is all but unanimous belief here that you *cannot* subject the South to the Union. Even they who are your partisans and advocates cannot see their way to any such issue." He then added, rather ominously, that manufacturers are "anxious to obtain cotton and they will be all . . . pressing on our government the necessity of 'doing something.'"[23]

At this critical time, John Elliott Cairnes received his first letter from Sarah Shaw. Shaw and her husband, Francis, were both liberal reformers. In their younger days, they helped finance Brook Farm, the Transcendental utopian community in West Roxbury, Massachusetts. Her son-in-law, George Curtis, and his brother, Burrill, lived there for seventeen months before moving to Concord, which was known in the 1840s as something of a Transcendental mecca.[24] Sarah Shaw was strong-minded and idealistic. Like many New Englanders of her generation, she had been influenced by Transcendental philosophy early on. She once related that at age fourteen Ralph Waldo Emerson captured her "heart [and] soul." As she grew older, she "went to all his Boston lectures," and her "reverence for him grew with [her] growth" and "strengthened with [her] strength." Emersonian idealism became her guide in life.[25] Eventually, she would pass this idealism on to her son, Robert.

Both Shaw and her husband were dedicated abolitionists.[26] She had recently read Cairnes's *The Slave Power* and wanted to thank the author personally for his contribution to the cause. After introducing herself, she told Cairnes, "It's idle to say that we no longer care what you in the 'Mother Country' think or say of us. We do *care*," she insisted. When she read Cairnes's "treatise upon our mighty struggle for the Right," she felt "ready to forgive all the cold criticism and flippant insults that have reached us through the English Reviews and Press."

Shaw went on to explain to Cairnes that, because she was "born and bred in Massachusetts, . . . love and respect for England" was a part of her education. Unfortunately, like so many onetime Anglophiles, when the North's expectations of sympathy and support from England, "the Pioneer in Freedom," were not fulfilled, "the bitterness of the disappointment" was that much greater. She did find some solace, however, in the fact that several leading intellects and philosophical thinkers of England "have from the beginning seen and understood our position."[27] From this point forward, Sarah Shaw and Cairnes would develop an increasingly strong bond of friendship and mutual regard.

Such examples of Anglo-American amity were all too rare as transatlantic animosities continued to simmer. The *Philadelphia City Item* of June 28 announced that the new issue of the *Atlantic Monthly* was out and is "excellent and highly readable. . . . The *Atlantic*," the *Item* insisted, "is better than any one Magazine published even in England." Hawthorne's "Chiefly About War Matters," which appeared in the same issue, did not meet with the *Item*'s approval, however. The paper described the controversial piece, in which Hawthorne revealed his ambiguous feelings about the war and Lincoln, as showing "frivolity and insincerity."

The original version of Hawthorne's article, based on a recent visit to Washington, included comments on Lincoln that were so offensive to the *Atlantic*'s editor and publisher, James T. Fields, that he urged Hawthorne, who was a personal friend, to drop the passages. One of the most offensive focused on his description of the president's homely appearance and lack of formal education, qualities that were so often the target of British critics. Hawthorne described the president, whom he referred to as "Uncle Abe," as "a tall, loose-jointed figure" who was "about the homeliest man I ever saw." The president's "whole physiognomy," he noted, "is as coarse a one as you would meet anywhere in the length and breadth of the States."

Hawthorne also reported that Lincoln was a man who showed "no bookish cultivation, no refinement."[28] While Hawthorne attempted to offset these negative impressions by noting the president's honesty and tact, Fields was fully aware that the article, as it stood, would be deeply offensive to most of the *Atlantic*'s readership. It would also reinforce the negative views of Lincoln that already populated the British press. Like many others in New England, Fields was experiencing what his biographer calls a "growing bitterness toward his beloved England," and he was not about to offer the sneering cultural critics there more fuel from the pen of one of America's most estimable authors.[29]

In his letter to Hawthorne, Fields expressed concern about English readers of the *Atlantic* and noted, "Ticknor & I both think it will be politic to alter yr. phrases with reference to the President, to leave out the description of his awkwardness & general uncouth aspect. England is reading the Maga[zine] now & will gloat over the monkey figure of 'Uncle Abe' as he appears in yr. paper."[30] Hawthorne acceded to his editor's request, but even with the alterations the article, published under the pseudonym "A Peaceable Man," was offensive to many. In his response, Hawthorne indicated that he had omitted several passages that Fields "doubted the public could bear. The remainder is tame enough in all conscience, and I don't think it will bear any more castration." He also offered some advice to his liberal editor and publisher. "I think the political complexion of the Magazine has been getting too deep a black Republican tinge," he warned. "There is a time pretty near at hand when you will be sorry for it. The politics of the Magazine suit Massachusetts tolerably well (and only tolerably), but it does not fairly represent the feeling of the country at large."[31]

In the final version, which appeared in July, Hawthorne substituted tongue-in-cheek footnotes, ostensibly by a censorious editor, where deletions had been made. For example, in speaking of the meeting with Lincoln, he noted, "We are compelled to omit two or three pages, in which the author . . . gives his idea of the personal appearance and deportment of the President. The sketch appears to have been written in a benign spirit, and perhaps conveys a not inaccurate impression of its august subject," but the passage was deleted because "it lacks *reverence*."[32]

Throughout the article, Hawthorne told of what he saw as the negative and positive on each side of the struggle. Because of this, he was roundly criticized in the North, both publicly and privately, for his apparent lack of patriotism. Curtis was appalled by Hawthorne's cold indifference toward a war that so aroused the passions of his New England friends and neighbors. He wrote to Norton, "What an extraordinary paper by Hawthorne in the *Atlantic*! It is pure intellect, without emotion, without sympathy, without principle. . . . It is as unhuman and passionless as a disembodied intelligence."[33] Most of New England's writers and thinkers were now far too committed, emotionally and intellectually, to the great issues of the war to allow for any ambiguity, even the nuanced speculations of one of America's most respected authors. As indicated in Fields's letter to Hawthorne, the relentless drumbeat of criticism in the British press only added to their sensitivity on the matter.

That sensitivity was undoubtedly enhanced when, in a somewhat surprisingly hard turn to the right, *Fraser's Magazine* chose this same month to publish an absolutely damning piece attacking the North. The author was Hiram Fuller, an American expatriate with strong Nativist beliefs.[34] Fuller's argument was very much in keeping with that of British conservatives and their Southern counterparts. "The root of all the evil," he declared, is "Unrestricted Suffrage, which has rent the American Union asunder, and threatens to topple 'the Model Republic' into a hopeless heap of ruins." Abraham Lincoln, Fuller maintained, was a typical product of this defective system. He appealed to the crude masses precisely because "his reputation for 'rail-splitting' and flat-boating, with the 'electioneering anecdotes' of his coarse habits and vulgar familiarity," showed that he was one of them.[35]

As Fuller was fulminating bitterly against the dangers of universal suffrage in *Fraser's*, Edward Dicey was describing the advantages of "self-government" in glowing terms in *Macmillan's Magazine*. "The Free West" was the latest installment of his American travelogue. While the contours of New England resembled Old England in many ways, nothing in Dicey's homeland could have prepared him for the panoramic spectacle of the American West. "The one 'grand' thing about American scenery," he observed, "is its vastness; and so, to the American mind, mere size, simple greatness, has an attraction we in the Old World can hardly realize."

Dicey noted that in this rugged environment all men faced the same challenges on the same terms. The result was that "in the West all men are equal, as a matter of fact, not at all of abstract theory." Thus, "two propositions . . . about slavery have established themselves fully in the Western mind. The first is, that slavery in the West is fatal to the progress of the country; the second . . . is, that the existence of slavery at all is fatal to the peace and durability of the Union." Consequently, "the West draws the conclusion, that slavery must be abolished; and, if abolition should prove inconsistent with the Constitution, then the master-piece of Washington must be modified."[36] As Dicey's article suggested, there was now a growing consensus throughout the North that slavery must go, regardless of current constitutional protections. The conservatives' demand for a return to the status ante was now little more than wishful thinking.

The issue of democratic governance was also discussed in the *North American Review* of July, where John Stuart Mill's new study, *Considerations on Representative Government*, was the subject of a generally positive review.[37] However, there was one area of disagreement, and that was on the matter of universal suffrage. While Mill was generally in favor of it, the reviewer noted that the English scholar "depreciates . . . the extension of the suffrage to those who are too ignorant to vote intelligently." As a result, Mill would require a "test" at the point of registration that included both reading and math skills, which the writer felt was so rigorous it "would disenfranchise some of the younger graduates of our universities." "Mr. Mill," he reported, is also "in favor of granting two or more votes to persons who have attained certain prescribed standards of education."

The reviewer objected that Mill's system was decidedly tilted toward elites. In America, "there are many among those commonly termed 'self-educated' whose attainments in knowledge are larger and more valuable than those of the inferior members of the (so-called) learned professions," he insisted. Indeed, "there are not a few of the comparatively uneducated, whose conversance with affairs, shrewd judgment of men and measures, and sound discretion, would render their just claim to a plural vote superior to that of many persons of high reputation for such learning as is derived from books alone."[38] The reviewer might very well have had the self-educated Abraham Lincoln in mind. As the war evolved and emancipation and universal male suffrage were proposed as Union goals, the question of voting rights and qualifications would become heated issues.[39]

This difference of opinion between Mill and his *North American* critic highlighted the difference between British and American liberalism at this time. Eugenio Biagini writes, "Liberalism is often described as a body of strictly individualistic doctrines based on, and aimed at, the defense of personal rights and liberties, intended as 'absence of restraint.'" In light of this, he states that Mill was "the leading 'libertarian' of his day."[40] But this British form of liberalism had its limits. As Louis Hartz argues, Mill "advocated the power of plural voting for the educated elite in order to keep mass opinion in its place."[41] It is precisely this Victorian restraint that New England liberals now balked at. Leslie Butler claims that Mill's proposals for plural voting were seen by some Americans as "'elitist' and undemocratic," and "they gained almost no traction among the young transatlantic liberals" of New England. Such proposals stand, she suggests, "as a reminder of the limits that national differences set on political discourse: while American liberals hardly questioned universal manhood suffrage, British liberals hardly contemplated it."[42]

Meanwhile, events on the battlefield in America continued to have serious repercussions in Great Britain. When news of the failure of McClellan's Peninsula Campaign reached England, the reaction was dramatic. Minister Adams wrote to his son on July 18 that the Richmond news "has set all the elements of hostility to us in agitation, and they are working to carry the House of Commons off their feet in its debate tonight."[43] William Lindsay, who had supported William Gregory's earlier bid for Confederate recognition, introduced a motion in the House of Commons for British mediation to end the war in the interest of saving the textile industry.[44] Benjamin Moran, assistant secretary to Minister Adams, later recorded in his diary that during the debate James Mason, the Confederacy's emissary to Great Britain, was seated on the floor before the gallery, where he "spat tobacco . . . furiously . . . and covered the carpet."[45] Fortunately, Palmerston, ever cautious, spoke against the measure and it was withdrawn without a vote.[46] Ephraim Adams maintains that this "was the most critical period in the entire course of the British attitude toward the Civil War." In the fall of 1862, very few believed that a Union victory was even a remote possibility and, sooner or later, "European recognition would have to be given to the Confederacy."[47]

At this critical time, Harriet Beecher Stowe expressed her deep disappointment with the lack of support from British abolitionists in a letter to the Duchess of Argyll. "We tread the winepress alone," she wrote, while "they whose cheap rhetoric has been for years pushing us into it now desert 'en masse.'"[48] At home, Stowe, along with other abolitionists, began in earnest to urge the recruitment of Black troops, something that would prove of inestimable importance in the campaign for emancipation and, later, equal rights. Like others, she felt Lincoln was too slow on emancipation. Stowe's frustration and depression were shared by Sarah Shaw, who wrote to Cairnes telling him that "the disappointment in McClellan, the sickness in the army . . . the coming home of our poor wounded men, and the memory of our noble dead youth left behind, all tend to depress us."[49]

Members of the Saturday Club also felt strongly that the movement toward emancipation should be accelerated, not only because it was just but because they believed a more vigorous and robust emancipation policy would help win British support. Norton wrote to George Curtis at this time that he feared "the President is not yet quite conscious of the spirit of the people, and aware of the needs of the time." Unlike Emerson, who appreciated Lincoln's need for caution, Norton was becoming impatient. "Will Lincoln be master of the opportunities, or will they escape him? Is he great enough for the time?" he asked.[50] Very soon, Norton would have an answer.

In August, Dicey's fourth installment of his American travelogue, "The New England States," appeared in *Macmillan's*. In this piece, he reflected on America's now conflicted attitude toward its cultural identity. On the one hand, there was a strong desire to assert an identity distinct from that of Old England. In a dramatic change from pre-war attitudes, "an American is almost always offended if you tell him that America is very like England," Dicey reported. "He has a conviction . . . that his country ought to have a separate individuality." At the same time, "he has an opposite conviction, which I would not gainsay, that . . . he is the descendant of the England of Milton, and Shakespeare, and Bacon." According to Dicey, it was the war that caused "this conflicting state of sentiment," and he saw "little prospect" of "friendship between the two countries, till America has got what she is fast getting, a literature and a history and a past of her own." It was apparent that a second revolution was now well underway and the mother country was no longer a fit model for a nation newly recommitted to what Thomas Paine had called "the rights of man." New England's literati would continue to play an important role in propelling this revolutionary movement forward.

During his visit, Dicey was introduced to many of New England's most esteemed literary figures, thanks in part to the efforts of James T. Fields. "All over America, and above all in New England, literary fame and the reputation of learning are honoured to a degree we can hardly appreciate at home," Dicey observed. Because of this, in America "the literary mind represents the national mind more closely than would seem probable to us."

For Dicey, there was no question that in the ranks of the intellectual class, Emerson was the first among equals. "Hearing him . . . speak," he wrote, "I understood better than I had learnt from his writings the influence which Mr. Emerson has wielded over the mind of America, and how Concord had become a kind of Mecca, of which the representative-man of American thought was the Mahomet." Emerson was using that influence now in an effort to reshape American democracy along the liberal lines that he believed were most authentically and uniquely American. Dicey also met "the great poet of America," Longfellow, as well as Holmes and Lowell.

The Englishman was impressed with the Saturday Club and the warm fellowship enjoyed by New England's literati, something that was apparently rare among their British counterparts. "To anybody who knows anything of the literary world in England," Dicey wrote, "it will seem remarkable that all the men of literary note in Boston should meet regularly once a month, of their own free will and pleasure, to dine with each other; and still more so that they should meet as friends, not as rivals." The close fraternity of the Saturday Club that Dicey described had undoubtedly been enhanced by the war. The need to defend Northern American culture against an onslaught of British criticism and the shared determination to reinvent American democracy on a new, more liberal basis made them comrades in literary arms. Dicey closed with the hope that, despite McClellan's recent failure, England would not be tempted to interfere in America's conflict. Indeed, it seemed anomalous to him, given the fact that he was raised to believe "England was the home of the free," that his country would ever consider extending a hand to "the slave-owner and oppressor who looks to England for succor," but he could not rule out the possibility either.[51]

In the wake of McClellan's humiliating defeat, the *Saturday Review* called upon the North to give up what it considered the impossible goal of conquering the South. In a front-page essay titled "American Prospects," the *Review* did not explicitly demand British intervention, but it came close. The war, the writer insisted, was now a hopeless affair. "The rebels cannot possibly be conciliated," and "there is no longer a political motive for the invasion of the South." In light of this, the writer contended, England "after unparalleled patience with which neutrality has been maintained . . . has abundant right to protest against the savage folly of internecine war with the South."[52] Just what form that "protest" might take was not indicated.

A week later, Gladstone wrote to Lord Russell that mediation was justified because of the "frightful misery which this civil conflict has brought upon other countries" and because of the "unanimity with which it is condemned by the civilized world." Like most Englishmen at this time, Gladstone believed the North could not succeed in forcing the South to return to the Union and, therefore, the war was both futile and cruel. Additionally, nearly 75 percent of the textile workers in Great Britain were either idle or on short time. Regardless of their suffering, however, many English workers had come to see the American contest as New England liberals did: a people's war being fought to vindicate the principle of equal rights, regardless of class, caste, or race.[53] A growing number of them now openly supported Lincoln and the Union cause.

Around this time, Emerson recorded in his journal his concern about British intervention. The only way to prevent it, he believed, was a declaration of emancipation. European governments, he wrote, "dare not interfere for slavery, as soon as the Union is pronounced for liberty."[54] Emerson also speculated about the difficulty that even well-intended Englishmen had in understanding how, presently, the Union could be fighting both for and against slavery. "Our constitutionality," he recorded, "on which we so pique ourselves, of . . . fighting *for* slavery in the loyal states, and in the rebel states *against* it, is too technical for distant observers, & only supplies them with the reproach that our cause is immoral."[55] It was clear to many Northerners that the commitment to "constitutionality" and the preservation of slavery must give way if the nation was to survive.

Meanwhile, the war continued to go badly for the North, and there was little hope things would improve any time soon. Morale in the Union army was sinking. Ellen Emerson wrote to her cousin, "Mrs. Bowers sent over a letter from the Capt. who has lately been sent with the 32nd Regiment to Harrison's landing. . . . 'They are not afraid to fight again,' he says, but they are disheartened and feel as if they were not well-commanded, and scarcely expect to conquer. He says they look upon emancipation as the only help and see it avoided with disgust and surprise."[56]

With the military situation deteriorating and the threat of intervention growing, many felt the time had come for a dramatic policy change that would imbue the North with a sense of high purpose and also stave off European intervention. Motley wrote to his mother from his diplomatic post in Austria, "The only thing that saves us as yet from a war with the slaveholders, allied with both France and England, is the anti-slavery feeling of a very considerable portion of the British public." Because of this, he was convinced that "nothing but a proclamation of emancipation to every negro in the country will save us from war with England and France combined."[57]

The day after Motley penned his letter, Horace Greeley published "The Prayer of Twenty Million" in his *New York Tribune*. The prayer called upon Lincoln to use the powers granted in the Confiscation Act to liberate the slaves of those owners who were disloyal to the Union and to employ them in the war effort. Failure to enforce this act uniformly throughout the Union ranks, Greeley insisted, suggested a "mistaken deference to Rebel Slavery" that was immensely damaging to the Union cause. Two days later, Lincoln issued his famous "Reply to Horace Greeley," a statement that was a huge disappointment to those who were committed to the cause of general emancipation. Lincoln made it clear his primary and only goal was to preserve the Union. He told Greeley, "If I could save the Union without freeing any slaves I would do it, and if I could save it by freeing all slaves I would do it, and if I could save it by freeing some and leaving others alone I would also do that."[58]

The president's concise reply to Greeley may have been welcomed by some conservatives, but a closer reading of the document should have given them pause. As James McPherson observes, the reply offered "something for both radicals and conservatives—another hint that emancipation might be coming," but "it would happen only because it was necessary to save the Union." In this way, Lincoln "cloaked a radical measure in conservative garb."[59] Conservatives might also have taken note of the president's poignant final sentence: "I have here stated my purpose according to my view of *official* duty; and I intend no modification of my oft-expressed *personal* wish that all men everywhere could be free."[60] This "*personal*" wish would become increasingly prominent. As Ronald White notes, at this time "union and emancipation were coming together for Lincoln as the inseparable goals in a rebirth of the nation."[61]

The feeling in New England was the same. Attitudes toward slavery were changing. A week after the president's reply, Holmes, who had himself been a conservative on the matter at the outset of the war, reported to Motley in Vienna that "they were talking in the cars to-day of [Gen. John C.] Fremont's speech at Tremont Temple last evening. His allusions to slavery . . . were received with an applause which they would never have gained a little while ago. Nay, I think a miscellaneous Boston audience would be more likely to cheer any denunciation of slavery now than almost any other sentiment."[62] No doubt, the eloquent voices of New England's intellectual class that were resonating throughout the North, calling repeatedly for emancipation, had something to do with this dramatic change.

While New England liberals were becoming frustrated with Lincoln's failure to act decisively on emancipation, some Black leaders were becoming skeptical of the war effort. Writers in New York's *Anglo-African* magazine questioned whether Northern Blacks should contribute to it. Boston's Charles Lenox Remond was highly critical of the Lincoln administration's policies and questioned whether the war would be of any benefit to the slaves. However, other prominent Black leaders, like John Rock and William C. Nell, saw the war in a positive way, the latter referring to it as the "pure gold of the republic."[63] Soon Rock would dedicate his energies to raising Black recruits for the Union army. He told the volunteers that the war was being waged now for equal rights and that "we at the North . . . shall not be satisfied until we get equal rights for all."[64]

Boston's Black women also took an active part in the war effort. In November they formed the Fugitive Aid Society, in part at the urging of Elizabeth Keckley, Mary Todd Lincoln's dressmaker, who had founded her own Contraband Relief Association. The Boston group sponsored lectures by such notable Black leaders as Remond and Douglass, raised money and supplies for the needy, and hired Louise De Mortie, a popular Black singer, to perform for the "suffering sick, aged, and infants among the contraband at Washington."[65]

Norton wrote to Elizabeth Gaskell's daughter, "Meta" (Margaret Emily), around this time to express his continuing confidence that emancipation would be achieved. "Do not believe what you see in the '*Times*,' or in other papers, of discord or want of heart, or failure of resolution at the North," he told her. "We mean to save the Union . . . for the sake of Liberty and of civilization," and with this "the slavery of the black race in America will come to an end." He then added, "I am sorry, but not surprised at, the general misconception abroad of our position, our purposes, and our principles."[66]

Despite the confidence of liberals like Norton, it was a truly dismal time for the Union both at home and abroad. Longfellow wrote in his journal of "war and rumors of war and a sense of apprehension in the air, and sadness and general discomfort."[67] England was a constant worry, and the sons of New England, like many others throughout the North, continued to sacrifice their lives in a struggle that looked increasingly hopeless. Lincoln's recent reply to Greeley only seemed to underscore to the rest of the world that the Union cause lacked a high moral purpose. Most of the British intellectual and artistic class remained highly critical. John Ruskin told Norton in a letter, "As for your American war—I still say as I said at first—If they want to fight—they deserve to fight and to suffer—It is entirely horrible and abominable—but nothing else would do.—Do you remember Mrs. Brownings curse on America?" he asked. "I said at the time 'she had no business to curse any country but her own.' But she, as it appeared afterwards, was dying—and knew better than I against whom her words were to be recorded."[68]

At this point in the struggle, many in the North felt little enthusiasm for a war to preserve a Union with slaveholders. For some, the conflict appeared to be what the British claimed it was, a meaningless exercise in mass slaughter on a scale never before seen. The Union defeat at Second Bull Run (August 29–30) was just another bloody example. Shortly thereafter, Longfellow, whose son was in the army, reflected in his journal on the "great battle at Manassas. . . . The moon set red and lowering; and I thought in the night of the pale, upturned faces of young men on the battle field, and beards pointing to the skies, and the agonies of the wounded; and my wretchedness was very great," he wrote. "Every shell from the canon's mouth bursts not only on the field, but on far away homes, North or South, carrying dismay and death."[69] Many wondered how much longer this seemingly pointless carnage could go on.

Chapter 9

Lincoln Proclaims Emancipation as Race Takes Center Stage

The failure of McClellan's Peninsula Campaign had one positive result. It brought an end to the idea of a limited war for limited ends. As James McPherson notes, "from now on the North would fight not to preserve the old Union but to destroy it and build a new one on the ashes."[1] Much of the drive to achieve this new vision came from New England idealists. Henry Adams wrote to his brother Charles that he was convinced the war must go on until the South was utterly crushed and the institution of slavery extinguished. "I don't much care whether they are destroyed by emancipation, or . . . a vigorous system of guerilla war carried on by negroes on our side," Adams wrote. "We must ruin them before we let them go or it will all have to be done over again. . . . It is a battle between us and slavery."[2] George Curtis shared this view. In an article titled "The Coming Wrath" in *Harper's Weekly* on August 30, 1862, he called upon the North to commit itself to total war.

For the British government, the Union's second defeat at Manassas, coming on the heels of earlier defeats in the Seven Days' Battles, suggested that the time had come, again, to consider intervention. Palmerston wrote to Lord Russell that accounts of the recent battles "between the Confederates and the Federals show that the latter got a very complete smashing," and that soon Washington or Baltimore may fall into the hands of the Confederates. "If this should happen," he asked, "would it not be time for us to consider whether . . . England and France might not address the contending parties and recommend an arrangement upon the basis of separation?"[3]

A commitment to emancipation might change this equation. Not surprisingly, as the policies of the North verged more and more toward emancipation, the London *Times*'s criticism intensified. Charles Mackay and Francis Lawley, who were passionate supporters of the South, had replaced Bancroft Davis and William Howard Russell as the paper's American correspondents.[4] The *Times*'s animus toward the North may have been due, in part at least, to the fact that its manager, Mowbray Morris, was of West India planter stock and, according to one source, "blamed Britain's own abolition of slavery for the loss of his family's fortune." Now it seemed the same fate was about to be imposed on the South's innocent planters. Morris wrote to Charles Mackay that "the Northern Government and its policy are an abomination to me, and I greatly enjoy to hear them abused."[5] That abuse was now almost constant.

The North still had some friends in the British press. Edward Dicey, in "The Outlook of the War" in the September issue of *Macmillan's*, insisted that, despite conservative claims to the contrary, this was an antislavery war. Dicey pointed to such evidence as the abolition of slavery in the District of Columbia, which he argued was a sign of things to come. While acknowledging that there was still considerable prejudice against Blacks in some places in the North, he insisted that "in all the Northern States the negro is treated like a man" and "in most of the New England States, the black man has exactly the same rights and privileges as the white: and throughout the whole of the Free States the growth of public opinion is in favour of a more kindly treatment of the negro."[6]

In addition, Dicey reported that most Northerners now believed "the South must be reorganized and . . . the slave-owners . . . must be virtually removed, whether by ruin, exile, or confiscation, matters little." Echoing Emerson's call in his recent Smithsonian address for an "atomic restructuring" of Southern society, Dicey declared, "A social revolution must be accomplished, and a new system of society constituted in the South, in which slavery has no part or share." He insisted that this view was "really more rational" than any alternative.[7]

Dicey's articles were deeply appreciated by supporters of the Federal cause in England. John Stuart Mill praised them and the book that soon followed, *Six Months in the Federal States*, in a letter to a friend. Dicey "writes very judiciously, as well as with right feeling, and what he says of the North, being evidently a faithful transcript of what he has seen and heard, ought to have some influence," Mill wrote. He also noted that "the *Times* . . . is as bad as ever, and even more undisguised in the expression of its bad wishes."[8] Fortunately, there were now a few strong voices on the other side.

One that was becoming ever more prominent was that of John Elliott Cairnes, who published on September 22 a strongly worded letter to the editor of the London *Anti-Slavery Advocate*. In the piece, he argued that it was not the hostile and insulting articles appearing in American newspapers that were the cause of the growing hostility between the United States and Great Britain. Rather it was the bitter diatribes in the pages of "the *Times*, the *Morning Post*, the *Saturday Review*, and, above all, those of the Tory press." The "sustained torrent of fierce, unsparing denunciation" which "those papers have now for more than a twelvemonth poured forth," he wrote, have reached a level of "positive disgust and hatred."

Lately, this hatred was focused on Blacks. "The speeches of Mr. Beresford Hope" and "the articles in the *Times* . . . denouncing a policy of emancipation," Cairnes observed, all showed these conservatives were "in perfect accord" with Southern slaveholders in regard to "the grounds on which slavery is maintained," namely, that Blacks constituted a race "so essentially inferior to the whites as to be incapable of taking an equal part with them in the business of civil life."[9] Because this belief was now being challenged as the Union moved ever closer to emancipation, he argued, the heated rhetoric in the British press was becoming even more intense.

There were some conspicuous exceptions. Around this time, Mill assured Motley that "*Macmillan's Magazine* has from the beginning been steadily on the right side in American affairs." In his letter, Mill also made an important distinction, often missed by Northerners, between the policy of the British government and British public opinion as represented in the press. He pointed out that, thus far at least, the government "has felt more rightly . . . than a majority of the public," who have been agitated by the conservative press. The main obstacle to a more robust enthusiasm for the Northern cause, Mill believed, was the perception that "the reconquest of the South [is] impossible."[10] A major Northern victory would help dispel that assumption. On September 17, the day Mill penned his letter to Motley, the Union army attained that victory by a small creek in Sharpsburg, Maryland, known as Antietam.

Robert E. Lee's invasion of Maryland was intended to open the door for foreign intervention, something the British government was now seriously considering.[11] McClellan, with overwhelming numerical superiority and the added advantage of having Lee's battle plan in his possession, managed to eke out a narrow victory.[12] It was destined to be the bloodiest day of the war. The Union army suffered over 11,600 causalities and the Confederates over 11,700. But Lee was forced to abandon the field, so the Union could claim a technical victory. As a result, Confederate hopes for recognition were scuttled, for the time at least.

Among the many Union soldiers wounded at Antietam were Robert Gould Shaw and Oliver Wendell Holmes Jr. This had been the second time each of them was wounded in battle. Another son of New England, Charles Francis Adams Jr., was also a combatant. He escaped intact, but in a letter to his mother, written shortly after the battle, he described some who did not: "I told a Captain near me that the enemy had a perfect range of the road and he'd better be careful how he drew their fire and just as I uttered the words, r-r-r-h went a round shot through the bushes over my head, slid across Forbes and Caspar as they lay on the ground some thirty yards further on and took off the legs of three infantry men next to them."[13]

The carnage at Antietam was grotesque and the sacrifices great, but the victory allowed Lincoln to do what his liberal supporters on both sides of the Atlantic had been demanding for some time. On September 22, he issued his Preliminary Emancipation Proclamation, which declared that on the first day of the new year all slaves in rebel-held territory would become "forever free." Lincoln felt it was necessary to wait for a Union victory before announcing his proclamation in order to avoid the perception that it was an act of desperation.[14] The proclamation would have vast international consequences.[15]

Before making this proclamation, Lincoln discussed the measure with his cabinet. According to Doris Kearns Goodwin, Seward expressed a concern that "the proclamation might provoke a racial war in the South so disruptive to cotton that the ruling classes in England and France would intervene to protect their economic interests." She also notes, "Seward failed to grasp what Lincoln intuitively understood: that once the Union truly committed itself to emancipation, the masses in Europe, who regarded slavery as an evil, . . . would not be easily maneuvered into supporting the South," a point New England liberals had been making for some time.[16] Seward's concerns, however, were not totally unfounded. While the measure did not provoke European intervention, the reaction in England was overwhelmingly negative among the governing class.

The president couched his proclamation in legalistic terms. As a lawyer, he was concerned that his actions be consonant with his constitutional authority. He was already suffering criticism from conservative (and some liberal) defenders of the "Constitution as it is" for his press censorship and suspension of habeas corpus, and he did not want to give them more ammunition.[17] Lincoln based the proclamation on his Article II powers as America's "commander-in-chief" in a time of actual war.[18] This provided him with the authority to take all necessary measures to defend the nation against an aggressor. Since the slaveholders were making war on the United States, depriving them of a valuable resource like their slaves would be a proper action for the president to take.

The Preliminary Emancipation Proclamation also provided that "the executive government of the United States, including the military and naval authority thereof, will recognize and maintain the freedom of such persons, and will do no act or acts to repress such persons, or any of them, in any efforts they may make for their actual freedom."[19] These people would truly be, at last, "forever free." The president's bold action signaled a major turning point in the war, one that would have enormous consequences for the nation. As constitutional scholar Akhil Reed Amar puts it, "with the stroke of the executive pen, Lincoln changed the meaning of the war and the course of American history. No longer was the struggle merely to restore the Union as it was. Henceforth, it would be a war for Freedom alongside Union."[20]

New England liberals were ecstatic. Following the president's dramatic announcement, Norton wrote to Curtis exclaiming, "God be praised! I can hardly see to write,—for when I think of this great act of Freedom, and all it implies, my heart and my eyes overflow with the deepest, most serious gladness." With this act, he declared, "the war is paid for."[21] Curtis shared his euphoria. "Coming at this moment, when we were in the gravest peril from Northern treachery," he wrote, "the proclamation clears the air like a northwest wind. We know now exactly where we are. There are now none but slavery and anti-slavery men in the country. The fence is knocked over, and straddling is impossible."[22] When the news reached Concord, Bronson Alcott recorded in his journal that the proclamation put "a new face on the war."[23] The Emerson household was also pleased but a bit worried by the fact that the measure would not take effect for three months.[24] Secretary of State Seward, knowing that Adams Sr. had been pushing for such a bold move for some time, wrote to the minister that the "interests of humanity have now become identified with the cause of our country."[25]

The strategy of New England liberals for some time had been to hype incremental steps, such as the abolition of slavery in the District of Columbia, in order to create pressure for further reforms by making them appear inevitable. The proclamation was no exception. *Harper's Weekly* on October 4 was unabashed in declaring that the "Proclamation of the President practically abolishes slavery throughout the United States after next New Year's Day." The writer, most likely Curtis, contended that, with emancipation in virtually all of the Confederate states, the border states "must abolish slavery, or it will abolish itself." All of this reflected a dramatic shift in national feeling, since "there was a time, not very long since, when a large majority of the Northern people would have opposed [emancipation] strenuously." Clearly, *Harper's* pointed out, "the war has produced a remarkable change in the opinions of educated and liberal men at the North," and this was having an effect on the rest of the nation. "How long it will take for these liberal views to permeate society and stamp themselves on the mind of the working class" the writer was not prepared to say. He was certain, however, that it would happen.

While the proclamation was enthusiastically embraced by Northern liberals, conservatives had a very different reaction. War Democrats protested loudly, some claiming the measure made Lincoln a "Military Dictator," who had given in to "our shrieking and howling abolition faction." Peace Democrats were also outraged. The *Chicago Times* declared the proclamation "an act of bad faith to every conservative man in the North ... a monstrous usurpation, a criminal wrong, and an act of national suicide." One New York paper asked, "Shall the working classes be equalized with Negroes?"[26] The newly established and decidedly liberal Boston *Commonwealth* offered on October 4 a terse summary of the views expressed in conservative journals. "By a careful perusal of the *Boston Post*, *Courier*, and *Herald*, and the *N.Y. Express*, *Journal of Commerce*, and *Herald*," the writer observed, one might conclude they were reporting "the latest news from Hell."

The *Commonwealth*, which was read on both sides of the Atlantic, would be a strong liberal voice throughout the balance of the war. It was born out of an effort to provide Charles Sumner with popular press coverage, including detailed notices of his numerous speeches and addresses.[27] The Democratic papers in Boston had excluded him, and even the Republican *Daily Advertiser* paid him little attention. In order to help him out, some of Sumner's wealthy Boston friends, including businessmen Amos A. Lawrence and George Luther Stearns, along with abolitionist Dr. Samuel Gridley Howe (a member of the Saturday Club), agreed to finance the operation. One of the *Commonwealth*'s major goals was to promote popular support for emancipation.[28] The journal extended its reach in

1863 when Moncure Conway traveled to England. He reported regularly on English public opinion and controversial figures like Thomas Carlyle.[29]

When news of the president's proclamation reached England, the British governing class reacted with shock and outrage. Ephraim Adams reports that the London press was uniform in "treating the proclamation with derision and contempt and no other one situation in the Civil War came in for such vigorous denunciation."[30] Rather than an act of moral courage, English critics claimed it was obviously a desperate military measure.[31]

A major reason for this reaction was the belief that Lincoln's bold act might lead to a global movement for human rights that would have a destabilizing effect throughout the British Empire. Henry Hotze's *Index* was quick to remind Englishmen of this possibility, claiming Lincoln's emancipation declaration would lead to rebellions throughout the empire comparable to that in India in 1857.[32] Other journals made the same comparison. Howard Jones points out that Lord Russell, William Gladstone, and others in Palmerston's cabinet "feared that emancipation would incite a wave of slave revolts that would grow into a race war," potentially igniting similar uprisings in the empire. Russell was especially concerned "about the Sepoys of India." This apprehension, Jones suggests, "weighed heavily on the minds of British legislators as well."[33] Dean Mahin makes a similar point. "The upper classes' reaction . . . to the proclamation," he states, "seems to have been influenced by concern about native uprisings in the British Empire. . . . Most upper class Englishmen had relatives or friends in the British colonies and vivid memories of native uprisings, especially the Great Mutiny in India in 1857–58."[34] Don Doyle notes that this concern was widely voiced in the British press, where some writers even invoked "comparisons between Lincoln and Nana Sahib, the murderous leader of India's Sepoy Rebellion."[35]

The London *Times* published on October 6 the full text of the proclamation along with a report from their New York correspondent. The president's proclamation, he wrote, "is considered a blunder by all except extreme Abolitionists. . . . The Democratic party are opposed to it as illegal, unconstitutional, and unjust, while Republicans are divided in opinion." The following day, the *Times* published a second report that predicted Lincoln would ultimately step away from this radical "revolution," which was surely their hope.

In another article on October 12, the *Times* noted that the conservative candidate for governor of New York, Horatio Seymour, was of the opinion that "if the Union can only be restored by aid of a servile war, and the utter extermination of the Southern people . . . it is not worth the price to pay for it." The writer added that if Seymour wins the election, "common sense will have a chance to be heard" and the president will be strengthened to take a stand against the "revolutionary faction that is fast driving him into unknown depths of revolutionary madness."[36] Despite such intense conservative resistance, however, it was clear that the "second Revolution" liberal New Englanders were promoting had made a dramatic advance.

Reactions to the measure in Great Britain became even more heated as fears of a bloody "servile insurrection" throughout the South were amplified in the press. The *Times*'s pronouncements, especially, became highly inflammatory, focusing on the president himself. On October 21, the paper asked: "Is the name of Lincoln ultimately to be classed in the catalogue of monsters, wholesale assassins and butchers of their kind? . . . When blood begins to flow and shrieks come piercing through the darkness, Mr. Lincoln will wait until the rising flames tell that all is consummated, and then he will rub his hands and think that revenge is sweet."[37] The *Edinburgh Review* of October referred to the proclamation as Lincoln's "cry of despair," and *Blackwood's* the next month called it "monstrous, reckless [and] devilish" and asserted that it "justifies the South in raising the black flag, and proclaiming a war without quarter."[38] The British satirical magazine *Punch* even ran a cartoon showing a very devilish-looking Lincoln about to throw his "last card" (a black spade depicting the face of a Black man) atop a powder keg in a poker game with a neatly dressed Confederate adversary.[39]

British diplomacy was also impacted. On October 10, William Stuart, the British chargé in Washington (Lord Lyons had been granted a temporary leave), erroneously reported to Lord Russell that "the Proclamation of Emancipation seemed to be causing many in the Union armies and the border states to desert to the South."[40] Lord Russell felt the time had come for England to intervene to end the slaughter and also to prevent a bloody servile insurrection. Palmerston, Russell, and Gladstone were all leaning strongly toward mediation for the first time. Even Richard Cobden, a stalwart supporter of the Union, believed that the proclamation would only lead to increased carnage and that the North would "half ruin itself in the process of wholly ruining the South." He also felt, like his conservative adversaries, that emancipating and arming the Black slaves could only serve to bring about "one of the most bloody and horrible episodes in history."[41]

The Confederate cause was now at its zenith in Great Britain, at least among the conservative governing class. A September 26 report from Henry Hotze to Confederate secretary of state Judah Benjamin noted that the "sympathies of the intelligent classes are now intensified into a feeling of sincere admiration to which even the few presses that continue hostile to us can not altogether withhold utterance." Opinions among the English working class, however, were different. As Hotze reported, "There is only one class which as a class continues inimical to us—the Lancashire operatives."[42]

This situation was truly surprising since operatives in the textile industry were suffering, more than any other group in England, the painful effects of what was now a full-blown "cotton famine." However, in what would prove to be one of the most important developments in the war, the proclamation confirmed to the British working class that Lincoln was truly committed to universal human rights and the dignity of free labor. As a result, their feeling of affection for this "common man" president and the cause he represented grew considerably. Their strong, sympathetic support would prove invaluable to the Union cause.

Despite the chorus of abuse in the English press, the Preliminary Emancipation Proclamation did have English supporters in addition to the Lancashire operatives. English abolitionists applauded the measure and discounted the conservatives' claim that emancipation would lead to servile insurrection.[43] Intellectuals like John Stuart Mill were pleased. He wrote to Motley that he, like other British liberals, thought the state of affairs in America had improved considerably as a result of the Union victory at Antietam, but "still more by Mr. Lincoln's anti-slavery proclamation, which no American . . . can have received with more exultation than I did." He also noted that the measure "has only increased the venom of those who, after taunting you for so long with caring nothing for Abolition, now reproach you for your Abolitionism as the worst of your crimes."

The sources of this criticism, Mill wrote, were predictable. It was always "some deeply-dyed Tory . . . to whom slavery is rather agreeable than not, or who so hate your democratic institutions that they would be sure to inveigh against whatever you did." Mill also assured Motley that the North still had many stalwart friends in England. The "Liberal party . . . are naturally your friends and allies," he insisted. They will "return to that position when once they see that you are not engaged in a hopeless, and therefore . . . unjustifiable contest." Additionally, "there are writers enough here to keep up the fight," among them "Cairnes, and Dicey, and H. Martineau, and Ludlow, and Hughes."⁴⁴

British criticism of the president's proclamation continued in conservative journals, but there were also public defenders in the liberal press, which generally reflected the views of the lower and middle classes. Typical was the *Morning Star*, which declared on October 6 that Lincoln's proclamation was "indisputably the great fact of the war—the turning point in the history of the American Commonwealth—an act only second in courage and probable results to the Declaration of Independence."⁴⁵

In response to this new threat, British conservatives launched a fullthroated frontal assault on the North's growing liberalism. In the October issue of the *Quarterly Review*, uber-conservative Lord Robert Cecil attacked Lincoln, the Union cause, and democracy itself. Cecil maintained that it was "impossible to continue to believe that the North were crusading for abolition, in the face of the President's reiterated denials, and of the inhuman treatment which negroes were constantly receiving at Northern hands." If any proof was needed to confirm this scepticism," Cecil argued, "it has been supplied by the President's recent proclamation. That he should have reserved Emancipation to be the military resource of his extreme necessity, shows how little he cared for it as a philanthropist."

Cecil also contended that it was only those "whose iron-sided fanaticism no facts can penetrate" who now "maintain that the democracy has worked well. Most men," he said, "are now agreed that it has failed." This was due in part to the fact that Northerners were "infamously led. It has been well said that a regiment of asses with a lion at their head, will do more than a regiment of lions with an ass at their head." Lincoln's "poverty of greatness" testified to the weakness of "democratic institutions." "Political equality," Cecil argued, "is not merely a folly—it is a chimera. It is idle to discuss whether it ought to exist; for, as a matter of fact, it never does."

Cecil's model of ideal governance was assuredly that of present-day conservative England. He maintained that "every community has natural leaders, to whom, if they are not misled by the insane passion for equality," the populace "will instinctively defer." These natural leaders were easily distinguished. "Always wealth, in some countries birth, in all intellectual power and culture, mark out the men to whom . . . a community looks to undertake its government. They have the leisure for the task, and can give to it the close attention and the preparatory study which it needs," something British conservatives frequently said of Southern leaders also.⁴⁶

Other British journals contributed to the growing drumbeat of conservative attacks on the idea of equality, especially racial equality. The *Edinburgh Review* in October argued that, despite the recent proclamation, Northerners had no real love for Blacks, and even if the North were to triumph, "the change to the negroes would be only a change of masters." Since North and South were thus both morally complicit, if it were "manifestly for the advantage of England to recognize the Confederacy," the writer argued, "their morality, for which we are not responsible," should not stand in the way.[47] For English conservatives, the mere immorality of slavery would not be a bar to doing business as usual with the South.

The unfriendly attitude toward the North, so evident in major British journals and newspapers, was also reflected in statements by certain individuals in the British government. William Gladstone, Palmerston's chancellor of the exchequer, favored British intervention because he believed Confederate independence was a fait accompli. Like most Englishmen, he did not see how the North could ever control the South, even if it was victorious.[48] It is also possible Gladstone sympathized with Southern slave owners because he came from a slave-owning family in the West Indies, and, like many English conservatives, he did not support the decision to abolish slavery in the empire in 1833.[49]

Whatever his motivation, Gladstone, as the *Times* reported on October 9, stated in a speech at Newcastle-on-Tyne that the Confederates have "made an army; they are making, it appears, a navy, and they have made what is more than either—they have made a nation." As a result, Gladstone asserted, "we may anticipate with certainty the success of the Southern States so far as regards their separation from the North."[50] Lord John Russell, the foreign secretary, agreed. Like Gladstone, he believed the South was simply too big to be permanently subdued by force of arms.[51]

The same issue of the London *Times* offered praise for a recent speech in Parliament by John Roebuck where he called the people of the North "the scum and refuse of Europe."[52] Roebuck, like William Gregory, was a strong supporter of the Confederacy and a proponent of recognition. In a recent speech before his constituents at Sheffield, he was outspoken in his demand that England intervene in the American war out of self-interest. The August 16 *Spectator* reported that Roebuck described the people of America as bullies who are "insolent and overbearing." Therefore, "Mr. Roebuck rejoices that the union is split into two, and will be split 'into five.'" Roebuck also asserted that England can "make friends of the South" even though, as the *Spectator* observed, the Southerners "governed the Union for over thirty years, and insulted us all that time."⁵³

That the British were now seriously considering the possibility of intervention seemed clear from Gladstone's public comments. On October 13, Lord John Russell circulated a memo in the cabinet arguing that the European powers should "propose an armistice in America." Sir George Cornewall Lewis, secretary for war, advised against this and noted that Britain could not afford a costly war in North America, which would be the inevitable consequence of intervention.⁵⁴ Lewis suggested waiting for the outcome of the congressional elections in November to see if there was support in the North for a move toward peace. Additionally, although acceptable to most in the governing class, Southern slavery was still a grave moral issue with the general public, one that weighed against intervention because support for the South unavoidably meant support for slavery. Ultimately, Lewis's argument prevailed, and Palmerston decided against intervention at this time.

Interest in the fall elections was growing in the North as it was in England. Lincoln's emancipation policy had sharpened differences between liberal and conservative factions, and Southerners hoped the Lincoln administration would be weakened as a result. The *Daily Picayune* noted that "the political elements in the North are in a ferment. The conservatives and the radicals are preparing to measure strength. Party antagonisms after being ignored for a year and a half are re-appearing."⁵⁵

The cautious editors of the *North American Review* felt this tension. They were concerned with preserving the integrity of the Constitution and resisted the policies of radicals like Charles Sumner. The current rush toward emancipation was unnerving for them. The journal warned in October of the potentially deleterious effects of such a dramatic measure, contending that the United States was not fighting a war for emancipation, even if the "ultra abolitionists, in and out of Congress," would like to make it so. Such a move, the writer insisted, would compromise the entire war effort. "All the accounts from the army uniformly represent that the soldiers . . . have neither part nor lot in these projects for universal emancipation." He then offered the following testimony from "an educated and intelligent [Union] colonel of a regiment that has seen hard service. 'Let it once be understood that this is a war of emancipation of the negroes,'" warned the unnamed officer, "'and three quarters of the army would lay down their arms.'" The *North American* was certain that any effort to impose emancipation would amount to "a revolution on the part of the North," which, of course, was exactly what New England's liberal reformers hoped it would be.[56]

In their effort to defend the Constitution "as it is," some conservative Democrats also defended slavery. The Boston *Courier* revealed the extent of this strategy in an October 13 article titled "People's Nominations." In promoting conservative candidates, the article included a reminder of the North's willingness, before the outbreak of hostilities, to tolerate slavery where it already existed. The paper supported this position while opposing Lincoln's recent Preliminary Emancipation Proclamation. The election slogan of the "People's Party" was "The Union, The Constitution, The Enforcement of the Laws."

The next day, the *Courier* published a short article attacking abolitionism. It argued that "the difference between secession and Abolition is simply this—the one strikes at the throat of the Union with a drawn sword—the other mixes a cup of deadly poison for it to drink." As the *Courier* made clear, not everyone in Massachusetts was in a liberal state of mind. In his journal, under the heading "People's Party," Emerson observed, "The Proclamation has defined every man's position. In reading every speech . . . a few words show at once the animus of the men, shows them friends of slavery." What this revealed, Emerson noted, was that "the battle ground is fast changing from Richmond to Boston." This "seems to promise an extension of the war," he wrote, "for there can be no durable peace, no sound Constitution, until we have fought the battle & the rights of man are vindicated."[57] Emerson and his liberal New England cohorts were prepared to continue that struggle on both sides of the Mason-Dixon Line.

The division caused by Lincoln's emancipation policy was evident throughout the North. Whereas New England was generally supportive, despite the protests of the business class, the West was more inclined to be conservative on the issue of slavery. Economic factors also played a role. On October 27, Governor Oliver P. Morton of Indiana warned Lincoln that, presently, "it was a staple of every Democratic speech that . . . New England is fattening at our expense; that the people of New England are cold, selfish, [and] money-making and through the medium of tariffs and railroads are pressing us to the dust."[58] This feeling was strong enough that some disaffected Westerners proposed establishing an independent Northwestern Confederacy. Lincoln's liberal policy on emancipation only added to this discontent. Two weeks after the proclamation went into effect, the Democrats in the Indiana legislature passed a resolution against it.[59]

These tensions grew as New England liberals continued their vigorous support of emancipation and other policies relating to the treatment of freed Blacks and their future in a reinvented American democracy. In another of his Lounger columns in *Harper's Weekly*, George Curtis declared that Lincoln's proclamation was "an act which is in itself simply just, but which in its results becomes sublime." The proclamation, he contended, was far more than just "a military measure, dictated by common sense." For Curtis, the act had a distinct moral and spiritual quality. "It is a national purification," he declared. "Its ultimate result is permanent peace and prosperity, founded upon the only principle that can secure either."[60] That principle was justice for all.

The *Boston Weekly Transcript* took an even more extreme position. The paper argued that "the war has now become a struggle for national existence . . . which is to leave us either a great free power or a great slave power. . . . God means not to let us off with any half way work." It was time for the North "to take the most radical ground possible—to assume that this is a war for the subjugation or the extermination of all persons who wish to maintain the slave power—a war to get rid of slavery and of slave-holders, whether it be constitutional or not." The president was clearly moving in that direction. Lincoln, the *Weekly* insisted, was "the Abraham of a new political dispensation."[61]

Emerson agreed. He celebrated Lincoln's bold act in a public lecture at the Parker Fraternity on October 12. The following month it was published in the *Atlantic Monthly* under the title "The President's Proclamation." The manuscript for the address included a passage that did not appear in the published version. It indicated the important role played by reactionary British critics in furthering the emancipation movement. "We can read many things through the eyes of others which we cannot see with our own," Emerson observed. "The men in the street by no means think Emancipation a primary duty. . . . But the moment they meet the Englishman or the Frenchman and would reproach him with the virtual aid he gives to slavery, they are prepared to show that the North is for liberty, that this is substantially a war for freedom, and that all the honest and civil portions of mankind ought to be with us. Could they only convince themselves of that whenever they labor to convince the foreigners!"[62] Eventually, most of them would.

Although approval was growing steadily in America, foreign opinions of emancipation continued to be largely negative. John Stuart Mill in his earlier letter to Motley noted that he heartily approved of Lincoln's action, but in England there were those who now considered abolitionism "the worst of your crimes." In the letter, Mill also named several English liberals who strongly supported the North, all of whom by now were familiar to New Englanders. Among supportive journals, he named the *Daily News*, *Macmillan's*, the *London Star*, and the *Westminster* and *London Reviews*.[63] *Fraser's* was conspicuous by its absence.

Mill's review of Cairnes's *The Slave Power* appeared in the October issue of the *Westminster Review*. In it, Mill questioned why presently in England, a nation that prided itself on the abolition of slavery from its empire, "the general voice of our press, the general sentiment of our people, [is] bitterly reproachful to the North, while for the South, the aggressors in the war, we have either mild apologies or direct and downright encouragement?" This, he noted, "is not only from the Tory and anti-democratic camp, but from Liberals, or *soi disant* such."

In answer to this conundrum, Mill suggested that not all English constituencies were truly antislavery. "It must be remembered," he stated, "that though the English public are averse to slavery, several of the political and literary organs . . . are decidedly not so. For many years," Mill declared, "the *Times* has taken every opportunity of throwing cold water . . . on the cause of the negro." However "Liberal on the surface," the *Times* is "imbued with a deeply-seated Tory feeling, which makes it prefer even slavery to democratic equality; and it never loses saying a word for slavery, and palliating its evils" (504). The war in America, it seemed, was certainly redefining liberalism in Great Britain.

While Mill was penning his essay, Elizabeth Gaskell's daughter, Meta, expressed both sympathy and support for the North in a warm letter to her friend Charles Eliot Norton. The letter showed the close, personal connection that the novelist (a Unitarian liberal) and her family felt with Norton and other New England liberals. "We never hear of any American news without thinking how it has first fallen on your ear," she wrote, "and if it is good news for the North, we rejoice with you; and grieve so for you if it is bad. Mamma and I are staunch Northerners, and fight for you in words whenever we hear Southern sympathy expressed."

Gaskell also told of "the great distress prevailing in Manchester for want of cotton." While this "is very sad to see," she wrote, "it lends us as much blessing as sorrow" because "the spirit of the poor people is so patient and brave—they can turn from their own misery and want to think with heartfelt pity of the sufferers in the American War." Remarkably, the support for the Northern cause of these workers and their families remained firm, even though it is "the chief cause of their own distress."[64] The continuing support of British workers, like those in Manchester, would prove critical in the months ahead.

Lincoln's announcement of his Preliminary Emancipation Proclamation in September 1862 was a major inflection point in the war for both the United States and Great Britain. The debate over race and human rights would intensify greatly in the months ahead as Northern liberals grew more outspoken in their demand for a reinvention of democracy that would guarantee freedom and equal rights to all. In response, British conservatives would become increasingly strident in their opposition to that demand and to the rising tide of liberalism at home and abroad.

Chapter 10

Midterm Elections Focus on Race

In the North, the Preliminary Emancipation Proclamation widened considerably the gap between conservative Democrats and liberal Republicans and made race a major issue in the November midterm elections. Democrats campaigned against the proclamation and its author, declaring that "this is a government of white men, . . . established exclusively for the white race."[1] It also brought out strong antiwar sentiments, as reflected in the formation of the Peace Party in Massachusetts.[2]

The Copperhead faction of the Northern Democratic Party vigorously opposed the liberals' effort to turn the war into a second revolution.[3] The elections were also influenced by anti-draft feelings, the suspension of habeas corpus, and the suppression of political opposition. When the voting was over, Democratic victories were many, but not as many as expected.[4] Still, some feared the election results might weaken the president's resolve. Norton wrote to Curtis that the situation was now "iffy" and "the worst of the *ifs* is the one concerning Lincoln." He was "very much afraid that a domestic cat will not answer when one wants a Bengal tiger."[5] Despite their many victories, Massachusetts conservatives were bitterly disappointed in the reelection of Radical Republican Charles Sumner, who had received strong support from Emerson and fellow members of the Saturday Club.

Across the Atlantic, the London *Times* declared on November 21 that the midterm elections amounted to a vote of no confidence in Lincoln's administration. The president has shown himself to be "unfit" as a war leader, the paper charged, pointing to the "indecision, and procrastination and general feebleness" that had marked Union military operations, "for which he is ultimately responsible." Not surprisingly, the *Saturday Review* declared that the democratic gains represented a triumph for conservatives and a clear defeat for liberals. "Mr. Lincoln avowedly 'yielded to pressure' when he issued his proclamation of liberty to the slaves," the journal asserted. "Pressure may now make him withdraw it; a little more pressure may possibly frighten him into negotiations for peace."[6]

This possibility was seen as a real danger by British liberals. As Allan Nevins indicates, most of the liberal journals and leaders in England believed that "any retreat from the proclamation would be the most deplorable event in history."[7] To help prevent this from happening, the British Emancipation Society was established on November 11, headed by none other than John Stuart Mill. Its membership, which totaled 340, included such distinguished individuals as John Bright, Richard Cobden, William E. Forster, John Elliott Cairnes, Richard Davis Webb, Francis W. Newman, Thomas Hughes, Edward Dicey, Lord Houghton, and Goldwin Smith.[8] Smith would soon emerge as a major liberal voice.

The society began to organize huge rallies almost immediately. As a result, according to one historian, it was impossible to ignore "the support of British workers and middle-class Radicals for Northern democracy." It was also at this time that Goldwin Smith became "the leading Oxford protagonist of the Union cause."[9] Like others in the group known as "university liberals," Smith's commitment to liberalism was enhanced significantly by the war and the transatlantic alliance with New Englanders such as Emerson, Lowell, Norton, Higginson, Holmes, Motley, and members of the Adams family, men who constituted "a comparable intellectual group."[10]

Meanwhile, in Washington, the English chargé, William Stuart (who had temporarily replaced Lord Lyons), watched the elections carefully in anticipation that a strong vote for Democrats would signal an opportunity for intervention.[11] Stuart was especially enthusiastic about the opportunity a Democratic victory would present. When the final results for the fall elections became known, Stuart concluded that a clear Democratic victory had been won. He told Russell, "We might now recognize the South without much risk to ourselves."[12]

Russell was pleased with the news, but a more discerning look at the results showed that the Democratic victory was not as sweeping as Stuart thought.[13] For one thing, Nevins points out, Massachusetts provided a strong endorsement for Lincoln and his emancipationists policies, as "Sumner and John A. Andrew, two thorough-going radicals, carried everything before them." The Peace Party candidates were crushed in the process as Governor Andrew, "the Miles Standish of the Bay State," ensured that Massachusetts would remain "a pillar of strength for the Union."[14] Emerson and other members of the Saturday Club were pleased and reassured by this triumph, which they had helped bring about. Their extensive lecturing and writing in promotion of Lincoln and the policies of the Radical Republicans undoubtedly had an effect. Sumner had recently joined this elite fraternity, and Andrew would soon follow, along with James T. Fields. Through them, Massachusetts became the intellectual wheelhouse of liberal democracy.

After the dust settled, it was seen that Democratic gains in the midterm election were substantial but not overwhelming. When Lord Lyons returned to the United States following his sojourn in London, he quickly sized up the situation. The liberal Republicans, he concluded, were still very much in charge and the South had no desire to return to the Union. Consequently, as he reported to Russell, it was his considered opinion that "foreign intervention, short of the use of force, could only make matters worse here."[15]

Other European leaders continued to assess the situation. Napoleon III had been in contact with the Confederate envoy, John Slidell, in late October. He became convinced that the time was right for the European powers to intervene in the American war. Very shortly, he proposed that France, England, Prussia, Austria, and Russia suggest an armistice to the Americans. In response, Lord Palmerston called a meeting of his cabinet on November 7, a meeting that could potentially decide the fate of the American Union.[16] As he had earlier, Secretary for War George Cornewall Lewis argued against British intervention in a fifteen-thousand-word memorandum that was actually written by his stepson-in-law, William Vernon Harcourt.[17]

Harcourt later submitted a series of letters to the London *Times* under the pseudonym "Historicus," outlining the argument against intervention in detail. One of the more compelling points made was that, after a year and a half of intense fighting, the Confederacy had not succeeded in winning its independence. "Historicus" reminded English and Southern readers alike that "Rebellion, until it has succeeded, is Treason" and that "the only real test of independence is final success."[18] Because of this, neutrality remained the best policy. These arguments, along with the fall election results, were ultimately convincing. Palmerston and his cabinet rejected the French proposal for a collective European intervention and made their decision public.[19]

In his "Annual Message to Congress" on December 1, Lincoln made it very clear to those skeptics who doubted his resolve that the fall election results did not alter his intention to implement his proclamation, as planned, on the first day of the new year. His words on this occasion served to imbue his action with a moral idealism that the largely technical Preliminary Emancipation Proclamation lacked. "Fellow-citizens, *we* cannot escape history. . . . The fiery trial through which we pass, will light us down, in honor or dishonor, to the latest generation," the president declared. In defending his proclamation, Lincoln emphasized the justice of the measure, not merely its expediency. "In *giving* freedom to the *slave*, we *assure* freedom to the *free*—honorable alike in what we give, and what we preserve. We shall nobly save, or meanly lose, the last best, hope of earth. Other means may succeed; this could not fail. The way is plain, peaceful, generous, just—a way which, if followed, the world will forever applaud, and God must forever bless."[20]

Lincoln believed the war was slowly bringing forth a new and better America. Like Curtis in his earlier Lounger essays, he held that "the dogmas of the quiet past, are inadequate to the stormy present. . . . As our case is new, so we must think anew, and act anew." While admitting "the occasion is piled-high with difficulty," the president insisted, "we must rise to the occasion," and he was determined to lead the way.[21] The "new" thoughts and "new" actions he was contemplating would prove truly revolutionary. Ultimately, this revolution sought to establish freedom and equal rights for all, a goal that was vigorously resisted on both sides of the Atlantic by those who enjoyed the benefits of the status quo.

Meanwhile, the effects of the Emancipation Proclamation continued to be felt, even in the Deep South. Enslaved Blacks played an important role in spreading the word. One of them, George Washington Albright of Mississippi, recounted that "the plantation owners tried to keep the news from us," but the "Washington government . . . organized an underground information service to inform the slaves of their freedom. The slaves themselves had to carry the news to one another." Albright took pride in the fact that at the tender age of fifteen, his "first job in the fight for the rights" of his people was "to tell the slaves that they were free" and "to keep them informed in readiness to assist the Union armies whenever the opportunity came."[22] These underground activists named their operation "Lincoln's Legal Loyal League."²³ As the Union army advanced deeper into the South, many thousands of them eventually carried on the struggle as Union soldiers.

In spite of evidence to the contrary, the London *Times* published a December 1 report by Francis Lawley, their pro-Southern correspondent in Richmond, that claimed all the Blacks there detested the Yankees, and everywhere he went he saw evidence of "negro fidelity" to their masters.²⁴ Lawley's reporting was rarely accurate and always pro-Southern. Unfortunately, the *Times* relied on him almost exclusively for news of Confederate affairs, a practice they would later regret.²⁵

The *Times*'s other American correspondent, Charles Mackay, was even more pro-Southern and anti-Northern in his reporting. When John Delane (editor) and Mowbray Morris (manager) brought Mackay on board, they advised him to keep in mind the anti-Northern policy of the paper. Mackay's reports in the *Times* consistently emphasized the North's military failures, its discontent with the war, and Lincoln's policies, all of which was helpful to the Democrats' political strategy. These reports also helped reinforce conservative attacks on the Union cause in England. In light of this, Nevins asserts, "No single person did more during the war to create misunderstanding and animosity between Britain and America" than Charles Mackay, but Lawley was certainly a close second.²⁶

The *Times*'s manipulation of news about the war involved omission as well as deliberate misrepresentation. Their political reporting on the debate in England routinely excluded arguments and details favorable to the North. Thus, when Matthew Arnold wrote to his mother about his brother-in-law William Forster's recent speech, where the Liberal MP had expressed strong support for the Union cause, he told her, "Somehow or other I missed William's speech at Bradford—I did not know which day it was to be and I look at the *Times* very hurriedly—but was there much about it?"²⁷ There wasn't. The *Times* had simply ignored the speech. However, the London *Daily News* published a report on the speech where they referred to Forster as "the most prominent man in the House on the American question."²⁸

Eventually, Arnold realized that by reading only the *Times* he was not getting an accurate view of the political debate in Great Britain regarding American affairs. A week later, he wrote to his mother again: "How odd about Wm Forster's speech. Of course I saw nothing that was in the *Daily News*, for I see no daily paper but the *Times*, and read of that only the indispensably necessary. But it shews how unscrupulously they treat the public (if they dare) as to anything that does not accord with their own views."[29] The *Times* followed this policy throughout the war, much to the chagrin of Union supporters on both sides of the Atlantic.

Northern allies in Great Britain continued to worry about the harsh and now nearly constant criticisms appearing in the pages of some of the country's most prestigious newspapers and magazines. They were determined to counteract those criticisms. A relatively new voice, Goldwin Smith—an Oxford scholar, a liberal, and a staunch anti-imperialist—was attracting notice at this time in England. The Union cause won Smith's support early on. As his biographer reports, he regarded "the United States as the greatest achievement of his race, [and] he was consumed by mingled hope and curiosity about its future, and watched the struggle with the anxiety of an American."[30]

Around this time, Mill wrote to Cairnes to report that he had recently heard from a "strong Lancashire abolitionist," who told him that the tone of public opinion in Manchester and Liverpool had improved recently. The commercial class had gone from sympathizing with the South to indifference. "I fancy that before long they will come round still more to the right side," the correspondent wrote. "As regards the working classes," he noted, "their opinions on the American question have not altered in the least, notwithstanding the enormous increase of the distress."[31] As Mill's letter confirmed, following Lincoln's recent proclamation on emancipation, the working class in England had come more and more to embrace the Union cause as their own. They believed that by fighting against slavery, the North was also fighting for the dignity of labor and the workingman everywhere.

The provisions of the proclamation were to take effect on New Year's Day, and the Manchester correspondent informed Mill that a great meeting was scheduled for December 31, which was "the last day of slavery, in order to send an address of the working men of Lancashire to President Lincoln."[32] The growing support of the English working class was also noted by Minister Adams. He wrote to his son Charles in late December that these workers "see in the convulsion in America an era in the history of the world, out of which must come . . . a general recognition of the right of mankind to the produce of their labor and the pursuit of happiness."[33] The liberal democracy that he and other New England idealists envisioned, Adams believed, would eventually become the standard for the world.

Emerson promoted the same notion in his lecture "Perpetual Forces," which he delivered at least fifteen times throughout the fall and winter months of 1862–63. In this lecture, Emerson looked to a postwar America. "How then to reconstruct?" he asked rhetorically. "Since nothing satisfies men but justice," first and foremost, you must "leave slavery out." In addition to freedom for all, Emerson took the rather extraordinary step of calling for equal voting rights, regardless of race. "Let us stifle our prejudices against commonsense and humanity," he declared, "and agree that every man shall have what he honestly earns, and, if he is a sane and innocent man, have an equal vote in the state, and a fair chance in society."[34] It was undoubtedly statements like this, both early and late, that led Black intellectuals like William C. Nell to refer to Emerson as one of the "ever-to-be-honored friends of equal rights."[35]

Not everyone in the North was prepared at this time for such a breathtaking liberal vision. Lincoln himself had not yet articulated a policy calling for total emancipation, let alone universal voting rights. Indeed, Black suffrage would never receive more than a limited and highly qualified endorsement from him.[36] Most Northerners, including the majority of Emerson's audience, shared these reservations. Three days after his impassioned address, a Democratic paper in Albany, the *Argus*, described Emerson's lecture as "a re-hash of his Abolition sophistry" and pointed out that "when he argued in favor of forcible emancipation, a few old ladies and gentlemen applauded; but when he insisted that the Negro should have 'an equal chance with the white man,' even they were indignantly silent."[37]

Emerson realized that what he was proposing was at odds with the Constitution "as it is," but that did not bother him or his liberal cohorts. They felt the times required extraordinary measures. A rigid respect for a flawed and fatally compromised compact, they believed, should not be allowed to deter real moral progress. In his journal notes for "Perpetual Forces" he wrote, "I speak the speech of an idealist. I say let the rule be right. If the theory is right, it [does] not so much matter about the facts." He added, "All our action now is new & unconstitutional, & necessarily so," which, Emerson well knew, was "enough to drive a strict constructionist out of his wits."[38] Clearly, progress was being made, but the war still was not won.

Meanwhile, on the war front, Lincoln replaced George McClellan with Ambrose Burnside on November 7.[39] There had been widespread dissatisfaction with McClellan's lack of aggressiveness. His failure to follow up his technical victory at Antietam by pursuing and destroying Lee's retreating army was a severe disappointment to the president. Lincoln's act of faith in appointing Burnside was based on his positive performance in actions along the coast of North Carolina. Burnside himself, however, did not feel qualified to assume command of the Army of the Potomac.[40] He was right. Burnside developed a reasonable battle plan for an attack on Lee's army in Fredericksburg, Virginia, but the implementation of the plan was deeply flawed. The result was a disaster. When the fighting came to an end on December 13, there were nearly thirteen thousand Federal casualties, with Confederate losses about a third of that number. The horrific carnage of the battle was so appalling it sent shock waves throughout the North.

The losses in the Battle of Fredericksburg were not merely statistics to Emerson and his Saturday Club friends. Longfellow wrote a hasty note to Charles Sumner asking if he had any information about his nephew Stephen, who had been wounded in the battle. Fortunately, as Sumner later reported, the wound was not serious and Stephen was recovering well.[41] Others were not so lucky. George Curtis wrote to Norton, "On Saturday afternoon my brother Joe fell dead at the head of his regiment, ending at twenty-six years a stainless life in the holiest cause and in the most heroic manner. God rest his noble soul, and grant us all the same fidelity!"[42]

Sarah Shaw relayed the news of the death of her son-in-law's brother to John Elliott Cairnes. In her letter, she also reported that her sister's only son had been killed in a later engagement in North Carolina and that "another nephew left his young wife near her confinement, & joined the army with her full consent. Her child was born, when anxiety brought on fever & her young husband got leave to come home in time to see her die." All of this brought great sorrow and "a grief-ful atmosphere in which we live," she wrote. Suffering such as this made the harsh criticisms of the British press even more deeply reprehensible and morally intolerable to many in New England and throughout the North. As Shaw told Cairnes, "some writer in *Blackwood's* called this war a 'screaming farce.' A strange farce, indeed, for we poor actors."[43]

There was a strong and immediate reaction in Washington to the Fredericksburg disaster. It left Lincoln deeply depressed as Radical Republicans demanded a more effective prosecution of the war so as to avoid a compromise that would restore the Union without abolishing slavery.[44]

The Battle of Fredericksburg did have one positive result. The loss meant that the war would continue and with it the push toward emancipation. The enlistment of Black soldiers, something both British and American liberals were calling for, would be a key component in that struggle. Even before the battle, the British *Spectator* had published positive reports on the performance of the early contraband regiments. "They have shown remarkable spirit," the paper noted. In their first action in Florida, "they landed under a heavy fire and dispersed their enemies, and behaved altogether with the most ardent enthusiasm and courage during this, their first military trial."

The *Spectator* then echoed the thinking of many Northern liberals in declaring that presently the "statesmen of the North . . . are drifting blindly, and almost reluctantly, into an emancipation policy; and so may lose half the political fruits of it. . . . The *New York Tribune* is right in saying that the very first step of the Union should be to give full privileges of Union soldiers [to US Colored Troops], and absolutely enforce treatment of prisoners taken amongst them by the South in all respects as prisoners of war."[45] Very soon, that policy would be instituted as the first USCT regiments in the regular Union army were formed.

The crushing defeat at Fredericksburg coming on top of the Democratic gains in the midterm elections led to a growing concern among some liberals that Lincoln might be inclined to rescind his proclamation before it could be fully implemented on January 1. However, John Murray Forbes was reassured by a friend, Republican representative Charles Sedgwick, that Lincoln had recently stated in a conversation with Secretary Stanton that he "could not stop the Proclamation if he would, and he would not if he could."[46] In an effort to reinforce the president's resolve, Forbes was able to persuade the presidential electors of 1860 to sign on to a letter to the president calling upon him to follow through on his emancipation policy, which they referred to as "the greatest act in American history."[47]

Like his Saturday Club associates, Forbes was convinced that, for the oppressed slaves, the proclamation would be a clarion call to freedom and an invitation to fight. With this in mind, he had one million copies of the document printed on small slips, one and a half inches square, to be distributed to the Union troops, who would then "scatter them about among the blacks while on the march." Charles Sumner expressed his approved of the plan in a letter to Forbes on Christmas Day. New England idealist that he was, Sumner also reported that he had "exhorted the President to put into the next [that is, final] Proclamation some sentiment of justice and humanity," which Lincoln did.[48] In his response, Forbes encouraged Sumner to pressure Lincoln to issue "General Orders" in conjunction with the proclamation that would allow the government "to use the negro in every respect as a man, and consequently as a soldier, sailor, or laborer, wherever he can most effectually strike a blow against the enemy."[49]

While there was concern about the effect the enlistment of Blacks might have on morale in the Union army, some were willing to allow the experiment in light of the added strength it would afford. One soldier who was serving in New Orleans at the time wrote, in a letter home, he believed the proclamation would encourage slaves to flee to the Union lines in large numbers. He then added, "I have felt more strongly than ever that the negro should be armed and do their part in the suppression of this rebellion; or at least let the trial of negro prowess be made and if a failure let it be discontinued."[50] In America, he believed, everyone should be given a fair chance.

Whether due to the needs of the army or the encouragement of liberals in Congress and elsewhere, or whether he simply considered it the right thing to do, Lincoln chose this time to make a historic decision. He called Charles Sumner to the White House on Christmas Day to confer with him about the final wording of the proclamation. He accepted Sumner's suggestion that his justification for the proclamation include not only military necessity but also the fact that it was "an act of justice and humanity, which must have the blessing of a benevolent God."[51] He informed Sumner that he was now prepared to enlist Black troops as well. With these two measures, Lincoln would dramatically change the character of the war.

As promised earlier, a huge gathering of Manchester workingmen occurred on the last day of the year to celebrate Lincoln's Emancipation Proclamation. The event, as R. J. Blackett reports, was "organized, financed, and dominated by the working class." Their commitment to the cause was influenced by firsthand reports they heard from African American lecturers and their experiences with racial discrimination. Almost forty of these lecturers were active in Great Britain at this time, including Andrew Jackson, the former coachman of Jefferson Davis. These African Americans contributed greatly to the campaign to win support for the Union cause among the British working class.[52]

As reported in the *Manchester Guardian* on January 1, 1863, the group's proclamation, a copy of which was sent to Lincoln, declared,

"This meeting, recognizing the common brotherhood of mankind and the sacred and inalienable right of every human being to personal freedom and equal protection, records its detestation of negro slavery in America, and of the attempts of the rebellious Southern slaveholders to organize on the great American continent a nation having slavery as its basis."[53] Lincoln was greatly touched. As Allan Nevins puts it, he could see that when "the liberal sentiment of America decreed emancipation; the liberal sentiment of Britain responded."[54] He also understood that even voteless men, provided they were determined, united, and persistent, could have an influence regardless.[55]

While English workers and liberal Northerners were celebrating Lincoln's proclamation and calling for the immediate enlistment of liberated slaves and freedmen, in the South, Jefferson Davis declared that any Blacks "captured in arms" would be handed over to state authorities, where they would be punished "according to the laws of said states." This could only mean execution or enslavement. The dignity and rights afforded combatants in uniform were not to be afforded to Black Union soldiers.[56]

Despite their recent victory at Fredericksburg, the Charleston *Daily Courier* in "The Crisis" on December 31 warned Southerners against complacency. "The North is not exhausted and remains determined," the paper opined. "They have lost hundreds of thousands of men, and expended hundreds of millions of money . . . but they are not yet quite convinced of the impossibility of the undertaking, and they will bear more severe discomfitures and groan under more direful calamities before they will consent to abandon the infamous work."

The *Courier*'s warning would prove accurate. The North was now committed to a "total war," one that would change forever the character of democracy in America. That commitment would entail unimaginable suffering for both sides as the fortunes of war rose and fell for each. On the last day of 1862, as celebrations of emancipation were being prepared in Boston and elsewhere, Rebecca Meade received the news that her only son, John E. Meade, had died while serving with the Confederate army defending Petersburg, Virginia. The inscription on his tombstone declared, "Sustained by Christian faith, he faltered not in duty and was contented thus early to yield up his life in full assurance of blissful immortality." He was just twenty-one.[57]

As the conflict in America intensified, liberals and conservatives in England remained deeply engaged in their own struggle, the result of which would have a dramatic effect on the evolution of democracy there. Additionally, Great Britain's conduct in the war and the relentless criticism in the English press had opened up a vast cultural and political divide between England and the North. By the close of this year, the cultural identity that most Northerners once believed they shared with "the mother country" was, literally, a thing of the past. Mutual respect and admiration had been displaced by mutual recrimination and hostility. The situation would only grow worse, much worse, in the tumultuous year ahead.

Chapter 11

1863

As the Civil War Becomes a Second Revolution, Conflict with Great Britain Looms

In the event-filled year that was 1863, the fortunes of war shifted dramatically. A Union victory at Gettysburg shattered Lee's once invincible army, devastating Southern morale and sending shock waves through the ranks of Confederate supporters in Great Britain. Similar victories at Vicksburg and Port Hudson put the Union firmly in control of the Mississippi, thus splitting the Confederacy. At Port Hudson and, later, Fort Wagner, the Union's new Colored Troops distinguished themselves in combat, thus affirming their manhood and the key role they played in a war that looked more and more like a crusade to affirm the universal rights of man.

British conservatives were appalled by these developments. The British establishment worried over what it would mean for the future of the empire. They responded with bitter vitriol toward all measures that would challenge the principles of human inequality and white supremacy on which that empire stood. The British working class, however, became equally adamant in their support of the Union in what they now believed was an international struggle for human rights.

Adding to all this, before the year was out, tensions between Great Britain and the United States would rise to a crisis level once again. This time the issue was the building of Confederate warships in British shipyards. This activity was in direct violation of the country's Foreign Enlistment Act, which forbade the "fitting out and equipping" of warships for use by foreign nations. This situation eventually brought about a diplomatic confrontation that most believed could only lead to war.

The new year in Boston began with joyful celebrations of Lincoln's Emancipation Proclamation, which went into effect, as promised, on January 1, 1863. There was a huge gathering at the Music Hall, where Emerson read his "Boston Hymn," which he had composed for this very special occasion. One member of the audience described it as "a hymn of Liberty and Justice, wide and strong, and musical."[1] The jubilant crowd gave three cheers for Lincoln and three cheers for William Lloyd Garrison, editor of the *Liberator* and a major figure in the abolition movement. Until recently, Garrison had been the object of odium and derision for many but, as George Fredrickson notes, at this point in the war, "everyone, it appeared, had become an abolitionist."[2] The official program included the names of several members of the Saturday Club. Among them were Longfellow, Holmes, Whittier, and Fields. The large and diverse audience also included a number of Black Bostonians.[3]

A similar celebration was held at Tremont Temple, where Frederick Douglass was the featured speaker. Following the ceremony, the predominantly Black audience adjourned to Boston's leading African American church, Twelfth Baptist, where the celebration continued for some time.[4] New England liberals knew that a truly great victory had been won, despite the limited nature of the proclamation. The *Boston Daily Evening Transcript* declared, "Slavery from this hour ceases to be a political power in the country. . . . Such a righteous revolution as it inaugurates never goes backward."[5] Many realized that the war to save the Union had become a revolution.[6]

Approval of Lincoln's bold proclamation was nearly universal among liberal thinkers and reformers throughout the North. The *Boston Semi-Weekly Advertiser* on January 3 cautiously approved, "not unmindful of the immense advantages in the prosecution of the war gained to us by this measure." One of those important advantages was that "we shall now have thoroughly on our side the immense support which springs from the cordial sympathy of the moral sense of the whole world." The January 7 *Boston Weekly Transcript* saw the measure in an even more idealistic way: "To save a nation is its immediate object; to give liberty to three millions of human beings—liberty to live and earn an independent livelihood as men, will be its humane effect."

New England Transcendentalists, both Black and white, had been arguing from the beginning that the war required a moral justification. In his pamphlet "The Soldier of the Good Cause," published shortly after the disaster at Bull Run, Charles Eliot Norton had stressed the moral aspects of the struggle. Black activist John Rock insisted in a speech just months later that those who sought to "fight without an object" were expressing "the sentiment of the cotton brokers and secession sympathizers of Boston." Rock argued that the war effort required an "*active* idea" that would impart transcendent meaning to the conflict and render it a cause worth dying for.[7] That "active idea" had now been clearly defined.

Not surprisingly, Northern conservatives, like their British counterparts, were appalled by the president's action. The *Boston Post* declared on January 2 that the measure was illegal and done at the behest of "fanatics." It would do more harm than good because "it only embitters and divides the North while it unites and strengthens the South." The *Boston Courier* that same day condemned the president's action because it would undoubtedly result in "a John Brown raid on a gigantic scale" throughout the South. The *Boston Statesman and Weekly Post* declared on January 9, "The President has no right, by the laws of war, to proclaim the emancipation of the slaves in those sections not under the immediate control of the Federal armies. A paper declaration," the *Post* argued, "cannot . . . change relations that are fundamental without most terrible and bitter revolution." That "revolution" was already well underway and gaining strength every day, fostered and encouraged by New England's intellectual class.

The influence of this liberal group was now obvious enough that it brought condemnation from conservatives throughout the North. A meeting of the Democratic Union Association, held in New York City on January 13, drew a large and animated audience. The keynote address was delivered by Representative Samuel Cox of Ohio, the leader of the conservative Democratic caucus. The group had been formed to promote the goals of Northern conservatism, and Cox came prepared.[8] He had a national standing as the opposition leader in Congress.[9] Cox and his conservative colleagues were determined to turn back the New Englanders' effort to change forever the American social, political, and cultural landscape. Their demand to end slavery and establish equal rights was abhorrent to these conservatives, and Cox attacked them with a fury.[10] His vitriolic presentation attracted considerable public attention.

Cox titled his address "Puritanism in Politics," a title that indicates, like so many other commentaries throughout the war, a fusion of culture and politics.[11] In this speech, which was published in its entirety in several Democratic newspapers both North and South, as well as in pamphlet form (which is the source here), Cox specifically blamed New England for the Emancipation Proclamation. He warned that the region's liberalism was now threatening to infect the entire nation. Indeed, Cox claimed that the most formidable threat to the nation actually came from the Northeast, not from the South. "New England," he asserted, "may be accounted smart in intellect, cunning in invention and energetic in industry. She may boast of her libraries, schools, churches and press . . . but such smartness may be unable to comprehend the machinery of a State. It may bring—nay, it has already brought—crash and confusion where better minds evolved beauty and harmony."

In his lengthy address, Cox drew a direct line of descent from the early Puritan settlers of New England to the Transcendentalists to present-day reformers.[12] These included Theodore Parker, Wendell Phillips, Governor Andrew, and Charles Sumner, all of whom he described as the "spawn of Transcendentalism." It is somewhat ironic that Cox cast them as aristocratic snobs and elitists, even though, as he indicated, their agenda was focused on emancipation and equality. "It is always understood," he stated sarcastically, "that what is for the common defence and public welfare is to be decided by the Brahmins of Boston! It being also further understood that we Sooters[13] of the West—being of another and inferior caste—are obliged to confess the infallibility of the Brahaminical decision. It is under just such doctrines that proclamations of anti-slavery issue. Other sections are not to be consulted." Cox insisted that "had the Central, Western and Border States been consulted, the proclamation never would have been issued: and by their help, it never can or shall be executed." All of this malicious mischief, Cox said, "is the direful result of these intermeddling purists of New England."

Cox then identified the source more specifically. "It comes from that coterie known around Boston as Transcendentalism. Its first organ was the devil. . . . Its most clever exponent was Emerson. It has its priests, high and low, . . . [from] the great [William Ellery] Channing, . . . to the little [William Henry] Channing, who foists himself into the Senate room at Washington of Sundays, to preach that Abolition hate and retail such slander against the Democracy as the powers at Washington seem most to relish."[14]

The essence of Transcendentalism, according to Cox, was "the absorption of God and nature in man, and that man, the Brahmin or the Puritan, believes in nothing but the soul. The soul of man is God and nature. No matter, *no color*, nothing but the soul in man; he is all; it is all." Cox saw an integral relationship between this Emersonian concept of the Transcendental oneness of mankind and the liberal idea of racial equality. "Do you wonder, therefore, that since he [Emerson] makes the negro a part of himself, that he holds him to be his equal?" he asked rhetorically.[15] This idealistic idea of spiritual oneness and equality, Cox insisted, led directly to the Emancipation Proclamation.[16] The Transcendentalists' emphasis on racial equality was an evil that threatened the entire nation, according to conservatives like Cox. A year later, he would take to the floor of the House to denounce "the new system, called by the transcendental abolitionists, *Miscegenation*." In the fall election, the Central Campaign Committee of the New York Democratic Party published a pamphlet, "Miscegenation Endorsed by the Republican Party," which attacked Emerson specifically for promoting the view that "the negro is better than the white man."[17]

The growing conservative backlash against New England's liberal culture was manifested in a number of other ways. The liberal *Boston Weekly Transcript* reported that Clement Vallandigham of Ohio, a Copperhead Democrat and bitter critic of the Lincoln administration, recently indicated a willingness, a desire even, to remake the Union with New England excluded.[18] The article noted that conservatives were offended not only by New England's "political principles" but also "her literature, her social life, and her relative worth as a type of modern Christian nation." By contrast, and somewhat ironically, the political and cultural values of conservative Northern Democrats like Cox aligned more with the oligarchic South than the democratic North. The same was true for their conservative British counterparts, who, the *Transcript* asserted, were "in sympathy with the most tyrannical despotism the world has ever seen." A day earlier, the paper reported that Governor Seymour of New York "has sketched a plan of a Copperhead winter campaign" that could have "proceeded from South Carolina instead of New York."

Reactions to the proclamation in England followed the same pattern as earlier. Liberals were thrilled and conservatives were outraged. The effect on the working class, however, was especially remarkable. Young Henry Adams wrote to his brother Charles that the proclamation "is creating an almost convulsive reaction in our favor all over this country. The *London Times* [is] furious and scolds like a drunken drab," while the "vast mass of the lower orders" offered enthusiastic support for the Union cause. British workers, he noted, were now "making common cause with us."

All of this was a revelation to Henry Adams. "I never quite appreciated the 'moral influence' of American democracy," he wrote, "nor the cause that the privileged classes in Europe have to fear us, until I saw how it works. . . . A vast mass of the lower orders . . . go our whole platform and are full of the 'rights of man.'" As in America, there was a revolution arising in Great Britain. "You can find millions of people who look up to our institutions as their model and who talk with utter contempt of their own system of Government. . . . I will not undertake to say where it will stop," he added, "but were I an Englishman I should feel nervous."[19] This nervousness would grow stronger as the war and the campaign for human rights it brought continued.

There were huge pro-Northern gatherings throughout England at this time where resolutions were passed in support of the Union, liberty, and equality. One of the largest was at London's Exeter Hall. Richard Cobden was delighted to see such support for the Union. The gathering at Exeter Hall, he later told Sumner, "has had a powerful effect on our newspapers and politicians. It has closed the mouths of those who have been advocating the side of the South. Recognition of the South, by England, whilst it bases itself on negro slavery," he declared, "is an impossibility."[20] British workers were energized by what they saw as the Union's effort to assert the principle of equal rights regardless of class, caste, or race. At a rally in Manchester, a speaker declared that the people of the North were "not merely contending for themselves but for the rights of the unenfranchised in this and every other country." He was certain that if the North succeeds, "liberty [will] be stimulated and encouraged in every country on the face of the earth," which was, of course, the British governing class's greatest fear.[21]

Military service for African Americans was an important step in ensuring that this effort would not fail. This was reflected in British workingmen's newspapers, which, one scholar notes, expressed the belief that "the pathway to citizenship was now open to African Americans. The *Birmingham Daily Post* reported that the Proclamation had made African Americans think about the United States as 'their country as well as that of the white man.'"[22] Those same newspapers also maintained that the British upper classes were opposed to the proclamation for selfish reasons. Slavery in America, they argued, only served to reinforce inequality in England, and they attacked the London *Times* for being on the wrong side in the matter.[23]

Leading British liberals like John Stuart Mill felt the same way. Mill applauded the proclamation in a letter to Motley. He reported that "a decided movement in your favor has begun among the public, since it has become evident that your GOVT. is really earnest about getting rid of slavery."[24] This, he noted, was not readily acknowledged in most British journals because too often these reflected the "accidental interests or sympathies of some one person." Thus, "the *Sat. Review* . . . is understood to be the property of the bitterest Tory enemy America has, Beresford Hope."[25]

A new strategy began to emerge among Southern sympathizers in Great Britain. In an effort to blunt the positive impact of the Emancipation Proclamation, they argued that Blacks would not benefit from freedom. At the same time, they began to promote the idea of a modified form of slavery, a sort of perpetual serfdom.[26] Additionally, for the first time ever, the London *Times* offered on January 6 a specific, religiously based argument in defense of the institution of slavery. The *Saturday Review* did the same. Many people on both sides of the Atlantic were taken aback by what they viewed as the *Times*'s blatant moral perfidy. In America, the report caused shock waves to ripple through the Northern press. The *Chicago Tribune* reprinted the entire article on January 28 under the heading, "The London *Times* Defends Slavery on Scripture Grounds."

The *Times* article also attacked abolitionist clergy who "fulminate over the North American continent," calling for "the emancipation of every slave in the Union, not as a . . . contingent measure, . . . but as an absolute dogma, founded on principle, to be carried into instant effect." Just as Southern slave owners had done for years, the *Times* denied that the moral position taken by these reformers was supported by Christian scripture. "They preach with the bible in their hands, [but] in that book there is not one single text that can be perverted to prove slavery unlawful."

Despite such efforts, or perhaps because of them, more British abolitionists were now warming to the Union cause. An article in the London *Daily News* offered harsh criticism of the hypocrisy of the British upper class for their "languid indifference" to the plight of the slaves. It was now "the turn of the common people" to speak, and at Manchester "they have made a good beginning," the paper reported. Idealism was prominent, with speakers referring to the "'sacred and inalienable rights of every human being,'" and "the 'common brotherhood of mankind.'" Such words, the writer noted, were "big with the hopes of the many, but an offence and foolishness to the privileged few." Race and class, so important to the elites, were no barrier to these simple people, who, "possessing little more than our common humanity, . . . prize that above artificial distinctions of class or color."[27]

These expressions of solidarity with the oppressed of the world by members of Britain's working class were a serious cause of concern for conservatives. For them and their American counterparts, "playing the race card" would become increasing important in their effort to hold back what was threatening to become a liberal tsunami. As the debate on the American Civil War turned more and more on issues of race, an old theory known as scientific racism found new currency in conservative circles. Members of the governing class now sought to "prove" that distinctions of race were not "artificial," as the Manchester workers believed. Their intent was to show that Blacks were naturally inferior through the deployment of arguments they claimed were based on science.[28]

As a means to this end, a new society was founded by scientific racists who rejected monogenism, the idea of a common ancestor for the human species. The idea of monogenism was promoted by Charles Darwin. It had garnered wide acceptance following the publication of Darwin's classic study, *Origin of Species*, in 1859. The idea that the human family evolved from a common ancestor had strong moral as well as biological connotations for those engaged in a debate over racial equality. Monogenism was widely accepted by members of the prestigious London Ethnological Society because of the sound science supporting it. Those who wished to promote the concept of separate origins for each race, "polygenism," subsequently abandoned that group and formed the Anthropological Society of London.

Polygenetic theory had been around for some time. Its chief proponent in America at this time was the charismatic Harvard professor Louis Agassiz, a founding member of the Saturday Club. His racialist thinking found few friends among that liberal set. Emerson, who liked the personable Agassiz, simply dismissed his racist view as inconsistent with the moral laws of the universe as he knew them. For Emerson, those laws were affirmed by the best scientific thinking of the day. In his journal, he commented, "I fear Agassiz takes too much time & space in denying popular science. He should electrify us by perpetual affirmations."[29] Agassiz's chief scientific adversary was also a distinguished Harvard professor, Asa Gray, who would later become a member of the Saturday Club himself.[30] As noted earlier, during the war Gray became a strong supporter and personal friend of Charles Darwin.[31]

Agassiz's writings on polygenetic theory were promoted by the Anthropological Society of London, along with similar works by Robert Knox (*The Races of Men*), Josiah Nott (*Types of Mankind*), and George

Gliddon (*Indigenous Races*).[32] Together, Agassiz, Morton, and Nott formed the core of what came to be known as the "American School." All of their works argued for polygenism in one way or another, and these provided the basis for "scientific racism."[33] George Morton (1799–1851) was the de facto leader of the American School. Morton became famous for his cranial studies, where he measured the size, shape, and volumetric capacity of skulls that were deemed representative of the various races. Relying primarily on his measurements of cranial capacity, which he equated with brain size, Morton ranked groups that he identified as "races." The actual number of groups considered to be races varied greatly in the nineteenth century. Morton identified five and offered the following ranking: Caucasian on the top and Ethiopian (African) on the bottom, with Mongolian, Malay, and American (that is, Native American) in the middle.[34] Morton's study was widely accepted as scientifically accurate, and it was highly influential in the nineteenth-century debate over race. As one historian reports, Morton's "infamous craniometric studies provided a rallying point for the polygenist movement as objective proof for the diverse origins of mankind and the superiority of the white race."[35]

All of these works insisted on absolute distinctions between the races and a hierarchy of abilities that always placed the Caucasian at the top and all others below in a descending order, with Black Africans at the bottom. George Gliddon coined the terms "monogenist" and "polygenist" to describe the two competing theories.[36] It was Josiah Nott, however, who became known as the most dedicated proponent of polygenism at midcentury. His theory was eagerly embraced by those seeking a scientific, rather than a purely biblical, justification for slavery. The influence of science was growing as the century progressed, and scientific racism seemed to answer a need. In a "scientific" justification of Black servitude Nott offered a sociological application of his biological theories. While maintaining, unequivocally, that "the Anglo-Saxon and the negro races are . . . distinct species," with the former vastly superior to the latter, it was but a short step to the conclusion that "the negro attains his greatest perfection, and also his greatest longevity, in a state of slavery."[37]

From its beginning, the Anthropological Society of London was rife with Southern agents and supporters. Henry Hotze was one. His *Index* frequently ran articles attacking Darwin's common stock theory and its "brotherhood of mankind" implications, while promoting the work of the society's polygenists. Hotze employed their theory of racial inferiority in an effort to undermine British opposition to slavery. The new society had its own publication, the *Anthropological Review*, edited by James Hunt, a thirty-year-old medical doctor who became an outspoken advocate of the new "science."[38] The *Review* was unique among English publications in that it overtly supported both the Confederacy *and* the institution of slavery. Because of this, one correspondent suggested to scientist Thomas Huxley that Hunt "is paid by the Confederates to lie as he does."[39] This assumption was basically correct.

From the time of its founding, it was evident that the primary goal of the Anthropological Society of London was to destroy the belief that "the negro is a man and a brother."[40] This purpose was made clear in ways that went well beyond the realm of pseudoscience. The skeleton of a so-called savage was hung in the window of the society's meeting hall, and the mace with which meetings were called to order featured the head of a Black person with a human thigh bone clamped between its teeth. Very soon the organization, with some 700 to 800 members, became known as the "Cannibal Club."[41] Henry Hotze was delighted with the new society. He managed to place three of his paid agents on its governing council and consistently promoted the society in the pages of the *Index*.

Around this time, James Hunt made several outrageous claims in a popular pamphlet titled "The Negro's Place in Nature" in an effort to "demonstrate" "Negro" inferiority. His malicious intent was so obvious that he was immediately attacked as a racist.[42] Among the more bizarre claims were that "the hair [of a Negro] is very peculiar—three hairs, springing from different orifices will unite into one," and that the "ape-like Negroes had elongated heels and could not stand like men."[43] Such absurd claims—presented as scientific evidence—were just too much for Thomas Huxley. A gifted biologist, Huxley (grandfather of Aldous) took his science seriously. He was opposed to slavery not out of sentimentalism but because he believed it degraded the entire human family. He was also a friend and supporter of Charles Darwin.[44] Darwin himself hated slavery and its proponents' desire to "make the black [an]other kind, sub-human, a beast to be chained." He came from a family with strong antislavery ties, but rather than enter the public arena to offer polemics against slavery, he instead hoped to subvert it with his science. Throughout the public debate, Asa Gray became Darwin's most effective American advocate. The pages of the *Atlantic Monthly* were always open to Gray's scientific arguments supporting Darwin's views.[45]

All of this was highly controversial, especially in the context of the Civil War, where issues of emancipation and equal rights were now thoroughly intertwined with race. Darwin appreciated Gray's advocacy, and the two became friends at this time as a result. Their relationship grew throughout the war years. Darwin wrote to Gray frequently with questions about the war and political and military matters, as well as the ongoing battle with Agassiz and his racist supporters. Darwin's work proved to be of great value as the war gradually turned into a crusade to abolish slavery and to promote human rights. Indeed, Huxley once commented that *Origin of Species* was a veritable "Whitmore gun in the armory of liberalism."[46]

Huxley eventually decided to take on the polygenists directly. He blasted Hunt's pamphlet, "The Negro's Place in Nature," ridiculing his ludicrous claims about physiology as base ideology masquerading as science. English liberals loved it. Newspaper headlines proclaimed "Professor Huxley an Abolitionist," and articles described him as one who believed in "equal rights for all men." Science, pseudoscience, and politics now occupied the same intellectual space as liberals declared that Huxley had made "his physiological definition of the Negro's place among men equivalent to an earnest plea for Negro emancipation."[47] This intellectual war about race had serious implications on both sides of the Atlantic for those determined to maintain the principle of white supremacy. Some British critics now tacitly acknowledged the importance of this principle to the continuing stability of the British Empire. They pointed to the recent violent uprising of the Sepoys in India as an example of what can happen when that principle is challenged.[48]

Social and cultural consequences came with the rise of scientific racism in Great Britain. It brought about a new emphasis on the exclusiveness of "gentility." In the 1840s and 1850s, accomplished Black antislavery speakers like Frederick Douglass and Henry "Box" Brown made successful tours of England. Everywhere, they were well received, their lectures well attended and positively reviewed in the popular press. They were seen as "gentlemen" and welcomed into polite circles.[49] However, many elites were now led to believe that it was impossible for any Black person to rise above his presumed genetic limitations. If Blacks were irredeemably inferior, then they must be excluded from the company of the upper classes. "Once the assumption was made that blacks could only perform laboring tasks and never approach gentlemanly status," Douglas Lorimer notes, "respectable Victorians simply applied to all men with black skins the same judgments, manner, and bearing that they adopted toward their social inferiors within English society." As a result, "a new inflexibility and contempt characterized English attitudes to the Negro," at least among the conservative upper class. On the other hand, this fact only made the working classes even more inclined to make common cause with the oppressed slaves, thus discounting what they considered "artificial distinctions of class or color."[50]

All of this, of course, served to further intensify British interest in the American war, especially as it continued to impact cultural and political norms regarding class, caste, and race in Great Britain. Correspondingly, American liberals were led to take a greater interest in social conditions in England, particularly those affecting the English working class, with whom they were increasingly aligned. *Harper's Weekly* reported on January 24 that "the working men of Manchester have made an important demonstration in support of the cause of the American Union, expressing at the same time their approval of the war and emancipation policy of President Lincoln. . . . The Mayor of Manchester presided . . . and the negro, Jackson, ex-coachman of Jeff Davis, was on the platform."

Later, in his letter "To the Workingmen of Manchester, England," Lincoln thanked the workers for their support. "I know and deeply deplore the sufferings which the workingmen at Manchester . . . are called to endure in this crisis," he wrote. "It has been . . . represented that the attempt to overthrow this government, which was built upon the foundation of human rights, and to substitute for it one which should rest exclusively on the basis of human slavery, was likely to obtain the favor of Europe." But that was not the case with the working classes, Lincoln noted. "Under these circumstances, I cannot but regard your decisive utterance . . . as an instance of sublime Christian heroism." These sentiments, he declared, "will excite admiration, esteem, and the most reciprocal feelings of friendship among the American people."[51] This transatlantic alliance of common people would only grow stronger from this point forward.[52]

In addition to the working class, the Union also continued to find support among England's liberal intellectuals and reformers. In a letter to Richard Webb around this time, Samuel Joseph May reported his gratification at the positive impact of the proclamation among British abolitionists. "We have much comfort & satisfaction in the changed aspect of affairs in G[reat]. Britain," he noted, "[that] the old, solid, antislavery feeling is stirring." But he complained, "Notwithstanding all this, England has, in the most forcible & ready way in which it can be done—short of an open alliance—ministered to, helped, & fed the slaveholders' rebellion,

& their project of a slaveholding Empire, from the first. This is a fact which can never be wiped out."[53]

Southern sympathizers in Great Britain tried to minimize the impact of the proclamation and the many public displays of support, like that at Manchester, that it brought forth. The *Saturday Review* referred to such public demonstrations as a "carnival of cant." Propagandist Hotze told his Confederate superiors in Richmond that "all persons of social and political respectability have held aloof" from such demonstrations, and the London *Times* referred to the throngs of working people who participated as lower-class "nobodies."[54]

But these "nobodies" were clearly having an impact. At the end of the month, Henry Adams wrote to his brother Charles, "The anti-slavery feeling of the country is coming out stronger than we ever expected." He reported that there had been a meeting at Exeter Hall the night before that was "likely to create a revolution, or rather to carry on a complete revolution." Support for the North among the working class was growing exponentially. As Henry noted, at the meeting "the enthusiasm for Lincoln and for everything connected with the North was immense."[55] In the weeks and months ahead, this support would grow even stronger, much to the dismay of the British governing class.

Chapter 12

British Conservatives React with Alarm as Race and Class Become Central Issues

On February 12, 1863, the London *Times* published Lincoln's letter, "To the Workingmen of Manchester," where he thanked them for their expression of support while noting the suffering they willingly endured. Around the same time, Richard Cobden informed Charles Sumner that the working-class response to the proclamation "shows how wide and deep the sympathy for personal freedom still is in the hearts of our people." He added that the recent great meeting at Exeter Hall "has had a powerful effect on our newspapers and politicians. . . . If an attempt were made by the government in any way to commit us to the South," Cobden asserted, "a spirit would be instantly aroused which would drive our government from power."[1] Henry Adams wrote to his brother Charles that the upper classes were more bitter and angry than ever. The strong popular feeling for the North, he said, is "gradually dividing the nation into aristocrats and democrats," something he believed "may produce pretty serious results for England."[2]

Since it was now undeniable that the North's position was against slavery and the South for it, British conservatives found themselves pushed into a corner. Some, like the *Times* and the *Saturday Review*, finally showed their true colors by arguing, as the Southerners did, that slavery was actually a positive good. *Fraser's* followed suit. Their February issue included another polemic by Hiram Fuller. It began with an argument that was now the common property of conservatives on both sides of the Atlantic. "Fern leaves cannot become rose bushes," Fuller wrote, "thorn trees cannot produce grapes; the ass cannot be converted into the horse, nor the negro into a white man. There is no such thing as Transubstantiation in nature; and there is no such thing as equality in man. All men are created unequal," he asserted, "and no man is born free—the primary proposition of the American 'Declaration of Independence' to the contrary notwithstanding."[3]

Because Fuller also wrote for Henry Hotze's Southern propaganda journal, the *Index*, some believed that he was actually a paid agent of the South.[4] Edward Peacock was one. Peacock was a British antiquarian, novelist, and liberal reformer.[5] Around this time, he began corresponding with Caroline Healy Dall, a liberal Boston Unitarian and feminist reformer who was dedicated to the antislavery cause. She had a substantial reputation as a lecturer and author, having recently published *Woman's Right to Labor* (1860) and *Woman's Rights Under the Law* (1861). Like other reformers of her generation, she was strongly influenced by Ralph Waldo Emerson, as well as Thoreau, Margaret Fuller, George W. Curtis, and other Transcendentalists. On occasion, she lectured in Concord, where she was treated to the warm hospitality of the Alcotts and the Emersons.[6]

It is not clear how Dall first came to know Peacock, but around this time she introduced him to her friend, Boston activist and reformer Lucy Stone. Stone eventually became a leader in the women's medical movement in America. She was in England at the time, pursuing her medical education. Stone wrote Dall that she "was admitted to the London Hospital. . . . This is one of the largest hospitals in London," she told her, "and I am the first woman who has ever entered it as a student." She also stated, "I sent your letters to Mr. Peacock as you directed and kept up an occasional correspondence with him till he came to London about three weeks ago."

Stone was at first a bit apprehensive about meeting Peacock because his letters showed he was a very "learned man," and she wondered if she could "talk freely with him, . . . but the moment I saw him," she wrote, "all my fears vanished. He is young, not much over thirty, . . . [and] a thorough reformer." She added that Peacock and his wife are "on the side of the North which makes it very pleasant for me to visit them." This was a welcome surprise for Stone because, as she told Dall, "nearly all the English people I meet, are very strongly on the Southern side and almost every new Doctor that I meet attacks me on the subject of the war . . . when I tell him that I am a northerner and abolitionist."[7]

Five days later, Peacock wrote a long letter to Dall that reflected the growing bond of mutual friendship and support between liberals in Old and New England. Peacock said, "I look on this conspiracy of the slave owning South as one of the foulest, if not the very foulest crimes in human history." He firmly believed that "woman's rights, education and all other social reforms are as nothing *now* compared with the liberation of our brothers and sisters from the most hateful bondage the world has ever seen."

Peacock also told Dall about his concern that popular opinion in England "has been directed almost entirely by persons who have sympathy with the Slave faction" and that "this has caused much ill-feeling against England in America." He correctly surmised that much of this was the result of the "desperate efforts" of Southern agents "to poison the public mind" by hiring English "conspirators . . . who are paid for publishing falsehoods." He was also concerned about the misinformation published by the London *Times*. "To a person like myself," Peacock wrote, "it seems grotesquely absurd for people to pin their faith on 'the leading journal,'" as so many of his countrymen did. Like other English liberals, Peacock was certain slavery would eventually give way, but he was "quite unable to see what the end will be." In the meantime, he was concerned that "the Democrats will succeed in patching up a peace with the slave owners in spite of all the efforts of New-England."

A particular worry at present, Peacock told Dall, was the insidious influence of the Southern propagandists as reflected in the articles appearing in highly regarded British journals. "Most probably you see *Fraser's Magazine*," he wrote. "If you do, you will not have failed to notice an article in the February Number . . . 'by a White Republican.' It is certainly one of the most abominable productions I ever read. The 'White Republican,'" he noted, "is believed to be a paid agent of the South."[8]

As the war of words continued, the London *Times* began to promote the idea that Lincoln's proclamation and notions of racial equality were not embraced by the majority in the North. Charles Mackay reported on February 23 that "the cry of immediate emancipation" by Lincoln's supporters "is simply their confession that they believe the prosecution of the war to be hopeless. If white men . . . are powerless to save the Republic, it is already a thing of the past." Mackay indicated further that "Mr. Lincoln's proclamation of freedom to the slaves has been fatal to the Union" because "the negro was never beloved in America," and even though he had "theoretical friends, who desired that he should not be chattel," even these, he claimed, were not "prepared to grant him social equality."

For conservatives, one of the most disturbing elements of the Emancipation Proclamation was that it provided for the enlistment of Blacks in the regular Union army. This was a significant and highly controversial development in the evolution of Lincoln's war strategy. It helped to change dramatically the status of Blacks in America. As James McPherson notes, "the Proclamation turned the Union army into a potential army of liberation," one that would now include former slaves.[9] New England liberals celebrated this development as a major step forward in the march toward universal emancipation.[10] Blacks also celebrated but noted that the measure was a long time coming. "The Black Volunteers," a poem by Fanny Jackson that appeared on the front page of the *Anglo-African* in May, welcomed "our brave volunteers" but also recalled that earlier, "their offers were spurned," as "Grim Prejudice vaunted their aid was not needed."[11]

As noted earlier, even before the proclamation, the Union army had been using Black "contraband" soldiers. Transcendentalist Thomas Wentworth Higginson led the 1st South Carolina Regiment, which was the first unit composed of freed slaves. In January, Colonel Higginson and his Black troops conducted a significant raid along a South Carolina river.[12] Later, in a report to the War Department on the performance of his troops, he stated, "The men have been repeatedly under fire; have had infantry, cavalry, and even artillery arrayed against them, and have in every instance come off not only with unblemished honor, but with undisputed triumph." As a result, "no officer in this regiment now doubts that the key to the successful prosecution of the war lies in the unlimited employment of black troops."[13] Higginson would later write extensively about his experiences with his Black regiment for the *Atlantic Monthly*.

About the time of Higginson's raid, Governor Andrew of Massachusetts received permission from the War Department to raise a regiment of Black volunteers for the regular Union army. This, ultimately, led to the formation of the Massachusetts 54th and 55th, the Federal army's first regular Black regiments. Initially, they were not given equal pay. Outraged, Charles Sumner argued vociferously against this injustice until it was finally, albeit belatedly, rectified.[14]

Governor Andrew succeeded in enlisting the perfect commander for the unit, Colonel Robert Gould Shaw. Robert was the son of Sarah Shaw, who had for some time been corresponding with John Elliott Cairnes. Sarah and her husband, Francis, were ardent abolitionists, and they were pleased when their son accepted command. As a boy Robert was surrounded by famous abolitionists.[15] He was a Harvard man, class of 1860. When the war started, Shaw joined the 2nd Massachusetts Infantry, where he served as an officer. He was twice wounded and saw action in the horrific Battle of Antietam.[16] Handsome and intelligent, Robert was a popular figure with Boston's intellectuals and reformers.

The idea of Black troops was still very controversial, even in liberal Massachusetts. It was a great coup for Governor Andrew when Shaw agreed to command the new regiment. Robert accepted the position only after a period of consideration, as the governor later indicated in a letter to Shaw's father.[17] Shaw took command of the 54th on February 15, 1863.[18] The 54th was popular with New England liberals, who supported it with both their pens and purses. Emerson was especially active in this effort, and he, along with Frederick Douglass and many other Black and white reformers, vigorously promoted the formation of Black regiments by making enlistment speeches and raising funds for regimental equipment.[19] They recognized the value of military service and the opportunity for African Americans it represented. Service in fighting units would allow them to demonstrate their intelligence, courage, dignity, and self-worth, as Douglass stressed in his call to arms, "Why Should a Colored Man Enlist."[20]

There was some fear at this time that both the proclamation and the enlistment of African Americans might have a deleterious effect on the morale of the Union army, which was already low following the disaster at Fredericksburg. An enlisted man serving in Louisiana at this time reported in a letter to his sister that "on Sunday night nearly thirty deserted from the regiment, three from our company. . . . There is a great deal of dissatisfaction in the Army," he wrote. "It is niggers and Old Abe all the time; they are not going to fight to free niggers, and they are not going to do this, and do that. The truth of it," he told her, "is they did not start from the right motive."[21] Eventually, however, the army's morale improved and before long, James McPherson reports, "most Northern soldiers had broadened their conception of liberty to include black people."[22]

Despite the good feeling among New England liberals regarding Lincoln's proclamation and the dramatic changes it was bringing, some still worried about the conservative backlash. In response, Boston liberals decided to organize a formal group to support the president's policies. On February 4, they established the "Union Club." An invitation had been sent out to potential members in late January. It was signed by John Murray Forbes and Charles Eliot Norton.[23] Members pledged "unqualified loyalty to the Constitution" and "unwavering support of the Federal government in suppressing the rebellion." A large circular from this time included the names of over 425 supporters and reads like a directory of New England's liberal establishment. Even the traditionally conservative commercial class in Boston was well represented.[24] Norton indicated in a letter to Curtis that "Our Union Club . . . promises well." But at the same time he acknowledged that "nothing will do us much good but victories."[25]

The private correspondence of some Englishmen at this time showed mixed reactions to the current state of affairs in America. Anglo-Irish poet Aubrey de Vere wrote to Norton that he was pleased with Lincoln's proclamation, but others remained skeptical. "The mass of Englishmen seem . . . to see everything in a *false perspective*," he told Norton, but "in Ireland [where he lived] I believe the masses are all for you! I think Irish in America have fought well for you." De Vere felt confident that "the time of compromise is gone by and that the North will forever shake off all responsibility as regards to slavery, come what may in the South."[26]

Earlier in the month, Norton received a letter from John Ruskin that took the opposite stance. It was sneering and brutal. "It is no use talking about your war," Ruskin declared. The idealism that was driving New England liberals looked to him like "a religious phrenzy" that was both "foolish and fearful. . . . If you want the slaves to be free—let their masters go free first—in God's name," he urged. "If they don't like being governed by you—let them govern themselves. . . . As for your precious proclamation," he added, "it is 'a gift of that which is not to be given / By all the assembled powers of earth and heaven'[27]—if I had it here," he told Norton, "there's a fine north wind blowing, and I would give it to the first boy I met to fly it as his kite's tail." Ruskin concluded his screed with an especially cruel afterthought: "As soon as I've got a house I'll ask you to send me something American—a slave perhaps. I've got a great notion of a black boy in a green jacket and purple cap—in Paul Veronese's manner."[28] Time would not temper Ruskin's ire.

Despite the setbacks in the midterm elections in the fall of 1862, the spring elections proved to be more positive for the Republicans and reassuring to those who wished to see the trend toward total abolition continue. The *New York Tribune* saw this as confirmation that the Copperheads were fading. It was now clear, Allan Nevins states, that "sentiment in support of a rigorous persecution of the war, and of a peace which required unconditional submission to the Union and to emancipation, was rising."[29]

All of this was rather remarkable in light of the fact that there was almost no progress on the battlefield. The aftershocks of the Union defeat at Fredericksburg continued to reverberate on both sides of the Atlantic. When a clash between Union and Confederate forces at Murfreesboro (Stones River) in Tennessee in late December ended in a deadly draw, news of the event provided a slight but welcome lift to the North.[30] In the meantime, Grant remained stalled before Vicksburg, a matter of considerable concern since major Union victories were the only sure way to discourage British intervention.

The building of Confederate warships in Great Britain, which had been a growing concern for some time, now became a critical issue. The British Foreign Enlistment Act forbade the building and arming of warships for a belligerent power. However, this prohibition had been routinely circumvented by arming vessels only after they departed British waters. The most notorious of these Confederate predators was the *Alabama*, which had been ravaging Union shipping from the time it entered service in September 1862.[31]

The Laird brothers' shipyard in Liverpool was now at work on two vessels, later known as the "Laird rams," which were clearly designed for war. They were ironclads, 230 feet long, steam powered, and equipped with twin revolving gun turrets. They were also fitted out with underwater rams, designed to penetrate the hulls of wooden ships. Such powerful weapons could be used to break the Union blockade and even to threaten Northern coastal cities like Philadelphia, New York, and Boston.[32] Their construction was closely watched by agents of the American government.

In response to the growing threat, on March 2 the US Congress passed a bill to authorize privateers. These were civilian ships that were allowed to take on armaments and prey on ships providing support to the enemy. This would pose a serious threat to British shipping and commerce.[33] As the situation became more grave, Charles Sumner warned the Duchess of Argyll that if work on the rams was allowed to continue, a war with England could not be ruled out.[34]

The British were also concerned with the gravity of the situation. Lord Russell saw the American act authorizing privateers as a serious threat to British interests.[35] When Lord Lyons protested the action to Secretary Seward, the secretary read to him a dispatch recently sent to Minister Adams, which noted that Confederate warships continued to be built in violation of British neutrality; this was "a last effort to arrest the evils which the present state of things have made imminent."[36] The situation would reach a crisis stage before the year was out. War with

Great Britain, once again a real possibility, became a source of constant concern in the North.

There was yet another disturbing sign that British commercial interests were affecting her war policy. On March 18, a cotton loan of £3 million went on the market in London and other major European exchanges. An investment in this loan was obviously an investment in the Confederacy and its fate. Therefore, it was a troubling turn of events when the American minister to Paris, John Bigelow, obtained a partial list of investors. Shockingly, the list included the names William E. Gladstone (Chancellor of the Exchequer), Alexander Beresford-Hope (cofounder of the *Saturday Review*), William Lindsay, MP (one of the Confederacy's staunchest defenders), John Laird, MP (co-owner of the shipyard where the Laird rams were currently under construction), William H. Gregory, MP (another Southern apologist), James Spence, and several other prominent members of the English establishment.[37] For many, this revelation confirmed the fact that England's "neutrality" was a farce.

It was around this critical time that Norton informed Curtis that his Boston friends were making arrangements "to secure the circulation of good telling articles from foreign and our own newspapers, to influence and direct public opinion. We propose to secure from one hundred thousand to five hundred thousand readers for two articles per week, and perhaps more." He told Curtis, "I shall be the 'editor,' so to say, with John Forbes and Sam Ward as advisers." Norton then asked Curtis to "send to me, marked, articles which you think should be thus circulated." He also noted, "I shall have frequent occasion to borrow from 'Harper,' or rather from you in 'Harper.'"[38]

Emerson also received an invitation to join this effort.[39] On March 10, a society was formed. The broadsheets they published would eventually reach over one million readers. Included among them were the editors and writers of many of the most influential newspapers in the North.[40] Norton eventually expanded the circulation list to include editors and others in Great Britain and France.[41] Both the organization and the publication became known officially as the *New England Loyal Publication Society*, which appeared on the masthead of every broadsheet. This was one of a number of such organizations being formed in cities throughout the North at this time.[42]

The roots of the Boston society extended back to the previous summer when John Murray Forbes first contemplated the benefits of such an effort.[43] He intended from the beginning that the content should be international in scope. One of the first items published was "A Voice from England," from the London *Daily News* of February 19. The article ridiculed a recent proposal to restore the Union "with the omission of New England," calling it "wild and absurd." "New England," the article stated, has been, more than any other area of the nation, responsible for the "preservation of the principles on which the Republic was founded." Since that time, "the substantial material of the national pride and hope has been the mind and character of New England."[44] The *Society* would distribute materials such as this for the balance of the war.

Now that limited emancipation had been declared, English abolitionists consistently identified the North as the antislavery side. New England liberals also promoted this idea, following their usual practice of hyping every positive development in the hope of precipitating another. On March 14, *Harper's Weekly* published a large and detailed illustration showing the recent "GREAT UNION MEETING AT EXETER HALL" that had so pleased Mill, Cairnes, and other British supporters. "It was one of the largest and most enthusiastic meetings ever held in London," *Harper's* reported. The article cited a witness to the event who stated that when "the crowd shouted 'Emancipation and Union!' . . . there broke forth the most tremendous outburst of popular enthusiasm it has ever been our fortune to witness."

The depiction of the war as a transatlantic campaign for human rights and the dignity of free labor was reinforced four days later when the *New England Loyal Publication Society* printed a "Letter of John Stuart Mill" that was recently sent to Union supporters in London celebrating Washington's birthday. He wrote that "the prospects of the human race are so deeply interested in the success of the great experiment which is working itself out in the United States that the lovers of freedom and progress in other countries feel whatever injures, and still more whatever dishonors America, as a personal calamity. Foremost among all things which injure and dishonor a country stands the personal slavery of human beings." The war, Mill indicated, while initially an effort to prevent the extension of slavery, was now aimed at its extinction. "*My hopes for the future welfare and greatness of the American Republic,*" he declared, "*were never so high as in this, to superficial appearance, the darkest hour of its history.*"[45]

The *Saturday Review* was well aware that such strong public support of the North by one of England's most respected and influential thinkers could be persuasive to many. Furthermore, now that the workingmen were expressing enthusiastic support for Lincoln while conservative aristocrats were condemning him, the divide in Great Britain was beginning to look very much like class warfare. In "Mr. Mill on America," the *Review* responded by arguing that Americans and Englishmen shared a tradition of liberty and lawful governance. "It is thus perfectly true," the writer insisted, "that we are all deeply interested in the success and honour of America, because the principles of their government are the principles of our government also. It is also true . . . that slavery is a reproach and dishonor to any nation in which it exists."

Following this perfunctory condemnation of the institution, a reversal of the *Review*'s recent defense, the writer argued that because slavery was lawful in the states where it existed, "the war in America now represents a situation where one side is attempting to impose its moral view upon the other, in violation of Constitutional law. Mr. Mill should know better than to take the side of the North," he declared. "The whole gist" of his *Essay on Liberty* is that "it is never expedient to attempt to force people into virtuous conduct." Casting the conflict as one that pitted subjective morality against objective law, the *Review* concluded that it was simply "absurd" to represent the war as "a struggle between aristocrats and democrats," even if that was exactly what it looked like.[46]

In the meantime, as the debate on race became more intense, both sides moved to more extreme positions. A conservative Ohio editor described the Emancipation Proclamation as "monstrous, impudent, and heinous . . . insulting to God as to man, for it declares those 'equal' whom God created unequal."[47] The *New York Caucasian* struck a similar note. The paper declared that "God Almighty has made the negro a different and inferior being and therefore assigned him a different and inferior social position wherever and whenever in juxtaposition with the superior white man."[48] On the other side, as one scholar points out, "the idea of equality—as a legal, political, and spiritual value—came to dominate the Transcendentalist and abolitionist understanding of the war."[49]

Race and equal rights were now pressing issues on both sides of the Atlantic. Black abolitionist Lewis Putnam defined the war as a struggle over the principle of "political equality and fraternity."[50] On March 21, the Boston *Daily Covenant* reported on a recent "discussion at the Sunday Institute" where the question considered was "Has American slavery benefitted the condition of the Negro race?" The proponent of the affirmative argued that "by being better fed and cared for they become better developed and more humanized," just as "wild horses and cattle and sheep, are [also] greatly improved by domestication. But the transmutation of a buffalo into an ox," he insisted, "is just as impossible as that of a Negro into a white man."

A March 6 report by Charles Mackay in the London *Times* described the growing racial divide in the North. The division, he wrote, was between those on one side "who maintain that Washington and Jefferson intended the Republic to be a Government of white men, and of white men only." The other side was "composed of philanthropists, preachers, lecturers, and zealots, who proclaim that they would ruin and slay every white man, woman, and child in the South, rather than acknowledge that the negro was not a brother, and not as fully entitled as themselves to political equality." These "zealots" also claimed they "would obey—a black President as implicitly as they would obey a white one, if, by the lawful agencies of that wondrous machine the ballot-box, Mr Frederick Douglass, or any other whole or half-caste negro were nominated to the perilous position." Name calling was common among conservatives in the current debate. " 'Wooly Heads,' " Mackay reported, "is the new name given to the Negrophilists and Abolitionists by the Democrats."[51]

Aware that the best way to counter such deep-seated bigotry was through a demonstration of the Black man's ability to fight side by side with white Union soldiers, New England liberals now lent their full energies to building up the Massachusetts 54th. While many in Boston pledged their support, some had their doubts. A letter from a Boston socialite to a friend recounted a recent visit from Henry Higginson, a cousin of Thomas Wentworth Higginson. Henry was serving with the 54th. "He has gone into the negro regiment . . . under Robert Shaw," she reported. "How I hope that undertaking may succeed; it is no use to ask people about their experience for half the men, like Edward Hooper and Robert Shaw, say the negroes behave with discretion and fidelity and the other half say they are utterly superficial and discipline is in vain."[52] Emerson spoke at a fundraiser for the Massachusetts 54th at this critical time and also donated to the cause.[53] The fundraiser was a big success, and the *Boston Advertiser* reported on March 21 that "quite a large sum was collected."[54]

In his speech at the event, Emerson responded to the bitter racism that now surfaced in the debate on the future of the Black man in America. The Boston *Evening Traveller* of March 21 wrote that Emerson told the audience, "We have kept the black man down until his name has become a synonym of all that is low and degraded." As a result "the hostility of races is a uniform fact." The only way to mitigate this evil, he observed, "is by a closer acquaintance between the opponents." One sure way to do that was through military service. Now that the government had finally "decided to organize negro regiments," Massachusetts was "endeavoring to do a part and to elevate the hitherto oppressed race to a position where they may strike for their rights." The writer added that Emerson was certain "that the black man would make a good soldier."

In addition to supporting the 54th, New England liberals continued to praise the accomplishments of Thomas Wentworth Higginson's regiment of contrabands in South Carolina. The *Boston Daily Evening Transcript* related on March 21 that "the Black Brigade of Col. Higginson bids fair to be as famous in the present war as the English first brigade, which rose into the 'jaws of death' on the Crimean peninsula."[55] The *Daily Advertiser* also reported on the same day that "the colored brigade, which is marching into Florida, is said to have been thus far successful."

Meanwhile, on the other side of the Atlantic, the Union cause was clearly in the ascendency among the masses in Great Britain, and the *Times*, which was read primarily by the elite, could not change that. The March 21 *Harper's Weekly* published a report on "a great demonstration at the Amphitheatre in Liverpool . . . in support of President Lincoln's Emancipation Proclamation. The Liverpool *Post* says that a more unanimous meeting was never witnessed on any question." On the other hand, the article noted, "the conduct of the Lord Mayor of London in feting Mr. Mason, the Minister of the Confederate Movement, was strongly reprobated." Back at home, Robert Shaw wrote to a friend, "People lately from England say the change of feeling there is a wonder—and they attribute it almost entirely to the proclamation."[56]

At the end of the month, John Bright delivered a "Speech before the Trades Unionists in London." He was joined by John Stuart Mill. In his address, Bright argued that the Civil War in America was truly a people's war and a moral crusade. It is "a question of freedom or slavery, of education or ignorance, of light or darkness," he declared. Bright strongly implied that class had a great deal to do with English feelings about the war. It was only the morally bankrupt "dynasties and aristocracies" of "privilege," he pointed out, that had the audacity to support the side of slavery.[57]

In responding to Bright on March 28, the *Saturday Review* felt compelled, once again, to refute the notion that there was anything like class warfare emerging in England. Bright's "denunciation of those classes, which he falsely stigmatizes as privileged, is culpably unjust and mischievous," the *Review* fumed. It was dangerous to proclaim "that all

Englishmen above the working classes are the enemies of the United States. If war should unhappily arise," the writer warned, "no small part of the blame will attach to the partisans who have habitually calumniated their own Government and country by echoing the vituperative falsehoods of the Northern Press."[58] Despite such retorts, or perhaps because of them, the rhetoric on both sides continued to escalate.

Sensitivities grew more acute as many in New England's intellectual class continued to experience the war on a personal level. It remained the central topic of discussion at the Saturday Club, where key figures in the conflict were frequently guests. Others were represented through their letters. The tone was at times bellicose. Nathaniel Hawthorne wrote to his English friend Henry Bright that he "went to the Club, last Saturday, and met all the usual set, besides some generals and colonels, fresh from the battle-field, war worn and wounded. The tone of feeling was patriotic, the mildest men and most abstract philosophers being, as it seemed to me, the most truculent. Emerson is as merciless as a steel bayonet, and I would not give much for a rebel's life if he came within a sword's length of your friend Charles Norton."

Hawthorne was, at this point, still the odd man out at such gatherings. He asked Bright, only half-jokingly, not to tell Norton "what I say, or he will turn his weapon against me. But seriously," he added, "this Club may fairly be considered as representing the most enlightened public opinion of New England, at least, if not of the whole North; and it is unreservedly and enthusiastically in favor of continuing the war, and steadfastly confident of the result."[59] This distinguished cadre of New England intellectuals was for some time fully committed to ensuring that this Civil War would, indeed, be America's second revolution, fulfilling, finally, the Founders' promise of freedom and equal rights for all.

Meanwhile, the now bitter divide between New England's liberal literati and their British cousins was strikingly evident in major essays appearing in *Fraser's*, the *Quarterly Review*, and the *Economist*, among others. The subject of race was central in *Fraser's* February "American Literature and the Civil War." The article argued that the literature of America was inferior to British literature because of the leveling effect of democracy. Like conservative Democrat Samuel Cox in his recent New York address, the author here took specific aim at New England.

According to *Fraser's*, the notion of universal equality embraced by the region's major writers had a deleterious effect on American culture, especially American literature. "Slavery has been proclaimed a crime by the preacher, the poet, and novelist," the writer observed, and "they are, as it were, maddened to do good, and to destroy evil." Such fanaticism was not conducive to the creation of great literature because it blinded one to the facts. Thus, "the poets of the Northern United States have judged slavery from their own mental and moral standpoint." As a result, "the care-free, hog-and-hominy, and possum-eating Negro is elevated, in the mind and heart of the poet, to his own plane," something that, presumably, could never happen with England's literary sages.[60]

The same issue of *Fraser's* included "Essays on Political Economy" by Norton's cranky friend, renowned English art critic, writer, and philosopher John Ruskin. Apparently, he felt that the time had come for him to speak out on an issue that had become a matter of national concern. In his essay, Ruskin defended the idea of a social hierarchy. For him, as for most Victorian elites, the notion of equality was simply absurd. The essay is a compelling example of the now stark differences between British and American ideas of culture and polity as articulated by one of Victorian England's most iconic figures.

Ruskin began by noting that the "sensibility" of a nation was indicated by "the fineness of its customs." By sensibility he meant "its natural perception of beauty, fitness, and rightness; or of what is lovely, decent, and just." For him, these qualities were "dependent much on race, and the primal signs of fine breeding in man." According to Ruskin, in any advanced civilization, the heavy labor was always done by those who were born to it. In some cases, these were slaves. In others, they were workers. The difference for Ruskin was in name only. As he artfully expressed it, "in the frame of a nation, nothing but the head can be of gold, and the feet, for the work they have to do, must be part of iron, part of clay. Foul or mechanical work," he observed, "is always reduced by a noble race to the minimum in quantity."[61]

For Ruskin, as for other Victorian elites, there was simply no dignity in physical labor. Like Southern "gentlemen," they considered it to be something that was "performed and endured, not without a sense of degradation, as a fine temper is wounded by the sight of the lower offices of the body." Because of this, he noted, historically, "the highest conditions of human society reached hitherto, have cast much work to slaves." If slavery was "to be done away with, mechanical and foul employment must in all highly organised states take the aspect either of punishment or probation. All criminals should at once be set to the most dangerous and painful forms." What "necessarily inferior labour remains to be done,"

Ruskin asserted, "falls to the lot of those who, for the time, are fit for nothing better," namely, the working class (442–43).

This division of labor was the natural order. There were, as Ruskin put it, "infinite differences between the natures and capacities of men; and these differing natures are generally rangeable under the two qualities of lordly, (or tending towards rule, construction, and harmony), and servile (or tending towards misrule, destruction, and discord); and, since the lordly part is only in a state of profitableness while ruling, and the servile only in a state of redeemableness while serving, the whole health of the state depends on the manifest separation of these two elements of its mind" (443).

While British workers were embracing the cause of the slave and demanding a more equitable role for themselves, Ruskin was confident that the foolishness of this notion would eventually come home to them. "The common insolences and petulances of the people, and their talk of equality," Ruskin wrote, are "but mere blindness, stupefaction, and fog in their brains." Once this fog cleared, they would naturally be inclined to exercise "patience in submitting to their true counsellors and governors" (446). As for America, it must learn discipline. On this matter, Ruskin was in total agreement with Matthew Arnold and Thomas Carlyle. To underscore his point, he quoted the latter's prediction that Americans will find that "stump-oratory, and speeches to Buncombe will not carry men to the immortal gods" (448).[62]

America's current democratic "constitutional arrangement" must be "with terrible throes, and travail . . . remodeled, abridged, extended, suppressed; torn asunder, [and] put together again." That process, it seemed, was well underway. "All forms of government are good," Ruskin argued, provided they observed the principles of natural hierarchy and social discipline (450). One can hardly imagine a social and cultural construct, short of an absolute dictatorship, more diametrically opposed to the liberal, democratic model that was being promoted throughout the North by the New England intelligentsia. On the other hand, Ruskin's idea of a proper social model could be seen as a virtual endorsement of Southern culture and Southern society.

As British conservatives amplified their criticism of the North's democratic culture, Northern liberals doubled down on their defense of it. They did this by promoting racial equality and equal rights, the inherent dignity of free labor and "the common man," and the importance of ideals. They also offered generous praise for America's home-grown authors and artists. Thus, while *Fraser's* and other English journals were carping about the crude inferiority of American literature, the *Commonwealth* ran a highly laudatory essay on April 10 on America's favorite "barbarian," Walt Whitman, "the rough singer of Brooklyn."

Meanwhile, the building of Confederate warships in British shipyards in violation of British law became a critical issue as work continued apace on the formidable Laird rams.[63] This situation, like the *Trent* crisis, became the subject of back-channel communications between Charles Sumner and Richard Cobden. Sumner told Cobden that the building of such ships posed a grave threat to his country and something had to be done to stop it. On April 2, in a letter marked "Private," Cobden responded. He told Sumner that "on receipt of your letter I communicated privately with Lord Russell, urging him to be more than passive in enforcing the law respecting the building of ships for the Confederate government." Russell told Cobden there was little he could do without proof that the ultimate purchaser was the Confederate government.[64]

Tensions continued to grow throughout the spring as the public rhetoric on both sides became increasingly heated. Around this time, Francis Newman, younger brother of the famous Cardinal Newman, expressed his concern in a private letter to Boston poet and novelist Epes Sargent. "The marvelous unanimity of Whigs & Tories in wishing success to your wicked rebels," he wrote, was pushing the two countries to the brink of war. "If our *nation* is consulted, it would rather vote down the House of Lords . . . rather than permit war with you." Knowing this, he declared, "what good care will be taken *not* to consult them." Despite this situation, Newman was confident that the will of the common people would still prevail because the political leaders "know too well the sympathies of the nation with the Free North to dare to take any active step to plunge us into war."[65]

Moncure Conway was now in England. His reports, which were published in the *Commonwealth* and also Greeley's *New York Tribune*, often described the indifference or hostility of Britain's literary giants. Around this time, he arranged a meeting with Thomas Carlyle. Conway later recounted in his *Autobiography* that Carlyle expressed the feeling that in America, "all was going wrong; our ballot-boxing, our negro emancipations, our cries for liberty, all showed nothing but that the nations [that is, states] were given over to believe a lie and be damned. . . . What the people were seeking," Carlyle insisted, "they would never obtain. Society was all wrong, and would go on getting worse." Conway also recorded that Alfred, Lord Tennyson was silent on the war because of the attacks on England in American newspapers, which he felt were "insulting and significant of a dominant puerility in America."[66]

In the North, attitudes toward Great Britain were now as hostile as at the height of the *Trent* crisis. *Harper's Weekly* recounted on April 25 that "every British dock-yard is now engaged in building steamers to capture and burn our merchant men, to run our blockade, and to bombard our defenseless sea-board cities." Meanwhile, "Lord Russell sees no ground" to stop such outrageous activities on the part of Southern sympathizers in Great Britain. "These events," the writer warned, "have very naturally aroused a general and intense hostility to England among all classes in this country." As a result, "there has never been a time when hatred of the English was so deep or wide-spread as it is at present."

The situation worsened when the Union army suffered another major defeat, this at Chancellorsville, Virginia (April 30–May 6). Still looking for a competent general to lead the Union forces following McClellan's dismissal, Lincoln appointed Joseph "Fighting Joe" Hooker to command the Army of the Potomac. His predecessor, Ambrose Burnside, had succeeded only in bringing disaster at Fredericksburg in December. He followed this up with the infamous "Mud March" in January. Burnside had planned on moving the army across the Rappahannock several miles above Fredericksburg to face the rebels once again, but heavy rains fell on January 20, turning the road to mud, into which the army ignominiously sank. Two days later, Burnside canceled the entire operation. Days after this he was replaced by Hooker.[67]

Although there were doubts about Hooker's fitness for the job, Lincoln's choices were limited, and morale did improve a bit under him. Unfortunately, at Chancellorsville, despite the Union army's considerable numerical superiority, a combination of Robert E. Lee's daring and Hooker's indecisiveness at a critical time in the battle resulted in another stunning victory for the Confederates. Following this, James McPherson reports, "Northern morale descended into the slough of despond."[68] There were now multiple sources of worry. Emerson's son, Edward, notes in his history of the Saturday Club that "the spring of this year was the darkest time of the war. The tide of the Rebellion seemed to be rising; the frightful sacrifice of our troops at Fredericksburg was recent, and the great failure of Chancellorsville was just coming on." In addition, "our finances were embarrassed. In the shipyards of Liverpool ironclad rams, against which our ports would be defenseless, were being built, unchecked, for our foe."[69]

In spite of these depressing developments, New England liberals understood that the longer the war went on, the more likely it was that the revolutionary reinvention of American democracy that they envisioned would be accomplished. The *Atlantic* continued to defend that cause against Northern defeatists and their British allies. Regardless of such opposition, this stalwart voice of New England liberalism remained confident that Northerners had the fortitude and the will to "put down the Rebellion [and] vindicate the majesty of the Law and sacredness of the Union." "Let us perform this duty fearlessly," the journal urged, "and leave the future with God."[70] That future would soon benefit from a new and potent addition to the American family, one whose arrival had been long delayed.

Chapter 13

New England Liberals Herald the Rise of the "African American"

British Critics Scoff

The principle of equality, New England liberals believed, was implied if not overtly stated in Lincoln's Emancipation Proclamation. Reunion on the basis of the status ante was no longer the object of the struggle. They believed that with the proclamation, America had taken a major step toward reinventing itself. There could be no turning back now. In the May issue of the *Atlantic Monthly*, David Wasson, a prominent second-generation Transcendentalist, gave voice to this idea.[1] His essay, "Shall We Compromise," stressed the importance of equality. It stood as a pointed riposte to Ruskin's recent "Essays on Political Economy," which insisted on inequality within a rigid social hierarchy.

Wasson argued that morality was the basis of social order and that universal freedom and equal rights were the hallmarks of a truly progressive and humane civilization. Rather than being truly civilized, the English model, like that of the South, was essentially a barbaric one, where those who have power use it to subjugate others. "This war," he wrote, "is an encounter between opposing tendencies in man—between the beast-of-prey that is in him and is always seeking brute domination, on the one hand, and the rational and moral elements of manhood . . . on the other."[2] Those who speak for the first, Wasson insisted, were on the wrong side of history.

The liberal women of the North also believed the war was part of a broader struggle for human rights everywhere, regardless of race or gender. Around this time, the Women's National Loyal League was formed, with Elizabeth Cady Stanton serving as president and Susan B. Anthony as secretary.[3] They made their liberal views clear in their "Address to the Soldiers of Our Second Revolution." It was prepared by Angelina Grimké Weld and published in the *National Anti-Slavery Standard* on May 30, 1863. Although born in Charleston, South Carolina, Weld, an ardent abolitionist, embraced the Puritan tradition of New England as a bulwark against the corrosive influence of slavery. "This war of slavery against freedom did not begin with the first shot at Sumter," she declared. "It began in 1620, when the Mayflower landed our fathers at Plymouth Rock, and the first slave ship landed its human cargo in Virginia. Then, for the first time," Weld asserted, "liberty and slavery stood face to face on this continent. From then till now, these antagonisms have struggled in incessant conflict."

Like Wasson, Weld insisted this was "a war of Principles" that had international implications. It is "a war upon the working classes whether white or black; a war against *man*, the world over. In this war, the black man was the first victim, the working man of whatever color the next." The war clarified the values on each side. "Now *all* who contend for the rights of labor, for free speech, for free schools, free suffrage, and a free government, securing to *all* life, liberty, and the pursuit of happiness, are driven to battle in defense of these or to fall with them," she declared. Indeed, for Weld and her liberal cohorts, "the South has waged this war against human rights," and the South must be defeated if those rights are to be secured. In this global struggle, it was now clear to many that the British had aligned themselves with the wrong side.

Confederate warships, both those already in service devastating Union shipping and those under construction in the Laird shipyards at Liverpool, remained foremost in the minds of many Americans at this time. With the rhetoric rising to the boiling point in the American press, sober minds on both sides of the Atlantic sought to turn down the heat. Richard Cobden wrote Charles Sumner on May 2 to assure him that "whatever may be the tone of his ill-mannered dispatches," Lord Russell "is sincerely alive to the necessity of putting an end to the equipping of ships of war in our harbors to be used against the Federal government by Confederates." In speaking of the most notorious of these predators, Cobden insisted that Russell was "*bona fide* in his aim to prevent the *Alabama* from leaving" and "was angry at the escape of that vessel." He obviously intended that Sumner would pass this information on to the administration, as he had done earlier during the *Trent* crisis. "It is necessary," Cobden told him, that "your government should know all this."[4]

Despite their often bellicose rhetoric, the prospect of a war with the United States over the issue of Confederate shipbuilding was not a welcomed one in the practical minds of most British conservatives. The possibility of swarms of Yankee privateers preying on British merchantmen, as well as the nightmarish fantasy of Union ironclads cruising up the Thames to terrorize London, tended to temper their rhetoric. The *Saturday Review* declared, "We in England . . . are desirous, by every means consistent with honour, to avert a war in which we should have to kill and injure persons speaking the English tongue, and which could not possibly do us any good whatever." The writer was also confident that "on the other side of the Atlantic . . . the Federal Government does not really wish to go to war with England." He was certain that the "topics of dispute between England and the Federal Government" will not "lead to grave results if they are discussed in a fair, temperate, and courteous manner."[5] That was the hope at least.

Throughout the month of May, Cobden continued as before to use his unique relationship with Sumner in an effort to defuse the growing tensions. Through this personal connection, he was able to function again as an unofficial go-between for the British government and the Americans. On May 22 he wrote again to Sumner. "I called on Lord Russell," he reported, "and read every word of your last long indictments against him and Lord Palmerston, to him. He was a little impatient under the treatment, but I got through every word." A half-hour conversation on the topic followed. Cobden told Sumner that just now in England "public opinion is recovering its senses" and "John Bull" is "becoming gradually reconciled. He . . . *now* begins to understand that he acted illegally in applauding those who furnished ships of war to prey on your commerce." Colden then assured Sumner, "*It will not be repeated.*"[6] It would take some months and a crisis, however, before the issue was finally resolved.

Meanwhile, Southern sympathizers in England sought to keep the pot boiling. John Roebuck criticized Union naval policy in a speech in the House of Commons. He was especially critical of American interference with British ships bound for neutral ports. The actions of the North, he claimed, were "unfit for . . . the civilized world." He also indicated that he was "prepared for war."[7] Around this time, John Stuart Mill wrote to Henry Fawcett, a British statesman and, like Mill, a respected economist. Mill told him that Roebuck's speech and others like it "were well calculated to provoke a reaction and . . . they have done so."[8] However, as Mill had hoped, Roebuck had finally overplayed his hand. Palmerston's government wished to *lower* the temperature in relations with America, and the prime minister made it evident that he did not appreciate such intemperate rhetoric at this critical time.[9]

In the meantime, on the war front in the West, Ulysses S. Grant began what would be a months-long siege of Vicksburg, Mississippi, on May 22. The Union army was in need of men and, on the same day, Secretary of War Edwin Stanton established the Bureau of Colored Troops. In England, conservative critics accused the North of racism and maintained that Black soldiers would be merely cannon fodder.[10] The enlistment of Blacks in the regular Union army had monumental implications. James McPherson contends that it "marked the transformation of a war to preserve the Union into a revolution to overthrow the old order," which is exactly what New England liberals hoped it would do.[11]

The Southern response was predictable. The *Liberator* reported on May 15 that the Confederate government had passed an ordinance "dooming to death or slavery every negro taken in arms, and every white officer who commands negro troops." This was a clear violation of international law and the protocols of civilized warfare, but British critics who had been so quick to condemn the Union for its "barbaric" tactics made no mention of it. In response, Lincoln asked General Henry Halleck to prepare an Order of Retaliation, which was issued on July 30. It declared that "the law of nations and the usages and customs of war as carried on by civilized powers, permit no distinction as to color in the treatment of prisoners of war." The Confederate ordinance was "a relapse into barbarism" that required a compelling response. "It is therefore ordered that for every soldier of the United States killed in violation of the laws of war, a rebel soldier shall be executed; and for every one enslaved by the enemy or sold into slavery, a rebel soldier shall be placed at hard labor."[12]

British liberals were pleased with the North's new policy on Black enlistments. Some, like Francis Newman, wished only that it would go faster. He wrote his Boston friend Epes Sargent, "The only thing that gives me uneasiness . . . [is] the apparent slowness with which you form black regiments." He added that the new policy did not change the thinking of English conservatives. "They come back to the old saying, '*I know* what the Northerners are made of, and what is their sentiment about the niggers.'" Newman concluded with a comment marked "*Private*." "I am sorry to say that my friend James Martineau [brother of Harriet] continues to talk for the South. He calls my lecture, 'clear, but unconvincing.' "[13]

The enlistment of Blacks in the regular Union army, along with the admirable performance of "contraband" soldiers earlier, helped bring about a sea change in how Northerners viewed Blacks. Authors in the North now began to depict Black people as romantic heroes. This year, novelist John T. Trowbridge published a romantic tale titled *Cudjo's Cave*. In it, he celebrated a "noble" Black protagonist who undergoes a variety of daring adventures. Trowbridge admitted that this was "a partisan book, frankly designed to fire the Northern heart."[14] His purpose was to project the image of a Black hero. With Colored Troops now bearing arms in defense of their country, Trowbridge felt free to take this bold step.

The dignity and strength of Black people were also on display at the Thirty-Eighth Annual National Academy of Design in New York City.[15] The works in this major exhibit of American art were another indication that American culture was moving away from European models. The presence of Blacks as a positive and integral element of that culture was now gradually being acknowledged as a result of the war.[16] A May 2 account of the exhibition by George Curtis in *Harper's Weekly* noted that "the war so absorbs the public mind . . . that as you ascend the staircase to the gallery . . . you will find yourself asking whether the noise of war has not reached the quiet studios of the painters."

Among the many items Curtis described was Henry Peters Gray's painting titled *American* (1862), where a "kneeling manly figure of a slave looks up into the eyes of the genius of America, who breaks his chains with one hand and offers him a sword with the other." It could have easily served as an enlistment poster for the Union army's new Black regiments. Curtis also pointed out Vincent Colyer's "Loyal Refugee," where the subject is "a slave boy escaping to [Union] lines." The picture, he declared, "opens the Exhibition with a thrill for we remember as we look at it that the flag of the United States is at last what it was meant to be, the flag of freedom to all mankind."

Curtis continued his commentary on the new exhibit in the June issue of *Harper's Magazine*. Of particular interest was the work of his friend and fellow New Englander, sculptor William Wetmore Story. Like Curtis, Story had many friends in the Saturday Club and recently enjoyed a dinner with them after returning from his long sojourn in Europe.[17] Curtis reported that Story "has lately completed probably the finest and most original of modern works in sculpture, 'The Libyan Sybil.'" The piece, which Story once described as his "anti-slavery sermon in stone," was destined to become one of his most admired works. It was exhibited at the London International Exhibition in 1862, where it was widely praised.[18]

The study presents a pensive and somewhat mysterious African female. She appears Athena-like in suggesting the complex qualities of wisdom and tenderness. "It is our peculiar interest in the African race at this time which nationalizes Story's statue of the Libyan Sybil," Curtis opined.[19] This major work by a major American artist was further evidence that the African presence was coming to be seen as an integral and positive element of American life.

Harriet Beecher Stowe made this point earlier in the *Atlantic Monthly* of April, where she revealed that the famous Black female abolitionist lecturer Sojourner Truth was the inspiration for Story's masterpiece. Stowe wrote, "Some years ago, when visiting Rome, I related Sojourner's history to Mr. Story." This history "worked in his mind and led him into the deeper recesses of the African nature,—those unexplored depths of being and feeling, mighty and dark as the gigantic depths of tropical forests. . . . A few days after, he told me he had conceived the idea of a statue which he should call the Libyan Sibyl." The result is captured in a description of the finished work from the *Athenaeum* that Stowe included in her article. "This Libyan woman is the closest of all the Sibyls," the account read. "She rests her shut mouth upon one closed palm, as if holding the African mystery deep in the brooding brain that looks out through the mournful, warning eyes. . . . Over her full bosom, mother of myriads as she was, hangs . . . [a] symbol. Her face has a Nubian cast, her hair wavy and plaited, as is meet."[20] It was this "Nubian" element that Curtis and Stowe both celebrated as indicative of a uniquely American work of art.

There were other signs of the emergence of a new American culture on display in the academy's exhibition, as Curtis noted in his *Harper's* essay. "While subject matter reveals nationality in landscape paintings," he observed, sculpture "reveals its time and country only by the characteristics of its subject," as was the case for Story. There were several examples "in the Academy Exhibition," he noted, including "the little clay group, *The Union Refugees*, by John Rogers. It is American," Curtis insisted, "for nowhere else does the sturdy form of the laborer have the full loftiness of man. It is not English, nor French, nor Italian, nor Swedish, but American."[21] For Curtis, such works reflected the values of America's liberal, democratic culture, the product of a racially diverse society of common people for whom labor was honorable and dignified, unlike imperial England and the aristocratic South. As Curtis was undoubtedly aware, Rogers produced several popular sculptures that reflected this diversity by depicting the strength and nobility of Blacks.

One of Rogers's most successful early pieces was *The Slave Auction* (1859), inspired in part by John Brown's famous raid. It features a strong and defiant Black man standing before an auctioneer. In describing the piece to a friend, Rogers wrote, "I have got a magnificent negro on the stand. He fairly makes a chill run over me when I look at him. He would be a capital fellow in a Harpers Ferry insurrection."[22] He later indicated that *The Slave Auction* "gave me probably more satisfaction than any other of my small groups."[23] Another popular piece was *The Wounded Scout: A Friend in the Swamp* (1864). In this sculpture, a badly wounded Union soldier is being helped to safety by a strong and determined fugitive slave. Like many others, Lydia Maria Child was deeply moved by the piece. Writing in the *Independent*, she declared, "There is more in that expressive group than the kind negro and the helpless white, put on equality by danger and suffering; it is a significant lesson of human brotherhood for all the coming ages."[24]

It was apparent to many that the growing demand for total emancipation and equal rights, coupled with the service of Black Union soldiers, first as contrabands and now as regulars, was giving rise to a new image of Blacks. Now, for the first time, their cause was the nation's cause. As "African Americans" they had a positive, even essential, role to play in fighting *for* that nation rather than *against* it as rebels and fugitives. The myth of "Negro inferiority" was gradually being displaced by images of courage and strength forged on the battlefield. This development would have profound social, political, and cultural consequences on both sides of the Atlantic. The acceptance of the African American as a member of the American family was vigorously promoted by the New England intelligentsia, even as the London *Times* and journals like *Blackwood's* and the *Saturday Review* disparaged it.

The number of Black soldiers continued to grow. Longfellow, like other members of the Saturday Club, was delighted to see that the Massachusetts 54th was taking shape rapidly. After observing the regiment marching on parade, he wrote the following in his journal: "In town. Saw the first black Regiment, or *Regiment of Blacks*, march through Beacon St!" The poet found the spectacle "an imposing sight; with something wild and strange about it, like a dream." It was a dream that was a long time in the making but now, "at last, the North consents to let the Negro fight for his freedom."[25]

Young Colonel Shaw was proud of his regiment. He wrote to John Malcolm Forbes that "the 54th has been a success from beginning to end. The drill & discipline are all that anyone could expect. Crowds of people came to our battalion drills & dress parades every afternoon, and we have heard nothing but words of praise & astonishment from friend & foe."[26] Robert's mother, Sarah, traveled to Boston to witness the send-off of the 54th. In a letter to Cairnes, she expressed her enthusiasm. "A thousand black men, with Enfield Muskets in their hands, marched through our streets on a bright and lovely morning. It was a splendid sight to see!" she told him. She knew this display of martial discipline and personal dignity would go a long way in changing America's perception of the Black man. "They conquered all prejudice by their manly soldierly bearing," she declared. Her son, by his willingness to lead these men, provided eloquent testimony to his confidence in them. "I will not trust myself," she told Cairnes, "to tell you of my feeling as I looked from the window upon my boy, 25 years ago a baby in my arms!" And then, in what would prove to be a prophetic moment, she added, "If I never see him again, I shall feel that he has not lived in vain."[27]

Several other prominent sons of New England rode off that morning along with the colonel. Henry James Sr.'s son, nineteen-year-old Garth Wilkinson, and James Russell Lowell's nephew, Charles Russell Lowell, had both accepted commissions in the new regiment. Young Lowell's fiancée was Colonel Shaw's nineteen-year-old sister, Josephine.[28] Both of Frederick Douglass's sons, Charles and Lewis, also volunteered for service in the 54th.[29] Eventually, another of Henry James's sons, Robertson James, would accept an officer's commission in the Massachusetts 55th, the second Black regiment formed in Massachusetts. Henry James Sr. later wrote that "the formation of the negro regiments affected us as a tremendous War measure," and the sympathies of the whole family were "all enlisted on behalf of the race that had sat in bondage."[30]

Cairnes wrote to Mrs. Shaw thanking her for the materials she recently provided. He also applauded "the progress of recruiting among the negroes" and "their behavior as soldiers," which showed that centuries of enslavement "has not crushed all manhood out of its victims."[31] The service of Black soldiers, as David Blight observes, was absolutely critical for the "recognition of [their] manhood and citizenship." That service would ultimately help determine "the meaning of race in an expanding American republic" and with it "the very future of black people in the society" and, one might add, in the world.[32]

On May 28, a large crowd had gathered to witness the departure of the 54th for the battlefront.[33] The course they followed through Boston's streets was the same route taken by Anthony Burns in his ignominious march back to bondage nine years earlier.[34] Not everyone in Boston felt inclined to celebrate this historic moment. The reactionary *Boston Pilot* was vile in its commentary on the new recruits. "One Southern regiment of white men would put twenty regiments of them to flight in half an hour," the paper declared. "Twenty thousand negroes on the march would be smelled ten miles distant. . . . There is not an American living that should not blush at the plan of making such a race the defenders of the national fame and power."[35] Members of Boston's exclusive Somerset Club hissed as the regiment passed by.[36] At one point, a group of roughnecks attempted to attack the men but was held back by police.[37]

These demonstrations of disdain were countered by the cheering of a large crowd that included Oliver Wendell Holmes, William Lloyd Garrison (who held a bust of John Brown in his arms), and Wendell Phillips. After marching on review past Governor Andrew and the Boston Common, the regiment continued down to Battery Wharf. Along the way, they sang Julia Ward Howe's "Battle Hymn of the Republic," published a year earlier in the *Atlantic Monthly*.

Governor Andrew's success in forming not one but two regiments of Colored Troops in Massachusetts led other Northern governors to follow suit. In less than a year, no fewer than ten more regiments were raised in Pennsylvania, New York, and surrounding states.[38] While New England liberals took pride in these new regiments, the feeling was far from universal in the Union army. One soldier wrote home to his family at this time from his post near Vicksburg to tell them he had been offered the position of first lieutenant in a "Miss. Reg. [of] Blacks." He turned down the opportunity, though, because he "thought it was much preferable to serve my Country with white men."[39] For many, however, that attitude would soon change as events in the war showed that Black soldiers could fight and die as bravely as their white comrades.

Harper's Weekly reported regularly on the progress of the Black soldiers. In "Union Troops" on June 20, the writer indicated that the army under Grant in the West continued to battle for control of the Mississippi. One of the main Confederate defenses was Port Hudson. After earlier, unsuccessful assaults, the position was attacked again on May 27, this time by a Union regiment of Louisiana Blacks. Although not successful, the regiments performed gallantly.[40] In a later article, *Harper's* offered praise for "the magnificent behavior of the Second Louisiana colored regiment at Port Hudson." The writer also pointed out that until recently "the bulk of the people of the United States" believed it was "unworthy of a civilized or a Christian nation to use in war soldiers whose skin was not white." Indeed, there was a nearly universal and "unchristian contempt of the blacks," but that was no longer the case.[41]

British feelings about the war were also beginning to change, at least a bit. Around this time, Francis Newman indicated in a letter to his Boston friend Epes Sargent that sympathy for the South was waning in Great Britain, although animosity toward the North remained strong. "Those who have substantially come round to your side," he wrote, "still go on moaning about the bloodshed & the ravage in a tone of *equal disapproval*, & cannot yet understand that . . . the South . . . alone is to blame; nay, not alone," he added. "Englishmen who have fostered the South share the blame largely."[42]

During this critical time, Norton's *New England Loyal Publication Society* continued to expand its subscription list, spreading words of hope and encouragement to an ever larger audience. As of early June, the organization was mailing out news and editorials to 1,223 recipients. On June 4, it published its first large-sheet broadside.[43] At this point, Norton invited George Bancroft, the distinguished historian and Democratic leader, to contribute. As noted earlier, although a conservative by nature, Bancroft was a staunch opponent of slavery and a War Democrat. He told Norton that, while sympathetic with his goals, "I do not think I had better write specifically for the press which you superintend with so much zeal, ability, and disinterestedness." Unlike Norton, Bancroft was uncertain whether slavery would finally be abolished. "I hope we shall come out of this war without slavery," he stated, "but as yet I cannot see that result clearly." Reflecting the recent dramatic changes in their status in American society, Bancroft expressed his belief that the decision will ultimately depend on Blacks themselves, but, he warned, "the white man will betray them, if he can."[44]

Moncure Conway continued to send reports home to the *Commonwealth* recounting his efforts to drum up support for the North, especially among English intellectuals. So far, the results were not encouraging. In "A Visit to Thomas Carlyle" (June 6), Conway reported that after an initial inquiry about his closest American friend, Ralph Waldo Emerson, Carlyle shared his views on "the great social problems of the hour." At that moment, Conway found himself "face to face with . . . a powerful Pessimist," whose "dreary skepticism" chilled him. He believed that the end result of the American war will be catastrophic and that "for such men as all this Liberty is producing, one may well be thankful that a good supply of powder and shot is preparing."

Later in the month, the *Commonwealth* published on June 19 Conway's account of his visit to "Cambridge University," where "the general opinion . . . was adverse to the North. Much of this," he noted, "is owing to the unwearied efforts of Rev. Charles Kingsley, who has lectured and written and talked on the side of the Southern oppressors until many of his once earnest friends such as [Thomas] Hughes and [Edward] Dicey speak of him as a 'lost leader.'" Kingsley's abrupt turn to the right, Conway surmised, was the result of a desire for personal gain. "He has given up his former brave testimonies for justice and Humanity, for a chaplaincy to the Prince of Wales and a reception amongst the aristocracy."

Charles Kingsley was a shocking disappointment to many New Englanders. He proved to be nearly as reactionary and racist as Carlyle. Kingsley rejected John Stuart Mills's argument for expanding suffrage in England on the principle of equal rights because he believed that people were *not* equal. According to Douglas Lorimer, "In Kingsley's view, Mill and others like him overlooked 'the harsh school of facts' which meant they 'disparage, if not totally deny, the congenital differences of character in individuals, and still more in races.'"[45]

Even though he was generally disappointed with the students and faculty at Cambridge, Conway did find some friends of the Union there. Among them "Mr. [Leslie] Stephen, Fellow of Trinity Hall who goes in June to America, and Dr.[William] Whewell, their president, and Mr. [Henry] Fawcett." These were but a small minority, however. The sad fact was that "the nobility are . . . against us; and so great is the disposition in all classes to truckle to them, that many professed abolitionists are glad enough to find excuses in our errors and . . . to oppose our cause." Very soon, developments on the battlefield would bring about a dramatic change in the course of the war, one that would have a significant impact on that cause.

Chapter 14

Union Victories and Colored Soldiers Change the Course and Complexion of the War

Confederate victories like that at Chancellorsville in May 1863 led to increased calls in England for intervention to bring about a cessation of hostilities. When these were repeatedly rejected by the Palmerston government, recognition became the alternative. On June 30, a motion calling for recognition was introduced in Parliament by John Arthur Roebuck.[1] It found little support from Palmerston's government, and John Bright virtually destroyed Roebuck in the debate. The motion was withdrawn on July 13 without ever coming to a vote.[2]

Roebuck's effort would prove to be the high-water mark of Confederate hopes for recognition. Prior to this, William Lindsay and Roebuck, on their own initiative, had met with Emperor Napoleon III, a move that was not well received back in England.[3] The perception was that the opportunity for such an action was long past. Ephraim Adams reports that "as in Parliament, so in the public press, immediate recognition of the Confederacy received little support."[4] The Tory *Examiner* (July 4) observed, "Mr. Roebuck was strong on every point but the fact. He showed many reasons for desiring the independence of the Confederacy, but he did not even attempt to show the independence had been achieved."[5]

At the same time, the Laird rams were still a deep concern and a continuing source of tensions. Samuel May suggested in a letter to his British friend Richard Webb that the growing crisis was beginning to strain relations even between the North and its British allies. While praising "Prof. Newman" as a supporter who, "of all Englishmen, has said the best and wisest & truest things of our war," May felt that Newman had "excused & defended England & the English Govt too far & too long. . . . I am not disputing the fact of the English common people being kind & right, & I exult in such noble men as Newman, . . . Cairnes, Mill, Hall, Forster, Hughes, etc. etc.," he declared, "but when we speak of *England* we mean the attitude of the *whole nation* in *the aggregate*, Govt & people." The former, he believed, had been terribly remiss "in regard to the piratical vessels built and fitted out in her ports to burn American ships and destroy American property."[6] May, like many other New Englanders, felt the situation was fast becoming intolerable.

With tensions growing, the risk of a naval war with the United States was now a more dire concern to British authorities than at the beginning of the war. One reason for this was the surprising and rapid development of ironclad ships in the Union navy. In a July article in the *Edinburgh Review*, Edward Plunkett, an expert on British naval affairs, pointed out that the Americans had made startling progress in this new technology. As a result, "those wooden walls which we have trusted in for centuries [have been] rendered useless." It was on these that England depended for much of her "internal peace and order." They provided "security at home" and "consideration abroad." In Plunkett's view, their loss could lead to "a most serious calamity."[7]

In addition to this new sense of vulnerability, the British had cause to be concerned over the deep animosity in America directed toward the once-beloved mother country. Evidence of this was everywhere. Oliver Wendell Holmes unleashed a bitter attack in a Fourth of July address ominously titled "The Inevitable Trial." After summarizing in blunt, critical terms the case against the British to date, he declared that the war had become an international struggle to defend the principles of universal freedom and equal rights. "Not to have fought would have been false to liberty everywhere," he declared. This fact explained the British opposition. They feared that "the two halves of this Union are the two blades of the shears . . . that will sooner or later cut into shreds the old charters of tyranny."[8] In his personal copy of the privately printed text, Holmes inscribed marginal notes that were probably late additions. "We know our enemies," he wrote, "and they are the enemies of popular rights. We know our friends, and they are the foremost champions of political and social progress."[9]

Like many others, Holmes also noted the growing respect for African Americans, now represented by the gallant Black soldiers adding their considerable strength to the cause of universal freedom. At one time, he observed, fugitive slaves were hunted through the streets of Boston, but just a few weeks ago, "a regiment of colored soldiers, many of them bearing the marks of the slave-driver's whip on their backs, marched out before the vast multitude, tremulous with newly-stirred sympathies, through the streets of the same city, to fight our battles in the name of God and Liberty."[10] Such a compelling sign of the growth of racial equality in the North was sure to be unnerving for the British governing class.

It was around this time that another English friend arrived in Boston, young Leslie Stephen, aspiring writer and future father of Virginia Woolf. Stephen had been a staunch defender of the North as an instructor at Cambridge where, as Conway had recently testified, there were many supporters of the Confederate cause. After several debates in which matters of fact were frequently in dispute, he decided to travel to America and learn the truth for himself.[11] Stephen came with letters of introduction from John Bright and Edward Dicey, the *Macmillan's* writer who had been so well received just a year before. With these, he was able to make the acquaintance of many of New England's most distinguished writers and intellectuals. Eventually, he would meet President Lincoln.[12]

As it turned out, Stephen arrived in America just at the time a major event was about to change dramatically the course of the war. On July 4, the *Saturday Review* reported on a Confederate "invasion in force of Maryland and Pennsylvania" under General Robert E. Lee. The Army of the Potomac under "Fighting Joe" Hooker was preparing to respond. Recognizing the potential geopolitical significance of these movements, along with Grant's continuing siege of Vicksburg, the article envisioned two possible strategic outcomes. "If Lee crushes Hooker, and Johnstone [*sic*] relieves Vicksburg," the writer postulated, "the right of the Government at Washington to suppress the rebellion will be, at last, seriously disputed." On the other hand, "if the Confederate armies should incur heavy reverses, the triumph of peaceable counsels may be indefinitely postponed."[13] Little did this writer realize that the matter had already been decisively settled in the most important battle of the war.

Lee's dramatic victory over Hooker at Chancellorsville in early May had reinforced the belief of conservatives on both sides of the Atlantic that the war was unwinnable for the North. In England, it brought renewed calls for recognition and even intervention. In the North, it emboldened Copperheads in their demand for a negotiated end to the war, while adding momentum to a growing peace movement. Another major victory over the mighty Army of the Potomac, especially one on Northern soil, could bring these efforts to fruition and frustrate Lincoln's commitment to emancipation and final victory. British conservatives were increasingly confident that such a victory was imminent. On July 9, the London *Times* predicted that Lee would soon capture Washington.[14]

Lee's army of almost 80,000 men was on the move in early June. Hooker put the Army of the Potomac, over 90,000 men, into play to shadow Lee's movement.[15] Lincoln saw this as an opportunity to confront and smash the Army of Northern Virginia in a definitive battle. Hooker, however, suggested avoiding Lee and storming Richmond. Lincoln began to doubt Hooker's resolve as a battlefield commander, and he replaced him with a competent but untested General George Meade on June 20.[16] Lee began to concentrate his forces in the area of Gettysburg, a small town that happened to be at the convergence of a dozen roads. When the first elements of his army arrived there, they were surprised to find two brigades of Union cavalry under the command of battle-worn and tenacious Colonel John Buford. They were able to hold the Confederate force at bay until the lead elements of Meade's forces could arrive.[17]

The Battle of Gettysburg began on July 1 and ended on July 3. It was the bloodiest battle of the Civil War, and it resulted in a resounding defeat for Lee's gallant but—as was now evident—not invincible Army of Northern Virginia. The three days of fighting produced over 51,000 casualties. Lee lost nearly half his army, and the Confederate cause was dealt a crushing blow from which it would never recover. The effect of the loss was amplified greatly by the news that the day after Lee's defeat, Vicksburg also fell. After a forty-six-day siege, General John C. Pemberton surrendered his army of 28,000 men to the forces of Ulysses S. Grant.

Unfortunately, the victory at Gettysburg was not as complete as Lincoln had hoped.[18] With his men exhausted, the ever-cautious Meade failed to deliver a final, crushing blow to Lee's retreating army, which would live to fight another day. As a result, the war would drag on for another two years, but a turning point had been reached. It was now clear to almost everyone that the Union would eventually prevail.[19] In Europe, especially England, the Union victories dashed all remaining hope for recognition or intervention of any sort. Moreover, the cotton famine had been relieved somewhat as alternative sources from other countries such as India and Egypt were developed. Additionally, a recent uprising in Poland against the Russians caused the English government to turn its attention to European affairs.

A month after the defeats at Gettysburg and Vicksburg, James Mason, the Confederate envoy, who had been effectively ignored by Lord Russell for some time, was withdrawn by the Confederate government.[20] Despite these positive developments for the Union, tensions between the United States and Great Britain remained high. The issue of the Laird rams was still unsettled, and the deep animosity that had been growing between the people of the North and those they now called simply "the English" had not abated. This bitterness was based as much on cultural as on political differences, and it was largely unchanged by developments on the battlefield. The central issue concerned the question of equality and human rights.

News of Lee's repulse at Gettysburg reached London on July 16. It was reported by the *Times* two days later as virtually a Southern victory since, untypically, the Northern army was on the defensive in the battle. By July 20, details concerning events at Gettysburg and Vicksburg had been received, and the *Times* finally acknowledged the significance of the Union victories. However, as Ephraim Adams reports, "efforts were made to prove that these events simply showed that neither side could conquer the other."[21] Eventually, the truth of the matter became apparent, and the English critics reacted predictably. In a letter penned on July 23, Henry Adams told his brother Charles that it "was just as though a bucket of iced-water were thrown into their faces. . . . As our success was great, so rose equally the spirit of hatred on this side. Never before since the *Trent* affair has it shown itself so universal and spiteful as now."[22]

As a result of the Union victories, universal emancipation was now a real possibility. This would, however, require truly revolutionary changes in the nation's Constitution. The path to such change would be a difficult one, but so was winning the war. The *Atlantic Monthly* in July presented both a moral and a legal argument for universal emancipation. The author, Robert Dale Owen, was a former congressman and social reformer from Indiana.[23] He argued that the Constitution of the United States was, like all things of human origin, "imperfect." Therefore, "it was by its founders properly made subject to amendment." Developments in the war showed clearly that change was now in order. "By the President's Proclamation some three millions of slaves have been already declared free," but those in the border states remain in bondage, Owen noted. "Can we maintain in perpetuity so anomalous a condition of things? Clearly not." Slavery must end, he insisted. The time had come for a constitutional guarantee of freedom and equality before the law for all.[24]

Such bold declarations were disturbing to both English and American conservatives. Things were clearly getting out of hand. A blunt clarification of sensible, traditional values was called for. Southern propagandist Henry Hotze argued in the London *Index* that "*the most dangerous dogma of modern times* and that which, unconsciously to the majority of those who accept it, underlies nearly every social, political, and religious heresy which mars our civilization, is the dogma of the equality of man."[25]

Two days later, the *Saturday Review* echoed this idea in a critique of Lincoln's brief remarks to a group of serenaders who had appeared spontaneously at the White House shortly after news of the victory at Gettysburg reached Washington. In his brief, extemporaneous address to the joyful crowd, Lincoln offered thanks to "Almighty God" that a great victory had been achieved against "a gigantic Rebellion" that sought "to overthrow the principle that all men are created equal." It was significant, the president noted, that it was on the Fourth of July that "the cohorts of those who opposed the declaration that all men are created equal, 'turned tail' and run." After expressing his appreciation "to the many brave officers and soldiers who have fought in the cause of the Union and liberties of the country from the beginning of the war," he concluded his remarks.[26]

The *Saturday Review* found this brief address offensive, especially Lincoln's statement on human equality. The writer argued that this notion was not only vulgar, it was also dangerous. "Mr. Lincoln's address to the serenaders," he observed, "apart from the grotesque oddity of a style in which simplicity is carried to the last extreme of homeliness . . . he has the assurance to pretend that the war of the North against the South is, and all along has been, a war on behalf of the immortal and 'self-evident' Fourth-of-July doctrine that 'all men are created equal.' To hear him, it is a war of abolitionism against slavery," the author declared. The fact that this idea was gaining ground in the North at a time when the military tide was clearly turning in its favor had serious implications for English elites. It now seemed, the *Review* noted, that "the North is in arms to assert and establish the civil and political equality of all men, and to make the negro a free and independent fellow-citizen of the white," a development at once both astounding and unnerving.[27]

The twin victories at Vicksburg and Gettysburg were a blow to the Copperhead Democrats and the agenda of the Peace Party in the North. Nevertheless, they remained dedicated to the conservative cause, which at this point developed an even deeper racist inflection. The *Boston Statesman and Weekly Post* of July 10 reported on a "Mass Meeting of Democrats in

Concord, N.H.," that was attended by thousands to press their demand for "the Constitution as it is, the Union as it was." Copperheads did their best to incite the masses to resist the effort to turn the war into a revolutionary human rights crusade. This, in combination with a growing resentment of the new conscription law, eventually culminated in the so-called "Draft Riots" in New York, Boston, and several other Northern cities. In addition to being anti-draft, these riots were also anti-government and anti-Black. The worst was in New York City July 11–17. The mayhem there resulted in many injuries and deaths as well as significant property damage. A half-dozen innocent Blacks were lynched, scores brutalized, and an African American orphan asylum was burned to the ground. The homes of George Curtis and Sarah Shaw were threatened.[28]

Eventually, several regiments of George Meade's army, fresh from the battlefield at Gettysburg, were rushed to New York, where they succeeded in restoring order. It was, at the time, the worst riot in American history. Over one hundred people were killed.[29] The riot in Boston, which broke out on July 14, was violent but less deadly than that in New York. Governor Andrew was attending the Harvard Commencement in Cambridge when the mayhem started. He returned to Boston on the instant and, after realizing the seriousness of the situation, called in elements of the Union army serving at the harbor forts and nearby training camps to restore order.[30]

For British critics, the riots offered further proof of the deeply flawed character of Northern democracy. Charles Dickens told a correspondent that his prediction that conscription would not succeed was borne out by the New York riots. "I still [take] the liberty to suppose that I [know] something of the [American] people," who "are the greatest and the meanest of scoundrels," he wrote.[31] The riots also caused concern among the friends of the Union in England. Elizabeth Gaskell wrote to Norton asking what it all meant. "It is so impossible to learn the truth here about anything in America, . . . Is not this violent resistance to the conscription in New York very bad?" she asked. Gaskell, as usual, wished to counter the bad press in England using information from her American friend. "Please write us a political letter," she urged.[32]

Leslie Stephen arrived in Boston early in the month, just in time to witness the impact of the formation of Black regiments. During his visit, he wrote detailed letters to his mother and his Cambridge colleague, British liberal economist Henry Fawcett, one of Mill's close associates and a fellow Union supporter. The purpose of Stephen's letters was to provide his English friends with firsthand evidence that he hoped would support the liberal cause.[33] "The first night I was here," Stephen told his mother, "I went to a public meeting where speeches were being made about a plan for providing for the families of the nigger regiments that are now being raised." An army chaplain "talked about the poor negro looking down at his blue pants and counting the glittering buttons on his coat—each button with the American eagle on it—and feeling a new manhood glowing all through his nerves. . . . I have also seen some fine-looking nigger soldiers, and am told that a nigger regiment [the 54th] left this place the other day amidst tremendous enthusiasm—which is remarkable, if true."[34]

Stephen also told his mother that he met Oliver Wendell Holmes Sr., who had recently delivered a feisty, anti-British Fourth of July address. In speaking of the war, Holmes told him his son had been wounded three times and was still in service. Stephen was impressed and told his mother, "From all I can hear and see, there never was a more atrocious lie than the common one of the [London] *Times* about these people [not] fighting themselves and getting Germans and Irish to fight for them. You can't speak about any one without hearing about his or her relatives' losses."[35] Among the most notable of the young New Englanders currently serving was Colonel Robert Gould Shaw. From the time he first arrived with his troops on the South Carolina coast, Shaw was eager to join the fray. He wrote his mother, "I want to get my men alongside of white troops, and into a good fight if there is to be one."[36]

He was about to get his wish. Union forces under General Quincy Adams Gilmore planned an attack on Fort Sumter in Charleston, where the war began. The first element of the operation was an assault on Fort Wagner, located at the mouth of the harbor on Morris Island. A force under General George C. Strong, with the 54th in the lead, was to attack at dawn on July 18. As Allan Nevins reports, "when Strong offered the regiment this post of honor, Robert Gould Shaw might have declined, for his Negro troops had been marching for two days through sand and marsh, in pitiless heat, and were worn out; but he accepted with exultation."[37] This was the moment they had all been waiting for.

When the order came to attack, Colonel Shaw moved his men out. As the troops reached the outskirts of Wagner, the rebels unleashed a storm of musket fire upon them, followed by hand grenades and artillery. Under the withering onslaught, many men fell. Nevertheless, eventually almost half the regiment succeeded in mounting the parapet and reaching the interior of the fort, where they planted the colors before being forced to retreat. The attack was a magnificent failure. Of the 600 men of the 54th who participated, 272 were killed, wounded, or captured. Henry James Sr.'s son Wilky was severely wounded.[38] Colonel Shaw died with his men, shot through the heart. When a request was later made for his body, a common wartime courtesy, a Confederate officer reportedly replied, "We have buried him with his niggers."

Robert Shaw's body was never recovered, but his family felt no remorse over the fact. His father urged against any further effort, saying, "We hold that a soldier's burial place is on the field where he has fallen."[39] The symbolism of the act was compelling. This commingling of Black and white corpses came to typify for many the brotherhood of mankind, here manifest in death as in life. The *National Anti-Slavery Standard* commented that "neither death nor the grave have divided the young martyr and hero from the race for which he died." *Harper's Weekly*, where Curtis (whose sister was Shaw's widow) would soon be serving as political editor, declared, "Where else could [Colonel Shaw] be so nobly and fitly buried? . . . Where should he be buried but with them?"[40]

This was a dramatic and historic event in the history of race in America. As Gary Scharnhorst notes, when Shaw was buried with his soldiers, "their common grave [became] a type of sacred sepulcher consecrated by blood." Very soon, at least nine poems memorializing Robert Gould Shaw's burial "beneath a pile of Negroes" were published in newspapers and magazines throughout the North.[41] Eventually, Shaw became one of the most famous heroes of the war.[42] The implications of the attack at Wagner and the burial that followed were telling. Both sides seemed to realize this almost immediately.[43]

The manly dignity displayed by Black soldiers, as well as their patriotism, was now frequently celebrated in the visual arts, with striking effect. One example, the chromolithograph *Come and Join Us Brothers*, depicted an African American unit at attention in full-dress uniforms as Black soldiers take possession of their new status, shown by their firm grasp of the American flag. As Harold Holzer and Mark Neely point out, in this image, "an African American was portrayed clutching the flag himself, perhaps for the first time in American iconography." Similarly, in *Storming Fort Wagner*, "the flag billowing at the apex of the design is held aloft by an African American, and the dead and dying soldiers falling beneath it are shown sacrificing their lives for it." Another, *The End of the Rebellion in the United States*, showed that "African Americans had, under that flag, raised themselves from shackled slaves to armed freedom fighters."[44]

While the North celebrated these Black warriors, they were disparaged and defamed in the South.[45]

The 54th's surviving troops took heart, even in the midst of defeat. They knew they had accomplished something extraordinary, something that would help determine the fate of the Black man in America and the fate of democracy everywhere. Sergeant-Major Lewis Douglass, son of Frederick, wrote to his fiancée two days after the battle. He told her that the 54th had now "established its reputation as a fighting regiment," and he assured her that "not a single man flinched. . . . I wish we had a hundred thousand colored troops," he said. "We would put an end to this war."[46] Eventually Douglass's wish, and then some, would come true. Wagner had clearly demonstrated to the world the courage and skill of Black soldiers.[47]

The impact of the battle was felt through the ranks and, in some cases, caused a dramatic turnaround in attitudes. In one instance a young enlisted man had earlier written to his father that "the niggers are used much better than the [white] soldiers, and there is not a soldier who does not hate the sight of a nigger. . . . I despise them like dirt." Just ten days later, after witnessing the attack on Fort Wagner, he wrote to his cousin from his camp at Hilton Head, South Carolina. This time, he expressed a very different opinion of his Black comrades. "When you hear any one remark that nigger soldiers will not fight," he told her, "please request them to come down here and judge for themselves. The 54th Mass Infantry 'colored' is as good a fighting regiment as there is. . . . This was proved at the charge on Fort Wagner."[48]

Coming in the wake of the racist-fueled draft riots in New York, the heroism of the soldiers of the 54th made an important statement. As James McPherson indicates, "Few Republican newspapers failed to point the moral: black men who fought for the Union deserved more respect than white men who fought against it."[49] The normally conservative *North American Review* acknowledged in July that Blacks in America were Americans, after all. In speaking against the Lincoln administration's recent proposal for the colonization of emancipated slaves, the *North American* indicated that the plan was simply unacceptable. The writer pointed out that, "though they love and honor [Lincoln] as their great benefactor and sincere friend, [the Negroes] are not attracted by the prospect held out to them. . . . They have no idea of being 'removed.' They deny that they are foreigners, and claim the privilege of remaining in their own country." The writer concurred with this view. "No one of a different race can plan acceptably for them. They must work out their own salvation, and they will do it in due time. We must have patience," he advised.[50]

The heroism of Shaw and his men was celebrated in England by friends of the Union. Elizabeth Gaskell published a personal memorial to Robert Gould Shaw in *Macmillan's Magazine*.[51] Even the London *Times* when it first reported on the attack on Fort Wagner indicated that "after a furious bombardment of the fort . . . repeated and desperate attempts were made to dislodge the Confederates." The *Times* went on to note that "two regiments of negro troops who participated in the attack are described as having fought with great bravery. It is stated that the sight of them so infuriated the Confederates that wherever they appeared the whole fire of the fort was concentrated upon them until they retired out of range."[52] Just one week later, September 10, the *Times* reverted to its more typical negativity. A "Letter to the Editor" asserted that "the North may have been able to make use of negro troops at Port Hudson and Fort Wagner; but, it is said, they only rushed on Southern cannon to avoid falling back on Abolition bayonets, and, if negroes are once called into the conflict, the 'docile and submissive' nature of the 'inferior creature' will make him a far more powerful instrument in the hands of his 'beloved master' in the South than under the lash of Northern tyranny."

Such propaganda was, by now, merely wishful thinking. Leslie Stephen wrote to his mother on July 21, "That emancipation must ultimately be the end of the war is becoming more and more certain. . . . Here is a neat fact for old [Henry] Fawcett to throw at any of the Spence school, as showing the progress of emancipation in the North." He then related the story of Shaw and the 54th. Stephen also told his mother he had met several Harvard people, "including Lowell, Holmes, Dana, and others," all Saturday Club men, as it turns out. He found them "really very pleasant, well-educated men," and all were "of some literary name." He also met Wendell Phillips and William Lloyd Garrison, the leaders of the antislavery movement. Stephen found both to be charming and sincere, not the "fanatics" that British critics often depicted them as being.[53]

While Stephen was writing home about his experience in America, Hawthorne reflected on English social conditions in a long article in the *Atlantic Monthly* in September. Seen in its historical context, "Outside Glimpses of English Poverty" was yet another indicator of the culture war between New and Old England that had been alternating between a simmer and a full boil for some time.[54] The article was based on Hawthorne's experience in England as American consul to Liverpool. It painted a truly gruesome picture of the dire conditions endured by the poor of England. Hawthorne recounted passing through a shabby neighborhood where the poor "lie down . . . [in] stifled and squalid rooms" at night or "sulkily elbow one another . . . when a settled rain drives them within doors" during the day. He found even "worse horrors than it is worth while . . . to admit into one's imagination." The children of these wretched poor were treated like "an impish progeny . . . below the common sphere of humanity. . . . It might almost make a man doubt the existence of his own soul," Hawthorne wrote, "to observe how Nature has flung these little wretches into the street and left them there, so evidently regarding them as nothing worth, and how all mankind acquiesces in the great mother's estimate of her offspring." These innocent children, who resembled the walking dead, had "been buried under this dirt-heap, plunged into this cesspool of misery and vice!" And no one seemed to care.

Hawthorne concluded this disturbing piece with a reflection on the vast disparity between the privileged rich and the wretched poor in the very heart of the great English empire. The wealthy aristocrats, he noted "live on their abundance in one of those stately and English homes, such as no other people ever created or inherited, a hall set far and safe within its own private grounds." "All this fair property," he noted, "seemed more exclusively and inalienably their own because of its descent through many forefathers."

Such splendid luxury in a land with such excruciating poverty begged the question of social justice. "Is or is not, the system wrong," Hawthorne asked, "that gives one married pair so immense a superfluity of luxurious home, and shuts out a million others from any home whatever?" Like others among his liberal New England friends, Hawthorne predicted that there would be a day of reckoning. "One day or another, safe as they deem themselves, and safe as the hereditary temper of the people really tends to make them," he warned, "the gentlemen of England will be compelled to face this question."[55] It was statements such as these, emanating with increasing frequency from democratic America, that kept British conservatives like Robert Cecil up at night.

Hawthorne was not alone in such negative feelings toward the mother country. Throughout the summer, anti-British sentiment swelled in New England, due in part to the continuing devastation caused by Confederate raiders built in British shipyards. Moreover, with its busy ports, the people of New England felt a special concern regarding the possible escape of the Laird rams, which were now nearing completion. If these powerful vessels of war were allowed to take to sea under Confederate command, the coastal towns and cities of New England could be at risk. With tensions growing, Sumner warned John Bright in a letter that "your Government recklessly and heartlessly seems bent on war."[56]

In the midst of the crisis over the Laird rams and the simmering anger toward England, Emerson's longtime friend, British literary lion Thomas Carlyle, dropped a bombshell. The August issue of *Macmillan's Magazine* included his "Ilias (Americana) in Nuce" (The American Iliad in a nutshell). In this brief squib of barely a hundred words, Carlyle depicted the characters "Peter of the North" and "Paul of the South" as beating each other's brains out because one hired "servants by the month or the day" and the other hired "servants for life."[57] Carlyle, like Ruskin and other British conservatives, believed there was little difference between slaves and working people, and this was his way of satirizing what he considered the foolishness and irony of the American conflict. He saw the war as a great tragedy involving the "self-murder of a million brother Englishmen, for the sake of sheer phantasms, and totally false theories upon the Nigger." On one occasion, he referred to the war as "Nigger-Agony."[58]

Like other Victorian elites, Carlyle believed American democracy was founded on a fundamental falsehood, namely, that all men are created equal. In his view, British governance was more enlightened because it recognized a natural hierarchy based on "difference."[59] Carlyle wrote to his brother in November 1862 that he looked "with a pity and awe . . . on the Consummation of Constitutional Palaver and Universal Suffrage, and our poor Yankee Brothers tearing one another in pieces about Nothing at all."[60] The expression of this view in his "Iliad" ignited a firestorm of criticism.

Northerners were outraged by this latest evidence of British spitefulness and the continuing and unforgivable perfidy of the British intellectual and artistic classes. Carlyle's views on slavery were well known before this and, not surprisingly, he was a favorite with Southerners and their English supporters. His reported comments at social gatherings and his conversations with visitors added to the negative feeling.[61] This latest blow, however, was particularly resented not only because it came at a time of growing tension between Great Britain and the United States but also because Carlyle had once been deeply respected by New England poets and thinkers, especially the Transcendentalists.[62]

English liberals were also offended. Frederick Denison Maurice, a British Christian Socialist, felt compelled to respond. In an August 8 *Spectator* essay, he made it clear that Carlyle's opinion, which was shared by most English conservatives, was an anachronism in a world where truly progressive nations embraced the principle of universal freedom. Maurice opined that "T. C.'s dealings with the 'Nigger Question' have not been fortunate. Some years have passed since he favored us with a pamphlet under that title, in which the most defective side of his philosophy came uppermost, asserting . . . the inherent right of the white man to force from the black man an amount of work satisfactory to the white man's mind." It was just this kind of thinking that aligned Carlyle, Ruskin, Kingsley, Cecil, and other prominent conservatives with the Confederacy.[63]

There were many heated responses to Carlyle in the weeks and months that followed as the bitter acrimony between New and Old England continued to reveal the now vast differences between the two cultures. The *Commonwealth* was among the first, on August 21. In "Carlyle and Emerson," the author noted, "Two literary men now living have more influenced thought among people who speak English than any in this century. They are Thomas Carlyle and Ralph Waldo Emerson. . . . We print today the latest public utterance of both those men." What the journal reprinted was Emerson's "Boston Hymn," wherein he expressed a strong condemnation of kings, aristocrats, and slavery, side by side with Carlyle's "Ilias." Six days later, the *New England Loyal Publication Society* did the same. In an accompanying editorial, Norton asserted that Carlyle's quip was yet another example of English feeling regarding the war that showed "a spirit of ignorance, arrogance, and inhuman indifference to the cause of liberty and justice."[64] Not since the American Revolution had the differences between the two cultures been so sharply defined.

The *Liberator* of August 28 also reprinted Carlyle's "Ilias," along with a letter by "General Thompson" addressed to "the Working-men" of England. Thompson described Carlyle's piece as an insult to the dignity of labor. "This is the stuff the men are made of, who refuse you the ballot," he told them. They believe, Thompson asserted, that the difference between the condition of a British workingman and that of a Southern slave—"who is whipped as many times a day as suits his masters, who is not allowed marriage except as a dog may be, whose children are sold in different markets like suckling pigs"—is that one is "hired by the month or day, and the others are hired for life." This "outrageous and insulting falsehood," Thompson declaimed, was "thrust into your faces under disguise of [a] joke and literary slang."[65] The workingmen of England, however, were not laughing.

Carlyle's equating of American slaves with British laborers provided yet another strong incentive for those laborers to embrace the Union cause. The support of these voteless men was critical in the continuing effort to blunt the South's influence with the British governing class. Cobden wrote to Sumner at this time that "Confederate agents . . . have pressed for recognition on England and France with persistent energy from the first." The fact that the British government had not given in to this pressure, "considering how much more we have suffered than other people from the blockade," was remarkable. "This," he said, "I attribute entirely to the honorable attitude assumed by our working population."[66]

With the growth of the alliance between British laborers and the North, two things began to happen in the British press. The first was that fewer conservatives were willing to claim that the war was *not* about slavery. The second was that the argument shifted more and more to the claim that Blacks were racially inferior. The conservative talking point was that they may not deserve to be slaves, but they were still naturally inferior and, like inferior races everywhere, they both require and benefit from the guidance of a superior race. This argument was employed by the British governing class to justify their imperial polity—both morally and pragmatically—while holding the advancing forces of democracy at bay. As John Ruskin had recently confirmed in his *Fraser's* essay, "Political Economy," the subordination of inferiors was a principle that also applied to the British working class, since "slave" and "laborer" were interchangeable terms.

Reactions to Carlyle's piece continued throughout the month and beyond. Cyrus Bartol, a Transcendental Unitarian clergyman and an influential figure in Boston's religious and intellectual circles, felt the time had come to hold these so-called "liberal" English thinkers and writers to account.[67] On August 14, he wrote to Emerson. "This unfriendliness of English scholarship to our cause,—is it not worth seriously considering & noticing?" he asked. "[James] Martineau & even Tennyson are against us—Carlyle makes himself a public shame— . . . Ought there not to be an address of the literary men of this country to their Order across the sea, on the ground which learning, philosophy & poetry should take in the premises which touch them as well as legislation and politics?" Bartol then specifically suggested that Emerson might "put into the press a truly friendly letter to Carlyle." Alternatively, Emerson could prepare a statement for publication in the *Atlantic Monthly*. Whatever the case,

Bartol insisted, "I hold it critical that you should draw it up, whether it be an article simply, or a manifesto signed by yourself, Bryant, Whittier, Lowell, Whipple, Holmes, etc."[68]

Emerson, it seems, was in no mood to write a "truly friendly letter" to Carlyle. As with Ruskin and Norton, the war was putting a tremendous strain on what had been a warm transatlantic friendship. At this point, Emerson had actually ceased corresponding with Carlyle. The *Macmillan's* piece was apparently just too much to take. Nor did Emerson write the *Atlantic* manifesto that Bartol suggested. Instead, he chose the lecture platform for his response. In a presentation titled "Fortune of the Republic," which he would repeat numerous times throughout the winter lecture season, Emerson utterly castigated his old friend, pointing to him as a sellout to the corrupting forces of the Old World that dominated British culture. "In his youth," Emerson noted, Carlyle "announced himself as a 'theoretical sansculotte fast threatening to become a practical one.'" But now he was "practically in the English system, a Venetian aristocracy, with only a private stipulation in favor of men of genius."[69]

Despite the continuing moral and material support provided by the British, it was clear the Confederates' situation was deteriorating quickly. The London *Examiner* was highly critical of a rumor circulating in England that the South was preparing "to enlist half a million of negroes."[70] The Confederate government would presumably promise "freedom and fifty acres at the end of the war" if the Blacks served faithfully. Emancipation in America was already viewed as threatening to the stability of the British Empire, whose oppressed indigenous populations, it was believed, would surely take note. Any effort at voluntary emancipation in the South would be an even worse blow to British interests than an act imposed by the North through the force of arms.

Not surprisingly, the *Examiner* described the idea as both "monstrous and impracticable." The writer pointed out that "the proportion of the black soldiery to the white [in the Confederate army] would be similar to that of the Sepoys to the British army before the mutiny," a reference sure to strike fear in the hearts of many Britons.[71] As it turned out, the rumor was just that. However, the time would eventually come when the Confederacy would actually do the unthinkable and endorse a policy providing for the enlistment of Black soldiers.[72]

The argument for equal rights had been given a big boost by the courageousness of the Massachusetts 54th and also by the New York riots, which exposed racism as an affront to the nation's character. An August 5 article in the *Boston Weekly Transcript* declared that through their heroic conduct "the 54th Massachusetts . . . have added one more argument to sustain the policy of raising negro regiments." The writer was confident "there is not a person in the loyal States,—if we except the brutes, ruffians and assassins of the New York mob—who can read the accounts of the assault without feeling his prejudices insensibly giving way before such examples of fortitude and daring."

It was now clear to almost everyone that the key element in promoting freedom and equality for African Americans was service in the Union army. No one recognized this more than Blacks themselves. John Stuart Mill wrote to Henry Fawcett that "everything now looks encouraging, both for the success of the North, and for the cause of Negro emancipation." Fawcett had been sharing with Mill the letters of Leslie Stephen. Mill was grateful and noted that they "contained some very interesting information which I have seen nowhere else," which was precisely what Stephen hoped would result from his trip. "Nothing that has come from America has so strongly impressed me," Mill stated, "as the manifesto of the Committee of negroes to induce their fellow negroes to enlist." This manifesto was the result of a gathering of African Americans in Poughkeepsie, New York, in July. What most impressed Mill was the idealism of the document. It called on Blacks to serve not out of mere self-interest for their race but also out of the realization that they would be fighting "for liberty, and humanity, and civilization, and that the improvement of the world would go back if the North did not prevail. Is that not noble?" Mill asked.[73]

The *Saturday Review*, on the other hand, was, as always, cynical when it came to such idealism. The *Review* claimed that "the semi-servile population" of Blacks in America "has neither military aptitude nor sufficient motive for fighting. The free negroes of the North are sufficiently intelligent to know that their service will be despised even when they are accepted," the recent and widely heralded example of Fort Wagner notwithstanding, apparently. The *Review* also noted, "General Lee . . . remains in the field at the head of a still powerful army, and appears to have resumed his former position, whence he is able to menace Washington and to protect Richmond."[74]

The war was obviously still far from over, which was actually a good thing if one's goal was to eradicate slavery forever and restore the Union on a radically new basis. Most New England liberals had believed for some time now that the abolition of slavery was certain and that it must be followed by the granting of equal rights. The means to that end would be a demonstration that African Americans were, in fact, the equal of whites. The Massachusetts 54th had shown the way, but it was just the beginning. On August 4 a circular distributed in Boston declared that "the prompt enlistment of colored men is all-important to the Union cause" and that the undersigned sought to "raise fifty thousand dollars" to support additional enlistments. It was signed by John Murray Forbes, Amos Abbot Lawrence, Samuel G. Ward, James T. Fields, and several other prominent citizens.[75]

Around this time, the *Atlantic Monthly* published an article contrasting Northern democratic equality and British class consciousness. The piece was penned by Francis Wayland, dean of the Law School at Yale and son of the president of Brown University. Wayland had recently visited London and the House of Lords. What struck the New Englander most about this august body was its conservatism, the common denominator of Great Britain's governing class. Wayland offered Lord Chesterton as representative. "The strong point of a Chesterton is what he calls his 'conservatism,'" Wayland wrote. "He values everything in proportion to its antiquity, and prefers a time-honored abuse to a modern blessing." Like other members of the House of Lords, Chesterton "would pity Adam, 'because he had no ancestors.'"

Given this, it was not surprising that "his lordship's bitterest hatred . . . [is] reserved for democratic institutions," against which "he wages a constant crusade. Democracy," Wayland explained, "is the *bête noir* of all the Chestertons. They attack it" because they "know that the theory of democracy is based on the equality of man, and that where democracy prevails a privileged class is unknown."

Unfortunately, aristocrats like Chesterton had a strong influence on Great Britain's foreign policy. As a result, "the ruling classes of England can have no sincere sympathy with the North, because its institutions and instincts are democratic." Conversely, Wayland observed, "they give countenance to the South, because at heart and in practice it is essentially an aristocracy." For British elites, the North stands as a "dangerous example of a successful and powerful republic, where every man has equal rights, civil and religious, and where a privileged order in Church and State is impossible." Therefore, Wayland concluded, its destruction "has become in the minds of England's governing classes an imperious necessity."[76] Very soon, these aristocrats would have additional cause for worry.

Chapter 15

Lincoln Affirms Commitment to Emancipation

Animosity Toward Great Britain Deepens

While the defeat at Gettysburg was a tremendous setback to the Confederates' fading hopes for British recognition, Southern sympathizers in England nevertheless continued their efforts to win support for their failing cause.[1] One of the most significant was the formation of the Southern Independence Association, which was announced in the *Index* on September 17. This propaganda organization was a coalition of two major Anglo-Confederate groups in Britain, the Manchester Southern Club and the Central Association for Recognition of the Confederate States.[2] The organization was formally established in October. It would remain an active force in promoting the Southern cause in England until nearly the end of the war.[3]

Promoting the South often meant attacking the North, especially its president. British critics continued to criticize Lincoln's public statements as indicative of the crude vulgarity they claimed was a reflection of the North's crude democratic culture. The American public, however, admired Lincoln's speech. At this point in his presidency, Lincoln had mastered a style best described as simple eloquence. Each new public utterance showed his uncanny ability to touch the minds and hearts of the American people.

A case in point is his "Public Letter to James C. Conkling." The letter was read at a mass meeting of "Union men" in Springfield, Illinois, on September 2. In it, Lincoln spoke directly in the first person to those who objected to the Emancipation Proclamation and his decision to allow

Black enlistments.[4] "You are dissatisfied with me about the negro. Quite likely there is a difference of opinion between you and myself upon that subject," he acknowledged. "I certainly wish that all men could be free, while I suppose you do not." Whatever the case, he assured them, "I have neither adopted, nor proposed any measure, which is not consistent with even your view, provided you are for the Union." Regarding the Emancipation Proclamation, he observed that some "say it is unconstitutional. I think differently." Regardless, "the proclamation, as law, is either valid, or is not valid. If it is not valid, it needs no retraction. If it is valid, it can not be retracted, any more than the dead can be brought back to life."

Lincoln also pointed out that "some of the commanders of our armies in the field who have given us our most important successes believe that the emancipation policy and the use of the colored troops constitute the heaviest blow yet dealt to the Rebellion, and that at least one of these important successes could not have been achieved when it was but for the aid of black soldiers."[5] He went on to address the question of motivation. "You say you will not fight to free negroes. Some of them seem willing to fight for you. . . . But negroes, like other people, act upon motives. Why should they do anything for us, if we will do nothing for them? If they stake their lives for us, they must be prompted by the strongest motive—even the promise of freedom. And the promise being made, must be kept."[6]

Lincoln's letter was a huge success. It was seen as a tour de force in both content and style. It was aimed directly at the hearts and minds of the people and clearly struck the mark. It was later reported that the letter was received "with the greatest enthusiasm" by an estimated 40,000 to 70,000 Union supporters attending the rally.[7] It was published in major newspapers throughout the country. Abolitionists were grateful for Lincoln's unambiguous commitment to emancipation. The *National Anti-Slavery Standard* reprinted the entire document on September 12 under the heading "A Letter from President Lincoln: His Promise in the Proclamation to Be Kept."

English allies praised the letter. The *Spectator*, which, though pro-Union, had been disappointed with the Lincoln administration's limited commitment to emancipation up to this point, was cheered by the president's clarity in expressing his opposition to slavery. "It is difficult to imagine anything more lucid, more oppressively clear" than the president's "letter to the Unionist League" the journal declared on September 19. The writer noted that its "almost brutal directness . . . is the specialty of working men's politics." The message was "couched in language the laboring masses can comprehend" and, therefore, "strongly tends to produce conviction." According to the *Spectator*, it was now manifest that in the mind of "the Western working man," which the president so effectively represented, "slavery, whether based on Scripture or born of avarice, is inconsistent with the existence of the Union." Lincoln's "letter is one more proof that freedom for the black is becoming one of their fixed ideas."[8]

Not surprisingly, the London *Times* ridiculed Lincoln's letter in a September 17 editorial. "How any man in his sober senses could have sat down to compose such a rhapsody as this, or having composed it could have read it over with gravity and ordered it printed, passes our comprehension," the writer declared. The document that the *New York Times* praised for its eloquence the London *Times* disparaged as "something between a prophesy and an oracular expression, with a dash of Yankee slang and terms of expression which remind us alternatively of Ossian, of the incoherent utterances of the 'Maori Chiefs,' and of schoolboy translations of corrupt choruses in Greek tragedy."[9]

The *Times* reference to the "Maori Chiefs," the leaders of the indigenous people of New Zealand, was especially telling. Whether intentional or not, it aligned Lincoln and his cause with those seen as the semi-civilized "others" who occupied the lowest levels of the social hierarchy in the British Empire. By extension, his cause was their cause, which was undoubtedly why the *Times*, and the rest of the conservative British establishment, both loathed and feared him and the liberal democracy that he now so effectively represented in his person and his speech.

Around this time, Leslie Stephen arrived in Washington after spending several days with the literary giants of New England, whom he clearly liked, especially Lowell. Now it was time to make the acquaintance of the nation's political leaders. He brought with him an introduction from an English hero. "The letter which [Henry] Fawcett got me from [John] Bright to Seward proved very useful," he told his mother. "Bright's name is . . . a complete tower of strength in these parts. They talked of him with extraordinary admiration." The letter opened many doors, including one to the White House. "Seward . . . took me in the morning to the President's house," Stephen wrote, "where I sat with old Abe and others for half an hour or so till all the cabinet was assembled and ready for business." Like so many others, he was impressed with Lincoln. "In appearance he is much better than I expected. He is more like a gentleman to look at than I should have given him credit for from his picture. . . . He has a particularly pleasant smile, a very jolly laugh, and altogether looks like a benevolent and hearty old gentleman," he reported. "I felt quite kindly to him."[10]

After concluding his visit to Washington, Stephen journeyed on to Philadelphia. In the course of his travels, he became aware of the strong feeling of animosity toward England that was now felt by almost all Northerners. These people "naturally feel very bitter about English sympathy having gone so strongly on the other side," he told his mother. Concern about the rams had only made things worse. In Washington, Seward had made a point of telling him that if England permitted the rebel rams to start, the United States would declare war, "a proposition which," Stephen stated, "I think not unlikely."[11]

The *Spectator* agreed with this grim assessment. The paper offered harsh criticism of the Laird brothers for defying the spirit, if not the letter, of English law by building ships that could plunge England into a war with the United States. According to the *Spectator*, this was exactly what the Confederates wanted. Everyone believes, the paper asserted, "that the Confederates strain every nerve to buy these ships out of their starved exchequer, far more for the sake of promoting a rupture between England and the North, than for any direct good that this homeopathic injury to the Northern commerce can effect for them."[12]

What Stephen and the *Spectator* did not know at the time was that Minister Charles Adams Sr. had already issued a stern warning to the British government. As Ephraim Adams reports, the minister indicated in a communication to Lord Russell on July 11 that if the rams were allowed to escape, the United States would consider that England was now a participant in the war. Russell responded that the British government had been advised that legally "they cannot interfere in any way with these vessels." Adams was becoming exasperated by such arguments, and on September 5, he wrote directly to Russell telling him bluntly that if the rams put to sea, "it would be superfluous of me to point out to your Lordship that this is war."[13] Unbeknownst to Adams, the British government was already taking steps to detain the rams.

On September 9, the Lairds were told not to move the nearly completed vessels, and on September 15, there was a public announcement of the detention. A message was sent to Washington informing the Lincoln administration of this decision, but it would take approximately two weeks to get there.[14] Meanwhile, Americans prepared, mentally at least, for a third war with Great Britain. Lowell wrote to his friend Tom Hughes to assure him that "the last thing we want is another war." However, he added ominously, "if the rebel ironclads are allowed to come out, there might be a change."[15]

The Northern press was rife with frightening rumors. *Harper's Weekly* reported on September 19 that "the rebel iron rams of Liverpool are described as of enormous strength, turreted, and furnished with every protection for the gunners. One of them . . . was reported to have sailed," and "the English government and people . . . [are] becoming alarmed of the breeches of international law which they had already sanctioned." The *Weekly* then reprinted an excerpt from the London *Times* on August 28 that stated, "We hold and acknowledge it unlawful to equip vessels of war for the use of a belligerent, we being neutrals, and yet every cruiser in the Southern States has been, as a matter of fact, sent to sea from this country."

In noting this unusual candor by the *Times*, Ephraim Adams speculates that, because "Delane of the *Times* was at this period especially close to Palmerston, . . . it is at least inferential that the editorial was an advance notice of governmental intention" to seize the vessels.[16] Whatever the case, it was clear that neither the *Times* nor the *Saturday Review* wanted England to go to war over this issue. Earlier, the *Trent* affair, where Confederate envoys were removed from a British ship, was a matter of English honor. The rams were simply a matter of business and should not become a casus belli.

With the help of Sumner's and Cobden's backdoor diplomacy, the crisis was resolved amicably. Having detained the rams, the following month the British government purchased them for the Royal Navy.[17] The brinksmanship on England's part, however, was unnerving to Americans already burdened by the continuing stress of the war. Like the *Trent* affair, the bad feelings generated by this crisis deepened significantly the anger felt toward Great Britain.

The British government's action was a hard pill for England's Southern sympathizers to swallow. Not surprisingly, English liberals praised the move. The *Spectator* declared, "Earl Russell has seldom done a wiser, never a braver, public act than the stoppage of Mr. Laird's steam rams. He knows . . . how great will be the annoyance of the friends of the South. . . . To stop the rams was to defy three-fourths of the Conservative party," but it was the right thing to do. In taking this prudential action, England had been true both "to her interest and her principles."[18]

Lincoln's determination to hold true to his proclamation's promise of freedom contributed to growing support among England's antislavery ranks; moreover, the absence of any signs of the bloody slaughter and "servile insurrection" critics had predicted no doubt served as well. Linking opposition to slavery with the dignity of labor also resulted in growing support from England's working class. This trend would be enhanced by expanding the overseas operation of the *New England Loyal Publication Society*, an idea that had been proposed earlier by John Murray Forbes.

On September 20, Samuel Ward wrote to Norton that Forbes, who was in England at the time, wanted to raise money for distributing the publication there. Three days later, Forbes wrote to Norton with details of his plan. "As to English diffusion," he stated, "it strikes me as desirable to make up our first number in each week with just so much reference to English issues & needs as we can without trouble & send always the first number to an English press." He included a lengthy list of proposed European recipients.[19]

It was undoubtedly with this coalition in mind that Northern liberals now frequently alluded to the plight of English workers. George Curtis used his September 12 Lounger column in *Harper's Weekly* to call attention to the "Social Condition of the English People." He spoke of a "very remarkable book with this title" that had just been published by Harper Brothers. Somewhat like Hawthorne's recent *Atlantic* piece, the study showed that "the present condition of England, which seems superficially so enviable, is but a veneer of prosperity over the most radical ignorance, vice, and discontent." Inevitably, John Bull's "trial hour" will come, Curtis declared. "His fate hangs upon a tribunal in which he cannot bribe the judges." Meanwhile, the American government "fights the battle of liberty and equal rights for every people, . . . which inspires hope in the laboring class, and hate in the governing class of England."

Curtis and other American liberals were quickly coming to the belief that America's Civil War had now, in effect, become a proxy for class warfare in Great Britain. The *Atlantic*'s review of Dicey's *Six Months in the Federal States* observed, "Our only supporters in England are those men who recognize at the heart of our contest that genuine principle of Liberty which is not to be limited to caste or race. And it is only by hastening to justify their confidence that we can win to our own cause the great people they address."[20] Despite growing optimism regarding an inevitable Union victory, however, it was not at all clear that a military victory over the South would translate into a political, social, and cultural victory for the principles of liberal democracy. The problem at the moment was that the people of the free North were not yet themselves fully reconciled to the concept of full equality, regardless of "caste or race." That debate would continue.

The September issue of the *Atlantic* included a long essay on the reconstruction of the South. The article was anonymous, but almost everyone knew it was the work of Charles Sumner. With a Union victory on the horizon, Sumner envisioned a complete restructuring of what Emerson once referred to as the "atomic social constitution of the Southern people," beginning, of course, with the abolition of slavery.[21] What Sumner left unsaid in his long treatise was what, exactly, the status of emancipated slaves would be in a reconstructed South. Would they have the full benefits of citizenship? Would they have equal political and civil rights? Would they be allowed to vote? Anyone who had been paying attention to the evolution of the thinking of New England's liberals knew the answer to all of these questions was "yes." The conservative pushback on Sumner's radical proposal was not long in coming.

One of the most detailed rebuttals came from the Washington *National Intelligencer*, which found the proposal to be fundamentally unconstitutional. The Federal government had no power over the states themselves, the paper argued. Moreover, to treat the states like territories (which Sumner had proposed) would be to acknowledge that they had seceded as states, which would, effectively, be an acknowledgment of their right to do so. Even more radical in the eyes of the *Intelligencer* were the implications of Sumner's proposal in regard to the Blacks of the South. If the freedmen were acknowledged as citizens, the writer asked, could they demand a citizen's right to vote and also to hold office? The very thought was shocking for conservatives. The paper questioned whether Sumner and his radical New England allies really wanted "a piebald Senate and House of Representatives, composed of 'black spirits and white' to regulate the destinies of the great American nation?"[22] Obviously, most Americans were not yet ready to embrace racial equality.

The military tide shifted a bit in late September when the Confederates achieved a tactical victory in the western theater at Chickamauga, Georgia, on September 19 and 20. A large element of the Union army under General William Rosencrans clashed with a strong Confederate force led by Braxton Bragg and supported by James Longstreet. After two days of intense fighting, Rosecrans was forced to withdraw to Chattanooga. The bloodiest battle in the western theater resulted in staggering losses on both sides. The Union forces sustained 16,119 casualties and the Confederates 18,274, which amounted to 28 percent of each army's total strength.²³ After the major defeats of midsummer, Southerners now took heart, but many realized their strength was being sapped. The Union maintained overwhelming strategic advantages, despite its many losses. Confederate generals were often criticized for not following through on tactical victories, but by this point in the war their reserve strength had been totally depleted.²⁴

The victory at Chickamauga also heartened, for a time at least, Confederate supporters in England. London *Times* correspondent Charles Mackay reported from New York on October 5, "The long line of Northern good fortune has had its turning." According to Mackay, this most recent action showed that the government in Washington, "filled with conceit" and afflicted with the mania of past successes, was willing to "fritter away" Federal forces "in remote and unconnected expeditions." Predictably, the *Saturday Review* told a similar tale, declaring that "the tide of success seems to have turned once more in favor of the South. . . . At every side and at every point there is some success more or less for the Confederates."²⁵

The North's English friends, however, were not easily discouraged by such claims. At this point, most still anticipated a Union victory. The only question now was whether the liberals' agenda would be fully accomplished before that happened. John Stuart Mill wrote to Henry Fawcett at this time to thank him for forwarding reports from Leslie Stephen. "The tidings from America may be considered good," he told him, but he worried that "if the war ends too soon, it may end without the complete emancipation of the slaves; but if it is ended by the aid of 40 or 50,000 negro soldiers, and after another year's experience of enfranchised negroes growing cotton and sugar for wages, not only slavery will be extinguished, but the South will probably settle down into a free country much more easily than is supposed, and the anti-negro feeling in the free states will have, in great measure, disappeared." The only thing left to deal with then would be "the exasperation of the Americans against England."²⁶

Mill believed that this exasperation was the result, in large part, of the perverse criticisms and deliberate misrepresentations found in publications like the *Times* and the *Saturday Review*. He wrote to a friend that "in the pro-Southern English papers which I see, the facts favorable to the Northern side . . . are always suppressed, and in the *Times* and *Saturday Review* the grossest lies told, in simple recklessness of assertion without knowledge." A particular offender is "that poor gobeamouche [gullible person] Mackay, in the *Times*, who simply retails the stuff he hears from a disreputable clique at New York, almost all of them personally interested in slavery either through commerce or politics."[27]

Mill was certainly right about Mackay, who was known to hold strong pro-Southern views. Mackay was well aware that his boss, managing editor Mowbray Morris, felt a robust animus toward the free North, so he routinely sent reports that were thoroughly negative in tone and content. Mowbray was pleased with these and told Mackay, "Your views are entirely in accordance with those of the paper and, I believe, of the majority of this country."[28] The other *Times* reporter in America, Francis Lawley, was just as bad, if not worse. He reported mainly on events in the South, and those reports were always brimming with optimism. Lawley firmly believed the Confederacy had a right to independence, and his reporting consistently reflected his sympathy with Southerners.[29]

The *Atlantic*, which had always stood as a strong counter-voice to these, would now have a stablemate. Charles Eliot Norton wrote to Curtis on October 16 to tell him, among other things, that he had "just undertaken, in company with Lowell, the editorship of the *North American Review*." Their goal was to "put some life into the old dry frame of the Quarterly" and turn this venerable New England journal into an enlightened vehicle of progressive liberal thought.[30] Curtis was an obvious choice for contributions in that line. He was invited to write "on any national question you choose."[31] Norton used the October issue to promote a new journal "written by colored persons" at a private "Manual Labor School." The purpose of this journal, titled *The Student's Repository*, was "to cultivate and develop the latent talents, and elevate the intellectual, moral, and religious character of the colored people." "These objects are worthy ones," Norton declared, and he offered the new journal "a cordial welcome" as he commended it to the public.[32]

Norton also continued in his position as editor of the *New England Loyal Publication Society*, which now extended its reach to friends and allies in Great Britain. Poet Aubrey de Vere wrote to him around this time, thanking him for sending "those very interesting extracts from the American Press on various matters connected with the War & with English public opinion."[33] Keeping British allies well informed was important given the lies, misrepresentations, and omissions of major publications like *Blackwood's*, the *Saturday Review*, *Fraser's*, and the *Times*. Much of the information provided eventually made its way into friendly publications like the London *Daily News*, the *Spectator*, and *Macmillan's Magazine*.

Around this time, Francis H. Newman wrote to his friend Epes Sargent in Boston to offer encouragement. "I believe that your successes & the firm tone of such men as Sumner, . . . have reinforced the slumbering conscience of Earl Russell & his supporters in the cabinet against Lord Palmerston. This section of the ministers," Newman conjectured, "got the victory when the news came that the Mississippi was yours."[34] The working class also continued to provide significant support. Richard Cobden wrote to Sumner to caution him against making any blanket condemnation of the English, because this would be offensive to "the masses in England" who were aligned with the North.[35] Such condemnation should be aimed at the governing class, not the working class. Cobden's point was an important one. Forgetting that this was a "people's war" on both sides of the Atlantic would be a costly error.

Cobden was a cannier politician than Sumner in this instance because he did not lose sight of the fact that, to use a present-day colloquialism, "all politics is local." Largely as a result of the proclamation, the Union cause was now the cause of the British working class. Cobden also told Sumner that he "always thought that the negroes . . . will play an important part" in the war and that it was "in the interests of the negroes themselves all over the world . . . that the black man should be found fighting his own battle."[36] The phrase "all over the world" was an indication that the American war was a contest that would impact human rights everywhere.

In addition to the troubled relationship with Great Britain, the Union defeat at Chickamauga was a depressing setback for New England liberals. The fall elections were seen as a crucial test of Lincoln's policies, especially those relating to emancipation and Blacks. Copperhead leaders like Clement Vallandigham and New York governor Horatio Seymour relentlessly attacked Lincoln and his policies in racist terms. Conservative Democrats had played the race card before with success. In Ohio, they depicted the war as "an irrepressible conflict between white and black laborers." In the face of this threat, it was imperative that every vote cast "count in favor of the white man, and against the Abolition hoards, who would place negro children in your schools, negro jurors in your jury boxes, and negro votes in your ballot boxes!" In Pennsylvania, Copperheads offered subtle warnings about "political and social equality" for Blacks.[37]

On the positive side, the Union victories at Gettysburg, Vicksburg, and Port Hudson in the summer had convinced many that the Union still had the upper hand militarily, despite occasional setbacks like

Chickamauga. Also, the heroic conduct of the Massachusetts 54th at Fort Wagner and that of the Union's Colored Troops at Port Hudson, as well as the growing recognition of the importance of Black troops generally to the Union cause, undoubtedly took much of the bite out of the Democrats' appeal to racism. As a result, when the votes were tallied, Republicans were handed substantial victories in several big elections. Vallandigham went down to a resounding defeat in his bid for the governorship of Ohio, as did George Woodward in Pennsylvania. Significantly, in Ohio Republicans received 94 percent of the absentee soldier vote. Public opinion in the North was clearly changing in significant ways.[38]

Republicans saw the election results as an endorsement of emancipation. A Republican newspaper in Lincoln's hometown of Springfield, Illinois, commented that if a referendum had been held on the Emancipation Proclamation a year earlier, "there is little doubt that the voice of a majority would have been against it. And yet not a year has passed before it is approved by an overwhelming majority." A New York Republican called the election results a "great and blessed revolution."[39]

New England liberals were also overjoyed. Norton wrote to Curtis just days later stating, "I heartily and with all my heart rejoice with you in the results of Tuesday's elections." Those results, he believed, justified their "confidence in the intelligence and patriotism of our people." "The victory," Norton declared, "is the moral Waterloo of the rebellion. The end is in view,—with Union and freedom and peace."[40] The fall elections, as Allan Nevins points out, were "one of the important turning-points in the political history of the nation," and one that "few men would have predicted early in 1863."[41]

One of the reasons for the growing acceptance of the Republicans' human rights agenda was the influence of the New England intelligentsia. As we have already seen, publications like the *Atlantic Monthly*, the *North American Review*, the *Commonwealth*, *Harper's Weekly*, and the *New England Loyal Publication Society* helped spread their liberal views to a large audience both at home and abroad. Each of the last two alone reached over one million readers. When Curtis became the political editor of *Harper's Weekly* in December 1863, he made it known that he intended "by a gentle but continuously brave pressure" to transform *Harper's* from a "semi-Secession" journal "into an anti-slavery and Republican" one. The paper now had a circulation of over 130,000. With a readership this large, Curtis's biographer states, "the influence of his editorials and articles during the war years was enormous."[42]

Meanwhile, on the other side of the Atlantic, relations between the British working class and the North were given a significant boost in the fall by a famous American visitor from a distinguished New England family. Henry Ward Beecher was one of the most popular preachers in America. Wherever he spoke, huge crowds turned out. Like Lincoln, Beecher employed plain speech, common diction, and, at times, broad humor.[43] Like his sister, Harriet Beecher Stowe, Henry was a staunch abolitionist and a cofounder and longtime editor of the antislavery New York *Independent*.

When he arrived in England, Beecher visited the American legation and spoke with Minister Adams about his proposed lecture tour. He expressed the hope that his lectures might help "remove misconceptions and promote peace between the two nations."[44] Beecher toured England as a private citizen for almost two weeks, beginning on October 9. He spoke primarily to audiences of working-class Englishmen about the war. In most places he was warmly welcomed, but even in those places where he was not, Beecher showed an amazing ability to win over an audience.

Beecher's speech at Manchester was typical. He made a strong appeal to the shared values of the two nations, which, he said, lie in our "own doctrines of liberty" and "doctrines of human rights," for which the working people of Manchester also struggled. "The same blood is in us. We are your children, or the children of your fathers and ancestors," he told them.[45] A commitment to equality and human rights lay at the heart of the American war, Beecher declared. This was clearly reflected in the effort to bring about emancipation. He admitted that there had been "a vicious prejudice in the North against the negro," but he assured his audience that "it is a part of the great moral revolution which is going on that these prejudices have been in great measure vanquished." This revolution, Beecher told them, had come about in large part through the efforts of Blacks themselves. "No men on either side have carried themselves more gallantly, more bravely than the colored regiments that have been fighting for this government and for their liberty."[46]

Beecher's common theme throughout his tour was that "the American question is the working man's question all over the world."[47] Not surprisingly, this appeal to the British working class was not well received by the British governing class. The *Saturday Review* of October 17, in rejecting Beecher's plea that England should support "the cause of the North," accused him of promoting "spiritual tyranny," just as his Puritan ancestors had. The writer insisted that the Confederates had succeeded in establishing a nation, and they had the right to determine their destiny, good or bad, without interference from the North or from England, slavery notwithstanding.

The *Review*'s racism was never far off stage. Like the London *Times*, the writer declared that "the Emancipation Proclamation is a mere political trick, . . . that Abolitionism is a mere hollow after-thought, and that 'the popular enthusiasm' for the nigger in New York is the most absurd fiction and romance." He also used this opportunity to cast aspersions upon England's own lower classes who vigorously supported emancipation. "The strongest friends of the North are, in England, to be found . . . among the lower sections of the middle class," he declared. This, he claimed, was "a class in which the real principles of civil and religious liberty are least known."[48] As it became increasingly clear that Beecher's speeches were resonating with those "lower sections," the *Review* became even more critical. Two weeks later, the journal accused the popular preacher of agitating the lower classes in a deliberate attempt "to stimulate the vulgar clamor." Fortunately, the writer noted, "it is only in the United States that they possess political influence."[49]

British conservatives sought to downplay the effect of Beecher's appeal to the commoners. The satirical magazine *Punch*, another reliable ally of the Confederacy, offered an untypically sober commentary following his departure. "Mr. Beecher," the journal noted, "has sailed to America," where he will "tell Messrs. Lincoln and Seward . . . that large numbers of the uneducated classes" turned out to hear him, "and that the press has been very good-natured to him." However, the writer also hoped Beecher would report "that the educated classes are at the present date just as neutral in the matter of the American quarrel as they were before the reverend gentleman's arrival."[50] Beecher's plain speech and liberal ideas had clearly moved the masses and in so doing sent a faint but discernible tremor through the foundations of the British establishment. It was a sign of things to come.

Chapter 16

Lincoln Speaks for Equality

The Anglo-American Divide Widens

While the peaceful resolution of the Laird rams crisis lessened tensions, Northern animosity toward the British did not abate. It was at this time that Nathaniel Hawthorne published his reflections on England and the English in a book titled *Our Old Home*, based on his earlier *Atlantic* articles. It proved to be controversial. While presenting a largely positive view of British life, Hawthorne included a number of candid criticisms and unflattering commentary. For example, in the first chapter, "Consular Experiences," Hawthorne reflected on the now vexed question of the evolution of American character from its English origins. "When our forefathers left the old home they pulled up many of their roots, but trailed with them others, which were never snapt asunder by the tug of such a lengthening distance," he wrote. "Even so late as these days, they remain entangled with our heart-strings, and might often have influenced our national course like the tiller-ropes of a ship." But this influence declined over the years due largely to "the boorishness, the stolidity, . . . [and] the contemptuous jealousy" of the mother country, which eventually compelled "us to be a great nation in our own right."

Echoing the sentiments of his Saturday Club friends, Hawthorne declared that American independence was divinely ordained. "The Providence of God," he wrote, has a special "work for us to do," and "the massive materiality of the English character would have been too ponderous a dead-weight upon our progress." This separation was fortunate in another way: "The power of America wedded to the power of England would have made her invincible" and, therefore, free from the "otherwise immutable law of imperial vicissitude."[1] Because this did not happen, America was now a rival power rather than an empowering subordinate.

Such commentary, coming at a time of bitter feeling between the two nations, could not help but strike a nerve with most British critics. *Blackwood's* November response was typical. At the outset, the anonymous author, noting the warm and friendly title of Hawthorne's work, indicated that British readers expected to find themselves "favorably and indulgently depicted." Instead, they found the book "laden with all the prejudices of [Hawthorne's] nation," prejudices that were currently so rabid that they "amount almost to insanity." Given this disappointing tone, the reviewer wondered if such bitterness was caused by Hawthorne's sudden conversion to the cause of "Abolition and Extermination." Alternatively, he speculated that this change in Hawthorne "must be owning . . . to some sense of injury received at our hands, either personal or national." If so, the writer was not reluctant to return the favor. He wondered aloud "what so many intellectual and polished Americans," like Hawthorne, "can find to excite them" in support "of a system which floods the land with corruption for the sake of elevating a nonentity to the Presidency," a sneer that only further alienated American readers.[2]

Hawthorne was taken aback by the negative reactions to his book in England. Perhaps because he tended to avoid political debate and dissention of any sort, he may not have been fully cognizant of the deep acrimony that had arisen between New and Old England since the start of the war. Even his English friend Henry Bright took offense. In speaking of the book, Bright told him, "It was really too bad, some of the things you say, you talk like a cannibal."[3] In light of such unexpected comments, as well as a number of harsh criticisms in the English press, Hawthorne told Fields that the British "seem to think me bitter against their countrymen, and it is perhaps natural that they should, because their self-conceit can accept nothing short of indiscriminate adulation." Nonetheless, he remained puzzled that there should be such controversy surrounding a work he felt was not particularly good or "weighty." "I don't care about seeing any more notices of it," he wrote.[4]

At the same time, British conservatives continued to castigate the North as a brutal aggressor in a bloody conflict that it could not win. Curtis continued to answer these accusations, arguing that Northerners were fighting for freedom and equality in what was now undeniably a global movement for human rights. From his November Editor's Easy

Chair column in *Harper's Monthly*, he noted that "the commotion which began upon this continent two years ago now disturbs the world. Russia, Poland, Germany, Spain, France, England, and Mexico" were all roiled by recent events in the American war, which was "gradually assuming the aspect of a contest between continents, the Eastern representing ancient wrong, despotism, and monarchy, with an alliance of the slaveholding aristocracy upon this side of the sea, and the Western standing for eternal liberty, popular rights, and human equality." It was this very division, of course, that fueled English fears and English criticisms.[5]

Boston's liberal Unitarian journal, the *Christian Examiner*, reinforced Curtis's point in November as it took Charles Kingsley to task in a review of his novel *Two Years Ago*. Before the war, Kingsley was a respected writer known for his sympathy with the British working class. But it turned out he was also a bitter racist who despised Black people.[6] In "Cambridge and Kingsley on American Affairs," Reverend Samuel Robert Calthrop, who succeeded Samuel Joseph May as minister to the Unitarian Church in Syracuse,[7] condemned the Englishman for his inexcusable treachery in attacking the Northern cause at the very moment when the Union was striking a deadly blow at the heinous institution of slavery. Among other grievous offensives, Calthrop reported how Kingsley had recently argued in a Cambridge lecture that the South had a "moral right" to secede and that "it was clearly a 'moral wrong' on the part of the North to try to prevent it."[8]

It wasn't much later when the *Commonwealth* published an attack on another British writer once popular with Americans, novelist William Makepeace Thackeray, author of *The Virginians* (1857–59). When he visited the United States in the early 1850s on a lecture tour, Thackeray was well received wherever he went. George Curtis, writing in *Putnam's Magazine* at the time, referred to him as "a great, sweet, generous human heart."[9] This view changed dramatically when, with the advent of the war, it became clear that his sympathy was with the Confederacy. "Thackeray is no longer what he was when *Vanity Fair* revealed his genius to the world," the *Commonwealth* observed on November 27. When *Vanity Fair* was published, Charlotte Bronte described him as "'the first social regenerator of the day,' the very master of that working corps who 'restore to rectitude the warped systems of things.'" Unfortunately, as the *Commonwealth* writer noted, "No one now would speak of him so. The 'social regenerator' thinks slavery may be tolerated wherever the claret is good." In a recent article in "the *Roundabout Papers* . . . written long after the great struggle commenced in America, . . . this great Englishman, who is so fond of Medoc and of juleps, told the Southern slaveholders, that 'his eyes do not care to look out for faults or his pen to note them.'"

The growing drumbeat of criticism now directed at British writers was noted by the *Saturday Review*. The journal offered a defense against these "unwearied American assailants." "Some patriotic wiseacre has discovered that none of the popular English authors have expressed their sympathy" with the North, the *Review* noted. "Sir E. Lytton, Mr. Thackeray, and Mr. Dickens are angrily reminded that they have had millions of American readers, and they are threatened with a literary excommunication. . . . Not content with vituperating 'rebel slavemongers,'" these critics are "constantly turning round on unoffending bystanders" like "the not less hated English nation."[10]

As the culture clash continued, the perceived perfidy of several of England's most revered and respected authors became especially distressing to the New England intelligentsia, who had once considered them partners in the grand march of Western civilization. Their anger was reaching a critical breaking point. Some felt compelled to openly declare their disdain for formerly revered icons like Ruskin, Carlyle, Dickens, Thackeray, Kingsley, Arnold, and others who were now lamented as pathetic "Lost Leaders."

A major offensive came in the form of a lecture by one of New England's most respected literary and intellectual icons, Oliver Wendell Holmes. Holmes opened the fall lecture season in Boston with a bitter and vitriolic assault on British character and culture, coupled with a strident declaration of American cultural independence. He titled it "The Weaning of Young America."[11] Holmes began his oration with an indictment of the British for their unforgivable failure to sympathize with the nation's suffering during its hour of need. "A cup of cold water was all we asked for in the dread extreme of our national agony," he declared. But instead, during this time on the cross, England "filled a sponge with vinegar mingled with gall and held it out to us upon the end of a spear."

With rumors of impending warfare between the two nations circulating in the press, Holmes offered a blunt challenge to the British military. In speaking of the once-indomitable British navy, he declared that "our iron water-beatles are ready and willing to drive any of the butterfly three-deckers, the *Terribles* and *Thunderers* and all the rest, back into their dock-yards, and punch their ribs in after they get there." He pointed out that "the turreted iron steamer was practically unknown to naval history until" a year ago, "when the little *Monitor* revolutionized maritime warfare, leveled the wooden walls of old England, and placed a shield before the breast of free America."

Holmes went on to indict the British for their many offenses in a style reminiscent of the Declaration of Independence. Those offenses ranged from "the scandalously hasty recognition of the rebels as belligerents" to their "virtual complicity with the outlaws who plundered and sunk our ships on the high seas." "Every act done and left undone," he declared, "told us in unmistakable language—nay, burned it in flaming letters in our naked hearts"—that England was not America's friend.

After complaining about the failure of the "English church" to blast "with its anathema the rising barbarism" of the South, Holmes trained his fire on the humanists of the intellectual class, whom he believed made the unkindest cut of all in their failure to support the North in its fight against slavery, the ultimate crime against humanity. "Where," he asked, "is Lord Brougham, ex-apostle of the Diffusion of Knowledge," while "perpetual ignorance" is enforced upon the slaves. "Where is Dickens, the hater of the lesser wrongs of Chancery Courts, the scourge of tyrannical beadles and heartless schoolmasters? Has he no word for those who are striving, bleeding, dying to keep from spreading . . . a system which carries with it all the villainies and all the miseries that demons can imagine?" Of Tennyson he asked, "where is the Laureate, so full of fine indignations and high aspirations. . . . Has he a song for the six hundred, and not a line for the six hundred thousand?"[12]

New Englanders applauded this fierce indictment of the British. For some, it had been a long time coming, signaling, at last, an absolute break from the foul and outworn culture of the Old World. In its account of Holmes's address, the Boston *Daily Advertiser* observed that "a great change has evidently taken place . . . in the relations of our country and nation to the dynasties of the Old World, especially to the predominant power of England." The writer noted that the United States was now in the "final emancipation of American opinion from British, from Old World mastery," which is "marked by the rapid growth of our Intellectual Independence."

The bitter feeling toward England, now so pronounced throughout the North, was the result of a thousand wounds inflicted since the war began. "It was not so much anger as deep sorrow that filled the souls of those Americans who loved her best," the *Advertiser* pointed out. "They had overrated the civilization of the mother country—that was all." But apparently that was enough. "The lecture was fully appreciated by the audience," the writer reported, and they "frequently manifested their pleasure in bursts of applause."[13] Holmes had given vent to the feelings of the New England literati and many others toward Great Britain and the discredited representatives of her once-respected culture.

While this culture war between New and Old England was reaching a fever pitch in the fall of 1863, tensions on the political front had actually abated considerably. With events on the battlefield trending toward an ultimate Northern victory, and internal reports suggesting that British intervention in any form would have disastrous military and commercial consequences, Palmerston's government turned its attention to Europe. The "Polish question" was the issue of the hour. An uprising in Poland against the occupying powers there, especially Russia, upset relations among Europe's Great Powers. England watched developments closely and was concerned with Russian intent.

In a letter to his mother from his diplomatic post, John Lothrop Motley reported that "our poor people in Vienna are in an awful fidget, and the telegraph wires between London, St. Petersburg, and Paris are quivering hourly with the distracted messages which are speeding to and fro, and people are going about telling each other the most insane stories." One of the most disturbing rumors was that "Russia is to set up Poland as a kind of kingdom in leading-strings, when she has finished her Warsaw massacres."[14]

With developments such as these threatening, it is little wonder that Palmerston's government was growing less interested in the American war. Moreover, the fact that the Russian fleet was currently wintering in American ports encouraged the British to be less antagonistic toward their former colony. When the Russians entered the ports of San Francisco and New York in September and October, they were warmly welcomed by their American hosts.[15] They were now seen by many as pro-Union, and rumors abounded that Russia was prepared to provide naval aid to the United States should war break out with England.[16]

In addition, with Roebuck's motion for recognition defeated in June, and Mason recalled shortly thereafter, followed by the resolution of the crisis regarding the Laird rams, England seemed to detach itself from the American question more completely than at any time since the beginning of the conflict. Around this time, Captain Charles Chesney, professor of military history at Sandhurst College, predicted that, despite recent defeats, the South could resist Northern invasion indefinitely. Palmerston's government, it seemed, was prepared to wait that long for a conclusive result.[17]

Despite Great Britain's resolve to avoid entanglement in the American war, the *Saturday Review* warned that American "animosity to England" continued to grow and might yet result in open conflict.[18] The heated rhetoric that still emanated from the popular press only served to stoke the fires at a time when the governments of both nations sought to tamp them down. Moreover, the American war was causing a disruption in the British body politic, a source of growing concern among the governing class.

In "Messrs. Cobden and Bright at Rochdale," the *Saturday Review* attacked these two for their oft-repeated claim that the war in America was "an aristocratic rebellion against a democratic government." Particularly disturbing to this writer was Cobden's recent declaration that when "the aristocracy is pitted against the people in a physical contest, the aristocracy has always gone down under the heavy blows of the democracy," a belief New England liberals also held. The *Review* insisted Cobden was wrong on both counts. "There is no conflict of aristocracy and democracy" involved in the American conflict, the writer asserted, and "it is by no means true that an aristocracy has always gone down under the heavy blows of the democracy," the American Revolution notwithstanding.[19]

Regardless of who might be right, the American Civil War had precipitated an international debate on the relative merits of a cultural and political system that validated a hierarchy based on class, caste, and race, and one that held all men to be created equal. New England liberals and reformers, especially the abolitionists, had been insisting for some time on universal equal rights as essential to the survival of American democracy. Demonstrations of Black ability and character featured prominently in this debate. The Union's Colored Troops had proved their heroism, fortitude, and ability at Fort Wagner and Port Hudson in July. For many, this had settled the question of their fitness for military service and, by implication, all the rights of citizenship. As one Union recruiter from Emerson's hometown of Concord reported in a letter to his sister, a great shift in public opinion was under way. Writing from his recruiting office in Nashville, Tennessee, he reported that large numbers of slaves were fleeing their masters' plantations and enlisting in the Union army, which delighted him. In speaking of a Concord neighbor, he added, "I am glad that Geo Butrick has gone into a negro regiment. People seem to be coming round to niggers fighting."[20]

Military service was only part of the equation, however. In September, the *Atlantic* published "The Freedmen at Port Royal" by Edward L. Pierce, a Massachusetts reformer who was appointed by the Federal government to report on the experiment. Plots of land carved out of abandoned plantations were parceled out to freedmen who, for the first time in their lives, would reap the rewards of their own labor. At the outset of his article, Pierce noted, "Two questions are concerned in the social problem of our time. One is, will the people of African descent work for a living? And the other is, will they fight for their freedom? An affirmative answer to these must be put beyond any fair dispute before they will receive permanent security in law or opinion." While the second question was being answered in the affirmative on the battlefields almost every day, the answer to the first was being worked out now on the Carolina coastal plain. The Port Royal experiment had been a remarkable success, Pierce reported. "Begun in doubt, [it] is no longer a bare hope or possibility. It is a fruition and a consummation. The negroes will work for a living. They will fight for their freedom. They are adapted to civil society."[21]

In the now global struggle for human rights, perhaps no single event was more important than that which occurred on November 19 when Abraham Lincoln delivered his memorable Gettysburg Address at the site of the war's greatest battle. Lincoln understood from the beginning that this was a "people's war." As such, it was necessary to justify the enormous sacrifices being made by relating it to some great and noble principle—a principle so great as to be worthy of any sacrifice.

At the outset of the war, recognizing the conservative concern with preserving the Constitution "as it is" and the need to avoid alienating the border states, the conflict was cast exclusively as an effort to save the Union. As late as August 1862, Lincoln, in his famous open letter to Horace Greeley, indicated that the preservation of the Union was his singular goal. But, with the passage of time and the dramatic change in attitude toward African Americans that the war had brought about, it became clear to many that slavery was fundamentally incompatible with the principles upon which the nation was founded. To patch a peace without abolishing slavery would simply lay the groundwork for yet another conflict. New England liberals, especially those whose résumés included service in the antislavery movement, had been vigorously arguing this position for more than two years now. Lincoln's Emancipation Proclamation was a giant step in the right direction. However, it did not apply to *all* enslaved Blacks. And so it remained simply a war measure. To attempt to do more would be extra-constitutional.

New England reformers had no hesitation in challenging the Constitution when it stood in violation of moral law. They had been doing that consistently since the passage of the Fugitive Slave Law in 1850, a law Emerson insisted every honest citizen would break at the first opportunity. But Lincoln could not be as free as a poet or a philosopher in challenging the law of the land and the Constitution he swore an oath to defend. At the same time, it was clear he had always preferred the universal moral sentiment of the Declaration to the legal letter of the Constitution. In his famous debates with Stephen Douglas in 1858, Lincoln frequently invoked the Declaration of Independence, in one instance noting that "all this quibbling about . . . this race and that race and the other race being inferior" should be dismissed and the country should embrace the truth articulated by the Founders that "all men are created equal."[22]

At this point in the war, and with ample prodding and support from New England liberals and the radicals of his own party, Lincoln apparently felt the time was right to affirm that freedom and equal rights were the moral foundation of the Union cause and the defining principles of democracy itself. His comments to the serenaders on the Fourth of July revealed the kernel of his thinking, and the formal composition of his address undoubtedly took place over a relatively long period of time. He made some final revisions on the evening of November 18.[23]

The featured presentation of the day was that of former Massachusetts senator Edward Everett. At this time, Everett was considered one of the most distinguished orators in America. He was trained in the classics, which, for a time, he taught at Harvard. His two-hour presentation was a model of ancient eloquence wherein he recounted, detail by detail, the several heroic clashes that occurred over the three days of battle.[24] By contrast, Lincoln's remarks consisted of only 272 words and lasted only minutes. The estimated 15,000 people present that day were undoubtedly as surprised by his brevity as they were delighted by his message. A contemporary newspaper account indicated that his words drew applause no fewer than five times during the short address.[25]

In his presentation, Lincoln spoke in the simple American idiom for which he was now known. His words were short, direct, and moving. As one scholar notes, here "the sublime appears in the simplest dress."[26] Lincoln's subject was the idealism that had characterized the

American experience from the very beginning of the nation's history. He expressed this idealism in simple, organic tropes. His rhetoric was based on "principles rather than precedents" because what he argued for was unprecedented in American history.[27] His use of Saxon words was also significant.[28] In the cultural conflict generated by the war, this simple diction distinguished him as a common man, a Puritan at heart, not a Cavalier aristocrat. His voice was that of "the people," not of the formal statesman, the traditional spokesman of the governing elite so respected in England and the South.

In his powerful opening sentence, Lincoln stated unequivocally the principle from which the balance of his address flowed: "Four score and seven years ago our fathers brought forth on this continent, a new nation, conceived in Liberty, and dedicated to the proposition that all men are created equal." He went on to show how the war was a heroic effort to affirm the validity of this noble concept. It was this transcendent principle, he insisted, for which so many had sacrificed their lives, and he called upon all who believed in American democracy to ensure that "these dead shall not have died in vain—that this nation, under God, shall have a new birth of freedom—and that government of the people, by the people, for the people, shall not perish from the earth."[29]

Lincoln's reference to "a new birth of freedom" implied the passing of the old. As Ronald White asserts, at Gettysburg, Lincoln "was no longer, as in his inaugural address, defending an old Union but proclaiming a new Union. . . . Lincoln had come to see the Civil War as a ritual of purification. The old Union had to die" so there could be "a new Union and a new humanity."[30] The "second revolution" that Emerson and his New England circle had been demanding virtually since the outbreak of hostilities was now, it seemed, fully embraced by the president. Like the first, this second revolution was informed by noble ideals of freedom and equality, but unlike the first, this time these ideals would not be compromised.

Reactions to Lincoln's address were quite positive, even though he himself at first questioned its effectiveness. Everett wrote to him shortly after the event. "Permit me," he said, "to express my great admiration of the thoughts expressed by you, with such eloquent simplicity & appropriateness. . . . I should be glad, if I could flatter myself, that I came as near to the central idea of the occasion, in two hours, as you did in ten minutes." Many newspaper accounts were also flattering.[31] New England's liberal literati were immensely pleased with Lincoln's words.

One of the problems that Lincoln and other Unionists had been wrestling with for some time was how to defend the Union, and the Constitution on which it was based, without defending slavery at the same time. At the outset of the war, this anomaly was problematic for liberals who believed slavery was incompatible with democracy. For most Northerners, however, this was not a major issue early on. The war was about preserving the Union as it was, including slavery where it already existed. But all that had changed.

Lincoln effectively reconceived the Constitution by applying to it the spirit of the Declaration. As a result, Garry Wills maintains, that day "the crowd departed with a new thing in its ideological luggage, that new constitution Lincoln had substituted for the one they brought there with them."[32]

The most revolutionary element in this new Constitution was racial equality, which outraged conservatives. The Chicago *Times* of November 26 thoroughly castigated Lincoln for subverting the document he had sworn to defend. "It was to uphold this Constitution," the paper declared, "and the Union created by it, that our officers and soldiers gave their lives at Gettysburg. How does he, then, standing on their graves, misstate the cause for which they died and libel the statesmen who founded the government? They were men possessing too much self-respect to declare that negroes were their equals, or were entitled to equal privileges."[33]

Similarly, the *New York World* took umbrage at Lincoln's bold words and accused him of "gross ignorance or willful misstatement. *This* United States," the paper insisted, was not founded on the Declaration of Independence but is "the result of the ratification of a compact known as the Constitution," a document that said nothing whatsoever about equality.[34] But what was done was done, and it seemed likely to many that there was no way now for conservatives to preserve "the Constitution as it is" or "the Union as it was."

In England, the address was barely noticed.[35] The London *Times* published a December 4 report by its new correspondent, Antonio Gallenga. He wrote that the "imposing ceremony" was "rendered ludicrous by some of the luckless sallies of that poor President Lincoln." With comments such as this, Gallenga found little favor with American readers. Lowell had written his English friend Thomas Hughes in September that "the *Times* . . . has now sent over an 'Italian' to report on us—a clever man, but a double foreigner, as an Italian with an English wash over him. Pray, don't believe a word he says."[36]

While Lincoln's address precipitated a rhetorical storm on the home front, there was relative quiet on the battlefront in the fall of 1863. Lee and Meade maneuvered against one another in the eastern theater but accomplished little. The one bright spot for the Union was Grant's success in late November at the Battle of Chattanooga. In what became known as "The Battle Above the Clouds" (November 24), Grant was able to drive off Confederate forces under Braxton Bragg and restore Union control over Tennessee, thus reversing Rosencrans's earlier failures.[37]

With the Union now in control of the military situation, and the crisis of the Laird rams resolved, relations with Great Britain, on an official level at least, appeared relatively calm. Curtis noted this welcome change of tone in a November 28 *Harper's Weekly* essay titled "America and England." After pointing to the seizure of the rams and the positive commentaries on America by "Historicus" (William Vernon Harcourt) in the *Times*, Curtis felt "it is pretty clear that Great Britain means to avoid all occasion of trouble with this country." Nearing the end of a long and tumultuous year of living dangerously, enduring the sleights, offenses, and threats from the mighty British lion, Americans could now "rejoice that the sky is clearer" and "resolve to keep it so." Events, however, soon tested this resolve.

Chapter 17

1864

The "Negro Question" Spurs Intense International Debate

At the opening of the new year there was the usual lull in military activity as armies on both sides remained, for the most part, in winter quarters. Despite the lack of progress in the eastern theater, where the focus remained on Lee and the defense of Richmond, the momentum of the war continued to favor the North. With a Union victory presumably in sight, a good deal of attention, both home and abroad, was now focused on the fate of the millions of slaves who would eventually be emancipated. In America, the argument was over citizenship and civil rights, especially the right to vote. In England, the argument centered on the question of race itself.

With both their culture and their polity based on distinctions of class, caste, and race, the British governing class felt increasingly threatened by a liberal democracy that would be so bold as to enfranchise the very people whom a majority of the "civilized" world deemed hopelessly inferior. Indeed, if former slaves in America could be made citizens with full civil rights, then how could Great Britain justify withholding such rights from its own working-class citizens, to say nothing of the human rights of the millions of indigenous peoples in its far-flung empire? White supremacy was, after all, the glue that held the British Empire together. In an effort to slow the rising tide of democracy, British conservatives, recognizing that emancipation was all but inevitable, argued for a form of "regulated coercion," "serfage," or "predial servitude" that would deny

African Americans civil rights and would keep them bound to the soil and subject to the will of the "superior race."

Northern liberals resisted these efforts as they continued in their role as midwives to the nation's political and cultural rebirth. Their challenge now was to give shape and coherence to that new America. In his *Topical Notebooks*, where he gathered his thoughts for lectures and addresses, Emerson, the nation's most revered public intellectual, stated the principles that this new democratic society would embrace. They were the principles he and the majority of New England's intellectual class had been promoting since the firing on Fort Sumter. He listed them under the heading "The Scholar's Creed": "I believe in free trade; in universal suffrage; in public schools; that all men are born free & equal *quoad* the laws; that all men have a right to their life *quoad* the laws; in freedom of opinion religious & political." For Emerson and his New England cohorts, these principles distinguished American culture from its English counterpart in a way that had never before been quite so clear. In this second Revolution, America would experience a more complete victory over the British, one both political *and* cultural. Of course, the key to this rebirth was the destruction of slavery. Liberal New England had been leading the way on this, and Emerson believed that the "Greatness of New England consists in the confidence that slavery must end."[1]

Similarly, their friends in Old England realized that the fate of democracy in both countries was inextricably tied to the fate of Black people in America. The first *Edinburgh Review* of 1864 featured a lengthy (39 pages) article by Harriet Martineau titled "The Negro Race in America."[2] The essay began with the blunt declaration that "slavery in America has received its death-sentence" (204). What followed was the proof, beginning with an overview of the history of slavery that focused on the many slave insurrections that had occurred over time, including "the Southampton Massacre" in 1831, led by Nat Turner.

Martineau pointed out that despite cruelty and harsh punishments for their effort, many slaves "learned to read more or less, by hook or by crook," thus showing the innate human desire and capacity for mental self-improvement (208). They also possessed, like all people, a desire to be free. "The runaways were a standing evidence . . . that the idea of freedom was active in the negro mind" even before "Abolition was heard of" (211). While conservatives writing in the *Saturday Review*, the London *Times*, *Blackwood's*, and other prestigious British journals spoke of the intense hatred of Blacks by people in the North, Martineau here pointed to the fact that "seven years ago . . . the Legislature of Massachusetts declared the Common Schools open unconditionally to all the children in the State," regardless of race. This rule was soon accepted by institutions of higher learning, and Black students "are now seen even at Harvard University" (218). After making note of the bravery of soldiers such as those serving in the Massachusetts 54th, Martineau concluded that all this showed clearly that Blacks were fully capable of the same development as whites—intellectually, socially, and politically—once the yoke of slavery was cast off.

On the other side of the Atlantic, Emerson, George W. Curtis, and Frederick Douglass had all publicly proposed the enfranchisement of Blacks and other non-white citizens. The idea was gaining ground through the combined efforts of the New England intelligentsia, their abolitionist allies, and Radical Republicans like Senator Charles Sumner. Freedmen also joined the effort. As Eric Foner reports, even before the war ended, "free blacks and emancipated slaves came together in conventions, parades, and petition drives to demand the suffrage."[3] But there was still strong opposition, in both North and South, to such a revolutionary change. Sumner's biographer reports that the senator's "exertions in behalf of Negro rights during the Thirty-Eighth Congress [March 1863–March 1865] brought upon him fiercer and more widespread criticism than any he had encountered since his attacks upon slavery in the early 1850's."[4]

Conservatives were becoming anxious, as shown in their effort to turn back this tide of change, while liberal friends in Boston applauded Sumner's actions. His congressional opponents accused him of electioneering and of sponsoring measures designed to give "gratification to that ultra-radical sentiment" of New England so that he could "say that such and such laws have been passed in favor of the negro." Despite such criticism, Sumner and his allies remained committed to the cause of equality. They realized it was essential "to extend the suffrage to the Negroes . . . as a counteracting power to that of their former masters." Sumner vigorously promoted this position even though he was aware that Black suffrage was still unpopular throughout the North. He was disappointed that Lincoln was not doing more in this regard, and he informed fellow members of the Saturday Club that his opinion of the president at this time was "at least not higher than it was three years ago."[5]

Earlier in the month, on January 9, the *Liberator* ran a story about a rather remarkable development in attitudes among Americans living in England. "At the great Thanksgiving Day breakfast at St. James's Hall, where all loyal Americans here were present, . . . and where Minister Adams made a speech—the Thanksgiving prayer was offered by [Rev.] Sella Martin, a fugitive slave." This seemingly simple gesture had great significance. English abolitionist "George Thompson, who was present, said, 'If I had been told three years ago that I would have seen a fugitive slave acting as the clergyman for a gathering of all the Americans in London, and sitting at the table beside the Hon. Robert J. Walker [a Mississippi Democrat] and the American Minster [Charles Francis Adams], I would have believed the man who prophesied it a madman.'"[6]

The emergence of this new and compelling counternarrative was bringing rather dramatic change in England. Positive attitudes toward Blacks were steadily displacing ancient prejudices. Newspaper and journal articles critical of slavery and slaveholders were becoming more common. At this point, the North was unambiguously identified with emancipation and the South with slavery.[7] With no immediate crisis poisoning the waters, some previously tepid British liberals now felt free to side openly with the North. Thomas Hughes informed Lowell that "every man here whose judgment is worth a straw is for negro suffrage."[8]

The *Saturday Review*, like other conservative publications, was deeply concerned with this trend. It was seen as a threat to the central principle upon which the British Empire stood, the subordination of "inferior races," such as Blacks in the West Indies, Sepoys in India, or Aboriginal peoples in Australia. The *Review* offered a strong condemnation of such wayward thinking, especially when coming from highly respected British liberals like "Mr. Francis Newman."[9] English conservatives were also becoming increasingly concerned with the tendency of liberals there and in America to equate the cause of slaves with that of the English working class.

The *Review* decided to address this issue directly. "Slaves and Labourers" was remarkable for its conservative candor. Without apology, the author openly acknowledged, "The position of the English poor does approach that of the Southern slave."[10] While he agreed that the condition of both slaves and laborers could be improved, reformers in both countries should have faith that there will be "good results from the action of very general and indirect influences," such as "economic changes, and material inventions, and an increasing wish in the governing classes to do their duty." These would inevitably "bring about a very slow but still a perceptible improvement" (71).

But this improvement had natural limits. The working poor of England, for example, could never be allowed to sit side by side with their betters in public conveyances. While "religion teaches English gentlemen not to despise the poor," the *Review* noted, this did not rule out limiting the lower classes' interaction with their betters when necessary. Thus, "if five farm labourers took five seats in a railway carriage, an English gentleman filling the sixth would find it hard to stand the smell, however benevolent and pious he might be." Even the church itself was not immune to the need for limitations on Christian philanthropy. "It must have occurred to many attendants on the service of the English Church," the author opined, "that if the poor really came, in the 'thronging numbers' which are invited, the building would reek with a stifling vapor" (72).

Like most conservatives on both sides of the Atlantic, the writer insisted that the condition of slaves in America was actually quite good. "The planter, unless he is a bad man towards his slaves, feeds them well, and gives them medicine when they are ill," he claimed. "The house slaves are beloved by the family; the old nurse is its darling; the black coachman is the guide and friend of the little boys." Similarly, in England, while "the difference of station is always kept up, it is the business of the good rich man to comfort, protect, instruct; it is the business of the good poor man to accept all this comfort, protection, and instruction in a gentle and thankful spirit" (72).

All of this was as it should be, the writer insisted, because "this division between the master and slave, aristocrat and laborer has been dictated by God and as such is a fixed natural law." The idea that "all men are created equal" was simply gross blasphemy. "The English poor man or child is expected always to remember the condition in which God has placed him, exactly as the negro is expected to remember the skin which God has given him. The relation in both instances is that of perpetual superior to perpetual inferior, of chief to dependent, and no amount of kindness or goodness is suffered to alter this relation." To disrupt this God-given paradigm, the author said, would be an unpardonable sin that would inevitably bring disaster (72).

The *Review* warned that the accelerating movement in America toward establishing equal rights, regardless of race, was a threat to long-established English polity. Such liberal thinking must be rejected outright, both in England and America. "The language currently held in England, when a sweeping Reform Bill is proposed," the writer noted, "does not differ very widely" from the argument in America for Black enfranchisement. "It is absurd, wise men say, to suppose that the rude British hind can be made fit to vote by giving him a vote. He is not capable of using political power." It is because of this, he pointed out, that "the British Constitution very sensibly provides that he shall be governed by his betters. Thus the governing classes in England speak, and there is truth and justice in what they say [and] a Southerner would not recognise in it any great difference from much that he has heard at home" (72).

Arguments such as this help explain the strong, persistent opposition of British conservatives to emancipation and equal rights in America. The very structure of Great Britain's social and political organization was threatened by those movements, which is undoubtedly why British conservatives continued to press for British intervention even long after Palmerston's government made the practical and necessary decision to remain truly neutral.

While the *Saturday Review* was explaining why strict distinctions between the unwashed masses and their betters were imperative in a civilized society, President Lincoln opened the doors of the White House, the People's House, to those unwashed masses for the traditional New Year's reception. When the London *Times* reported January 19 on "the universal handshaking *levée* at the White House on New Year's day," it noted one element of this year's event that was new and somewhat shocking. "It was remarked as a novelty that there were no less than four negroes in the crowd, and that the President received them with special good humor. It is the first time in the existence of the Republic that a black man has dared to mingle in the throng on such an occasion."[11] The *Times* offered no further comment. The notorious "Thunderer" was apparently left speechless by this remarkable sign of the times. British liberals were delighted with this conspicuous example of democratic equality. Lincoln was truly a people's president, one who welcomed *all* citizens, regardless of class or color. In a letter to John Elliott Cairnes, John Stuart Mill observed, "things continue to advance in the right direction in America. It does one good to read of negroes at the President's levée."[12]

It was undeniable that in America attitudes toward race were changing rapidly, at least in the North. This fact was reinforced when the *Liberator* of February 5 reported on Frederick Douglass's "Mission of the War" address at Cooper Institute in New York City. Douglass was one of those "no less than four" who had attended the president's New Year's levée. The report indicated, among other things, that "Mr. D. gave us an amusing description of his recent visit to the White House, or of '*a Rail-splitter meeting a Nigger*,'" an event no one could have imagined before the war. Sarah Shaw also celebrated the growing acceptance of Blacks in American society. In a letter to Cairnes she indicated that "the change of feeling about the colored race seems nothing short of miraculous."[13]

James Russell Lowell, who was now co-editing the *North American Review* with Norton, also took note of how swiftly American opinions were changing in regard to the question of race. In January's "The President's Policy," he pointed out that "the progress of three years has outstripped the expectation of the most sanguine. . . . When it was first proposed to raise Negro regiments, there were many even patriotic men who were sure something terrible, they knew not what, would follow."[14] But it did not, and even greater changes were now forthcoming.

Lowell's *North American* essay was part of the liberals' campaign to ensure Lincoln's war measures would become permanent, despite continuing opposition. As George Fredrickson observes, "Abolition from military necessity would not guarantee a national commitment to racial equality" because many still saw it as "a useful tactic in a war fought for conservative nationalism."[15] Some believed the battle for emancipation had been won, but Lowell and his group knew there was much more work to be done if equal rights were to be assured and America's reinvented democracy placed on a sound footing.

By the fall of 1863 there could be little doubt in the minds of New England's liberals that they and President Lincoln shared essentially the same vision of a reconstructed America, one founded on the ideals of universal freedom and equal rights. In order to make this vision a reality, however, the president would have to be reelected, something which, in the winter of 1863–64, seemed unlikely. No president had been reelected since Andrew Jackson, and with a continuing stalemate on the battlefield and war-weariness throughout the North, support for Lincoln's renomination was eroding. David Herbert Donald notes that even among supporters, "talk of reelecting Lincoln . . . [was] desultory and not particularly fervent."[16]

Conservative Democrats were especially hostile toward Lincoln at this time for enlisting African Americans in the Union army. The Boston *Pilot* contended that the Black race was much happier "in slavery than freedom," and it condemned the "negrophilists" and "nigger-worshippers" who try to convince Blacks that they were the equals of whites. The paper strongly supported the growing opposition to Lincoln. "Call them Copperheads—or any other ungentlemanly term you like," the *Pilot* declaimed, they are the only "true representatives of Republican freedom today in this country."[17]

Democratic opposition to Lincoln was also energized by resentment toward his liberal emancipation policies, which critics argued exceeded presidential authority and undermined the Constitution. Emerson felt it was time to speak out once again. His decision to publicly support Lincoln at this critical time was undoubtedly based on his personal regard for the man, as well as his perception of their shared values and goals regarding the future progress of the republic. In his lecture "Fortune of the Republic," which he repeated several times beginning in December 1863, Emerson celebrated the vision of America that Lincoln had described at Gettysburg.

It was, Emerson declared, a new day that dawns, bringing with it a "Second Declaration of Independence" that promised "liberty, land, justice, and a career for all men: and honest dealings with other nations."[18] He pointed to the progress being made by the newly emancipated freedmen. This progress, he insisted, had to go forward. "The steps already taken to teach the freedman his letters, and the decencies of life, are not worth much if they stop there." All Americans, he insisted, should support this effort in order to ensure every person has an equal chance in life. The result will be that which "the earth waits for,—exalted manhood, the new man, whom plainly this country must furnish."[19] Emerson was confident America's liberal democracy could reach this goal.

Around this time, Edward Peacock wrote a long letter to a friend, Boston reformer Caroline Dall, informing her that opinions in British universities were becoming more favorable toward the North. "Oxford is in many ways as much the centre of English opinion as London," he told her, and "opinion there has very much changed for the better since January 1863. Then but a small fraction of the advanced Liberals saw the true nature of the American contest. Now . . . almost all thinking persons, except a few political high churchmen like Mr Beresford-Hope, who have their crotchets about the hierarchical constitution of society . . . are strongly on the North's side."[20]

Firsthand reports from distinguished Englishmen also helped the Northern cause in England. Thomas Hughes noted in a letter to Lowell that Leslie Stephen had recently returned from his tour of America and that he was very enthusiastic "about New England and abolition." Hughes's letter also introduced another visitor, Edward Lyulph Stanley, a young English peer and Oxford graduate whom he described as a "Staunch

Northerner." Like Peacock, Hughes noted that public opinion in England was definitely turning in favor of the North.[21]

The *Saturday Review* remained concerned about this trend. A February 20 article with the revealing title "The Advantages of Slavery and the Slave Trade" complained about Harriet Martineau's recent essay in the *Edinburgh Review*. The author argued that, while slavery was, indeed, evil and certainly not the blessing Southerners claimed it to be, there was no way Blacks could ever be seen "as equal to the whites." Therefore, if emancipated (which now seemed a virtual certainty), it will be necessary that they be placed in "a system of regulated coercion which will display many of the features of villenage or predial servitude." Under such a system, Blacks would "remain attached to the soil," thus assuring their usefulness and the continued "supremacy of the whites."[22]

While British conservatives were offering their advice on how to keep emancipated Blacks in their place, Europe remained in turmoil as a result of the Polish uprising. The *Saturday Review* recognized that these were dangerous times. The journal warned on March 5 of the current peril and noted that if the English government was "bound to resist Austria and Prussia in arms," then "the Americans might probably take occasion to resent the injuries which they suppose themselves to have suffered in the matter of the *Alabama*." If this should happen, the writer declared, "a war with the United States . . . would be an unmixed evil. It is impossible to imagine a treaty of peace which, at the end of the contest, could leave England in a better position than at the beginning."[23]

This was clearly a concern for Palmerston's government. Ephraim Adams reports that "throughout these spring months of 1864, Lyons [the British minister in Washington] continued to dwell upon the now thoroughly developed readiness of the United States for a foreign war and urged the sending of a military expert to report on American preparations."[24] The *New York Herald* declared that the fact that the United States now possessed "a veteran army of close upon a million of the finest troops in the world" put the country into a position not only to "drive the French out of Mexico and to annex Canada, but, by the aid of our own powerful navy, even to return the compliment of intervention in European affairs."[25] While many would see this as simply Yankee bluster, there could be no doubt at this point that the United States had a formidable military, both on land and sea.

As English conservatives warned of the consequences of war with the United States, their liberal countrymen applauded developments in the American conflict that furthered their progressive agenda. The day after the *Saturday Review* article on English foreign policy appeared, Henry Bright wrote to Norton: "Whatever bad results your Civil War has had, it has at least had two happy ones, one the emancipation of the slave,—another the increasing interest which here is taken in everything connected with America, & which cannot but be for good."[26] The *Commonwealth* appeared to confirm that perception. Their English correspondent reported that "nothing is more remarkable and exhilarating . . . than the reverence with which the Simon-pure abolitionist is regarded here." They are seen as "the legitimate successors of the [William] Wilberforces and [Thomas] Buxtons, whose positions were among the highest in the land, and whose descendants are powers in Parliament. The American abolitionist is regarded as a nobleman."[27]

Even if somewhat exaggerated, it was clear there had been an important shift in English public opinion. The reason for this, according to the March 12 *Commonwealth*, was that "almost every American name that hitherto has been ever heard on this side of the ocean was the name of an abolitionist." New England literati were especially prominent. "Not one in twenty will be found ignorant of Emerson, Phillips, Garrison, Mrs. Stowe, H. W. Beecher, Sumner, Curtis, Mrs. Child, or Horace Greeley; and each of these names has an association with abolitionism." Because of this, the correspondent pointed out, "it is taken for granted that all our literary men are on that side."[28] The opposite might be said of Great Britain.

On the home front, the outlook on the war was improving somewhat. This month, Ulysses S. Grant was officially commissioned as "lieutenant general," a rank last held by George Washington. On March 17, he took command of the Union armies with the title "General-in-Chief of the Army of the United States."[29] There were high hopes for military success in the spring. After a string of disappointing leaders, Lincoln now had in place the Union's most competent and successful generals: Grant, William Tecumseh Sherman, and Philip H. Sheridan. The South, on the other hand, had suffered enormous losses the previous year and endured a long, hard winter on short rations.[30] The end could not be far off. For most Northerners, it could not come too soon.

War-weariness remained a concern, and the Copperheads were looking forward to an opportunity to deny Lincoln a second term. The *New England Loyal Publication Society* was determined this would not happen. Circulation reached 1,282 on March 1. The content of this broadsheet now consisted mainly of attacks on Copperheads and the Peace

Party, as well as positive reports on the activities of the Union's Colored Troops.[31] Those troops continued to garner a great deal of positive press, especially in New England.

With numerous reports of, and tributes to, the Black soldiers' courage, skill, and valor, antislavery feelings reached new heights in the North and also in Great Britain. English abolitionist George Thompson, now on an American tour, was greeted enthusiastically wherever he went. Samuel May wrote to Richard Webb that he recently heard Thompson speak in Boston: "He shows us how essentially friendly to our country & everything good in it is the great mass of the working, laboring, mechanic people of England including with them a very large body of the middling class & not a few of the best-educated minds."[32] The alliance between the English working class and the North would continue to strengthen in the year ahead.

While these major developments were occurring in America in the spring of 1864, the Palmerston government was too preoccupied with developments in Europe to take serious notice. The revolt in Poland had brought bloody Russian reprisals, while Prussia and Austria sent troops into Denmark. British public opinion was aroused by the invasion and, as Ephraim Adams puts it, there was a feeling in the country, "widely voiced, that Great Britain could not sit idly by while Prussia and Austria worked their will on Denmark."[33] Southern sympathizers in England now saw an opportunity. William Lindsay, still a strong supporter of the Confederacy in Parliament, felt that this was the time to propose yet another motion calling for British mediation in the American war.

The idea, implausible at best, was that Palmerston's government would approve the measure in order to ensure the support of Southern sympathizers in Parliament for its Danish policy. Lindsay wrote to James Mason, who was now back in Virginia, urging him to return to England. He also included the wording of the motion he intended to propose.[34] At the same time, Lindsay, Robert Cecil, William Gregory, James Spence, and other conservative Southern sympathizers called upon various organizations dedicated to Southern independence to join the effort to arouse public opinion on the matter. These included the Manchester Southern Club, the London Confederate States Aid Association, and the Southern Independence Association. The weakness of all these conservative organizations was that they appealed mainly to "persons of rank and gentlemen of standing," while the working class remained committed to the North.[35]

Nevertheless, with major British journals like the *Saturday Review* and the *British Quarterly Review*, as well as Henry Hotze's *Index*, at the ready, the conservatives took to the field once again.[36]

Part of the strategy involved the claim that Palmerston's government had caved in to American bluster in seizing the Laird rams and, earlier, the *Alexandra*. Cecil took the lead in January's *Quarterly Review*. He argued that England was no longer respected by the world powers. The problem was that England was now all talk and no action. "That appearance of warlike power which used to give dignity to its imperious tones no longer imposes upon its hearers. Its vehemence of language falls dead and impotent upon minds penetrated with the conviction that the storm which is assailing them is nothing but words—brave words possibly, but still only words."[37] Arguments such as this appearing in some of England's most prestigious journals undoubtedly made it very clear to Northerners that Southern sympathizers in Great Britain had no intention of giving up, or even moderating, their campaign for intervention. The *British Quarterly Review* made essentially the same argument in April, declaring, "The character as well as the *prestige*, of the British Government has . . . been seriously damaged" by Palmerston's capitulation on the issue of the rams.[38] The *Saturday Review* joined the propaganda campaign by criticizing the North's "degeneracy" and "barbarism" as it entered a new phase of "hard war" designed to bring the South to its knees by destroying its will to fight.[39]

By mid-month, this latest pro-Southern campaign, coupled with recent parliamentary maneuvering, had a depressing effect on young Henry Adams. He wrote his brother, "The idea is universal here that our armies are depleted and our last hour coming, while the tone of the sympathizers is more defiant than ever."[40] The European view of American affairs would always be inflected by the environment there, which was now thick with Southern propaganda appearing in the popular press. Things had a very different look from the American side. Around this time, Norton wrote to William Wetmore Story expressing his great confidence that the war was finally going well.

Story, however, who was back in Rome, had a starkly different perspective. "I would judge from your letter that America was just about the most wonderful place going, and that there was no such thing as corruption and money making and vulgarity there . . . that everything was done with noble means and aims and that the millennium was absolutely arriving now," Story wrote. "But somehow or other it does not look so to me at this distance—I think we shall get to our journey's end at last desolate in a ranshakley wagon . . . [with] a company of tobacco chewing, spitting and swearing speculators and politicians mixed up with spiritualists, enthusiasts and honest men, and all driven by a vulgar but well meaning driver who 'calhellates to do wot's rite.' " The problem was "we don't actually know what that is," Story complained. "The whole administration has been like the driving of a drunken coachman." In spite of such harsh commentary, he assured Norton that he was still "proudly American."[41]

Back in the United States, the New England intelligentsia felt far more positive in the light of recent developments. On April 8 the Senate passed the Thirteenth Amendment to the Constitution, mandating the abolition of slavery in the United States and all areas under its jurisdiction. The vote, 38 to 6, was significant.[42] It was now up to the House of Representatives, where there was substantial resistance, to do the same.

Lydia Maria Child was also feeling optimistic. In a letter to a friend, she celebrated the "marvelous and constantly increasing change in public opinion on the subject of slavery" that had occurred in the country over the past year.[43] A good part of this was brought about by the gradual acceptance of the use of Colored Troops in the Union army. *Harper's Weekly* reported on April 9 that "New York has sent off its second regiment of colored volunteers" to join the forces under Burnside. Many of these were former slaves. The *Weekly* also reported on atrocities recently committed by the Confederates against Black Union soldiers at Fort Pillow, something British conservatives failed to note while criticizing the Union army for its "barbaric" behavior.

There were about 557 Union soldiers at Fort Pillow, over half of them Black. On April 12, Confederate General Nathan Bedford Forrest surrounded the fort and demanded a surrender. When that was refused, he attacked in force. The Federals were overwhelmed, suffering the loss of 231 men killed. Northern reports indicated that the fort was surrendered almost immediately, but Confederate troops proceeded to massacre the helpless Black defenders en masse. In his memoirs of the war, Grant included part of a letter by Forrest that revealed his intention in allowing the massacre. "The river was dyed with the blood of the slaughtered for two hundred yards," the Confederate general wrote. "It is hoped that those facts will demonstrate to the Northern people that Negro soldiers cannot cope with Southerners."[44]

The Confederate atrocities were met with outrage throughout the North as the facts became known. *Harper's Weekly* of April 30 pointed to the "massacre of the black soldiers at Fort Pillow" as a clear indication "that in their fierce extremity the men who have been so long barbarized by Slavery have virtually raised the black flag." It was these same barbarians, who now "count upon the aid of Copperheads and Peace men at the North," who willingly aligned themselves with "the haughty aristocracy of the South." Undoubtedly with the support of English as well as Northern working men in mind, the author reminded readers that these were the aristocrats who believed "that laboring men of every color and nationality ought to be slaves and treated like cattle."[45]

The article predicted that this barbarism would elicit an even deeper commitment from Union soldiers, especially Colored Troops. Two months later, Charles Francis Adams Jr. confirmed this prediction. He was involved in the fighting before Petersburg, Virginia, at the time. Adams wrote to his father that the Colored Troops that were part of the Union force "were in high spirits; for the evening before in the assault they had greatly distinguished themselves. All admit . . . that the darkies fought ferociously, and . . . the cruelty of Fort Pillow is reacting on the rebels, for now they dread the darkies more than the white troops; for they know that if they will fight the rebels cannot expect quarter."[46]

In the meantime on the home front, Oliver Wendell Holmes launched another vitriolic verbal assault on the British in his April *Atlantic* article, "Our Progressive Independence." The essential difference between England and America, Holmes argued, was that one believed in equality and the other did not. He pointed out that America's long journey toward independence had begun with a revolution inspired by the idea of democratic equality and human rights. At the time, "the true-born Briton read as far as the first sentence of the second paragraph of the Declaration of Independence.[47] There he stopped, and there he has stuck ever since," Holmes asserted. "That sentence has been called a 'glittering generality,'—as if there were some shallow insincerity about it. . . . [But] 'glittering generality' or not," he declared, "the voice which proclaimed that the birthright of equality belonged to all mankind was the *fiat lux* [Let there be light] of the new-born political universe."

America was striving, for the first time, to apply that principle to men of all races. As a result, a true American democracy was now "threatening all the dynasties, menacing all the hierarchies, undermining the seemingly solid foundations of all Old-World abuses." As long as slavery existed in America, the English could take comfort in the idea that Americans, like them, did not truly believe in universal equality. But all that had changed as a result of dramatic and unanticipated (by most) developments in the war. Destroying slavery and proclaiming equal rights for all, Holmes declared, is the culmination of "our progressive independence," both political and cultural.

In conclusion, Holmes, like Emerson, insisted that because "American society founds itself upon the rights of civilized man," liberal America, not reactionary England, was now the ideal model for Western civilization. There is "no permanent safety for any nation but in the progressive recognition of the American principle," he declared. "The right of governing a nation belongs to the people of the nation; and the urgent duty of those provisional governments which we call monarchies, empires, aristocracies is to educate their people with a view to the final surrender of all power into their hands."[48] For New England liberals, this was the American dream. For British conservatives, it was the American nightmare.

Holmes's article, which reached a broad transatlantic audience, served as a stern rebuke to Victorian elites. There would be more to come in the months ahead. Emerson sent copies to Matthew Arnold, who expressed his gratitude. "It was a great pleasure to me to receive a letter from you," Arnold wrote. He recalled their meeting "some years ago" during Emerson's 1847 lecture tour. He told the New England bard that he could "never forget the refreshing and quickening effect your writings had upon me at a critical time of my life." Arnold included a copy of his *A French Eton*, which had recently been published in book form. The work offered some sharp criticisms of American culture, and Holmes's article would serve nicely as payment in kind. Arnold told Emerson that he hoped the American would "not be offended" by what he said about America. He thanked him "for the two numbers of the *Atlantic Monthly*" and noted that "the papers to which you directed my notice are certainly remarkable, thoughtful suggestive productions."[49] Despite this personal politeness, it must have occurred to both men that their views were, quite literally, worlds apart.

Chapter 18

Republican Radicals Declare Slavery Must Go

British Call for "Regulated Coercion"

In early May, the North suffered one of its worst defeats in the debacle later called the Battle of the Wilderness. At the same time, Matthew Arnold, writing in *Macmillan's Magazine*, maintained that the American war was ultimately a good thing because the conflict and the resulting breakup of the Union would (somehow) lead to the "disciplining and correcting" of the American people. Regarding the most pressing and morally significant issue involved in the struggle, he had nothing to say, other than to declare his indifference. "I put the question of slavery on one side," he wrote, because, depending on perspective, "one may wish this party or that to prevail."[1]

An article by Goldwin Smith appearing in the same issue of *Macmillan's*, titled "Has England an Interest in the Disruption of the American Union," focused specifically on the renewed talk of British intervention. Smith argued that intervention in American affairs would not be in England's best interest and that the nation would be better served with the United States as an ally rather than an enemy. He also condemned the surge in activity by the Southern Independence Association.[2] The group had recently published "Address from the People of Great Britain and Ireland to the People of the United States." It called for the North to make peace with the Confederacy. Attached were 300,000 signatures that were claimed to be from "men of all ranks, classes, religions and politics."[3]

The petition was published in the London *Times* on October 12. Following this, and in keeping with the de facto alliance between British and American conservatives, it was sent to Horatio Seymour, the Copperhead governor of New York, rather than Seward, the secretary of state. The hope was that Seymour "would place [it] before the people of the United States of America . . . with a view to secure the object of our appeal."[4] This propaganda ploy had been ignored by Seward since it was not approved by the British government.[5] Goldwin Smith published a strong retort as Northern supporters in England became bolder in their pushback on Southern sympathizers. In his "Letter to a Whig Member of the Southern Independence Association," he sought to leverage the now strong alliance between the North and the English working class. Smith pointed out that the Southern Independence Association specifically appealed to persons of rank and gentlemen of standing and that their interests were not those of the working class of Great Britain. Smith's pamphlet, Ephraim Adams reports, was "probably the strongest presentation of the Northern side and the most severe castigation of Southern sympathizers that appeared throughout the whole war."[6]

Meanwhile, on the battlefront, after a long lull and a series of indecisive minor skirmishes, Grant began to put into action his grand plan for advancing against the Confederates on all fronts simultaneously. For three days (May 5–7, 1864), Grant's forces were engaged in one of the bloodiest episodes of the entire war. When it was over, both armies were mauled and Grant had not achieved the victory he sought. The Battle of the Wilderness was a major Union disaster.[7] Throughout the seven days of battle, the Army of the Potomac alone lost more men than all Union armies combined in any previous week of the war.[8] War-weariness and general dissatisfaction with the state of things now combined, and it seemed probable that Lincoln would not be renominated, let alone reelected. Not surprisingly, during this time leading British newspapers and journals expressed their renewed confidence that Southern independence would be achieved, while predicting the defeat of Lincoln at the polls.

Ephraim Adams reports that from June 1864 to the end of the year, the London *Times* colored every report "to create an impression of the unlimited powers of Southern resistance."[9] Confederate sympathizers in England took heart at these inflated and flattering reports. One from the London *Times*'s "Confederate Correspondent" described the fighting near Spotsylvania and noted, "The Confederates are in splendid condition, and full of spirit and cheerfulness. They all realize the importance of victory, and are ready to endure any privation necessary to its achievement."[10]

Toward the end of the month, *Harper's Weekly* of May 28 reported on recent European developments in "The Schleswig-Holstein War." In a related article, "The American Question," the paper also revealed how Southern sympathizers in England continued to use the deteriorating situation in Denmark as a pressure point to get a more favorable policy from Palmerston's government regarding Confederate interests. Nevertheless, the writer reported, "the English Government declines to accede to the pressure for a Conference on American affairs. . . . Earl Russell, in a speech in the House of Lords, contended that it was owing to the vigilance of the Government that the Lairds had not plunged England into a war with the United States," and Palmerston wanted to keep it that way.

With the North now firmly identified with emancipation, and since most British conservatives did not wish to be seen as supporting the "foul blot" of slavery, the position of the Southern Independence Association was quickly becoming untenable. Despite the efforts of influential conservatives like Robert Cecil, Alexander Beresford-Hope, William Lindsay, and others to keep it afloat, Adams reports that "by the end of June, 1864, there was almost a complete cessation of meetings."[11] English public opinion was clearly changing, but the battle was not yet won.

Around this time, Edward Peacock wrote again to his Boston friend Caroline Dall. "Public opinion is still very much divided on American matters," he told her. "All the thinking liberals and a few high class Conservatives sympathize with you, but the great non thinking middle class go with the south because they think them 'gentlemen.' " These include "more than half the members of the *learned* professions." Southern propagandists like Hotze, Peacock noted, "have been worldly wise enough to see this and have paid for first rate talent to advocate their cause."

Knowing of Dall's strong interest in, and commitment to, the new social science movement in America, Peacock also commented on the current debate regarding race.[12] "I have been much amused by the controversy on the origin of the human race," he wrote. "There are some ignorant persons here who think that if it could be proved that the negro was a different species to ourselves, slavery etc. would follow as a matter of course," which was the essence of the conservative argument at present. "This is all nonsense as every thoughtful person must see," Peacock declared, "but trash of this order has much weight with many persons. Slavery is surely wrong because slaves are men and women, not because they are our distant cousins."[13]

The *Saturday Review* also joined the debate, another indication of the acute anxiety English conservatives felt regarding the growing demand in the North for equality without regard to race. In "The Negro Found Out," the *Review* noted that, because of the war, "the negro has been revealed in all his peculiar characteristics to the searching scrutiny of American and European criticism."[14] Each has had "opportunities of watching the daily habits and innate disposition of a race previously unknown save through exaggerated description" (748). As a result, the writer observed, presently in England "we hear great nonsense talked . . . about the American war and the anti-slavery sentiments of the Federal leaders. The whole thing is grossed in fraud," he insisted. "Not one in a hundred of the Northerners—perhaps not one in ten hundred—cares, or ever has cared, for the negro in the 'man and brother' sense of the word" (749). New England, the writer admitted, has been something of an exception to this rule.

Ignoring the recent testimony of English visitors like Edward Dicey to the contrary, the *Review* then described the Northern Black as "a citizen with curtailed and stinted rights of citizenship, a thing to flout and scorn and jostle out of the public highways of daily life." All of this, the author claimed, stemmed not from prejudice alone but from Blacks' innate inferiority. The Black man "is what he is, not through mere causeless prejudice and dislike" but "from his own incapacity to profit by favourable opportunities." He went on to insist that Northerners do not truly believe "all men are created equal" and that "no respectable party or body of Northerners honestly proposes to put the negro on a perfect level with white men," which might then have the unthinkable consequence of actually encouraging "the dusky pets of the platform to aspire to matrimonial alliance with white women" (749).

Meanwhile, in America, having replenished his forces following the disastrous Battle of the Wilderness in May, Grant began an offensive that would result in yet another Union disaster, the Battle of Cold Harbor (June 1–3).[15] Although the Federal campaign had failed, things were not exactly looking up for the Confederates. With Grant's forces surrounding their capital and settling in for a long siege and no possibility of British intervention, there was little cause for hope.

On July 1, the London *Times* reported that the Union army had surrounded the Confederate capitol. The *Times* speculated that if these developments resulted in "the capture of Richmond . . . and the reunion of North and South," it was likely this would "be followed by a declaration of war against Great Britain for the depredations of the *Alabama* and the *Florida*."[16]

The possibility of an American declaration of war on Great Britain was taken seriously by the British. The day after the *Times* report appeared, July 2, the *Saturday Review* indicated that a shooting war with the Americans was a very real and unnerving possibility and noted that there was now concern about "the defence of Canada." In light of this, the writer opined, it would be in England's best interest to follow policies that were least likely to provoke a conflict.[17]

It was around this time that Lincoln allowed Horace Greeley to meet with three Confederate representatives on the Canadian side of Niagara Falls. The purpose of this informal meeting was to discuss the possibility of peace negotiations. Lincoln was suspicious of the whole thing, but he did not wish to be seen as completely opposed to any peace effort. He provided Greeley with a "to whom it may concern" letter outlining the conditions to be met in any peace settlement. The first was the restoration of the Union, and the second, foremost in the minds of liberal New Englanders, was "the abandonment of slavery."

This second requirement apparently surprised many, despite the several steps that Lincoln had already taken in that direction. The Confederate emissaries rejected the offer and published Lincoln's letter in an attempt to embarrass him. His critics claimed that by offering what many would see as patently unacceptable terms, Lincoln was deliberately short-circuiting any effort to end the war through negotiation. Conservative Democrats seized upon this episode as proof that Lincoln had turned the war into an abolition campaign when its proper and only true aim, they insisted, was the preservation of the Union.[18]

Even some Radical Republicans turned on the president for what appeared to be just one more misstep in a long series.[19] Emerson, however, was delighted with Lincoln's words. He saw in them a clear articulation of a profound ideal that had global significance in the struggle for human rights. In his journal, he noted that when "certain memorable words[,] expressions that flew out incidentally . . . , as, for example, in Lincoln's letter, 'To all whom it may concern,' are caught up by men, go to England, go to France, [and] reecho thence with thunderous report to us, . . . they are no longer the unconsidered words they were," he wrote. "We must hold the government to them: they are powers, and are not to be set aside."[20] For Emerson, Lincoln had made it clear, intentionally or not, that slavery must be abolished in order to achieve a lasting restoration of the Union.

Emerson was right about the positive effect Lincoln's words would have in England, at least among America's allies there. The antislavery *Spectator* felt that "Mr. Lincoln never displayed his remarkable shrewdness to better advantage" than in this letter. As the writer noted, the president had now clearly stipulated that "the cause of the war must be finally removed" before peace can be restored. This, he acknowledged, will not likely please conservatives in the North any more than the slave owners in the South because "great masses of the Americans are still unjust in opinion toward the negro." However, even these people would have to recognize that "the society created by slavery and the society created by democratic freedom cannot exist side by side." Not surprisingly, the writer also wrote that this development "displeases the English friends of the South."[21]

Lincoln was able to recover a bit from criticism at home when he allowed James Gilmore and Colonel James Jaquess to travel to Richmond in July on a subsequent peace mission. The idea was suggested by Colonel Jaquess, known as the "Fighting Parson" because before the war he was a Methodist clergyman. Jaquess believed that by "acting on the Methodist element of the South he could bring about a peace that would be honorable to all."[22] The two succeeded in getting a meeting with Jefferson Davis, where they presented a statement of terms approved by Lincoln. As Gilmore later described the meeting, the terms included "Emancipation, No Confederation, and Universal Amnesty." Davis reportedly replied that amnesty only applied to criminals and "we have committed no crime."

Regarding emancipation, Davis stated, "You have already emancipated nearly the million of our slaves,—and if you will take care of them, you may emancipate the rest." But the North's primary goal in the war, the restoration of the Union, Davis rejected in anger. "*We will be free!*" he declared. "We will govern ourselves. We *will* do it, if we have to see every Southern plantation sacked, and every Southern city in flames."[23] Davis's words made it clear that at this point in the war it was reunion and not abolition, as the president's critics claimed, that was the primary obstacle to peace.

Upon his return, Edmund Kirke wrote up a full report of his interview with the hope of getting it into Greeley's *New York Tribune*. That was fine with Lincoln, but what he really wanted was to get it into America's most influential journal, the *Atlantic Monthly*.[24] Gilmore later wrote that after he read his account to Lincoln, the president asked, "'What do you propose to do with this?' 'Put a beginning and an end to it, sir, on my way home, and hand it to the *Tribune*,'" Gilmore answered. "'Can't you get it into the *Atlantic*?'" the president asked. "'No doubt I can, sir,' I replied." At this point, Charles Sumner, who was also present at the meeting, interrupted. He suggested Gilmore put a short account immediately "'into one of the Boston papers, and then, as soon as he can, the fuller report into the *Atlantic*.'" Lincoln agreed and told Gilmore to "send me the proof of what you write for the *Atlantic*.'" A short account subsequently "appeared in the *Boston Evening Transcript*," Gilmore later wrote.

What happened after that testifies to the rather extraordinary relationship that had developed by now between the liberal intelligentsia of New England and President Lincoln. "Two or three days afterwards Mr. James T. Fields handed to me the proof of *The Atlantic* article," Gilmore stated, "which I at once forwarded to Mr. Lincoln. He retained it seven days, and thereby delayed the issue of the magazine considerably beyond the usual period."[25] Eventually, it was published to the president's satisfaction, and it achieved the desired effect.

Delaying the publication of the *Atlantic Monthly* for a week was a sacrifice Fields and his liberal colleagues were apparently willing to make if it served the president's purpose in bringing this second American revolution to a successful conclusion. The details of this meeting were eventually published in an abbreviated form in several Northern newspapers, along with the far more complete and dramatic account, titled "Our Visit to Richmond," which appeared in the September issue of the *Atlantic Monthly*.

These did much to blunt the criticism that Lincoln initially endured following the Niagara meeting. The account also served to discredit the Copperhead notion that somehow peace *and* reunion could result from negotiations with the Confederacy. Nevertheless, conservatives still argued that the demand for emancipation was an obstacle to a peaceful settlement. Additionally, Democratic editorials continued to complain about thousands of white men dying to free the Blacks.[26]

As Democrats, Copperheads, and English conservatives continued to denigrate Blacks and disparage the cause of emancipation, New England liberals became even more fully committed to that cause as a moral imperative. Early in the month, on July 2, *Harper's Weekly* published engraved side-by-side prints depicting "The Escaped Slave and the Union Soldier." These images presented a dramatic contrast: the first depicts the slave, a seated wretch dressed in rags; the second is the same slave now transformed into a smartly uniformed Union infantryman standing confidently with his Springfield rifle in hand. The accompanying text read in part, "On the one side, the poor fugitive oppressed with the weariness of two hundred long miles of dusty travel, a journey interrupted by a thousand necessary precautions, and harassed by . . . suggestions of a fate more horrible than death if he is discovered; with his meager covering of rags about him: and on the other side, the soldier crowned with freedom and honor." The writer then asked, "Can we not at length have faith in that heroism which has been so gloriously illustrated at Wagner and Olustee and Petersburg and which, in the face of the Fort Pillow massacre, yet offers itself afresh . . . to a cause [that promises] his freedom?" *Harper's* continued to document such striking transformations, both in words and dramatic visuals, for the duration of the war.

Earlier in the year, Southern supporters in England had been discouraged by developments in the war. Now, however, with Grant bogged down in front of Petersburg, a Confederate army under Jubal Early threatening Washington, and Sherman stymied in his efforts to take Atlanta, their hopes were revived once again. Nevertheless, the Palmerston government was determined to maintain a policy of true neutrality.[27]

By this time, the loss of life and property throughout the South had taken an enormous toll. The Southern economy was ruined, inflation was rampant, and Confederate money was nearly worthless. "Defeatism," Allan Nevins notes, "could be found everywhere [in the South] by the autumn of 1864."[28] English supporters, however, were unaware of this because the London *Times* was reporting the opposite. The English also had a broader perspective and broader concerns. If the cause of the North was the cause of liberal democracy everywhere, then the cause of the South was the cause of conservatism everywhere, and they were loath to see it fail.

Morale in the North was also at a low point due to war-weariness and the lack of progress on the battlefield. Abolitionist editor Sydney Howard Gay wrote to a friend that he believed "people would vote today for any compromise that would bring peace without sacrifice of the Union." There was also, he sensed, a "growing party for peace at any price, even disunion." Gay believed Lincoln's "chances of reelection grow daily less & less, & the chances of any Copperhead traitor better and better."[29]

Despite such negativity, Lincoln remained committed to emancipation. However, he realized that this commitment, which was vigorously supported and encouraged by liberal thinkers and reformers throughout the North, particularly in New England, was alienating to Northern conservatives, especially in the West.[30] For a short time, Lincoln considered altering his policy to make emancipation secondary to reunion, implying, at least, that the latter could come without the former. When he tried out a statement to that effect on Frederick Douglass, whom he considered "one of the most meritorious men in America," the response was immediate. Douglass strongly objected. "It would be given a broader meaning than you intend to convey," he told Lincoln. "It would be taken as a complete surrender of your antislavery policy, and do you serious damage."[31] The president was apparently moved by this, and he ultimately decided there was only one path—to continue on the course that destiny so clearly mandated, regardless of the consequences.

With this, as well as a stalemate continuing on the battlefield and war-weariness eroding Northern resolve, Lincoln fully expected to be defeated in November. Consequently, just four days after his meeting with Douglass, he composed his famous "Blind Memorandum" and asked members of his cabinet to endorse it, sight unseen.[32] It read, "This morning, as for some days past, it seems exceedingly probable that this Administration will not be re-elected. Then it will be my duty to so co-operate with the President elect, as to save the Union between the election and the inauguration; as he will have secured his election on such ground that he can not possibly save it afterwards. A. LINCOLN."[33]

Lincoln believed that in all likelihood, his failed general-in-chief, George B. McClellan, would be the next president. The Democrats met in Chicago at the end of the month. Their platform, written largely by Peace Democrats and Copperheads, declared, "Justice, humanity, liberty and the public welfare demand that immediate efforts be made for a cessation of hostilities." Although the document went on to say that "the aim and object of the Democratic Party is to preserve the Federal Union and rights of the States unimpaired," it was not clear how this aim could possibly be accomplished short of winning the war.[34] On the last day of the month, the Democrats, as Lincoln expected, nominated George McClellan.[35]

Chapter 19

Atlanta Falls and Lincoln Rises

British Criticism Intensifies

On September 17, 1864, the London *Times* reported on the recent nomination of George McClellan as the presidential candidate of the Democratic Party. The dapper general was favored by the British establishment because he was more interested in ending the war than in ending slavery. Additionally, a Democratic victory would almost certainly result in a permanently sundered Union. McClellan also possessed personal qualities that endeared him to British elites: unlike his "vulgar" and largely self-educated opponent, he was "an officer and gentleman."[1] What British readers did not know at the time was that dramatic historic events had already occurred in America that would determine the outcome of the election and, ultimately, the outcome of the war.

After months of attacks and counterattacks that left the issue of victory in suspense, General William Tecumseh Sherman finally prevailed against the defenses of Atlanta, and the city fell to Union forces on September 1. General John Bell Hood and what remained of the Army of Tennessee evacuated the city. The following day Federal troops assumed full control, and Sherman informed the president that "Atlanta is ours, and fairly won."[2] Just days earlier, Fort Morgan on Mobile Bay, Alabama, had fallen to the Union navy under the command of Admiral David Farragut. The port was now firmly under Union control. This left the rebels with only one port open for blockade running: Wilmington, North Carolina.[3] After months of a bloody stalemate, the dynamic of the conflict changed dramatically. The war was, once again, clearly heading toward a Union victory, and the recently passed Democratic "peace platform" looked to some like treason. In response to these important victories, Lincoln declared a national day of celebration. On the same day, under the procedure that Lincoln had previously outlined, the loyal citizens of Louisiana voted to ratify a new state constitution abolishing slavery.[4]

Things seemed to be moving in the right direction for the president at last. While the New England intelligentsia were solidly behind Lincoln, he also enjoyed the support of the most distinguished Black abolition leaders in America. Sojourner Truth, after a cordial visit at the White House in October, remarked, "I felt in the presence of a friend and I now thank God from the bottom of my heart that I always advocated his cause."[5] Frederick Douglass, who had recently met with the president, sent a long letter of support to the *Liberator*, published September 23. In it, he declared, "Every man who wishes well to the slave and to the country should at once rally with all the warmth and earnestness of his nature to the support of Abraham Lincoln." Additional victories on the battlefield served to reinforce confidence that Lincoln would be reelected. This optimism was reflected in a gathering of the Saturday Club where, as Norton later informed Curtis, members heard a firsthand account from "an officer, just from Atlanta," who "told us some good stories of Sherman."[6]

Earlier in September, Lincoln penned a letter to a "Union Mass Meeting at Buffalo" where he stressed the critical importance of the thousands of Black men now serving with distinction in the Union ranks. "Any different policy in regard to the colored man, deprives us of his help, and this is more than we can bear," the president wrote. "We can not spare the hundred and forty or fifty thousand now serving us as soldiers, seamen, and laborers. This is not a question of sentiment or taste, but one of physical force. . . . Keep it and you can save the Union. Throw it away, and the Union goes with it." Lest there be any doubt about the matter, Lincoln showed an iron resolve on the permanence of emancipation. "Nor is it possible," he declared, "to retain the service of these people with the express or implied understanding that upon the first convenient occasion, they are to be re-inslaved. It *can* not be; and it *ought* not to be."[7] There could be no mistaking the president's meaning. He was determined that these people would remain "forever free" and that the Union would be preserved.

Across the Atlantic in Great Britain, Lincoln continued to enjoy the support of a number of liberal thinkers and reformers, along with the masses of the non-voting working class. Thomas Hughes, one of the North's most reliable English friends, wrote to Garrison that "the great majority of Englishmen . . . agree with me in thinking that Mr. Lincoln has proved himself thoroughly honest & trustworthy." He added that British liberals had "the deepest interest in American politics, and especially in the noble stand which you & others have made against slavery in the United States." Like other English liberals, Hughes saw the American conflict as the New Englanders saw it, that is, as a "great revolution" that had global significance.[8]

The *Liberator* continued to pay close attention to developments in England, as did other Northern journals. There was a lingering fear of British recognition, or even intervention, and recent debates in Parliament brought on by Southern sympathizers kept those fears alive. Two of the most active, William Lindsay and John Arthur Roebuck, were persistent in their efforts regardless of Union victories, or perhaps because of them.[9] What would turn out to be Lindsay's final attempt to win recognition was rejected by the House of Commons in July. Despite this humiliating failure, throughout the fall, he continued to lend public support to the Confederacy.[10]

As had often been the case, New Englanders, like many others in the North, associated the actions of British sympathizers abroad with Northern accommodationists at home. The *Liberator*, in "An English 'Peace-Party' Copperhead" (Sept. 9), noted that "Mr. Lindsay, . . . in seeking to induce the British government to make an offer of 'their friendly offices' to the two contending parties on this continent," sought thereby to "greatly strengthen the position of the PEACE PARTY" in the upcoming election. In the eyes of many Northerners, such an overt attempt by a member of a foreign government to influence an American election was just one more indication of the unholy transatlantic alliance of conservative reactionaries the war had given rise to.

The day after this report on Lindsay's effort, the *Liberator*, in "English Sympathy Acknowledged by the President" (Sept. 10), printed the official response of Minister Adams to the recent expression of support for Lincoln from the Manchester Union and Emancipation Society. The article indicated that Adams told the workers the document was received by the president "with the most grateful satisfaction." In expressing such support, he told them, they were "promoting the ultimate interests of the human race everywhere," another confirmation of the global significance of the American conflict.

With emancipation now likely, the London *Times* focused its attention on the racial debate. While the Northern press regularly reported on the exemplary performance of the Union's Colored Troops, the *Times*'s "special correspondent," Francis Lawley, stationed in the Confederate camp near Petersburg, reported that "the colored soldiers" engaged there did not "possess the courage [or] . . . share the emotion of the Anglo-Saxon." Indeed, these presumably hapless creatures have been "starved into the Federal ranks" on the belief that they will "gain a liberty which they can neither improve nor understand."[11] The *Saturday Review* added to the calumny on September 24. After reporting that the Union army had recently succeeded in recruiting some 200,000 men, the writer said, "Of the actual enlistments, a large portion will be almost worthless, because it consists of emancipated negroes."[12]

The continuing, gratuitous criticism of Lincoln and the Union cause in the British press led to an even greater appreciation of British supporters. As Goldwin Smith toured America, he was received enthusiastically wherever he went.[13] His biographer notes that during his visit, Smith "was impressed by the widespread belief in equality and the relative absence of class divisions" in the North. "In the United States equality seemed to him as much the rule of life as was inequality in Great Britain." Eventually, Smith was able to meet with Lincoln, "to whom he brought messages of sympathy and support" from English liberals.[14]

Meanwhile, with Sherman's army marching through the Southern heartland, Sheridan in virtual control of the Shenandoah Valley, and Admiral Farragut achieving a stunning victory at Mobile Bay, by the fall of 1864 it seemed quite certain that the collapse of the Confederacy was at hand. Grant continued to maneuver around Petersburg in his effort to move against Richmond. So far, he had only great losses and little success to show for the effort. However, his army was being replenished regularly with fresh troops, many of them Black, while Lee was losing men he could not replace. At the end of August, Lee sent James Seddon, Confederate Secretary of War, a desperate appeal for additional men, but none were to be had.[15] Under such doleful circumstances, some in the Confederacy were now seriously considering what was once unthinkable, conscripting slaves.

For Northern liberals, this was a win-win situation. One Bostonian, whose husband was a Union officer, wrote to a friend asking, "Did you see that article from the Richmond *Enquirer* [reprinted in the *New York Times*] saying the reserves of white men were all used up, two thirds of the army absent without leave, and nothing remained but to enlist the slaves?" This remarkable development could mean only one thing. The Confederate army was exhausted and apparently on its last leg. Additionally, if slaves were now conscripted to restore it, this would be a triumph for Unionists. "Men cannot be soldiers without being free," she wrote, "and to ask a black man to fight to sustain slavery was out of the question. I am glad they see what's what."[16]

The culture war between New and Old England had reached a consummation of sorts. In October's *North American Review*, Charles Eliot Norton announced that America had acquired a new and decidedly liberal national character, one free of British taint. As a result of a long, progressive process, he declared, "we . . . have changed from Englishmen to Americans."[17] Norton explained that "the chief external form in which nationality embodies itself is that of institutions." In America, these institutions were "founded . . . on the principle of respect for the rights of man," which are universal. In the new America created by the war, "every individual in the community" will be "assured of the possessions and enjoyment of all natural rights, of all the dignities and privileges of manhood" (524, 525).

For Norton and other New England liberals, Southern slavery was a legacy of feudal Europe. He argued, "In destroying slavery we are destroying the worst form of class privilege, and a base and spurious counterfeit of aristocracy." By so doing, he insisted, we "have our principles confirmed, and our confidence in our free democratic system quickened and made stronger." He admitted that this new America was still a work in progress: "Not yet are our people educated up to the great argument of their own principles." But he was confident that "as our people become more enlightened and more virtuous," the ideal America he and his liberal cohorts envisioned would become a reality (526–27).

Liberals like Norton deeply resented the ongoing de facto alliance between British and American conservatives. They were also outraged by British efforts to influence the American election and, thereby, the outcome of the war. *Harper's Weekly*, in "The British Lion Cheers for Chicago" (Oct. 15), castigated the London *Times* for bursting "into a shout of enthusiastic delight at the nomination of McClellan and Pendleton, and the principles which they have been selected to represent. We have always insisted, says the *Times*, that the North could not subdue the South, and the proof is the Chicago Convention and its nominations." As *Harper's* reported, according to the *Times*, peace could only come with disunion because "Southern leaders are not such fools as to relinquish what they have proved their ability to hold." In writing thus, the *Times* appeared to many Northerners to be virtually dancing on the nation's grave. Fortunately, as *Harper's* pointed out in a related article in the same issue titled "The London-Chicago View," "the successes of Grant and Sheridan, of Farragut and Sherman" substantially deflated the hopes of America's transatlantic enemies and spelled defeat for the foul forces of the London-Chicago axis.

Not surprisingly, the fall presidential campaign was strongly inflected by race. Copperheads continued to argue that, under Lincoln, the war to save the Union had become a war to free the slaves. Like their Southern counterparts, Northern Democrats pointed to the Emancipation Proclamation as proof that the administration's ultimate goal was always the abolition of slavery.[18] As the movement toward emancipation and, for many, equal rights, continued to gain ground, Democrats painted the entire society as giving way to licentiousness and racial degeneracy. Mark Neely reports that "miscegenation—a term coined by Democrats in 1864"—was used to symbolize widespread moral decay. "Every institution was tainted in these democratic eyes—schools, churches, and government alike. The public schools had a 'leprous disease' and 'moral plague.'" For these Democrats, even the churches seemed "completely abolitionized and could not be counted on to uphold private morality." The entire nation was now threatened by what they called the "corruption of race."[19]

Lincoln's support in New England, especially Massachusetts, remained solid but sober. Edward Emerson notes in his history of the Saturday Club that, while most members voted for Lincoln as "the best man who could be elected," some were "uneasy at again choosing, in that dangerous period, 'a pilot who waited to ask his crew's opinion.'"[20] Despite such reservations, there was really no alternative. As Sumner told an abolitionist friend, "Lincoln's election would be a disaster, but McClellan's damnation."[21]

When election day finally arrived, the results proved astonishing. Lincoln carried every Union state except Delaware, Kentucky, and New Jersey. His electoral victory was an astounding 212–21. He won the popular vote by almost half a million out of some four million cast. Remarkably, the soldiers of the Union army (who counted the *Atlantic Monthly* and *Harper's Weekly* among their favorite reading) gave a resounding vote of confidence both to the president and to the war, casting 116,887 for Lincoln and only 33,748 for McClellan, their former general-in-chief.[22]

Lydia Maria Child saw the election as a victory for grassroots democracy and the common people. In a letter to a friend, she applauded "the intelligence and reason of the people" in reelecting this plainspoken man, a position fully opposite that of recent British critics. "There is no beauty in him, that men should desire him," she wrote. "There is no insinuating, polished manner, to beguile the senses of the people; there is no dazzling military renown; no silver flow of rhetoric; in fact, no glittering prestige of *any* kind surrounds him; yet the people triumphantly elected him."

This was a remarkable victory for common people everywhere regardless of their race. Child "rejoice[ed] in having a rail-splitter for President and a tailor [Andrew Johnson] for vice president. I wish a shoe-black could be found worthy to be appointed Secretary of State; and I should be all the more pleased if he were a *black* shoe-black."[23] Emerson was also pleased with the outcome. It confirmed his faith in what he called humanity's "moral sentiment" and what Holmes called simply "the heart of the people." In a letter to a friend, Emerson expressed his "joy in the Election." "Never in history," he declared, "was so much staked on a popular vote."[24]

News of Lincoln's reelection would not reach London until the end of the month. In the meantime, prominent English journals continued to express their low opinion of the president and his emancipation policy. The *Saturday Review* opined on November 5 that America's "excuse for hating the Mother-country" was the fact that "its educated classes" did not support universal emancipation. This was because they believed emancipation to be both impractical and unworkable. "Mr. Lincoln and his friends" have never "taken the trouble to consider what is to be done with four millions of emancipated negroes," the *Review* pointed out. "They will certainly not be accepted as equals and fellow citizens either by the Northern or Southern whites."[25] Because of the assumption that equal rights was neither possible nor desirable, "the Negro question" in America remained an enigma for the *Saturday Review* and the English governing class generally.

This was due, in part at least, to the fact that British conservatives were unaware of the degree to which Northern attitudes toward Blacks had changed. The major reason for this change was the service of Black Union soldiers. When the Union army began enlisting former slaves, British critics, like those of the *Saturday Review* and the London *Times*, said they would never make good soldiers. When Fort Wagner, Olustee, and Port Hudson proved them wrong, they simply ignored or even denied the evidence. Black soldiers could never be anything more than cannon fodder, they insisted. That argument was dealt a severe blow when several Southern governors proposed the enlistment of slaves in the armies of the Confederacy.

This situation resulted in some awkward attempts at explanation by the *Saturday Review* and the *Times*. The *Review* on November 12 held that the South's slave soldiers would fight well if instructed to do so. Their natural fidelity and "instinct of submission" would ensure that they would neither turn on their masters nor flee to the Union lines and freedom. Additionally, this forced military service could be used as a transitional step to the replacement of slavery with a less offensive institution, such as serfage. Still, the idea of white masters arming their Black slaves made the *Review* a bit queasy, recalling the recent bloody Sepoy uprising in India. However, the writer pointed out that "the negroes probably like their masters better, . . . and their lower intelligence throws difficulties in the way of concerted rebellion."

Whatever the case, the author maintained that "almost every imperial race" (which, apparently he considered the Southerners to be, even though the *Review* frequently condemned the North for its "pursuit of empire") "has at some time used the services of auxiliaries who have generally been treated as subordinates and inferiors," and so, while "the masters may hesitate to part with their slaves, . . . they know the character of the negroes and their own power too well to dread any vexatious assumption of equality."[26]

As British conservatives attempted to explain what was once considered unthinkable, British liberals, like their American counterparts, wondered what the status of emancipated Blacks would be after the war. Poet Aubrey de Vere wrote to Norton following the recent Union victories and questioned if there was "any doubt about the abolition of slavery; & in this case what will follow? Will the emancipated Blacks work?" he asked. And "what course will things take when the war is over? . . . Do pray write at once & tell us all you can."[27] At this point, Norton could not say with any certainty what would follow the Union's expected victory. He was hopeful, however, that America could become a society that embraced both diversity and equality.

Goldwin Smith offered a very positive view of just such a society in a long letter published in the London *Daily News* on November 24. Smith had witnessed the presidential election while in Boston. He pointed out that, despite the fierce excitement of parties, "the election has gone off with perfect tranquility," thus contradicting repeated claims by English conservatives that democracy was actually mobocracy. "In the lowest wards the crowd at the polls was almost as orderly as a crowd going to church. . . . I can scarcely conceive a nation in the midst of a great political struggle more temperate, more orderly, more respectful of each other's rights, more observant of the law," he reported.

The mutual respect Smith witnessed extended up and down the social scale and included Blacks as well as whites. "In a country town to which I went in the afternoon," he wrote, "I saw negroes taking part in a town meeting, apparently on a perfect equality with the whites." In Boston, Smith "saw the negroes going up in the line of voters to the polls mingled with the first men in the place." Such an orderly, democratic election, conducted in the midst of a bloody internecine war, testified to the resilience of liberal democracy and affirmed the principle of equality, Smith believed. He assured his English readers that Northerners "have in them the love of their community and the devotion to their cause, which, after all the calamities and errors, will bring them out victorious."[28]

Meanwhile on the battlefront, Grant's policy of hard war was now having its effect. Although Sherman's victory in Atlanta and his subsequent devastating "March to the Sea" were a source of celebration to the Union's friends in England, conservatives there condemned it. Sherman hoped his success would impress foreign nations, especially Great Britain. He wrote to Grant that if "we can march a well-appointed army right through [Jefferson Davis's] territory it is a demonstration to the world . . . that we have a power which Davis cannot resist. This may not be war, but rather statesmanship."[29]

Sherman's famous march did have an effect on the morale of Southern sympathizers in England. The London *Times* was deeply discouraged by it. It was not only a demonstration of the Union's military superiority, but it was also draining the lifeblood from a rapidly expiring Confederacy. Nevertheless, as noted in the *History of the Times*, "Till the eleventh hour . . . The *Times* argued desperately that the great march could not succeed, that Savannah could not fall, and when the disaster could no longer be denied tried to minimize its importance."[30]

Tennyson saw Sherman's march as yet another example of Northern barbarism. His sympathy with the South was no doubt reinforced by occasional visits from various Southern "gentlemen." At this time, he wrote to a friend that he recently spent an evening in the company of "two Confederates, men of the finest gentlemanship, perfectly simple and noble-mannered." One of these was a familiar guest, John Reuben

Thompson, former editor of the *Southern Literary Messenger*, who was now a contract writer for Hotze's propaganda journal, the *Index*. Thompson later described his visit with the poet laureate in his diary. He noted that Tennyson "talked much of the American war, which he deplored, and of the Yankees, whom he detested."[31] Thompson later sent Tennyson a supply of Southern tobacco as a gift.

At this point, the alienation between the New England intelligentsia and their once-respected Victorian cousins, with few exceptions, was absolute. In his journal, Emerson reflected, more in sorrow than in anger, on the shocking perfidy shown by the English intellectual and artistic classes throughout the war. "Could we have believed that England should have disappointed us thus?" he wrote, "that no man in all that civil, reading, brave, cosmopolitan country, should have looked at our [second] revolution as a student of history, as philanthropist, eager to see what new possibilities for humanity were to begin." Instead, "every one squinted; Lords, Ladies, statesmen, scholars, poets, all squinted, . . . *Edinburgh, Quarterly, Saturday Review,* Gladstone, Russell, Palmerston, Brougham, nay Tennyson; Carlyle, I blush to say it; Arnold. Every one forgot his history, his poetry, his religion, & looked only at his shoptill" and "whether the stability of English order might not be in some degree endangered."[32]

This crass self-interest and the desire to preserve their imperial culture had led them, finally, into a de facto alliance with the Confederacy. "Every poet, every scholar, every great man, as well as the rich," Emerson noted, "to our astonishment cried, *Slavery forever! Down with the North! Why does not England join with France to protect the slaveholder?*" In the hour of America's, and the world's, greatest need, England's cultural elites proved feckless. Despite such perfidy, however, Emerson remained confident that the new America rising from the ashes of war "shall prosper, [and] we shall destroy slavery, but by no help of theirs."[33]

In late November, Emerson delivered a series of lectures on "American Life." Like Norton earlier, he reflected on the new national identity that was now emergent as a result of the war.[34] He began his lecture by noting that Lincoln's reelection virtually assured that the nation would remain united. However, this new Union, unlike its predecessor, would be united by something more than its geography. The ideals of a nation normally define its character, but in the past America's character had been blurred by the pernicious and divisive influence of slavery. With that influence now in eclipse, America's true national identity was coming into focus.

For Emerson, and for most other New England intellectuals, that identity was clearly liberal. In direct response to the sneering critics of Great Britain, he presented a grand vision of a society built on freedom, diversity, and human rights. He called for "Opportunity—doors wide open—every port open: if I could have it, free trade with all the world, without toll or custom-house; invitation as we now make to every nation, to every race and skin—white man, red man, yellow man, and black man; hospitality, a fair field, and equal laws to all."[35] For New England liberals, America's diversity was its strength and equal rights was the glue that held the nation together.

The liberal philosophy of New England continued to resonate with a growing audience of liberals in Old England. The *Commonwealth* (Dec. 31) reported in "Our English Letter" that "the *Atlantic Monthly* has a wide circle of readers here; and amongst its many fine papers, those of Col. Higginson are exciting admiration." Thomas Wentworth Higginson's "Leaves from an Officer's Journal" had recently appeared in the November and December issues of the *Atlantic*. Based on his experiences commanding a Black regiment, he wished to show how the "discipline," "ardent loyalty," and "courage under fire" of his Black troops, whose service was so critical in winning the war, were "remolding the destinies of the two races on this continent."[36] From a liberal perspective, this "remolding" was one of the great achievements of the war.

John Stuart Mill certainly felt this way. He wrote to Cairnes applauding the fact that "there is now the majority in Congress necessary for the Anti Slavery amendment of the Federal Constitution. The value of this last cannot be overrated," he wrote, "for it ensures not only that there will be no reunion retaining slavery, but that after reunion the Federal Courts will have a right to set aside any tricky legislation in the Southern States intended to reestablish Slavery under another name."[37]

Edward Peacock also celebrated these liberal achievements. He wrote to Caroline Dall at this same time, thanking her for her recent informative letter. He told her it "has been read to several fierce Southerners, English people of course, and haters of strong-minded women." The good news from America had a predictable effect. "Southern sympathizers are somewhat downhearted in this country," Peacock wrote. "I think that the idea now [is] that the South will have to submit to terms but that those terms will include *slavery*, states' rights, etc." Peacock, however, was confident the North would never "sacrifice the interests of humanity after that fashion." He went on to suggest that once the South was conquered, the North should seize the slaveholders' land and "establish the negroes on it as peasant proprietors. When that has been done, and the black men become rich," he wrote, "it will be found that its prejudice against color will die out." Such, at least, was his hope.

Mrs. Peacock added a note to her husband's letter that underscored the importance and effectiveness of the liberal transatlantic alliance that had been brought about by the war. She indicated that Dall's correspondence, by keeping them informed of developments in the war, allowed them to rebut Southern propaganda and the perversions of the British press, especially the London *Times*. In addition to the "several papers from you which I have duly read," she noted, "we take the *Commonwealth* published at Boston" and also "the *Atlantic Monthly*."[38] All of this was very helpful to British liberals, who were now engaged in their own civil war against a conservative establishment.

With a Union victory virtually assured, some English friends began to reorganize in order to better address the anticipated needs of a post-emancipation America. Mrs. Martin Taylor wrote to Samuel May to inform him that "the Ladies Emancipation Society has changed its name to 'The London Negro Aid Society.' We leave out 'Ladies' as several gentleman have joined our society—amongst others—J. S. Mill, M.P. [Mill had recently been elected to the House of Commons], Thomas Hughes, M.P., P. A. Taylor, M.P., [and] Professor Fawcett, M.P." She added, "Professor Cairnes was appointed President of our Society," which was a special "subject of gratulation" to her.[39]

Back in America, Emerson, in a lecture titled "Books," spoke of a new American society, one where everyone would have a fair chance for a share in the future. A full account of the address appeared in the *Commonwealth* on the last day of the year. According to the article, Emerson declared that "the greatest achievement of American Literature" was the Declaration of Independence. "The shaft-words of the preamble of the Declaration—'We hold these truths to be self-evident, that all men are created equal, endowed by their Creator with certain inalienable rights, among which are life, liberty, and the pursuit of happiness'—these words, little heeded at the time, deemed oratorical, lampooned by flippant rhetoricians in our day as 'glittering generalities,' have turned out to be the only immortal words, the fresh, the matin song of the universe."[40] That song now resonated on both sides of the Atlantic.

Chapter 20

1865

The Civil War Ends, but the Battle for Human Rights Continues

The final year of the war witnessed some of its most dramatic events, including the fall of Richmond and the surrender of Robert E. Lee's once invincible Army of Northern Virginia to Ulysses S. Grant's now all-conquering Army of the Potomac. Sherman finished his famous "march to the sea" and then turned his army northward to complete his devastating sweep through the South. But in the midst of the North's joyous celebration of victory came the devastating news of President Lincoln's assassination. Anger, sadness, and outrage followed as Northerners viewed the heinous act as the last gesture of a barbaric slaveholding society. In England, critics once vitriolic in their condemnation of Lincoln as a crude dictator now found much to praise in the martyred president. Northerners, however, were unconvinced of this newfound respect for their fallen hero. Animosity toward Great Britain remained intense.

Throughout it all, international attention was focused on the fate of some four million former slaves. As liberals in Congress passed the Thirteenth Amendment, abolishing slavery forever, conservatives at home and abroad sought to limit the civil rights of emancipated Blacks. British conservatives maintained their de facto alliance with Northern Copperheads and Confederates, the aristocratic "Cavaliers" who fought for a now lost but, presumably, still noble cause. They continued to argue that the "natural inferiority" of Blacks rendered them unfit for full civil rights and insisted that some form of "serfage," "predial service," or "enforced coercion" was necessary to ensure that the former slaves remained useful to themselves and society. After Lincoln's assassination, they found common cause with the nation's new president, Andrew Johnson, who was decried by liberals for his racist policies. Defeated in their effort to ensure slavery's survival, British conservatives sought to slow, if not completely halt, what had become an international movement for human rights.

Charles Eliot Norton and his liberal associates realized this was a defining moment in world history. In the January issue of the *North American Review*, Norton observed, "We are now entering upon an era in which the political principles which are distinctively American . . . are to have fuller scope and new development." Like other New England idealists, Norton held that those principles were "as old as the moral nature of man for they are simply the expression of the natural rights of man in society. The political equality of men, their right to equal justice and freedom, their right to self-government, their right to every means of self-development consistent with the general welfare,—these are the essence of the American system of democracy," which, Norton insisted, was now rightfully the world's standard for progressive government.[1] He associated Lincoln's commitment to universal liberty and equal rights, regardless of race, with the English workingman's struggle to obtain the same. The struggle for human rights, he argued, extended far beyond America's shores. The stubborn efforts of British conservatives to resist this liberal movement only reinforced the simmering anger toward Great Britain that many Americans continued to feel.

A major source of irritation was the persistent negative commentary on the war in the London *Times*, which, as Leslie Stephen noted, was considered "the voice of England." In a lengthy essay, published around this time, Stephen indicated that his "complaint against the *Times* is its total ignorance of the quarrel, and . . . its pouring out a ceaseless flood of scurrilous abuse, couched, indeed, in decent language, but as essentially insulting as the brutal vulgarities of the *New York Herald*."[2] The *Times*'s biographers confirm that throughout the war the paper was seen by many as "the main instrument of alienating public opinion in America." It was clear that the paper "had gone very far astray in its military and even its political estimates" in reporting on the war.[3]

The *Times*'s two American correspondents, Charles Mackay and Francis Lawley, were largely responsible for this. Although previously supportive, Mowbray Morris, the *Times*'s manager, now accused Lawley of "an error of judgment" in his reporting. "The worse feature in Southern affairs," he wrote, "is the growing discontent. We augur ill from this. I observe that you never notice the Opposition & always represent the Southern people as being unanimous. Are you sure you are right in this?" Morris asked.[4]

Morris had also become dissatisfied with Mackay's reporting and eventually fired him. In his letter of dismissal, Morris wrote that it was "brought about by your blind & unreasonable condemnation of all public men & measures on the Federal side, & your disregard of the remonstrances which I have frequently addressed to you against such a course. It is our opinion that the paper has suffered in reputation through your partial representation of affairs in the Northern States, & that our readers have been misled by your statements to take an erroneous view of the current of events."[5]

The charges against Mackay and Lawley were clearly justified, but Morris was being disingenuous in his failure to acknowledge that his own well-known animus toward the North, which he shared with the paper's editor, John Delane, had a strong influence on the paper's coverage of American affairs. Additionally, the *Times*'s predisposition to represent the opinions of England's governing class undoubtedly contributed to its misleading reporting on the American war and the fact that the paper now "suffered in reputation" on both sides of the Atlantic.

Other conservative English publications were equally complicit, but even with the Confederacy's rapidly deteriorating situation, they were unwilling to back away from their earlier positions. The *Quarterly Review* published in January yet another bitter attack on the North by Robert Cecil, one that rehashed many of the same complaints and accusations found in his earliest essays. Cecil acknowledged that "there has been recently a perceptible relaxation" of interest in the American war among his countrymen, but he noted that "the mass of educated men in England retain . . . sympathy for the South." While, admittedly, there were some who saw the war as a crusade against slavery, "their number is scanty and their authority insignificant."[6] Cecil left the English working class out of this equation. In his view, they simply did not count.

Meanwhile, the Confederates' military situation worsened, with Sherman ravaging the Southern heartland at will and Hood's army in Tennessee now virtually destroyed.[7] In light of this desperate reality, the *Saturday Review* once again endorsed the unthinkable: the use of Black troops by the Confederate army. This was a dramatic turnabout for British conservatives. As noted earlier, the idea of Black inferiority specifically and the concept of racial inferiority generally were key components in providing moral justification for the British Empire. The continuing subjugation of millions of indigenous, mostly dark-skinned peoples in far-off colonies was morally acceptable only if it was understood that these inferior "others" benefited from their subordination. Even a radical liberal like John Stuart Mill had once argued that, while "universal rules of morality between man and man" may apply to the treatment of a "barbarous people," they do not have the same rights as "civilized" people.[8] For Victorian elites, if slavery could not be morally justified, subordination most certainly could. The Civil War in America was now challenging even that proposition.

This fact was apparent to many. The measure "adopts the whole theory of the abolitionists," the *Richmond Examiner* fumed. "If a negro is fit to be a soldier, he is not fit to be a slave."[9] Georgia politician and Confederate army general Howell Cobb declared that "the moment you resort to negro soldiers . . . is the beginning of the end of the revolution. If slaves will make good soldiers our whole theory of slavery is wrong."[10] Of course, this very fact was being affirmed by the Union army's Colored Troops every day.

When first reported, the Confederates' intention to enlist slaves was only a rumor. However, General Lee himself confirmed the need to do so in a letter to the sponsor of the "Negro enlistment" bill in the Confederate Congress. Lee told the congressman that the measure was both expedient and necessary. "The Negroes," he wrote, "under proper circumstances, will make efficient soldiers." Lee was led to this conclusion by the compelling example of the Union army's Black regiments. "I think we could at least do as well with them as the enemy," he wrote. Lee then added an important point: "Those who are employed should be freed. It would be neither just nor wise . . . to require them to serve as slaves."[11]

The *Saturday Review* realized that this measure, if passed, would result in a profound change in Southern society. Indeed, it would precipitate "a great social revolution," because if you "grant freedom to negro recruits," it is "taken for granted that general emancipation must follow." Some British sympathizers believed emancipation would lead to British recognition of the Confederacy, but the *Review* admitted that, in effect, British foreign policy was driven more by pragmatism than morality. "There is no doubt that much popular prejudice would be removed by emancipation," the writer observed, "but England has withheld recognition, not because the South maintains negro slavery, but because it has not definitively succeeded in establishing its independence."[12] For England's governing class, slavery, or some other form of "serfage," remained the proper condition for all "servile races."

On January 31, 1865, the Thirteenth Amendment to the Constitution of the United States was passed by the House of Representatives.[13] Lincoln, having won an astounding victory at the polls in November, used his political capital and all of the resources of his administration in an effort to get the amendment through Congress. He also let it be known that he favored the enfranchisement of literate freedmen and all who had served honorably in the ranks of the Union army.[14] At this point, there was a general understanding throughout the North that this was a war for freedom. Eric Foner states, "Millions of northerners who had not been abolitionists before the war became convinced that securing the Union as an embodiment of liberty required the destruction of slavery."[15]

New England liberals viewed the passage of the Thirteenth Amendment as a major step in the ongoing reinvention of American democracy. A Boston merchant recorded in his diary the joyful sentiment resounding in the hearts of citizens throughout the Commonwealth. "Slavery is dead—dead—dead & the States are fast accepting the Constitutional amendment—Now will commence a new campaign" aimed at civil rights.[16] One of the first steps in that "new campaign" occurred on the day after Congress approved the Thirteenth Amendment, when Charles Sumner introduced a motion to make John Rock of Massachusetts the first Black attorney to be admitted to argue before the Supreme Court of the United States.[17] Sumner stood before the court as Rock's sponsor. Rock's admission, *Harper's Weekly* predicted, would "be regarded by the future historian as a remarkable indication of the revolution which is going on in the sentiment of a great people."[18]

That revolution took yet another major step forward when Charleston was occupied by units of Sherman's army, which now included Black regiments.[19] Although the city had virtually no strategic value for the South, its port having been effectively blockaded by the Union navy for more than a year, the symbolic significance of its fall could not be overestimated. The firing on Fort Sumter had signaled the start of the war. The occupation of the city by Union forces seemed to signal its end.

When news of the fall of Charleston reached England, it made a profound impression.[20] Not surprisingly, the *Saturday Review* attempted to minimize the significance of the event. The "evacuation of Charleston by the Confederates . . . possesses little military importance," the *Review* insisted on March 11. With the forced abandonment of the city, "it is probable that [General William J.] Hardee has joined [General Pierre G. T.] Beauregard with a welcome reinforcement." These troops could then be used "either for the defence of Richmond, or in preparation for a transference of the campaign to Alabama and Mississippi."[21]

In spite of this effort to be optimistic, there was no end game apparent in these moves that would be favorable to a rapidly collapsing Confederacy. Some British officials feared that a war between England and America was a real possibility now, if not a certainty. Palmerston ordered the Duke of Somerset, First Lord of the Admiralty, to make preparations for the defense of Quebec. Richard Cobden believed there were leading politicians in America who would welcome a war with England. Prudent persons on both sides of the Atlantic continued to urge restraint.[22]

The hostility that Northern liberals continued to feel toward the British governing class was shared, to a somewhat lesser degree, by English liberals. Around this time, Francis Newman wrote to his Boston friend Epes Sargent, expressing his exasperation with his conservative countrymen for the antagonism they still displayed toward the North. "I hope I am not unpatriotic," he wrote, "but I am alienated from our upper classes & our educated classes by these events to a degree I could never have imagined." He felt compelled to speak out because he believed it was important that men who were able to catch the public's ear should not "shrink to denounce the misconduct of our men & classes in power."[23]

Another British liberal, Aubrey de Vere, wrote to Norton to congratulate him on the great change in American politics and culture that New England liberals like him had done so much to bring about. "I do not know whether you who fought mainly for the cause of freedom were in the beginning the majority or the minority in the North," de Vere wrote, "but I have observed with much edification how Power went gradually into your hands as the struggle went on. . . . The principle of Freedom has worked itself out as the true question at issue."[24] Mill felt the same. In a letter to an American correspondent at this time, he expressed how pleased he was with the "moral progress" shown by the recent "annihilation of negro slavery." He saw this as an important step in the "complete regeneration of the political policy and thought of the country."[25]

While British liberals were celebrating the end of slavery, the London *Times* correspondent Charles Mackay, against all common sense and the indisputable evidence from the battlefield, predicted that the South would yet achieve a decisive victory. Regardless of recent setbacks, he was confident that "such energy will be infused into the heart of the Southern people as will speedily enable them to achieve a victory sufficient to overbalance their late losses, and bring upon the North a renewal of the cold fit of despondency which it suffered . . . when the war was pronounced a failure."[26] It was outrageous perversions such as this that finally led Morris, the manager of the *Times*, to fire the discredited Mackay. His pink slip had been mailed the day before he filed this story.[27]

The *Saturday Review* was a bit more realistic in its reporting. Anticipating a Northern victory, the journal turned its attention on February 4 to Reconstruction and the recent passage of the Thirteenth Amendment. Acknowledging that the slaves would now be free, the writer maintained that, in the absence of some form of regulated coercion, Blacks' natural inferiority virtually assured that they would "dwindle and decay" if forced into an "unrestricted competition with a superior race." For English conservatives, servitude would always be the natural condition for the world's non-white population.[28]

The prospect of war with the United States continued to be a concern for the British. The particular source of heightened tension at this time was a Confederate raid on the border town of St. Albans, Vermont. Crossing over from their base in Canada on October 19, a group of Kentuckians entered the town and proceeded to rob its banks, steal horses and wagons, and set fires before fleeing under gunfire from local authorities. Eventually, some of the raiders were captured by a pursuing posse on the Canadian side of the border, which was British soil. They were handed over to Canadian authorities. After a complex legal battle, a Montreal magistrate released the men on December 13. They quickly fled before new warrants could be issued. The incident caused yet another burst of outrage against the British throughout the North.[29] In response, Great Britain prepared for the worst.

As the *Saturday Review* reported on February 11, the British began to organize the Canadian provinces for their collective defense. The *Review* applauded this effort as testifying to the continuing "youth and vigor of the British Empire." "It is . . . well to know," the writer stated, "that Canada is on the alert, and that no long time will elapse before she will form part of a Confederacy which, even without the aid that this country would be prompt to render, will have no mean powers of self-defense."[30]

Palmerston's government was also growing concerned about the Confederates' unyielding efforts to have ships of war built in British shipyards. Two days after the *Review*'s article on Canadian defense appeared,

Lord Russell sent an official letter to James Mason and John Slidell, representatives of what he referred to as the "so-called Confederate government," commanding them to cease and desist from such efforts. The order indicated that "undue and reprehensible attempts" had been made by them "to involve her Majesty in a war in which her Majesty had declared her intention not to take part." These included "the unwarrantable practice of building ships in this country to be used as vessels of war against a state with whom her Majesty is at peace."[31] Russell's use of the phrase "the so-called Confederate government" was telling.

The situation in the South was desperate. Rumors of an Anglo-French intervention provided a flicker of hope for some, but diarist Mary Chesnut was more realistic. "As a ray of artificial sunshine, Mrs. Munro sent me a [Richmond] *Examiner*," she noted in her diary. "Daniel thinks we are at the last gasp, and now England and France are bound to step in. England must know if the U.S.A. are triumphant they will tackle her next and France must know she will have to give up Mexico." While the logic of the proposition was attractive, Chesnut, like many others, had given up the possibility of European intervention. "My faith fails me. It is too late. No help for us now—in God or man."[32]

In the North there was further evidence of a fundamental change in America's attitude toward Blacks that had been brought about by the war. Massachusetts would soon pass the first comprehensive public accommodation law in the nation's history. It forbade the exclusion of any persons from restaurants, inns, theaters, and places of amusement because of their color or race. Additionally, Senator Henry Wilson of Massachusetts introduced a bill that provided a fine of $500 against any railroad or steamship line in the United States that discriminated against Blacks.[33] The bill was eventually buried in committee, but it showed to all that times were certainly changing.

March brought Lincoln's second inauguration. The occasion was auspicious. No president had been elected to a second term since Andrew Jackson. Lincoln delivered his Second Inaugural Address on March 4. This now famous speech was, like his address at Gettysburg, both brief and eloquent. He spoke in a distinctly American idiom, the voice of the people.[34] The address had a quasi-religious quality. As Doris Kearns Goodwin notes, "More than any of his other speeches, the Second Inaugural fused spiritual faith with politics," something his New England supporters had been doing since the war began.[35]

Many historians emphasize the healing tone of Lincoln's address, pointing to expressions such as "with malice toward none; with charity for all . . . let us strive on to finish the work we are in; to bind up the nation's wounds." However, a closer examination shows that Lincoln's major focus was on slavery, the issue now in the forefront of all discussions of the war, both at home and abroad. He made it very clear in the address that the South had started the war. "Both parties deprecated war; but one of them would *make* war rather than let the nation survive; and the other would *accept* war rather than let it perish. And the war came."[36] The preservation of slavery, Lincoln indicated, had always been the South's goal. "One eighth of the whole population were colored slaves, not distributed generally over the Union, but localized in the Southern part of it. These slaves constituted a peculiar and powerful interest. All knew that this interest was . . . the cause of the war."[37]

Lincoln also made it unmistakable that he believed slavery was unjust and immoral. "Both read the same Bible, and pray to the same God; and each invokes His aid against the other. It may seem strange that any men should dare to ask a just God's assistance in wringing their bread from the sweat of other men's faces," he asserted, "but let us judge not that we be not judged." He pointed out that no one at the outset of the war anticipated it would result in the destruction of slavery. "Each looked for . . . a result less fundamental and astounding."[38] It seemed to Lincoln, in retrospect, that the destruction of slavery was foreordained by a just God, and that the enormous bloodshed caused by the war was the price to be paid to expiate this grave and grievous sin.

"American Slavery," he declared, "is one of those offences which, in the providence of God, . . . He now wills to remove." And, he added, "He gives to both North and South, this terrible war, as the woe due to those by whom the offence came." It may be that "God wills that it continue, until all the wealth piled by the bond-man's two hundred and fifty years of unrequited toil shall be sunk, and until every drop of blood drawn with the lash, shall be paid by another drawn with the sword." Only *after* this will it be possible to "bind up the nation's wounds."[39] Plainly, in Lincoln's view, this business was not yet done.[40]

The president's commitment to a new and more just America was reflected by the inclusion of Black guests among the dignitaries admitted to the White House for the inaugural reception. Frederick Douglass attended at Lincoln's personal invitation.[41] As later reported, Lincoln was greeting well-wishers when he was informed that Douglass had come by to congratulate him but had been turned away because of his color. Lincoln ordered that he be shown in immediately. He shook Douglass's hand and told him, "There is no man in the country whose opinion I value more than yours." Lincoln then asked what he thought of his address. Douglass described it as "a sacred effort." "I am glad you liked it," Lincoln replied, and Douglass then passed along the reception line.[42] As Stephen Oates reports, the event was truly historic. "It was the first inaugural reception in the history of the Republic in which an American president had greeted a free black man and solicited his opinion."[43] It was also the first time in American history that companies of Black soldiers marched in the inaugural parade.[44] America's second revolution continued apace, and the president was at the forefront.

Europeans took note of the change. In their report, the London *Times* commented at length on the large number of Blacks who joined their fellow citizens in celebration of the inaugural. "At least one-half of the multitude were coloured people, pouring in from far and near to 'assist' in the ceremonial of a day which to them and to many wiser people seemed the triumph of their race over a fast fading social prejudice and political injustice. . . . The negroes held their heads high," the report read, "as if they thoroughly understood that, under the beneficent sway of Abraham Lincoln, 'a man was a man for a' that'; if even he were not something better than a man—if his skin happened to be of the Ethiopian and not of the Caucasian colour."[45]

The *Saturday Review*, with a distinct change in tone, offered praise for Lincoln's address. The "document is mournful, religious and humble," the writer noted, "and it expresses no sentiment of anger or unkindness even to the armed enemies of the Union," as the president seeks "the nearest road to peace."[46] The reason for the *Review*'s emphasis on peace was undoubtedly its growing concern with the deep animosity of the American people toward England, an animosity that, while generated by the war, was not likely to end with it. The question now was: Will the Americans seek retribution for the mother country's perceived perfidy?

Around this time, British liberal Edward Peacock wrote to Caroline Dall to congratulate her on the recent capture of Charleston.[47] He told her that while "it is not of much military importance . . . the moral effect will be very great both with you and here." In England, "all things show that people here have made up their minds that the Rebellion is in a state of collapse."[48]

In response to the new reality created by the Thirteenth Amendment, just ten days before Peacock penned his letter, Lincoln signed the bill creating the Freedmen's Bureau. This was another truly historic event, the significance of which was not fully appreciated at the time. As James McPherson points out, the formation of "the Freedmen's Bureau represented an unprecedented extension of the Federal government into matters of social welfare and labor relations" in an effort to facilitate "the building of a new society on the ashes of the old."[49] Three years earlier, Emerson had predicted that emancipation would alter the "atomic social constitution of the Southern people."[50] That process was now going forward rapidly.

On April 2, after suffering heavy losses to Grant and Sheridan, Lee evacuated his haggard and severely depleted army from the defenses surrounding Petersburg and Richmond. The following day, the once proud capital of the Confederacy was occupied by a Federal army that included Colored Troops.[51] Before leaving, the rebels had set fire to everything of military value. As the fires spread, mobs rampaged through the city until Union troops restored order. When Lincoln was informed that the Southern capital was in Union hands, he replied, "Thank God that I have lived to see this! It seems to me that I have been dreaming a horrid dream for four years, and now the nightmare is gone."[52]

A week after Richmond was abandoned, Lee's exhausted army surrendered to Grant in the small town of Appomattox Court House, Virginia. In the meeting of the two generals, who were living symbols of their respective cultures, the contrast was striking. Bruce Catton, in his famous account of the historic moment, states that Robert E. Lee stood for "the old aristocratic concept" that he hoped "might somehow survive and be dominant in American life." This "concept" was, as Emerson had asserted, a remainder of America's English past. As Catton observes, Lee "embodied a way of life had come down through the age of knighthood and the English country squire." He "stood for the feeling that it was somehow of advantage to human society to have a pronounced inequality in the social structure. In short, Lee embodied . . . the aristocratic ideal."[53]

On the other hand, Catton notes, Grant was "everything Lee was not." He was "the son of a tanner on the Western frontier. . . . These frontier men were the precise opposite of the tidewater aristocrats. . . . They stood for democracy, not from any reasoned conclusion about the proper ordering of human society, but simply because they had grown up in the middle of democracy and knew how it worked. . . . No man was born to anything, except perhaps to a chance to show how far he could rise."[54]

This historic moment at Appomattox certainly signaled for many the triumph of democracy and the "common man" over aristocracy and a regime of privilege. *Harper's Weekly* summarized on May 20 the meaning of the event this way: "Lee surrendering to Grant is barbarous feudalism yielding to Christian civilization." Grant later wrote that he felt "sad and depressed at the downfall of a foe who had fought so long and valiantly, and had suffered so much for a cause," but that cause, he added, was "one of the worst for which a people ever fought."[55]

By mid-month, news of Richmond's fall and Lee's surrender had not reached the editorial offices of the *Saturday Review*, where a flicker of hope for the South still burned in the hearts of some. On April 15 the *Review* reported, "The fate of Richmond, if not the Confederacy, will probably be determined within a few weeks." According to this article, "as long as General Lee commands an unbroken army of veterans, the Confederate cause is not wholly desperate. . . . The coloured troops which guard the Virginia peninsula might easily be overwhelmed, nor would any serious obstacles intervene between the James and the Potomac." For this writer, "a march upon Washington would be preferable to surrender."[56] Ironically, this essay appeared on the same day the London *Times* reported that Richmond had fallen and was now occupied by the Union army, which, as noted, included a number of Colored Troops.

The fate of Lee's army, however, was still unknown. A week later, the *Saturday Review* recounted the event with words steeped in bitterness: "The Northern Americans naturally rejoice in the success which has been so anxiously desired, and so long delayed." With characteristic consistency, the *Review* offered praise for "the lofty courage" of the now defeated South while criticizing the "bawling rabble" of the North. From the perspective of English conservatives, the triumph of the democratic North over the aristocratic South represented the triumph of the vulgar masses over the enlightened elites. Thus, the *Review* predicted, "wherever Federal occupation extends, the dregs and the scum of the people will welcome the conquerors." The author expressed concern that the North might turn its mighty military against Great Britain.[57] For British conservatives, the triumph of "mob rule" in America could only have dire consequences for the "civilized" nations of the world.

British liberals were, of course, thrilled by these dramatic developments. Goldwin Smith wrote to Norton. "I do indeed rejoice with you over this crowning victory of our cause," he told him. "Like you, I trust that the work of war is now nearly done." Smith believed, as did his American friends, that the Union victory would aid the cause of democracy in England. "The old fortress of Feudalism will not long withstand the force of your example," he wrote. "It quakes already."[58]

British reformer Richard Webb also celebrated the triumph of Northern democracy. After hearing the good news, he wrote to Caroline Weston to offer congratulations and to remind her of the North's many English friends. "The bulk of the English working classes and the great majority of the most eminent Englishmen . . . have been all along on your side," he told her. On the other hand, the opposition consisted largely of "the aristocratic & clerical parties who have felt that the success of a great Republican nation was dangerous to the permanence of their class positions."[59]

Edward Peacock agreed. He wrote Caroline Dall, "You American liberals . . . can hardly be aware" of how a Northern victory "will react upon the less enlightened civilization of the old world." It will have a beneficial effect "in a manner you can hardly conceive in spreading the principles of true democracy among our people."[60] Around the same time, John Bright wrote to a friend expressing "the exultation we feel that the great strife is over, & that *white & black* on the American continent are alike free!"[61] Human rights were now, it seemed, the common cause of common people everywhere.

Three days before Peacock penned his letter, as the North was basking in the glow of victory, tragedy struck like a bolt of lightning with the shocking news of Lincoln's assassination. The joy felt by Union supporters on both sides of the Atlantic turned to deep sorrow. On the evening of April 14, the president and Mrs. Lincoln went to Ford's Theatre in Washington to see a popular comedy, *Our American Cousin*. The play, first produced in 1850, was about a clash of cultures that occurred when a young and unsophisticated American male traveled to London to meet his aristocratic English cousins. Given the bitter cultural conflict between America and the mother country over the past four years, the play must have seemed especially relevant to American audiences. As the president watched the play from his balcony box, he was approached from behind and fatally shot by John Wilkes Booth, a popular actor and fanatical, though covert, supporter of the Confederacy. Lincoln was the first president ever to fall prey to an assassin, and his death the following day came at the moment of his greatest triumph.

News of the event sounded through the nation like a thunderclap. As Lowell reported, it "echoed along the wires through the length and breadth of a continent, swelling all eyes at once with tears of indignant sorrow."[62] Lincoln's death was a blow to all who loved him and the democratic values he stood for. At a somber public service in his hometown of Concord, Emerson told his fellow townsmen that he doubted "any death has caused so much pain to mankind."[63]

English liberals also felt the impact. John Stuart Mill wrote to an American friend, reformer and journalist Parke Godwin.[64] "I had scarcely received your note of April 8, so full of calm joy in the splendid prospect now opening to your country & through it to the world when the news came that an atrocious crime had struck down the great citizen," a man who "had gradually won not only the admiration but almost the personal affection of all who love freedom & appreciate simplicity & uprightness." Mill took some solace in the fact that Lincoln "did live to see the cause triumphant & the contest virtually over."

Regarding his countrymen, Mill reported that the "horror of the crime & sympathy with your loss seem to be almost universal, even among those who have disgraced their country by wishing success to the slaveholders." He hoped these sentiments "may be received in America as some kind of atonement or peace-offering," especially now, when many of his countrymen were concerned about the possibility of war between the two nations. While he was personally confident peace would prevail, he acknowledged that "there is a portion of the higher & middle classes of Great Britain who so dread & hate democracy that they cannot wish prosperity or power to a democratic people."[65]

Elizabeth Gaskell, who was closer to the working class than Mill, felt the loss personally. She wrote to Norton, "My heart burnt within me with indignation & grief" as she read the news. "Every one is feeling the same. I never knew so universal a feeling."[66] Three days later, her daughter, Margaret Emily (Meta), told Norton that the death of Lincoln "has roused the sympathy of the people here in an extraordinary way."[67] Edward Peacock's wife, Lucy, felt the same. In a letter to Caroline Dall she described Lincoln as a shining knight whose "solemn vow of knighthood was 'to fight only in the cause of God, to be the protector and champion of the oppressed, the widow, and the fatherless.' "[68]

Two days after Mrs. Peacock penned her letter, the London *Times* reported how quickly "details of the rash and bloody deed of last night" traveled "hundreds of thousands of square miles" to "a thousand American cities, linked together by a network of lightning."[69] Only now, after his death, did the paper acknowledge Lincoln's real qualities. Mowbray Morris, the *Times*'s manager, admitted to a friend that Lincoln had been one of "England's best friends." The paper even publicly rescinded one of its most oft-repeated calumnies, declaring that Lincoln was "as little of a tyrant as any man who ever lived."[70]

On the day the *Times* published the news of Lincoln's assassination, Goldwin Smith wrote to Norton that this tragedy signaled "the death-knell" of slavery. He also described an unusually emotional (for Englishmen) reaction to the president's death throughout the country and in the halls of Parliament. "Never did I see the ice which generally covers the feelings of this people more completely broken up than on the arrival of the last news from America," he wrote. The compensation for this loss, if there could truly be any, was that "slavery has doubly killed itself in striking this blow."[71]

Ephraim Adams reports that "all of England united in expressions of sympathy and horror."[72] The loss of Lincoln was felt most deeply among the British working class, who had come to both love and support the noble figure who had done so much by his personal example and his formal policies to validate the dignity of labor and the potential of common people. They continued to promote the principles of liberal democracy at home and abroad. The working class now expressed their support for the enfranchisement of the freedmen, a measure that correlated with their own political goals. "A Working Man" of Ashton explained, "We have a general impression among us that the once despised and enthralled African will not only be set free, but enfranchised, . . . and when the slave ceases to be, and becomes enfranchised free men . . . then the British workman's claim may be listened to."[73]

Before the assassination, journals in England and in the North had already gone to press with several articles reflecting on matters of major concern to both nations. In the April *North American Review*, Lowell discussed the pressing issue of race and civil rights in post-war America. Recently, he pointed out, the Southerners themselves had virtually acknowledged the wrongness of their racist views, "though they certainly did not so intend it." That acknowledgment came in the "last proposal of Davis and Lee for the arming of slaves. . . . Once arm and drill the negroes, and they can never be slaves again," Lowell observed. The proposal, made out of desperation, at once swept away both the ancient biblical and the modern pseudoscientific arguments for Black inferiority.

"All the Scriptural arguments, all the fitness of things, all the physiological demonstrations, all Mr. Stephen's corner-stones, Ham, Onesimus, heels, hair, and facial angle, all are swept out, . . . into the inexorable limbo of things that were and never should have been."

After suggesting that all freedmen be provided the means for self-support through the appropriation of public lands in the South, Lowell raised a more fundamental question, namely, "Will it be enough to make the freedmen landholders merely?" In addition to economic enfranchisement, "must we not make them voters also," he asked, in order that "they may have that power of self-protection which no interference of government can so safely, cheaply, and surely exercise in their behalf? We answer this question in the affirmative," Lowell declared, "for reasons both of expediency and justice." Indeed, for Lowell and other New England liberals, "our answer to the question, What are we to do with the negro? is short and simple. Give him a fair chance. We must get rid of the delusion that right is in any way dependent on the skin, and not on inward virtue."[74] New England liberals ramped up their campaign for Black suffrage. The *Commonwealth* on April 22 warned that without it, "the Southern States will make such laws as will allow the freedmen only to be 'hewers of wood and drawers of water,' and, uniting with Northern copperheads," the Southerners, once again, "will control the legislation of the country."[75]

In an effort to prevent this, Emerson's friend and liberal reformer George L. Stearns published a pamphlet arguing for "The Equality of All Men Before the Law." He distributed 50,000 copies throughout the North at his own expense.[76] At the same time, Frederick Douglass thundered from the platform that "slavery is not abolished until the black man has the ballot."[77] Anything less than full and equal rights would condemn former slaves to the kind of second-class citizenship that free Blacks had endured in many places before the war. Initially, New England liberals were convinced Andrew Johnson shared their values, and Lincoln's. Throughout the war, the Tennessean was as adamant as they in his opposition to the undemocratic social structure of the South. Wendell Phillips, now a leader in the fight for Black suffrage, was confident that Johnson was also an advocate of the cause. "I believe in him," Phillips declared. "I believe he means suffrage."[78]

At the annual meeting of the Emancipation League in Boston on May 29, the speakers were unabashed in their display of radicalism, sure that the new president would be receptive to their appeal for Blacks' civil rights, including suffrage. They were shocked when they later learned that, on the same day, Johnson had approved a reconstruction plan for North Carolina that did *not* include such a measure. This was just the beginning. On June 13, he approved an identical plan for Mississippi.[79] It was clear the new president had no intention of enfranchising emancipated Blacks. The Civil War was over, but the battle for equal rights would go on.

Epilogue

The American Civil War wrought profound changes in both the United States and Great Britain. In America, it brought about a new national identity, one that included, for the first time, Americans of African descent.[1] The promise of liberty and equality for all men was codified in law. The Thirteenth Amendment to the Constitution destroyed slavery forever. The Civil Rights Act of 1866, the first statutory definition of American citizenship, spelled out the rights to which all Americans are entitled, regardless of race. The Fourteenth Amendment, ratified in 1868, guaranteed equal justice to all, and the Fifteenth, ratified in 1870, forbade states from making race a qualification for voting. With these dramatic changes, the liberal vision of America that had been the dream of progressive New Englanders throughout the war became a reality—in principle if not in fact.

These major victories did not mean that the war for equal rights in America had been won. Far from it. For New England idealists equal rights were a moral imperative, but for many others in the North they were simply a matter of political expediency. The South had been converted only by force.[2] When Reconstruction ended in 1877 and the last Union troops were withdrawn from the South, white Southerners began to pass Black Codes that stripped away most of the civil rights of African American citizens. Eric Foner points out, "Southern leaders sought to revive the antebellum definition of freedom as if nothing had changed. Freedom still meant hierarchy and mastery; it was a privilege, not a right."[3] As one Mississippi planter wrote, "a man may be free and yet not independent." Or, as a Kentucky newspaper put it, "*free*, but free only to labor."[4] A reign of terror by the Ku Klux Klan ensured that whatever rights remained could not be exercised without the risk of violence, or even death. The lynching of Blacks became an international disgrace.[5]

The real cause of the war, it seemed, had quickly faded from the national memory. Echoing the rhetoric of British conservatives, Southerners created the myth of the "Lost Cause," recasting the conflict as an assault of a "free mobocracy of the North" against a "slave democracy of the South." Exhausted by the long and costly war, the rest of the country turned their backs to these developments. People wanted a return to "normalcy." Ultimately, reconciliation between the North and the South was purchased by the sacrifice of Black civil rights.[6] As James McPherson notes, these developments have led many historians to conclude that "the equalitarian achievements of the Civil War were built on a foundation of sand," which gave way very quickly as the prejudices of the past once again commanded the present.[7] Little, it seemed, had changed. According to some, the liberal voices of reform that so dominated New England's intellectual landscape fell silent once the war was won.

Louis Menand, for example, in his Pulitzer Prize–winning study *The Metaphysical Club*, argues that the American Civil War was largely an alienating experience for those who lived through it. It represented "not just a failure of democracy, but a failure of culture, a failure of ideas." For Menand, Transcendental idealism expired on the bloody battlefields of America's most devastating and costly war, a war that, in his words, "swept away almost the whole intellectual culture of the North."[8]

While it is true, as Menand shows, that after the war American pragmatism was on the rise, the liberal ideals and the commitment to reform that had been forged in the early history of New England and tempered in the fires of war were not obliterated. The idealism that energized New England's intellectual class remained a potent force in the post–Civil War period. Emerson, Norton, Higginson, Curtis, Lowell, Dall, Child, and other New England liberals continued their reform efforts throughout the period.[9] Emerson, nearing the end of a long career, lent his voice and prestige to liberal causes, especially that of the freedmen.[10]

Emerson spoke at the newly founded law school at Howard University in Washington, DC, in January 1872. He had been invited by the school's dean, John Mercer Langston, a freedman from Virginia who was educated at Oberlin College. Emerson described the school in a letter to his wife Lidian as "an important college for the colored men." In his lecture, Emerson told his audience of young Black scholars that he was very glad "to see this institution" and that he was "very happy in hearing the many details of the design [and] of the actual direction and management" of it. "It certainly is making a movement of great promise in the country," he observed. "It is one from which great good may be expected."[11] While his ostensible subject was "What Books to Read," Emerson's message was primarily about individual human dignity and the importance of self-reliance, an idea at the core of his Transcendental philosophy. "Every mind that comes into the world," he told the young Black men, "has its own specialty . . . a disposition to attempt something of its own." It was their obligation to bring that special something forward to improve their world.[12]

This message was also taught by Black Transcendentalists. Together, these idealists knew that they had accomplished a great deal. William C. Nell visited Concord in 1867 to re-engage with his fellow reformers, especially Emerson and Alcott. He enjoyed this opportunity to experience their physical as well as philosophical proximity. Nell wrote to a friend afterward that he had a delightful time at their "Fraternity Picnic in Walden Woods," the site of Thoreau's famous hermitage, and a place where he had hosted abolitionist gatherings and harbored fugitive slaves.[13] After Emerson's death in 1882, the legacy of Transcendental idealism lived on.

Moorfield Storey was a dedicated Emersonian who frequently invoked the bard's words and example in his campaign against racism at home and abroad.[14] Storey was a Harvard graduate, distinguished lawyer, and, eventually, president of the American Bar Association. He was also a consummate liberal idealist who served as the first president of the American Anti-Imperialist League, which was founded in 1898 to protest the establishment of an American colonial empire following the Spanish-American War.[15] As a young man, Storey enjoyed a close personal relationship with the Emerson family and was frequently a guest at their home in Concord. He served for a time as Charles Sumner's private secretary. Storey learned from Sumner, an experienced mentor, that the fight for equal rights in America was a never-ending one. Eventually, he joined forces with W. E. B. Du Bois, another New Englander and the first Black person to earn a PhD at Harvard.

Du Bois was a powerful writer and a committed idealist who, like Storey, was influenced early on by Emerson.[16] He was a leader in the Niagara Movement, an organized effort to promote the civil rights of African Americans. In October 1907, as the Niagara Movement struggled to advance the cause, Du Bois wrote to Storey applauding his anti-imperial and anti-racist views. Storey told Du Bois that he was familiar with his writings and was supportive of the goals of the Niagara Movement. Eventually, the two joined forces. When the National Association for the Advancement of Colored People (NAACP) emerged as a formal organization in 1909, Du Bois served as director of publicity and research and Storey as president, a position he held until his death at age eighty-four in 1929.[17]

Storey and Du Bois carried the abolitionists' idealism into the twentieth century. Following in the tradition of Frederick Douglass, whom he admired, Du Bois became, in the words of his biographer, "the premier architect of the civil rights movement in the United States."[18] The successes of that movement, James McPherson notes, were built "on the foundation laid down . . . by the abolitionists." Their efforts had culminated in the Thirteenth, Fourteenth, and Fifteenth Amendments, which Eric Foner describes as "sleeping giants to be awakened by subsequent generations."[19] These changes affirmed, for the first time, that the Declaration's assertion "all men are created equal" applied to everyone. "The importance of this accomplishment," Foner insists, "ought not to be underestimated."[20] It was, indeed, a tremendous achievement, truly the "second revolution" that the New England liberals envisioned during the war. This eventually led to many other landmark reforms such as woman suffrage, civil rights, voter protection, and marriage equality, to name but a few. Its consequences continue to reverberate to the present day. And its effects were not limited to the United States. The Civil War ended with a victory for democracy and human rights in America that resonated throughout Europe and the rest of the world as common people elsewhere demanded equal human rights.

Even before the war ended, James Russell Lowell predicted that the changes it would bring would be felt throughout Europe and the rest of the world. "Our example and our idea," he proclaimed in an essay in the *North American Review*, will "react more powerfully than ever on the Old World, and the consequence of a rebellion, aimed at the natural equality of all men, will be to hasten incalculably the progress of equalization over the whole earth."[21] The progress that Lowell anticipated manifested very early in England. Ephraim Adams reports that in the parliamentary election held in July 1865, "not a single member who had supported the cause of the North failed of re-election, several additional Northern 'friends' were chosen, and some outspoken members for the South were defeated."[22]

Minister Charles Adams saw this development as a clear victory for the liberal cause and a bitter defeat for conservatism. "This period marks an era in the political movement of Great Britain," he observed. "Pure old-fashioned conservatism has so far lost its hold on the confidence of the country that it will not appear in that guise any more." Adams predicted there would be "decided progress in enlarging the popular features of the [British] constitution, and diminishing the influence of the aristocracy." In all of this, he saw "the influence of our institutions." With the Union victory, "the progress of the liberal cause, not in England alone, but all over the world, is, in a measure, in our hands."[23]

Reactionaries in Great Britain fought against the trend. Earl Russell's Reform Bill of 1866 was defeated by a coalition of conservatives who wished to preserve the status quo, "government of the wise" as they called it, but they were swimming against the tide. They were soon forced by popular demand, in some cases reinforced by rioting, to pass a bill that was even more liberal than the original. Great Britain, it seemed, was experiencing its own revolution. As Ephraim Adams succinctly puts it, "the Reform Bill of 1867 changed Great Britain from a government by aristocracy to one by democracy. A new nation came into being. The friends of the North had triumphed."[24]

But this triumph was incomplete. In Great Britain, as in America, conservatives continued to fight a rear guard action against the growing demand for racial equality, which they still saw as a standing threat to the empire. James Hunt, president of the Anthropological Society of London, railed against his many liberal critics in his 1867 Farewell Address. He ridiculed them as people who suffered from what he called the "rights-of-man mania" and whose "defective reasoning power" had led them to a pernicious belief in "absolute human equality," which, he contended, was "a sham and a delusion."[25] It would take two world wars and the example of Mahatma Gandhi and others to disabuse British imperialists of this view.

Throughout the post–Civil War period, the New England intelligentsia never forgot their British friends—or their British enemies. The deep alienation between the iconic representatives of New and Old England that was caused by the war did not end with it. In his first letter to Leslie Stephen after the war, Lowell confessed he had not written earlier because he had "an almost invincible repugnance to writing again to England. I share with the great body of my countrymen in a bitterness (half resentment and half regret) which I cannot yet get over," he wrote. "I cannot forget the insult so readily as I might the injury of the last five years." He was especially angry at England's "taking every opportunity to *tell* us how disagreeable and vulgar we are." Then, slipping into an Americanism of the type disdained by proper Victorians, Lowell declared, "What really *riled* me was the quiet assumption that we hadn't, couldn't, and had no right to have, a country over here."

But Americans did have a country, a democratic country, Lowell insisted, and it was "democracy itself that makes us strong" because it acknowledged the common people regardless of their color and even if they appeared "vulgar." "I don't understand your English taste for what you call 'respectability,'" he added. "I should call it 'whitechokerism,' thinking, as I do, that one thing worth striving for in this world is a state founded on pure manhood, where everybody has a chance given him to better himself, and where the less costume and the more reality there is, the better."[26] This would remain the goal of succeeding generations of liberals of all races and genders in the many struggles that lay ahead.

Notes

Introduction

1. "Cornerstone Speech," Mar. 21, 1861, American Battlefield Trust, www.battlefields.org/learn/primary-sources/cornerstone-speech.
2. *CWL* 7:23.
3. *Atlantic Monthly*, Apr. 1862, 507.
4. *Atlantic Monthly*, Apr. 1864, 506.
5. "The President's Proclamation" (1862), manuscript, bms Am 1280.207 [7], HL.
6. Blight, *Frederick Douglass' Civil War*, 14.
7. Bolt, *Victorian Attitudes*, 157.
8. "American Literature and the Civil War," *Fraser's Magazine*, Apr. 1861, 519.
9. Jan. 23, 1863, *AL* 1:243, 244, 245.
10. Mill, "The Slave Power," 504.
11. *Culture and Imperialism*, xii, xiii.
12. *Culture and Imperialism*, xiii.
13. See Fish, "Rise."
14. Mott, *American Magazines*, 1:748–49.
15. Huntington, *Clash*, 67.
16. "American 'Degeneracy,'" *Spectator* (London), July 12, 1862.

Chapter 1

1. Wirzbicki, *Higher Law*, 5, 25, 53.
2. von Frank, "Mrs. Brackett's Verdict," 397.
3. Several American reformers, including Emerson, Wendell Phillips, and Frederick Douglass, encountered Chartists while visiting Europe. Their support contributed to the formation of a strong connecting link between European and

American liberalism (Wirzbicki, *Higher Law*, 125; Koch, *Emerson*, 130; Gougeon, "Emerson and Great Britain," 181ff).

4. Gohdes, *American Literature*, 145; Koch, *Emerson*, 23.

5. Quoted in Murray, *Matthew Arnold*, 70.

6. ArL 1:7. In *English Traits*, Emerson indicates that he told Thomas Carlyle during a visit to Stonehenge that eventually America would be "the seat and center of the British race . . . and that England, an old and exhausted island, must one day be contented, like other parents, to be strong only in her children" (*ECW* 5:49).

7. Koch, *Emerson*, 130. For more on Emerson and the Chartists, see Gougeon, "International Struggle" and "Emerson and Great Britain."

8. *EJ* 10:310–11.

9. A deeply informed and detailed study of Matthew Arnold and Victorian Liberalism is Malachuk, *Perfection*.

10. Quoted in Poirier, *Renewal*, 5.

11. Lawrence Buell sums up this difference succinctly. Referring to the "immense difference" between "Arnold's goal of cultural awakening by a top-down approach and Emerson's commitment to cultural awakening by energizing independent individuals," he concludes that "Emerson's notion of how a cultural order might follow from this looks serendipitous if not positively anarchic alongside the comparative programmaticism of Arnold" (*Emerson*, 103).

12. Speaking of the North-South conflict, Anne C. Rose observes that "culture, when reintegrated into a full view of the war, should be considered one of its causes" because "culture does not simply offer commentary on events but works as a force of central importance" (*Victorian America*, 14). Such was the case in the cultural warfare that erupted between New and Old England.

13. Austin, *Fields*, 26.

14. Tebbel and Zuckerman, *Magazine*, 24.

15. Butler, *Critical Americans*, 35.

16. Sedgwick, *Atlantic Monthly*, 100, 101.

17. Menand, *Metaphysical Club*, 68.

18. Austin, *Fields*, 300.

19. Howe, *Atlantic Monthly*, 16.

20. Austin, *Fields*, 27.

21. Austin, *Fields*, 31.

22. Of the group mentioned earlier, only Higginson was not a member of the Saturday Club.

23. *HLL* 1:204; Austin, *Fields*, 26.

24. The group always had a liberal inclination. For example, Dana, who was an outcast from most of Boston's Brahmin society because of his active role in the antislavery movement, was a founding member of the club, which he referred to as "an important and much valued thing" (Amestoy, *Slavish Shore*, 221).

25. Butler, *Critical Americans*, 44.
26. Myerson, "George William Curtis."
27. Leslie Butler indicates that after his promotion to political editor of *Harper's Weekly* in 1863, Curtis "flexed his editorial muscles and turned a periodical that once spoke for conservative Democrats into one of the strongest supporters of the Lincoln administration" (*Critical Americans*, 65).
28. Tilton, *Amiable Autocrat*, 268. Lawrence Kaplan reports that when Motley left for Austria, "he made himself an unofficial ambassador among his English friends for the American cause in the Civil War" ("Brahmin," 14).
29. *ML* 1:342.
30. Houghton, *Wellesley Index*, 2:303-4.
31. Houghton, *Wellesley Index*, 1:310, 313.
32. "United States through English Eyes," 285, 286.
33. "Chronicle of Current History," 135, 137. Ephraim Adams notes that "in 1860 the Liberal movement in England was at its lowest ebb since the high tide of 1832" (*Great Britain*, 2:276). John Bright and Richard Cobden were leaders of the Radical Liberals in the mid-nineteenth century. They sought to break what one critic calls "the stranglehold of an heredity aristocracy over church and state" (Stapelton, "Introduction," 7).
34. W. Craft to S. J. May, July 17, 1860, Antislavery Collection, BPL.
35. H. Martineau to [Richard Davis?] Webb, c. Sept. 22, 1860, Antislavery Collection, BPL.
36. Martineau's column in the *National Anti-Slavery Standard* was titled From Our European Correspondent. It was published from April 9, 1859, to March 12, 1862. Martineau, *Writings*, 140.
37. This venerable journal had been established in 1802 as "an instrument of enlightenment and social reform." As such, the journal spoke "for authority, as well as for freedom." One of its major interests was political economy. Houghton, *Wellesley Index*, 2:417-18.
38. Kinser, *Civil War*, 92.
39. Kinser, *Civil War*, 1-12.
40. "The Political Crisis in America," Nov. 1860, 59.
41. Sept. 24, 1860, *NL* 1:210, 211.
42. "The Election in November," 492, 494.
43. "Election in November," 499-500.
44. For the religious debate over slavery, see Lowance, *House Divided*. Scientific racism will be discussed in detail later.
45. For more on the Transcendental concept of universal intuitive truth, see Gougeon, *Emerson & Eros*, 97, 126, 154ff.
46. "The Fugitive Slave Law" (1854), *EAW* 86-87.
47. *EAW* 61.

48. *EAW* 67.

49. *EJ* 11:248. In a speech in 1856, former congressman and Massachusetts senator Rufus Choate denounced the "glittering and sounding generalities that make up the Declaration of Independence" (Brown, *Rufus Choate*, 1:215).

50. Randall Fuller argues that Northern writers "helped to create a literary culture that would play a significant role in the escalation of hostilities. . . . Among the complex and interwoven causes of the U.S. Civil War . . . was an indigenous and influential literature that demanded moral transformation from society. The writing of Emerson and his contemporaries . . . helped to propel the country into war" (*Transformed*, 9).

51. "Election in November," 501, 502.

52. *EJ* 14:363.

53. Nov. 19, 1860, *ML* 1:355.

54. Black, *Memoir*, 9. In his memorial on Lincoln, Emerson would observe that Lincoln's "occupying the chair of state was a triumph of the good sense of mankind, and of the public conscience. This middle-class country had got a middle-class president, at last" (*EW* 11:334).

55. The idea that Lincoln might have had Black racial characteristics was noted by others. In 1863 Thomas Carlyle received a visitor from Virginia, Ms. Rose O'Neal Greenhow. In her diary, Ms. Greenhow recorded that Carlyle "talks a great deal, is deeply interested in American affairs and [is] a most noble advocate of the South." Carlyle asked her a number of questions, including "what sort of a looking animal was Lincoln—I endeavored to do justice to his appearance," Ms. Greenhow wrote, "whereupon Mr C arose from his seat . . . and [said] Soulouque [president of Haiti] the flat nosed negro of Haty and Abraham the railsplitter of United States are a worthy pair to stand side by side in history" (quoted in Kinser, *Civil War*, 39, 40). In the political summer of 1860, the proslavery press depicted Lincoln as a lover of Black women and being the missing link between Blacks and whites (Fuller, *Book*, 220).

56. Black, *Memoir*, 10, 11, 38.

57. Dean Mahin reports that the British minister in Washington, Lord Lyons, informed Lord Russell, in a dispatch in May 1860, that Lincoln was "a rough Westerner, of the lowest origin and little education." Later, he described Lincoln as a "rough farmer who began life as a farm labourer and got on by a talent for stump speaking." William H. Russell, American correspondent for the London *Times*, was struck by Lincoln's unusual appearance and in his description of the new president emphasized his ungainly arms and legs and his "thatch of wild republican hair." Another English correspondent for the *Spectator* noted of Lincoln that "you would never say he was a gentleman." By contrast, Mahin points out that at this time "the leadership of both British political parties . . . was drawn mainly from person's with noble titles. In 1861 the British cabinet consisted of three dukes, two earls, one viscount, two other lords, and several baronets and knights" (*One War*, 28, 32).

58. Black, *Memoir*, 14–15.
59. All quoted in Crawford, *Anglo-American Crisis*, xxxii–xxxiii.
60. "Chronicle of Current History," 822.
61. "Chronicle of Current History," 822.
62. McPherson, *Battle Cry*, 258, 259.
63. S. May to R. Webb, 1860, Antislavery Collection, BPL. Richard Webb was a staunch supporter and lifelong friend of William Lloyd Garrison. He came to the abolition movement as a result of reading Harriett Martineau's *The Martyr Age in the United States* (Martineau, *Writings*, 335n137). Webb published a British edition of Frederick Douglass's *Narrative of Frederick Douglass*.
64. Gougeon, *Virtue's Hero*, 262fn22.
65. Printed circular, dated Dec. 10, 1860, Amos Abbott Lawrence Papers, MHS. This circular carries the names of twenty-one prominent citizens. The Personal Liberty Law sought to formally nullify an original provision of the US Constitution requiring that any "person held to Service or Labour in one State . . . escaping into another . . . shall be delivered up on Claim of the Party to whom such Service or Labour may be due" (article 4, section 2). This provision had been effectively nullified in the decades following ratification by popular resistance in the free states. Many passed "Personal Liberty Laws" specifically designed to protect runaway slaves. The Massachusetts law was devised by Charles Sumner and Richard Henry Dana Jr. (Donald, *Sumner*, 2:223).
66. O'Connor, *Civil War Boston*, 46–47.
67. *EJ* 15:111.
68. Dec. 11, 1860, *NL* 1:211, 212, 213, 214, 215.

Chapter 2

1. Sandars, "Chronicle of Current History," 133–34.
2. M. M. Bevington reports that "in the first few months of the war the *Saturday* deprecated the folly of the South in desiring separation" (*Saturday Review*, 72). As noted earlier, much of the English opposition to a Southern Confederacy at this time was based on opposition to slavery. Robert May maintains that "shortly before the Civil War began, human bondage went against the grain of what we today might call world opinion" (*Atlantic Rim*, 17).
3. This article was reprinted in the *Living Age*, Jan. 5, 1861, 57, which is the source here. Archives of the *Living Age* magazine can be found at *The Online Books Page*, https://onlinebooks.library.upenn.edu/webbin/serial?id=livingage.
4. "English Institutions and American Opinion," Jan. 5, 1861, 3. This article was reprinted in the *Living Age*, Mar. 2, 1861, 573–74.
5. "The Seceding American States," Jan. 12, 1861, 27.
6. "The Bearings of American Disunion," Jan. 12, 1861, 30, 31, 32.
7. Quoted in Sideman and Friedman, *Europe*, 27–28.

8. "The Dis-United States." This article was reprinted in the *Living Age*, Mar. 23, 1861, 758.
9. *Saturday Review*, Feb. 16, 1861, 160, 161.
10. "The Impending Crisis in America," 431–32. This journal was generally liberal. Founded in 1845, its philosophy emphasized freedom. It promised for the outset that "on all public questions" the journal "would be the advocate of freedom—freedom in the largest sense—freedom in Education, freedom in Trade, freedom in Religion—freedom and fairness in everything," tempered by a concern for moderation and reason (Houghton, *Wellesley Index*, 1:114).
11. "Impending Crisis," 432, 436.
12. "The Election of President Lincoln," Apr. 1861, 572.
13. "The True Issue Between North and South," Apr. 13, 1861, 395.
14. "The American News and Its Lessons," Apr. 20, 1861, 394.
15. Jones, *Union in Peril*, 5.
16. Feb. 10, 1861, *NL* 1:217. Charles Eliot Norton's importance in the transatlantic dialogue that played out during the war can scarcely be overestimated. Donald Hall states that "quite possibly Norton was the most important link in this transatlantic network" of liberal thinkers ("Victorian Connection," 87). Leslie Butler argues that Norton "played an indispensable and unparalleled role" in this network. She also points out that in his early travels Norton made the acquaintance of another American with a strong interest in Europe, George William Curtis. "The two men travelled together from the Continent to England, dining, talking, touring cathedrals, and forming the basis of a fast and enduring friendship." Both would play key roles in the cultural conflict precipitated by the war (*Critical Americans*, 43, 44, 47, 50).
17. Feb. 15, 1861, A. H. Clough to C. E. Norton, Charles Eliot Norton Papers, HL.
18. Mar. 10, 1861, A. H. Clough to C. E. Norton, Charles Eliot Norton Papers, HL.
19. Dec. 15, 1860, 762–63. Quoted in Bevington, *Saturday Review*, 272. This attitude was shared by other conservative Victorian journals. Marchand states that the *Athenaeum*, for example, "was never enthusiastic about Emerson" and was "antithetic to Transcendentalism" (*Athenaeum*, 79n210).
20. Jan. 1, 1861, C. P. Cranch to J. S. Dwight, Antislavery Collection, BPL.
21. "The Election in November," 500, 501, 502.
22. Feb. 16, 1861, *ML* 1:360.
23. "Oration Delivered Before the New England Society in the City of New York at their semi-annual anniversary," Dec. 22, 1855, printed pamphlet, Holmes Papers, HL, 44). For Emerson, see Gougeon, *Virtue's Hero*, 219–20.
24. Mar. 5, 1861, *NL* 1:219–20.
25. Mar. 22, 1861, W. J. Stillman to C. E. Norton, Charles Eliot Norton Papers, HL. For more on Stillman, see Garrison, "Stillman."

26. Mar. 26, 1861, S. J. May to R. Webb, Antislavery Collection, BPL.
27. For more on Emerson's antislavery career, see Gougeon, *Virtue's Hero*.
28. Fredrickson, *Inner Civil War*, 50.
29. Jan. 28, 1861, ArL 2:49. Arnold's criticism of the North during the war and the conspicuous absence of criticism of the South or slavery has been noted by modern critics. Some, like Sidney Coulling, have gone so far as to suggest that "there was a fundamental bond of sympathy between Arnold and the South that helps to account for his idealizing, not to say romanticizing, the Civil War and especially the Confederate cause" ("Matthew Arnold," 40, 41).
30. Jan. 14, 1861, S. J. May to R. Webb, Antislavery Collection, BPL.
31. "Peace-Be Still," Jan. 5, 1861.
32. "Speech of Hon. J. R. Barrett of Missouri, Delivered in the House of Representatives, February 21, 1861," *Daily Democratic Union*, Apr. 7, 1861.
33. Susan-Mary Grant notes that Theodore Parker and Ralph Waldo Emerson were among the individuals who were "active in the creation of a northern critique of the South that the Republicans seized on and developed in the run-up to the election of 1856" (*North Over South*, 78).
34. CWL 4:263, 271.
35. Adams, *Great Britain*, 1:50.
36. Campbell, *English Public Opinion*, 42.
37. Mar. 15, 1861, ML 1:364.
38. "Events in America," 258.
39. Donald, *Lincoln*, 292.

Chapter 3

1. Scudder, *Lowell*, 2:10.
2. Conway, *Autobiography*, 2:88–89.
3. Quoted in Emerson, *Early Years*, 255–56.
4. Lawrence Buell reports that New England's "most prestigious literary magazine, the *Atlantic Monthly*, and its most prestigious publishing house, Ticknor & Fields, were overwhelmingly . . . sponsored and dominated by groups of Unitarians who together formed a kind of interlocking directorship whose fraternal networking became publicly concretized for the region's literati most conspicuously by the inauguration of Boston's Saturday Club" ("Literary Significance," 164).
5. Robinson, *Warrington Pen Portraits*, 259, 263.
6. James McPherson notes that at the outset a majority of Northerners felt they were fighting "to maintain the best government on earth" and that the war "had nothing to do with slavery" (*Battle Cry*, 311, 310).
7. Apr. 26, 1861. Quoted in Karcher, *First Woman*, 446.
8. ECW 7:27.

9. "The Colored People Want to Fight," Apr. 24, 1861.
10. "Meeting of Colored People," Apr. 24, 1861 (emphasis in original).
11. "The Colored Citizens," Apr. 25, 1861.
12. Even without legal sanction, irregular Black militias were formed in Massachusetts beginning in the 1850s following the passage of the Fugitive Slave Law (Wirzbicki, *Higher Law*, 178–81).
13. *Atlantic Monthly*, Feb. 1861, 245.
14. "The Duty of the Citizen," Apr. 24, 1861.
15. Apr. 22, 1861, Aubrey de Vere to C. E. Norton, Charles Eliot Norton Papers, HL.
16. "Why We Talk About England," *Harper's Weekly*, Jun. 22, 1861. Ironically, all of the living figures Curtis alluded to here would offer only criticism of the North throughout the war.
17. Stafford, *Literary Criticism*, 123.
18. Donald Read maintains that the "Southern plantocracy was favourably regarded by the British aristocracy as the transatlantic equivalent of itself" (*Cobden and Bright*, 226).
19. Russell was considered by many Northerners to be a Southern sympathizer. In a letter to the British minister to the United States, Lord Lyons, in January 1861, Russell declared, "The best thing now would be that the right to secede should be acknowledged, & that there should be a separation" (quoted in Sebrell, *Persuading John Bull*, 18).
20. "American Belligerents and European Neutrals," May 11, 1861, 462.
21. Campbell, *English Public Opinion*, 31. The Queen's Proclamation was soon followed by similar declarations by Emperor Napoleon of France (June 10, 1861) and the government of Spain (June 17, 1861). Robert May points out that Lincoln's administration was not pleased with the initial European position on the war. "By proclaiming neutrality, European nations recognized the Confederacy's belligerent status, which meant that the Confederacy had the right to arrange loans and buy arms abroad" (*Atlantic Rim*, 6).
22. "Great Britain's Neutrality and Our Enemies."
23. Quoted in Sideman and Friedman, *Europe Looks*, 28.
24. In Arnold, *Democratic Education*, 385, 160.
25. "Arnold's Popular Education of France," Oct. 1861, 581–82.
26. It took approximately two weeks for communications to cross the Atlantic.
27. ArL 2:96. Arnold was always sensitive about his American reviews, in part because, as John Raleigh points out, "he always thought of the United States as constituting an audience as well as England" (*Matthew Arnold*, 7).
28. May 23, 1861.
29. *National Review*, July and Oct. 1861, 465, 466. Don Doyle reports that at the outset "Europeans were genuinely puzzled by the Union's conservative, legalistic position and lack of moral purpose in waging war" (*Cause of All Nations*, 69).

30. June 5, 1861, *CCD* 9:163.

31. June 3, 1861, S. J. May Jr. to R. D. Webb, Antislavery Collection, BPL, emphasis in original.

32. "England and the Rebellion," June 8, 1861.

33. June 5, 1861, Lowell Papers, BPL.

34. May 29, 1861, and June 6, 1861, Henry Wadsworth Longfellow Papers, HL.

35. Quoted in Beckett, *War Correspondents*, 22–23.

36. This letter was later reprinted in the *National Anti-Slavery Standard*, June 22, 1861.

37. J. E. B. Munson reports that "within a year of publication, one English publisher estimated that one and a half million copies of *Uncle Tom's Cabin* were circulating in Britain and her empire." Much of this was due to the pirated editions that proliferated in the absence of an effective international copyright law ("Book," 40, 42).

38. Hamand, "'No Voice,'" 4.

39. June 14, 1861, *ML* 1:372.

40. June 11, 1861, *DL* 9:425.

41. June 10, 1861, *GL* 654, 655, 656, emphasis in original. Despite these early concerns, Gaskell's biographer reports that, regarding Norton's commitment to "the value of the individual and the negro's right to freedom and suffrage" and "the principle of equal rights"—key elements in the New Englander's liberal agenda—he and Gaskell "were obviously in complete sympathy" (Hopkins, *Gaskell*, 227).

42. "America: Is the Success of the North Possible?," June 29, 1861, 702.

43. "The Causes of American Bitterness," June 15, 1861. This article was reprinted in the *Living Age*, July 20, 1861, 188.

44. Looby, "Introduction," 13.

45. Ethan Kytle indicates that "Higginson's turn to antislavery violence drew directly upon his own religious and philosophical beliefs, namely Transcendentalism" (*Romantic Reformers*, 327). Looby maintains that Emerson was "one of Higginson's most important intellectual and spiritual mentors" ("Introduction," 3).

46. "Nat Turner's Insurrection," *Atlantic Monthly*, Aug. 1861, 187.

47. Higginson wrote a number of stories about his experiences as a commander of Black troops for publication in the *Atlantic Monthly*. These essays, later published as *Army Life in a Black Regiment* (1870) have been referred to collectively as a "document in desegregation" (Meyer, "Introduction," 21).

48. Sept. 27, 1861, Letters of Capt. Richard Cary, 2nd Mass V. I, MHS.

49. "Chronicle of Current American History," July 1861, 130.

50. McPherson, *Battle Cry*, 497–98.

51. Williams, *I Freed Myself*, 3.

52. July 13, 1861. This article was later reprinted as "What English Abolitionists Want" in the *Living Age*, Aug. 17, 1861, 442.

53. *Atlantic Monthly*, Nov. 1861, 640. It would be another two years before Black men would be enlisted in the regular Union army, but this was obviously an important step in that direction.

54. Houghton, *Wellesley Index*, 1:8. Michael Michie notes that "*Blackwood's Edinburgh Magazine* was formed to vigorously promote broad conservative principles and to do it with style" ("'On Behalf,'" 120).

55. Hugh Dubrulle reports that the journal's proprietor, John Blackwood, was so dedicated to the Southern cause that he would on occasion rewrite articles on the war submitted to the magazine, often after asking James Mason, the Confederacy's envoy in Great Britain, to review the manuscripts (*Ambivalent Nation*, 70).

56. "The Disruption of the Union," July 1861, 130, 131. Michie states that *Blackwood's* had a "reputation for acerbic commentary" that would be "a constant irritant to American readers during the war" ("'On Behalf,'" 130).

57. Cecil was the brother-in-law of Alexander James Beresford-Hope, cofounder of the *Saturday Review*. During the war, he would become one of the principle financial backers of pro-Southern activity in Britain (Blackett, *Divided Hearts*, 100, 65, 67).

58. Roberts, *Salisbury*, 46. Roberts also notes that Cecil "refused to accept such a concept as the inalienable rights of man" (47).

59. Quoted in Steele, who points out that "nothing in his political life . . . made [Cecil] more anxious or depressed" than the American Civil War "and its outcome" (*Lord Salisbury*, 39, 26).

60. "Democracy on Its Trial," *Quarterly Review*, 249.

61. *The Social Significance of Our Institutions* (1861), 9, 10, 13, 34. The address was later published by Ticknor and Fields as a pamphlet, which is the source here.

62. *CWL* 4:438.

63. McPherson, *Battle Cry*, 312.

64. "The American Civil War," July 20, 1861. This article was reprinted in the *Living Age*, Aug. 24, 1861, 502.

65. "Mr. Jefferson Davis's Message," Dec. 14, 1861, 597, 598.

66. *Daily News* (London), July 19, 1861. This article was reprinted in the *Living Age*, Aug. 24, 1861, 506.

67. July 7, 1861, *ML* 2:4.

Chapter 4

1. McPherson, *Battle Cry*, 336, 347; Nevins, *War for the Union*, 1:214–23.
2. July 21, 1861, *ML* 2:21, 23, 24.
3. *EL* 9:55.
4. Conway, *Autobiography*, 1:335. Conway came from a slave-owning family in Virginia. He described his life as a "pilgrimage from pro-slavery to anti-slavery

enthusiasm." Having been influenced by Emerson's writings, he converted from Methodism to Unitarianism/Transcendentalism. He graduated from Harvard Divinity School in 1854 (Mott, *Biographical Dictionary*, 53).

5. July 26, 1861, *NL* 1:237, 238.
6. Quoted in Cary, *Curtis*, 148.
7. Turner, *Norton*, 170.
8. *EL* 5:253, 254.
9. Bennett, *London Confederates*, 30; Nevins, *War for the Union*, 2:244.
10. Campbell, *English Public Opinion*, 59; Jones, *Union in Peril*, 57. The Sept. 4 *Times* quote is from Crawford, *Anglo-American Crisis*, 123. On August 10 the paper reported that "the reverse at Manassas caused deep mortification and despondency in Washington."
11. Aug. 6; Crawford, *Anglo-American Crisis*, 119.
12. Stapelton, "Introduction," 7.
13. Quoted in Crawford, *Anglo-American Crisis*, 120.
14. Quoted in Crawford, *Anglo-American Crisis*, 127, 135–36.
15. Anonymous, *History of the Times*, 2:359, 366, 367.
16. Dowling, *Norton*, 59.
17. *DL* 9:452.
18. Kinser, *Civil War*, 127.
19. Aug. 28, 1861, *GL* 664, 665.
20. Aug. 15, 1861, W. W. Story to C. E. Norton, Charles Eliot Norton Papers, HL.
21. Quoted in James, *Story*, 2:61, 69.
22. Howard Jones reports, "Russell's letters printed in the New York *Herald* and the *Times* of London [had] . . . a profound impact on both sides of the Atlantic. His graphic accounts of Union forces in full disarray earned him the contempt of northerners as 'Bull-Run Russell' while giving the lie to the official claim that the Army of the Potomac had merely beat a strategic retreat" (*Union in Peril*, 61).
23. Sept. 7, 1861, *AL* 1:39.
24. Jones, *Union in Peril*, 61.
25. "Cotton and Civil War," Aug. 10, 1861, 869.
26. This letter was reprinted in the *Living Age*, Oct. 5, 1861, 381.
27. *Macmillan's*, Aug. 1861, 414–15, 416.
28. Stowe, *Independent* (New York), Aug. 1, 1861. Reprinted in *National Anti-Slavery Standard*, Aug. 10, 1861.
29. Quoted in Collini, *Public Moralists*, 140.
30. Collini, *Public Moralists*,141.
31. Aug. 18, 1861, *MCW* 15:738–39.
32. Charles Eliot Norton Papers, HL.
33. Charles Eliot Norton Papers, HL.
34. McPherson, *Battle Cry*, 353; Foner, *Fiery Trial*, 341.

35. McPherson, *Battle Cry*, 355, 356, 357; Williams, *I Freed Myself*, 3. Silvana Siddali points out that the Confiscation Acts "paved the way in the northern public mind for Lincoln to issue his Preliminary Emancipation Proclamation and . . . [gave] that proclamation a force and a power that Americans had hitherto disdained in verbal pronouncements" (*Property to Person*, 249).

36. Aug. 22, 1861, Rebecca Meade to John E. Meade, Southern History Collection, WL. Andrew Ward reports widespread slave resistance growing throughout the South at this time. "South Carolina was rife with insurrections at the beginning of the war," while "in Louisiana, slave uprisings doubled in 1861." In Mississippi, "whites hanged dozens of blacks and their white allies on suspicion of plotting insurrections" as slaves set fires to the courthouse and several homes in Yazoo City (*Slaves' War*, 162).

37. McPherson, *Battle Cry*, 352–54.

38. Douglass, *Selected Speeches*, 448.

39. "The American Disunion," Sept. 6, 1861. The article is reprinted in Adams, *Slavery*, 56.

40. *TL* 1:169.

41. Sept. 7, 1861, H. Bright to C. E. Norton, Charles Eliot Norton Papers, HL.

42. "England" and "British Opinion on the War," *Harper's Weekly*, Aug. 31, 1861.

43. William Porcher Miles Papers, Wilson Special Collections Library, University of North Carolina at Chapel Hill, http://finding-aids.lib.unc.edu/00508/; Heidler, *Civil War*, 1328–29.

44. July 20, 1861, R. Bunch to W. P. Miles, Southern History Collection, WL.

45. Campbell, *English Public Opinion*, 54.

46. Fergusson was a Conservative. The Honorable Robert Bourke would be elected to Parliament as a Conservative in 1868 (Bennett, *London Confederates*, 140).

47. July 27, 1861, W. Gregory to W. P. Miles, Southern History Collection, WL.

48. Sept. 12, 1861, R. Bunch to W. P. Miles, Southern History Collection, WL.

49. Barnes and Barnes, *American Civil War*, 1:126, 127.

50. Mahin, *One War*, 56.

51. Quoted in Dickey, *Our Man in Charleston*, 46.

52. These articles are discussed in chapter 6.

53. Aug. 23, 1861, Creecy Family Papers, 1861–65, Southern History Collection, WL.

54. "The American Union, and the Duty and Power of the North to Maintain It," Oct. 1861, 469, 472.

55. "Our Relations with America," Oct. 1861, 471.

56. "Democracy Teaching by Example," 395–96.

57. "Our Sympathies with America," Oct. 5, 1861, 339.

58. Sept. 7, 1861. Martineau, *Writings*, 151, 152.

59. Nov. 6, 1861, R. Webb to A. W. Weston, Antislavery Collection, BPL.
60. Chesnut, *Mary Chesnut's Civil War*, 242, 245.
61. Oct. 11, 1861, S. May to R. Webb, Antislavery Collection, BPL.
62. McPherson, *Battle Cry*, 362.
63. O'Connor, *Civil War Boston*, 82.
64. Bundy, *Nature of Sacrifice*, 192.
65. Bundy, *Nature of Sacrifice*, 184, 192. Carla Bosco reports that by the mid-1850s, following the passage of the Fugitive Slave Law, Harvard had become a bastion of antislavery feeling ("Harvard University," 246).
66. Duberman, *Lowell*, 220–21.
67. Gura, *American Transcendentalism*, 298; Heidler and Heidler, *Civil War*, 28. Like Emerson, Ellis graduated from Harvard, both the College and the Divinity School. He was the editor of the *Christian Examiner*, a liberal publication that served as the official voice of Unitarianism.
68. "Why Has the North Felt Aggrieved with England," 616.
69. "The Northern States of America," Nov. 5, 1861.
70. The phrase "multitudinous monarch" refers to the belief of English conservatives that America was a "mobocracy."

Chapter 5

1. Jones, *Union in Peril*, 81, 83.
2. Adams, *Great Britain*, 1:205.
3. Nov. 18, 1861, *AL* 1:71.
4. See von Frank's *Trials of Anthony Burns* for a comprehensive, detailed account of the Burns affair and its significance, especially for New England Transcendentalists.
5. Shapiro, *Dana*, 116, 118, 121–22.
6. Howard Jones indicates that in the public banquet in Boston, "Governor Andrew crowed that the captain has 'fired a shot across the bow of the ship that bore the English lion's head.' The House of Representatives thanked Wilkes 'for his brave, adroit, and patriotic conduct in the arrest and detention of the traitors'" (*Union in Peril*, 91, 94).
7. Emerson, *Early Years*, 257.
8. Emerson, *Early Years*, 274, 284-85.
9. Emerson, *Early Years*, 288.
10. Donald, *Sumner*, 2:31.
11. Emerson, *Early Years*, 288.
12. Dec. 3, 1861, *AL* 1:78.
13. Jones, *Union in Peril*, 85, 86, 88; Foreman, *World on Fire*, 191ff.

14. Quoted in Adams, *Great Britain*, 1:217.
15. Sept. 30, 1861. This article was reprinted in the *Living Age*, Jan. 11, 1862, 108.
16. Sebrell, *Persuading John Bull*, 45.
17. Quoted in Carroll, "American Civil War," 96.
18. Quoted in Carroll, "American Civil War," 97.
19. Nov. 29, 1861. Bright, "Letters," 148.
20. Dec. 5, 1861. Bright, "Letters," 150, 151.
21. Dec. 7, 1861. Bright, "Letters," 153.
22. Dec. 13, 1861, C. F. Adams Sr. to R. H. Dana, Dana Family Papers, MHS.
23. Dec. 3, 1861, *DL* 9:531.
24. Dec. 27, 1861, R. M. Mason to Amos A. Lawrence, Lawrence Papers, MHS.
25. Dec. 11 1861, *CCD* 9:368.
26. James, *Story*, 2:105, 106.
27. Dec. 8, 1861, *ArL* 2:107.
28. Quoted in Donald, *Sumner*, 2:37.
29. Dec. 24, 1861. Sumner, *Letters*, 2:90.
30. Doyle, *Cause of All Nations*, 149.
31. Quoted in Donald, *Sumner*, 2:39.
32. Jones, *Blue & Gray Diplomacy*, 105–6.
33. Emerson, *Early Years*, 257.
34. Read, *Cobden and Bright*, 222.
35. Emerson, *Early Years*, 288.
36. Nevins, *War for the Union*, 1:386; Donald, *Lincoln*, 320.
37. Dec. 5, 1861, E. Wigham to S. May, Antislavery Collection, BPL.
38. Dec. 7, 1861, W. Robson to F. J. Garrison, Antislavery Collection, BPL.
39. Dec. 31, 1861, R. Webb to C. Weston, Antislavery Collection, BPL.
40. "The President's Message," July 20, 1861. This article was reprinted in the *Living Age*, Aug. 24, 1861, 496.
41. James, *Story*, 2:111.
42. James, *Story*, 2:108.
43. "The American Question," 6.
44. Adams, *Great Britain*, 2:187, 193; Bourke would become an early organizer and supporter of the Southern Independence Association. Eventually he was elected to Parliament as a Conservative in 1868 (Bennett, *London Confederates*, 120).
45. "A Month with the Rebels," 757, 758, 762.
46. Doyle, *Cause of All Nations*, 348. For more on the background of this report and its publication, see Hughes, "'Personal Observations.'"
47. [Fergusson,] "Some Account of Both Sides of the American War," Dec. 1861, 768–79.
48. For an informed analysis of this important book, see O'Connor, *American Sectionalism*, 140–48.

49. Blackett, *Divided Hearts*, 138.

50. Ritchie Watson indicates that because of the pervasiveness of "the southern fantasy of a pure or nearly pure Norman race . . . Dixie's reactionary defenders . . . viewed massive immigration not as a sign of progress but as one of racial and social decay" (*Normans and Saxons*, 87).

51. Bennett, *London Confederates*, 39, 118. John Waller argues that Dickens's views closely paralleled those of Spence and that his sympathies were clearly with the South ("Charles Dickens," 535, 537, 543).

52. Quoted in Blackett, *Divided Hearts*, 139.

Chapter 6

1. Henry Wadsworth Longfellow Papers, HL.
2. "A Glance Beyond," Jan. 1862, 253.
3. "The Close of 1861," Jan. 1862, 131–32.
4. A similar argument was made by Thomas Carlyle earlier in "The Negro Question" (1849), later republished as "The Nigger Question" (1853). It would be repeated frequently by conservative critics on both sides of the Atlantic throughout the war as proof that emancipation would be deleterious to both slaves and their white masters.
5. "Sewall's Ordeal of Free Labour," Jan. 1862, 64.
6. "Loyalty," Jan. 1862, 174.
7. Ferguson, *Empire*, 121–28. Southerners at the time saw the Sepoys as similar to Black slaves who needed to be mastered to be made useful. See Bilwakesh, "'Their Faces.'"
8. Jan. 1, 1862, A. Evans to wife, Augustus Coutanche Evans Papers, 1861–63, Southern History Collection, WL.
9. "The Convulsions in America," Jan. 1862, 121.
10. Charles Hodge (principal of Princeton Theological Seminary), "England and America," *Princeton Review*, Jan. 1862, 150, 147, 149, 156, 153.
11. Donald, *Sumner*, 1:384.
12. Donald, *Sumner*, 2:33, 34, 114.
13. Jan. 10, 1862, *AL* 1:99.
14. "England, America, and Europe," Jan. 11, 1862, 31.
15. Dunn, *Froude*, 2:337.
16. Jan. 10, 1862, *TL* 1:173.
17. Jan. 6, 1862, *R-NC* 68, emphasis in original.
18. Jan. 31, 1862, *AL* 1:107.
19. *EJ* 15:186–87.
20. Forbes was a close friend of the Emerson family. His son William would marry Emerson's daughter Edith after the war. Forbes was an able and competent

businessman who was deeply involved in the building of America's railroads and other major commercial enterprises. He was also an abolitionist, a supporter of free labor, and a staunch Union man.

21. Richardson, *Emerson*, 551.

22. Garry Wills maintains that Lincoln's "dialectic of ideals struggling for their realization in history owes a great deal to the primary intellectual fashion of his period, Transcendentalism." In fact, he later describes Lincoln as "a Transcendentalist without the fuzziness." Wills traces this Transcendental element in Lincoln from Emerson through George Bancroft and Theodore Parker (*Lincoln at Gettysburg*, 103, 174, 103–4).

23. Conlin, "Smithsonian Abolition Lecture Controversy." Other lecturers in the series included Wendell Phillips, William Lloyd Garrison, and Henry Ward Beecher.

24. The lecture was divided into two parts: "American Civilization" (*Atlantic Monthly*, Apr. 1862) and "Civilization" (*Society and Solitude*, EW 7:19–34). The quotes here are from the former.

25. Emerson's belief in the importance of the American laborer permeates his works. Neal Dolan point out that, "from early to late," Emerson's writings offer "a sustained hymn in praise of labor" (*Emerson's Liberalism*, 114).

26. Emphasis in original. Emerson was undoubtedly aware that "Ich dien" was the official motto of the Prince of Wales, the heir apparent to the British throne. It appears in the prince's heraldic badge. As used here, the term is deeply ironic, given the demeaning view of laborers held by British aristocrats.

27. The relationship between the cause of free labor and the cause of the slave was understood by Northern reformers early on. In 1849 the Massachusetts Anti-Slavery Society declared that "the rights of the laborer at the North are identical with those of the Southern slave." The idea took hold. In 1850, following the passage of the Fugitive Slave Law, the New England Workingman's Convention passed a resolution declaring the act "an infamous usurpation, and a despotic enactment" (quoted in Wirzbicki, *Higher Law*, 139, 156).

28. "American Civilization," 502–11.

29. *MCW* 18:105.

30. "The Contest in America," *Fraser's Magazine*, Feb. 1862, 259. John Compton argues, "Mill believed that the intellectual, and, ultimately, physical struggle to eliminate the illiberal institution of slavery would force the American public to reflect on and rearticulate the nation's founding principles," which this study confirms ("Emancipation," 222–23).

31. "The Prospects of Slavery, as Affected by the Success of the North and that of the South Respectively," *Economist*, Feb. 15, 1862, 170–71.

32. Allan Nevins states, "The best intellectual leaders of the kingdom were on the Northern side." In addition to Mill, he included the "Manchester Liberals"

Monckton Miles, Goldwin Smith, and Thomas Hughes, as well as John Elliott Cairnes (*War for the Union*, 2:249ff).

33. Howard Jones reports, "Foreign Secretary Russell tried to temper relations with the Union by announcing that, effective 6 February 1862, British waters were no longer open to privateers or warships from either Union or Confederacy" (*Blue & Gray Diplomacy*, 114).

34. Quoted in Kinser, *Civil War*, 34.

35. Feb. 3, 1862, quoted in *HLL*, 2:159–60, 162, 163.

36. Feb. 10, 1862, W. W. Story to C. E. Norton, Charles Eliot Norton Papers, HL.

Chapter 7

1. Nevins, *War for the Union*, 2:73.
2. Jones, *Union in Peril*, 104.
3. Feb. 11, 1862, *Mary Chesnut's Civil War*, 286.
4. Mar. 21, 1862, *AL* 1:122.
5. Bennett, *London Confederates*, 140; Jones, *Union in Peril*, 105.
6. Feb. 21, 1862, Henry Wadsworth Longfellow Papers, HL.
7. Handlin, *George Bancroft*, 93.
8. Emerson, *Early Years*, 283. Stewart Winger maintains that Bancroft, "the most widely read American historian of the antebellum period, was full of Romantic notions" that eventually had an impact on Lincoln (Winger, *Lincoln*, 11). His history also "struck sympathetic chords within Transcendentalist ranks" (Mott, *Biographical Dictionary*, 13).
9. Quoted in Handlin, *George Bancroft*, 271.
10. Howe, *Bancroft*, 2:151.
11. Mar. 1862, S. May to R. Webb, Antislavery Collection, BPL.
12. Mar. 27, 1862, E. Wigham to S. May, Antislavery Collection, BPL.
13. Frank Luther Mott indicates that "the Harpers were Democrats, but their magazine was earnestly nonpartisan. It was anything but a 'journal of opinion.'" However, the Civil War, which was "a fiery ordeal for *Harper's*," changed all that (*American Magazines*, 1:392). Curtis would be a major force in bringing about this change.
14. Editor's Easy Chair, *Harper's Monthly Magazine*, Feb. 1862, 407–8.
15. "The Young Man from the Country," *All the Year Round*, Mar. 1, 1862, 541, 542.
16. Mar. 16, 1862, *DL* 10:53–54.
17. McPherson, *Tried by War*, 87.
18. Quoted in Donald, *Sumner*, 2:51.

19. *CWL* 5:144–45.
20. Karcher, *First Woman*, 457.
21. Quoted in Cary, *Curtis*, 53.
22. Mar. 8, 1862, *NL* 1:252.
23. "The President of the United States," *Harper's Weekly*, Mar. 22, 1862.
24. "*Blackwood* on Rebellion," *Philadelphia City Item*, Mar. 8, 1862.
25. Almost all of the major British magazines were printed and distributed in American editions (Mott, *American Magazines*, 1:748–49).
26. Mar. 21, 1862, R. Meade to John E. Meade, Southern History Collection, WL.
27. McPherson, *War on the Waters*, 96–105.
28. Quoted in Jones, *Union in Peril*, 110.
29. Apr. 4, 1862, *AL* 1:123.
30. Quoted in Sebrell, *Persuading John Bull*, 87.
31. Williams, *I Freed Myself*, 5.
32. McPherson, *Struggle*, 164.
33. Both sources quoted in McPherson, *Struggle*, 165.
34. June 21, 1862, Forbes, *Letters*, 1:317–18.
35. June 1, 1862, *EL* 9:76.
36. Mar. 25, 1862, *EEL* 1:266.
37. *EJ* 15:229.
38. Apr. 21, 1862, *EL* 9:73.
39. Mar. 16, 1862, *ML* 2:71.
40. Mar. 19, 1862, *NL* 2:253.
41. In a letter to Elizabeth Gaskell, Macmillan explained, "I think you will do me credit for no lack of sympathy with the American cause, when you remember that our *Magazine* has stood almost exclusively among the magazines, and stands with few public prints of any kind, in advocating the cause of the North" (Jan. 18, 1862, *Letters*, 102).
42. Edward Dicey, "Three Weeks in New York," *Macmillan's*, April 1862, 456, 459, 463.
43. Apr. 3, 1862, W. H. Newt (?) to W. P. Miles, Southern History Collection, WL.
44. Jones, *Union in Peril*, 118; Nevins, *War for the Union*, 2:93; Foner, *Fiery Trial*, 342.
45. *EEL* 2:275, 278.
46. Quoted in Pickard, *Whittier*, 449.
47. Apr. 20, 1862, *LongL* 4:276.
48. Jones, *Union in Peril*, 109, 118.
49. Apr. 8, 1862. Quoted in Dunn, *Froude*, 2:340.
50. McPherson, *War on the Waters*, 55.
51. May 16, 1862, *AL* 1:143.

52. May 16, 1862, *AL* 1:147, 148, 149.
53. May 22, 1862, *AL* 1:152.
54. May 14, 1862, G. Curtis to C. E. Norton, Charles Eliot Norton Papers, HL.
55. Mott, *Biographical Dictionary*, 272–73.
56. "Slavery, in Its Principles, Development, and Expedients," 639.
57. Jones, *Union in Peril*, 123.
58. Nevins, *War for the Union*, 2:91, 114, 116.
59. Jones, *Union in Peril*, 148.
60. McPherson, *Battle Cry*, 496.
61. Andrew Taylor argues that New England, especially Boston, played a unique role "in the creation of an American intellectual class." At the outbreak of the Civil War, Emerson declared that "'Boston commands attention as the town which was appointed in the destiny of nations to lead the civilization of North America.'" *Thinking America*, 4.
62. Curry, *Blueprint for Modern America*, 9.
63. Curry, *Blueprint for Modern America*, 74. Manisha Sinha argues that during the war "abolitionists and their Radical Republican allies pushed the Lincoln administration from nonextension to abolition to black rights" (*Slave's Cause*, 543). As shown here, many of the most influential of these allies were New England idealists.
64. McPherson, *Battle Cry*, 496, 506, 507.
65. Nevins, *War for the Union*, 2:94.
66. "This Country Must Be Saved," *Daily Democratic Union*, May 13, 1862.
67. Adams, *Great Britain*, 2:95, 84.
68. Edward Dicey, "Washington During the War," *Macmillan's*, May 1862, 17, 19, 23.
69. Dicey, "Notes of a Tour Through the Border States," *Macmillan's*, June 1862, 144, 145, 149, 139.
70. Jones, *Union in Peril*, 131.
71. "The Terms on Which Massachusetts Will Furnish Recruits," June 4, 1862.
72. McPherson, *Battle Cry*, 492.
73. Concord, MA Selectman's Report (1861–62), pp. 4, 5, CPL.
74. Weinberg, *Cairnes*, 23.
75. June 24, 1862, *MCW* 15:784, 785.
76. Editor's Easy Chair, *Harper's Monthly*, Aug. 1862, 421.
77. Trollope, *North America*, 2:52.
78. Trollope, *Four Lectures*, 33, 34.
79. Emerson, *Early Years*, 257.
80. Bennett, *London Confederates*, 43.
81. Burnett, *Henry Hotze*, 1, 20, 21.
82. May 15, 1862. Quoted in Young, *Colonial Desire*, 137.
83. Sebrell, *Persuading John Bull*, 58.

84. Sebrell, *Persuading John Bull*, 85.
85. Dufour, *Nine Men*, 277.
86. Quoted in Brown, *Victorian News*, 63. Edward George Geoffrey Smith-Stanley, 14th Earl of Derby, was the leader of the Conservative Party.
87. Quoted in Sebrell, *Persuading John Bull*, 85.
88. Sebrell, *Persuading John Bull*, 131.

Chapter 8

1. McPherson, *Battle Cry*, 464, 470.
2. Jones, *Union in Peril*, 127, 129, 130.
3. July 8, 1862, *EL* 5:280. As noted earlier, of Lowell's four nephews, three died in the war.
4. July 4, 1862, *AL* 1:161, 162.
5. Jones, *Union in Peril*, 132.
6. "Foreign Intervention," June 31, 1862.
7. Adams, *Great Britain*, 2:33.
8. *CWL* 4:426.
9. McPherson, "'Whole Family,'" 133.
10. McPherson, *Battle Cry*, 500.
11. McPherson, *Negro's Civil War*, 156–60; Williams, *I Freed Myself*, 82–83.
12. Quoted in White, *House Built by Slaves*, 58.
13. See Burlingame, "African Americans."
14. Burlingame, "African Americans," 54.
15. Quoted in White, *House Built by Slaves*, 60.
16. "Truth Versus Twaddle," *Harper's Weekly*, June 21, 1862.
17. Curtis, "American Doctrine," 99, 100, 102, 103.
18. July 31, 1862, *NL* 1:254.
19. Milne, *Curtis*, 116.
20. Howard Jones maintains that "despite denials by both the Union and the Confederacy, slavery was emerging as the focal point of the war" (*Blue & Gray Diplomacy*, 121).
21. Jones, *Blue & Gray Diplomacy*, 120–21.
22. Jones, *Blue & Gray Diplomacy*, 120–21.
23. July 11, 1862. Cobden, "Letters," 306, 307.
24. Bundy, *Nature of Sacrifice*, 277; Mott, *Biographical Dictionary*, 58; Delano, *Brook Farm*, 72.
25. Quoted in Waugh, "'Sacrifice,'" 59.
26. Duncan, *Death and Glory*, 7.
27. July 12, 1862. Quoted in Weinberg, *Cairnes*, 131.

28. Quoted in Fields, *Yesterday*, 99, 100.
29. Tryon, *Parnassus Corner*, 270.
30. Quoted in Tryon, *Parnassus Corner*, 263.
31. Quoted in Wineapple, *Hawthorne*, 350. See also Mellow, *Nathaniel Hawthorne*, 556.
32. "Chiefly About War Matters," *Atlantic Monthly*, 47, emphasis in original.
33. Quoted in Cary, *Curtis*, 156.
34. Campbell, *English Public Opinion*, 148. Waldo Dunn reports that Fuller published five articles in *Fraser's* during the war, all of them highly critical of the North. He was a native of Massachusetts, but "his outspoken utterances in favour of the South made it necessary for him to leave his native country. Settling in England, he did his utmost to promote the Southern cause" (Dunn, *Froude*, 2:334). All of Fuller's articles were extremely bitter and caustic.
35. "Universal Suffrage in the United States, and Its Consequences (By a White Republican)," *Fraser's Magazine*, July 1862, 21–22, 28.
36. "The Free West," July 1862, 179, 190, 191.
37. Mill's essay was published in England in 1861. An American edition followed in 1862.
38. "Mill on Representative Government," *North American Review*, July 1862, 242.
39. Eric Foner points out that "as democracy triumphed, the intellectual grounds for exclusion [from the right to vote] shifted from economic dependency to natural incapacity" (*American Freedom*, 71). This "natural incapacity" was often a euphemism for racial exclusion.
40. Biagini, "Liberalism and Direct Democracy," 21.
41. Hartz, *Necessity of Choice*, 152.
42. Butler, *Critical Americans*, 116. Foner holds race was also a factor for Mill. "Even Mill's argument for universal freedom, in his great work *On Liberty* (1859), applied 'only to human beings in the maturity of their faculties.' The immature included not only children but entire 'races' of less than 'civilized' peoples, deficient in the qualities necessary in the democratic citizen" (*American Freedom*, 71). Alex Zakaras also points to Mill's "elitism" in the matter of voting rights and his assumption that in a "'natural' social order . . . democratic citizens deferred to the moral authority of the educated" (*Individuality*, 193).
43. July 18, 1862, *AL* 1:166.
44. Bennett, *London Confederates*, 141.
45. Quoted in Jones, *Union in Peril*, 134.
46. Jones, *Union in Peril*, 135–36.
47. Adams, *Great Britain*, 2:34, 73.
48. July 31, 1862. Quoted in Hamand, "'No Voice,'" 12, 15.
49. Weinberg, *Cairnes*, 138.

50. July 31, 1862, *NL* 1:255.
51. Dicey, "The New England States," *Macmillan's*, August 1862, 284, 287, 288, 289, 289–90, 295.
52. "American Prospects," Aug. 23, 1862, 205.
53. Jones, *Union in Peril*, 155, 156.
54. *EJ* 15:207.
55. *EJ* 15:209.
56. Aug. 14, 1862, *EEL* 1:293.
57. Aug. 18, 1862, *ML* 2:81.
58. *CWL* 5:388.
59. McPherson, *War That Forged a Nation*, 119.
60. *CWL* 5:389, emphasis in original.
61. White, *Eloquent President*, 151.
62. Aug. 29, 1862, *HLL* 2:167. As indicated in chapter 5, earlier in the war, Fremont had been relieved of his command for declaring general emancipation in Missouri.
63. Quoted in Wirzbicki, *Higher Law*, 251.
64. Wirzbicki, *Higher Law*, 253.
65. Wirzbicki, *Higher Law*, 249.
66. Aug. 30, 1862, *NL* 1:255–56.
67. Aug. 1862, Henry Wadsworth Longfellow Papers, HL.
68. Aug. 28, 1862, *R-NC*, 73. "A Curse for a Nation," one of several antislavery poems by Elizabeth Barrett Browning, appeared in *Poems Before Congress* (1860) as prologue to "The Curse." Ruskin here ignores the actual point of the poem—i.e., that slavery is America's curse.
69. Sept. 1, 1862, Henry Wadsworth Longfellow Papers, HL.

Chapter 9

1. McPherson, *Battle Cry*, 489.
2. Sept. 5, 1862, *AL* 1:182, 183.
3. Sept. 14, 1862. Quoted in Sideman and Friedman, *Europe Looks*, 174–75.
4. Beckett, *War Correspondents*, 4, 5.
5. Sept. 4, 1862. Quoted in Beckett, *War Correspondents*, 4, 5.
6. Four New England states, Massachusetts, New Hampshire, Vermont, and Maine, allowed Blacks to vote on an equal basis with whites (Bergman, *Chronological History*, 68).
7. "The Outlook of the War," 414, 417–18.
8. Sept. 17, 1862, *MCW* 15:795.
9. "Estrangement Between the United States and Great Britain." This letter was reprinted in the *Living Age*, Nov. 15, 1862, 328, 329.

10. Sept. 17, 1862, *MCW* 15:796, 797.
11. Nevins, *War for the Union*, 2:222.
12. Union soldiers found a copy of Lee's orders in a field near Frederick, Maryland, where it was apparently dropped by one of Lee's subordinates (see McPherson, *Battle Cry*, 537).
13. Sept. 25, 1862, *AL* 1:186.
14. Goodwin, *Team of Rivals*, 468.
15. McPherson, *Battle Cry*, 545.
16. Goodwin, *Team of Rivals*, 468.
17. Leonard Curry indicates that there was substantial conservative opposition to the concept of emancipation, and to Lincoln's proclamation, in both the House and the Senate (*Blueprint for Modern America*, 71–74).
18. Amar, *America's Constitution*, 356.
19. *CWL* 5:433–34.
20. Amar, *America's Constitution*, 356.
21. Sept. 23, 1862, *NL* 1:256, 257.
22. Sept. 25, 1862. Cary, *Curtis*, 158.
23. Sept. 24, 1862. Alcott, *Journals*, 349.
24. Sept. 25, 1862, *EEL* 1:300.
25. Sept. 26, 1862. Quoted in Adams, *Great Britain*, 2:100.
26. All quotes are from Holzer, *Lincoln*, 409.
27. Donald, *Sumner*, 2:73–74.
28. O'Connor, *Civil War Boston*, 110; McPherson, *Struggle*, 79; Abbott, *Cotton and Capital*, 95.
29. Sanborn, *Recollections*, 2:264–65.
30. Adams, *Great Britain*, 2:100.
31. Burnett, *Henry Hotze*, 22.
32. Young, *Colonial Desire*, 138.
33. Jones, "History and Mythology," 30, 55.
34. Mahin, *One War*, 131.
35. Doyle, *Cause of All Nations*, 241.
36. "The Civil War in America," Oct. 12, 1862. Seymour won the election and thereafter became a conservative thorn in the side of those liberals promoting this "revolutionary" change.
37. Quoted in Sideman and Friedman, *Europe Looks*, 192.
38. Quoted in Adams, *Great Britain*, 2:103; Ewan, "Emancipation Proclamation," 15.
39. Oct. 18, 1862, reproduced in Klinefelter, "Lampooned in London," 28.
40. Quoted in Jones, *Union in Peril*, 264n24.
41. Jones, *Union in Peril*, 8, 150, 176.
42. Quoted in Burnett, *Henry Hotze*, 17.
43. Neely, *Union Divided*, 150.

44. Oct. 31, 1862, *MCW* 15:800, 801–2.
45. Quoted in Nevins, *War for the Union*, 2:270.
46. "The Confederate Struggle and Recognition," 536, 543, 545, 547.
47. "The American Revolution," 558, 594.
48. Nevins, *War for the Union*, 2:268.
49. Nevins, *War for the Union*, 2:183.
50. Quoted in Bennett, *London Confederates*, 137.
51. Jones, *Union in Peril*, 7–8, 22.
52. Nevins, *War for the Union*, 2:246.
53. "Mr. Roebuck on the American War," Aug. 1, 1862. This article was reprinted in the *Living Age*, Sept. 27, 1862, 615.
54. Adams, *Great Britain*, 2:50–51; Jones, *Union in Peril*, 189–91.
55. "The Northern Elections," Oct. 9, 1862.
56. "The Character of the Rebellion and the Conduct of the War," 523, 529, 530.
57. *EJ* 15:292, 293.
58. Quoted in Dowling, *Norton*, 41.
59. Dowling, *Norton*, 41.
60. "The Proclamation," Oct. 11, 1862.
61. "The Necessity of Emancipation," Oct. 22, 1862.
62. Emerson Papers, HL.
63. Oct. 31, 1862, *MCW* 15:800, 801.
64. Oct. 21–31, 1862, M. Gaskell to C. E. Norton, Charles Eliot Norton Papers, HL.

Chapter 10

1. Quoted in Neely, *Union Divided*, 16.
2. Lawson, *Patriot Fires*, 8.
3. McPherson, *Battle Cry*, 494.
4. Jones, *Union in Peril*, 199, 206, 207; McPherson, *Battle Cry*, 561; Weinberg, *Cairnes*, 150.
5. Nov. 12, 1862, *NL* 1:258.
6. "Republicans and Democrats," Nov. 22, 1862, 623.
7. Nevins, *War for the Union*, 2:271.
8. Weinberg, *Cairnes*, 68.
9. Adelman, *Victorian Radicalism*, 38, 39, 57, 58.
10. Harvie, *Lights of Liberalism*, 108–9. Unfortunately, after the war it became clear that Smith's liberal views did not extend to all minorities. For Smith's antisemitism, see his "New Light on the Jewish Question," *North American Review* 153, no. 2 (1891): 129–43; and Isaac Besht Bendavid, "Goldwin Smith and the Jews," *North American Review* 153, no. 3 (1891): 257–71.

11. Jones, *Union in Peril*, 187.
12. Jones, *Union in Peril*, 206.
13. McPherson, *Battle Cry*, 561–62.
14. Nevins, *War for the Union*, 2:305, 306.
15. Quoted in Jones, *Union in Peril*, 207.
16. Nevins, *War for the Union*, 2:270.
17. Jones, *Union in Peril*, 210–11.
18. Quoted in Jones, *Union in Peril*, 211.
19. Nevins, *War for the Union*, 2:270.
20. *CWL* 5:537, emphasis in the original.
21. *CWL* 5:537.
22. Albright quoted in Ward, *Slaves' War*, 108.
23. Williams, *I Freed Myself*, 115.
24. Quoted in Beckett, *War Correspondents*, 73, 74. See also Foreman, *World on Fire*, 305–11.
25. Anonymous, *History of the Times*, 2:379.
26. Nevins, *War for the Union*, 3:246.
27. Nov. 27, 1862, *ArL* 2:166.
28. Nov. 27, 1862, *ArL* 2:166n2.
29. Dec. 3, 1862, *ArL* 2:168.
30. Wallace, *Goldwin Smith*, 28.
31. Dec. 16, 1862, *MCW* 15:810.
32. *MCW* 15:810.
33. Dec. 25, 1862, *AL* 1:221.
34. *ELL* 2:300.
35. Quoted in Wirzbicki, *Higher Law*, 55. In 1857, Nell, a Boston printer, published a lithographic print of the "Heralds of Freedom" that placed Emerson alongside other abolition stalwarts such as William Lloyd Garrison, Wendell Phillips, and Samuel J. May (Yacovone, *Samuel Joseph May*, 87).
36. Oates, *With Malice Toward None*, 424–25.
37. Quoted in *LL* 2:288.
38. *EJ* 15:301.
39. McPherson, *Battle Cry*, 569–70.
40. McPherson, *Battle Cry*, 570.
41. *LongL* 4:304.
42. Dec. 15, 1862. Quoted in Cary, *Curtis*, 160.
43. Dec. 31, 1862. Weinberg, *Cairnes*, 158, 159.
44. Goodwin, *Team of Rivals*, 486.
45. "The Policy of a Negro Army for the North," Dec. 13, 1862.
46. Dec. 22, 1862. Forbes, *Letters*, 1:345.
47. Dec. 24, 1862. Forbes, *Letters*, 1:348.
48. Forbes, *Letters*, 1:348, 349.
49. Dec. 27, 1862. Forbes, *Letters*, 2:350.

50. Letter, ca. Dec. 18, 1862, James Taylor Graves Papers, NL.
51. Quoted in Donald, *Sumner*, 2:97.
52. Blackett, *Divided Hearts*, 81; Blackett, "Pressure," 70, 71.
53. Quoted in Foner, *British Labor*, 40.
54. Nevins, *War for the Union*, 2:274.
55. Nevins, *War for the Union*, 2:248.
56. O'Connor, *Civil War Boston*, 130.
57. "Petersburg, VA—Cemeteries: Blandford Cemetery (Part 3)," USGenWeb Archives, http://files.usgwarchives.net/va/petersburg/cemeteries/blandford03.txt.

Chapter 11

1. Quoted in Gougeon, *Virtue's Hero*, 292.
2. Fredrickson, *Inner Civil War*, 113.
3. O'Connor, *Civil War Boston*, 127.
4. McFeely, *Frederick Douglass*, 236, 237.
5. Goodwin, *Team of Rivals*, 501.
6. McPherson, *Struggle*, 221.
7. Quoted in Wirzbicki, *Higher Law*, 240.
8. Fear of the consequences of universal emancipation was especially acute among Midwestern conservatives like Cox. As George Fredrickson relates, there was a general concern that "Midwestern states might at some point be inundated by a flood of Negroes pouring across the Ohio River. This sense of a black peril . . . haunted the popular imagination of the Midwest and reached panic proportions when the Civil War brought the prospect of emancipation" (*Black Image*, 134–35). Cox's address is a clear reflection of that panic.
9. Lindsey, *"Sunset" Cox*, 49.
10. John Ashworth relates that Democrats were opposed to all liberal measures, but "most of all they detested the Republican's Emancipation Proclamation. They yearned for the Union that had existed before the War, rather than the new nation that Lincoln and his party seemed to be forging" (*Slavery*, 341).
11. Mark Neely emphasizes that the "central focus" of Cox's address "lay on slavery and the threat of racial equality." Because the liberal culture of New England supported vigorous opposition to the one and solid commitment to the other, "the bulk of the speech deal[s] with cultural issues" (*Boundaries*, 84, 83).
12. Cox's cultural genealogy was correct. According to Lawrence Buell, Transcendentalism is basically "a re-energized expression of Puritan spirit" ("Literary Significance," 169).
13. A "sooter" is one who removes soot from the outside of a boiler, hence, a common laborer.

14. While serving as a chaplain to the US House of Representatives, William Henry Channing was outspoken in his opposition to slavery. On one occasion he invited Henry Highland Garnet to deliver a sermon there. Garnet was the first Black minister ever to do so (Wirzbicki, *Higher Law*, 235).

15. Peter Wirzbicki notes, correctly, that Emerson's notion of the all-encompassing divine Over-Soul "encouraged an implicit egalitarianism" (*Higher Law*, 78). In "Self-Reliance," Emerson declared, "My blood is in every man, and every man's blood is in me" (*ECW* 2:41). For more on Emerson's belief in racial equality, see Gougeon, "Emerson and Race."

16. Cox, *"Puritanism in Politics,"* 5, 7, 11.

17. Quotes from Wirzbicki, *Higher Law*, 249.

18. "Vallandigham Democracy," *Boston Weekly Transcript*, Jan. 14, 1863. McPherson reports that "in January 1863 the president told Senator Charles Sumner that he feared 'the fire in the rear'—meaning the Democracy, especially at the Northwest—more than our military chances" (*Tried by War*, 171).

19. Jan. 23, 1863, *AL* 1:243, 244, 245. Betty Fladeland indicates that the workingman's movement in England felt a sympathetic relationship with the plight of the slaves as early as the 1830s. That feeling began to crystallize with the Chartist movement ("'Our Cause,'" 69–71).

20. Feb. 13, 1863. Quoted in McPherson, *Tried by War*, 60.

21. Feb. 24, 1863. Quoted in McPherson, "'Whole Family,'" 145. For more on the history of working-class support for Lincoln, see Logan, "Bee-Hive Newspaper."

22. Quoted in Wilson, "'Beginning of the End,'" 236.

23. The official history of the London *Times* notes that at this time "English opinion . . . was now clearly divided; pro-Northern sentiment gathered strength. The side which *The Times* supported . . . was now the losing side and also that which, according to all traditions of British humanity, was the wrong side" (Anonymous, *History of the Times*, 2:382).

24. Jan. 20, 1863, *MCW* 15:828.

25. Jan. 26, 1863, *MCW* 15:826, 827, 828.

26. Lorimer, "Anti-Slavery Sentiment," 411.

27. "Voices of British Working Men," *Daily News*, Jan. 2, 1863. This article was later reprinted in the *Living Age*, Feb. 14, 1863, 328, 329.

28. Douglas Lorimer states that "historians of science have found this rise of scientific racist thought a perplexing and disturbing development, for it would appear scientists created a pseudo-science or new mythology of race." This phenomenon is less perplexing, however, if one takes into account "the social and political context in which these ideas developed" (*Colour*, 131).

29. *EJ* 14:128. See also Walls, *Emerson's Life in Science*, for an excellent discussion of Emerson's views of the racial theories of his day, as well as Gougeon, "Emerson and Race"; and Rossi, "Emerson."

30. Walls, *Emerson's Life in Science*, 174.
31. For more on Gray's friendship with Darwin, see Fuller, *Book*, 223–30.
32. George Fredrickson recounts the early history of scientific racism. He points out, "During the 1840s and 1850s the conclusions of scientists on the nature and extent of racial diversity came for the first time to play an important role in the discussion of black servitude" (*Black Image*, 71; see also 71–96). During the Civil War, this movement would reach its apogee.
33. Dewbury, "American School," 122, 124.
34. Dewbury, "American School," 127.
35. Dewbury, "American School," 124.
36. Desmond and Moore, *Darwin's Sacred Cause*, 322–3, 333, 288.
37. Quoted in Dewbury, "American School," 139, 141.
38. Desmond and Moore, *Darwin's Sacred Cause*, 333, 332.
39. Quoted in Lorimer, *Colour*, 149.
40. Quoted in Desmond and Moore, *Darwin's Sacred Cause*, 332. Douglas Lorimer states that the "extreme racism" of James Hunt and his fellow scientific racists "was tied to a rejection of egalitarian values and a preference for an even greater degree of authoritarianism within English society" (*Colour*, 156).
41. Desmond and Moore, *Darwin's Sacred Cause*, 340.
42. Bolt, *Victorian Attitudes*, 6.
43. Quoted in Desmond and Moore, *Darwin's Sacred Cause*, 335.
44. Desmond and Moore, *Darwin's Sacred Cause*, 274, 334.
45. Desmond and Moore, *Darwin's Sacred Cause*, xvii, 324.
46. Desmond and Moore, *Darwin's Sacred Cause*, 331. The statement becomes even more poignant when one considers that British-made Whitmore sharpshooter rifles were just then being purchased by the Confederate army. Darwin was providing another type of weapon, which was no less potent, to the Northern side.
47. *Caledonian Mercury*, Mar. 7, 1864; "Professor Huxley and the Anthropologists," *National Reformer*, Mar. 12, 1864; both quoted in Desmond and Moore, *Darwin's Sacred Cause*, 336.
48. The idea persisted as long as the British Empire did. Lord Cromer (Evelyn Baring), British controller-general in Egypt, in 1908 declared that "subject races" benefited from British governance. As one historian notes, "This racist point of view was widely shared among British politicians and the British public" (Brantlinger, *Taming Cannibals*, 9).
49. Lorimer, *Colour*, 46–47.
50. Lorimer, *Colour*, 60.
51. Jan. 19, 1863, *CWL* 6:64–65.
52. Doyle, *Cause of All Nations*, 246.
53. Jan. 12, 1863 [?], S. May Jr. to R. D. Webb, Antislavery Collection, BPL.
54. Quoted in Doyle, *Cause of All Nations*, 248.
55. Jan. 30, 1863, *AL* 1:251.

Chapter 12

1. Feb. 13, 1863. Cobden, "Letters," 308–9.
2. Feb. 13, 1863, *AL* 1:252.
3. "Negroes and Negro Slavery in the United States," 192.
4. Bennett, *London Confederates*, 45.
5. Troy J. Bassett, "Author: Edward Peacock," *At the Circulating Library: A Database of Victorian Fiction, 1837–1901*, September 4, 2024, http://www.victorianresearch.org/atcl/show_author.php?aid=235.
6. Dall, *Daughter of Boston*, xi, 260–61, 289.
7. Feb. 1, 1863, L. Stone to C. Dall, Dall Papers, MHS.
8. Feb. 6, 1863, E. Peacock to C. Dall, Dall Papers, MHS.
9. McPherson reports that "the idea of putting arms in the hands of black men provoked greater hostility from Democrats and border-state Unionists than did emancipation itself" (*Tried by War*, 158).
10. Donald, *Sumner*, 2:119.
11. Quoted in Richards, *Battle Lines*, 96.
12. O'Connor, *Civil War Boston*, 134.
13. Quoted in McPherson, *Negro's Civil War*, 168, 169.
14. Donald, *Sumner*, 2:154.
15. Duncan, *Death and Glory*, 6.
16. Shaw, *Child of Fortune*, 11, 12, 14.
17. Feb. 7, 1863, J. A. Andrew to F. G. Shaw, Letters to Francis G. Shaw, MHS.
18. O'Connor, *Civil War Boston*, 124.
19. Blight, *Frederick Douglass' Civil War*, 157–59; Gougeon, *Virtue's Hero*, 296–98.
20. Richards, *Battle Lines*, 92.
21. Jan. 21, 1863, C. W. Colby to sister, Carlos W. Colby Collection, NL.
22. McPherson, *Cause and Comrades*, 124.
23. O'Connor, *Civil War Boston*, 142; Turner, *Norton*, 178.
24. Circular [large] 1863, "Union Club of Boston," Amos Lawrence Papers, MHS. Thomas H. O'Connor notes, "once the war was an accomplished fact, the city's businessmen . . . rallied 'round the flag and supported the Lincoln administration" (*Civil War Boston*, 233). Many of these gentlemen now joined the Union Club to support emancipation and the Lincoln administration (Abbott, *Cotton and Capital*, 101).
25. Feb. 26, 1863, *NL* 1:261.
26. Feb. 25, 1863, A. de Vere to C. E. Norton, Charles Eliot Norton Papers, HL.
27. A slight misquote from the Wordsworth sonnet "On a Celebrated Event in Ancient History."
28. Feb. 10, 1863, *R-NC* 75–76. Paul Veronese (1528–88) was a painter of the Italian Renaissance and a favorite with Ruskin. See Ruskin, *Works*, 16:xl.

29. Nevins, *War for the Union*, 3:154, 155, 156. Leonard Curry notes that "by the end of the Third Session of the Thirty-seventh Congress," the future seemed clear. "Congressional enactments plus the emancipation proclamation . . . had charted the course of America's future development. The Negro would be free" (*Blueprint for Modern America*, 74).

30. McPherson, *Battle Cry*, 582.
31. McPherson, *War on the Waters*, 112.
32. Jones, *Union in Peril*, 28; Mahin, *One War*, 177, 176.
33. Nevins, *War for the Union*, 3:485; Adams, *Great Britain*, 2:138.
34. Apr. 26, 1863. Donald, *Sumner*, 2:115.
35. Adams, *Great Britain*, 2:138.
36. Seward quoted in Adams, *Great Britain*, 2:139.
37. Sebrell, *Persuading John Bull*, 128.
38. Jan. 30, 1863, *NL* 1:259–60.
39. *EL* 9:104.
40. O'Connor, *Civil War Boston*, 142.
41. Turner, *Norton*, 178–79.
42. Lawson, *Patriot Fires*, 115.
43. Lawson, *Patriot Fires*, 115.
44. Mar. 17, 1863, Records of the *New England Loyal Publication Society*, BPL.
45. Mar. 21, 1863, Records of the *New England Loyal Publication Society*, BPL, emphasis in the original.
46. "Mr. Mill on America," Mar. 7, 1863, 302, 303.
47. Quoted in McPherson, *Battle Cry*, 594–95.
48. "The Most Unreasoned Delusion the World Ever Saw," January 17, 1863.
49. Wirzbicki, *Higher Law*, 245.
50. Quoted in Wirzbicki, *Higher Law*, 244.
51. Quoted in Beckett, *War Correspondents*, 93–94.
52. Mar. 15, 1863, G. Heath to F. Lee, Francis Lee Papers, MHS.
53. Mar. 24, 1863, *EL* 5:318, 320.
54. Luis Emilio records that "the members of the committee contributed liberally. . . . Included on the list of subscribers were some of Massachusetts's most distinguished citizens, like R. W. Emerson, James T. Fields, Governor Andrew, Samuel May and his wife, Professor Agassiz, and John Gorham Palfrey" (*Brave Black Regiment*, 15, 16).
55. This telling comparison with the heroic British soldiers in Tennyson's famous "Charge of the Light Brigade" would be recognized by many American conservatives who saw England as the ideal model of civilization.
56. Mar. 23, 1863, R. G. Shaw to C. F. Morse, Robert Gould Shaw Letters, MHS.
57. Bright's address was later published by the *New England Loyal Publication Society* (Mar. 26, 1863), which is the source here.

58. "Mr. Bright on America," 389, 390.
59. Quoted in Masur, *"Real War,"* 167, 177–78.
60. "American Literature and the Civil War," 519.
61. "Essays on Political Economy," 441, 442.
62. From Carlyle's "Latter-Day Pamphlets" (1850).
63. McPherson, *War on the Waters*, 202–3; Adams, *Great Britain*, 2:143; Mahin, *One War*, 168.
64. Cobden, "Letters," 309, 310.
65. Apr. 20, 1863, F. W. Newman to E. Sargent, Antislavery Collection, BPL.
66. Conway, *Autobiography*, 1:397, 407. Many of Tennyson's American friends were Southerners, and he supported them in thinking "the dispossession of slave-owners unjust." Tennyson was at heart a conservative, like most of the Victorian literary class. When speaking with the queen in 1867 about the soon-to-be-passed Reform Bill, he expressed his fear that "Universal Suffrage and vote by ballot would be the ruin of us" (Ormond, *Tennyson*, 146).
67. McPherson, *Battle Cry*, 584.
68. McPherson, *Battle Cry*, 584.
69. Emerson, *Early Years*, 312.
70. "No Failure for the North," April 1863, 501, 504.

Chapter 13

1. Wasson lived in Concord for a year and a half and became associated with Franklin Sanborn and other antislavery activists there (Sanborn, *Sixty Years*, 30–31; Gura, *American Transcendentalism*, 280–83).
2. *Atlantic Monthly*, May 1863, 650, 651, 653.
3. Faulkner, *Lucretia Mott's Heresy*, 180–81.
4. Cobden, "Letters," 310–11.
5. "Belligerents and Neutrals," May 2, 1863, 549.
6. Cobden, "Letters," 311, 312, emphasis in original.
7. Quoted in *MCW* 15:860n5.
8. May 17, 1863, *MCW* 15:860.
9. Campbell, *English Public Opinion*, 169.
10. Blackett, *Divided Hearts*, 229.
11. McPherson, *Battle Cry*, 565.
12. Quoted in Goodwin, *Team of Rivals*, 551.
13. May 15, 1863, F. W. Newman to E. Sargent, Antislavery Collection, BPL. As noted earlier, James Martineau was a Southern sympathizer. Newman's lecture was "President Lincoln's Good Cause," a copy of which he included with his letter.
14. Quoted in Fahs, *Imagined Civil War*, 178.

15. The mission of the National Academy of Design, founded in 1829, was "the promotion of American Art through education and exhibition" and to display the works of "artists who helped create an American culture and aesthetic" (Dearinger, *Paintings and Sculpture*, vi).

16. Harold Holzer and Mark E. Neely Jr. present many examples of positive images of Black people that were produced during the war by such notable artists as Thomas Nast, Eastman Johnson, and Edwin White. Some of these reached an even wider audience when reproduced as lithographs by Currier and Ives. In these works, virtually for the first time, Blacks "gained honest or even sympathetic portrayal" (*Mine Eyes*, 247, 236–61).

17. Emerson, *Early Years*, 298.

18. "The Libyan Sibyl," *The Met*, http://www.metmuseum.org/art/collection/search/12650.

19. *Harper's Magazine*, June 1863, 133.

20. "Sojourner Truth, the Libyan Sibyl," *Atlantic Monthly*, Apr. 1863, 481.

21. *Harper's Magazine*, June 1863, 133.

22. Quoted in Wallace, *John Rogers*, 81.

23. Quoted in Gates and Bindman, *Image of the Black*, 176.

24. Quoted in Gates and Bindman, *Image of the Black*, 212.

25. May 28, 1863, *LongL* 4:329n4.

26. June 3, 1863, R. G. Shaw to J. M. Forbes, Shaw Letters, HL.

27. June 4, 1863. Weinberg, *Cairnes*, 164.

28. Richardson, *William James*, 54, 55.

29. Blight, *Frederick Douglass' Civil War*, 167.

30. Quoted in Croce, "Calming the Screaming Eagle," 20.

31. June 21, 1863. Weinberg, *Cairnes*, 166.

32. Blight, *Frederick Douglass' Civil War*, 14. James Horton notes that the idea that Blacks were less manly than whites was common, even among white reformers. He reports that "Theodore Tilton . . . insisted that blacks were, in fact, a 'feminine people. . . . The negro race is the feminine race of the world'" ("Defending," 14).

33. Duncan, *Death and Glory*, 1.

34. McPherson, *Struggle*, 206.

35. Quoted in Duncan, *Death and Glory*, 86.

36. Duncan, *Death and Glory*, 86–87.

37. Richardson, *William James*, 54.

38. McPherson, *Struggle*, 206, 207.

39. June 9, 1863, C. W. Colby, Letter, Carlos W. Colby Collection, NL.

40. McPherson, *Battle Cry*, 637–38.

41. "Negro Troops," June 20, 1863.

42. June 10, 1863, F. Newman to E. Sargent, Antislavery Collection, BPL.

43. Earlier mailings had been in the form of smaller printed slips. Records of the *New England Loyal Publication Society*, BPL.

44. June 15, 1863, G. Bancroft to C. E. Norton, Records of the *New England Loyal Publication Society*, BPL.

45. Lorimer, *Colour*, 155.

Chapter 14

1. Campbell, *English Public Opinion*, 169.
2. Nevins, *War for the Union*, 3:491.
3. Bennett, *London Confederates*, 49–50, 141–42; Jones, *Blue & Gray Diplomacy*, 296.
4. Adams, *Great Britain*, 2:173.
5. "Recognition." This article was reprinted in the *Living Age*, Aug. 1, 1863, 238.
6. July 1, 1863, S. May to R. Webb, Antislavery Collection, BPL.
7. "The Navies of France and England," 166–67.
8. Holmes, *Writings*, 8:97.
9. "Oration, 4th of July (1863)," Oliver Wendell Holmes Papers, HL.
10. Holmes, *Writings*, 8:97.
11. Zink, *Leslie Stephen*, 30.
12. Maitland, *Leslie Stephen*, 107, 108, 118, 119.
13. "America," 7, 8.
14. Adams, *Great Britain*, 2:176.
15. McPherson, *Battle Cry*, 646, 647; Nevins, *War for the Union*, 3:91–95.
16. McPherson, *Battle Cry*, 651, 652.
17. McPherson, *Battle Cry*, 653.
18. McPherson, *Battle Cry*, 665.
19. McPherson, *Battle Cry*, 665.
20. Jones, *Union in Peril*, 226, 227.
21. Adams, *Great Britain*, 2:178.
22. *AL* 2:58, 59, 60.
23. "Robert Dale Owen," *Encyclopedia Britannica*, June 20, 2024, https://www.britannica.com/biography/Robert-Dale-Owen.
24. "The Claims to Service or Labor," 116, 116–17, 125.
25. "The Natural History of Man," July 23, 1863. Quoted in Burnett, *Henry Hotze*, 25.
26. *CWL* 6:119–20.
27. "American Statesmen at Home," July 23, 1863, 118–19.
28. Milne, *Curtis*, 119.

29. McPherson, *Battle Cry*, 610.
30. O'Connor, *Civil War Boston*, 140.
31. Aug. 9, 1863, C. Dickens to Wilkie Collins, *DL* 10:281.
32. July 28, 1863, *GL* 709.
33. Zink, *Leslie Stephen*, 30.
34. Throughout his correspondence, Stephen refers to African Americans with what modern readers consider a slur, despite the fact that he was an English liberal and strongly antislavery. He used the term consistently as the equivalent of "Blacks," without the strong pejorative connotations associated with the word today.
35. Maitland, *Leslie Stephen*, 110, 111.
36. July 6, 1863. Shaw, *Child of Fortune*, 374.
37. Nevins, *War for the Union*, 2:526.
38. Duncan, *Death and Glory*, 113.
39. Quoted in McPherson, *Battle Cry*, 687.
40. Quotations from Scharnhorst, "Soldier to Saint," 315–16.
41. Richards, *Battle Lines*, 218fn31.
42. Scharnhorst, "Soldier to Saint," 316, 317.
43. Eliza Richards notes that the "symbolization" of the event was "nearly instantaneous . . . due to the rapid production and circulation of newspaper reports, editorials, and poems that celebrated the soldiers' bravery under fire" (*Battle Lines*, 93).
44. Neely and Holzer, *Union Image*, 235.
45. Scharnhorst, "Soldier to Saint," 310.
46. Quoted in Shaw, *Child of Fortune*, 389, 390.
47. The November issue of the *Atlantic Monthly* included Louisa May Alcott's story "The Brothers," which celebrated the manly heroism of the Black soldiers who fought and died at Fort Wagner (593).
48. Sievens and Silber, *Yankee Correspondence*, 86.
49. McPherson, *Battle Cry*, 687.
50. "Liberia College," July 1863, 111.
51. "Robert Gould Shaw," Dec. 1863, 113.
52. "Latest Intelligence, America," Aug. 8, 1863.
53. Maitland, *Leslie Stephen*, 113, 114, 115.
54. This was one of twelve essays based on Hawthorne's experience in England that were published in the *Atlantic Monthly* beginning in October 1860. Together, they would be published in book form as *Our Old Home* in September 1863 by Ticknor & Fields (McFarland, *Hawthorne*, 279).
55. "Outside Glimpses of English Poverty," 38, 51.
56. Aug. 4, 1863. Quoted in Donald, *Sumner*, 2:117.
57. "Ilias (Americana) in Nuce," 302.
58. Quoted in Straka, "Spirit of Carlyle," 50.

59. Kinser, *Civil War*, 19.
60. Kinser, *Civil War*, 36.
61. John Waller reports that Carlyle "talked in his well-known explosive manner to anybody who took the trouble to visit him at his Cheyne Row residence, and a troop of persons, including a number of Americans, did this. Some of these hurried forth from Cheyne Row to spread the news of what Carlyle had said" ("Nutshell Iliad," 18).
62. Henry Adams, when speaking of Carlyle's fall, noted, "Demolition of one's idols is painful, and Carlyle had been an idol" (*Education*, 131).
63. "T. C. and the Slaves." This article was reprinted in the *Living Age*, Sept. 5, 1863, 476–77.
64. Records of the *New England Loyal Publication Society*, BPL. Emerson kept a copy of this broadside in his personal papers, now on file at HL.
65. "Thompson on Carlyle."
66. Cobden, "Letters," 313.
67. Mott, *Biographical Dictionary*, 14.
68. Aug. 14, 1863, C. Bartol to R. W. Emerson, Cabot Papers, SL.
69. *EAW* 141.
70. "Desperate Southern Project," Sept. 12, 1863. The *Spectator* also reported on this rumor in "The Secession Policy in Collapse," Sept. 12, 1863. Both articles were reprinted in the *Living Age*, Oct. 17, 1863, 130, 131.
71. This article was also published in the *Living Age*, Oct. 17, 1863, 130.
72. The Confederate Congress approved a measure to enlist Black soldiers in February 1865 (McPherson, *Battle Cry*, 837).
73. Aug. 24, 1863, *MCW* 15:876, 877.
74. "America," Aug. 15, 1863, 206.
75. Aug. 4, 1863, Circular, Lawrence Papers, MHS.
76. "An American in the House of Lords," 151, 152.

Chapter 15

1. Sebrell, *Persuading John Bull*, 137.
2. Sebrell, *Persuading John Bull*, 137.
3. Sebrell, *Persuading John Bull*, 141, 180–81.
4. Donald, *Lincoln*, 456. Ronald White observes that the speech was delivered "in vernacular American English," and notes further that Lincoln's "plain talk was part of his departure from the high-toned oratory that dominated much political speech in the first half of the nineteenth century" (*Eloquent President*, 202).
5. On August 3, 1863, General Grant had written to Lincoln in response to his inquiry about the performance of Colored Troops. "I have given the subject of

arming the negro my hearty support," Grant wrote. "This, with the emancipation of the negro, is the heaviest blow yet given the Confederacy." Quoted in White, *Eloquent President*, 205.

6. *CWL* 6:406–10.
7. White, *Eloquent President*, 217.
8. "Mr. Lincoln's Letter." This article was reprinted in the *Living Age*, Oct. 17, 1863, 137–38.
9. Quoted in White, *Eloquent President*, 220, 221.
10. Maitland, *Leslie Stephen*, 119, 120.
11. Maitland, *Leslie Stephen*, 122, 120.
12. "Messrs. Laird's Iron Rams and the Foreign Enlistment Act," Sept. 5, 1863. This article was reprinted in the *Living Age*, Oct. 10, 1863, 91.
13. Quoted in Adams, *Great Britain*, 2:144.
14. Adams, *Great Britain*, 2:145, 146.
15. *LL* 2:333.
16. Adams, *Great Britain*, 2:145.
17. Bennett, *London Confederates*, 64; McPherson, *War on the Waters*, 203.
18. "The Seizure of the Steam Rams," Oct. 17, 1863. This article was reprinted in the *Living Age*, Nov. 21, 1863, 381, 382.
19. Sept. 23, 1863, Records of the *New England Loyal Publication Society*, BPL.
20. *Atlantic Monthly*, Sept. 1863, 397.
21. "Our Domestic Relations, or How to Treat the Rebel States," 519, 588.
22. Quoted in Donald, *Sumner*, 2:137, 138.
23. McPherson, *Battle Cry*, 672–76; Bowman, *Civil War Almanac*, 170.
24. Nevins, *War for the Union*, 3:375.
25. "The War in America," Oct. 3, 1863, 443.
26. Oct. 14, 1863, *MCW* 15:689–90.
27. Oct. 23, 1863, J. S. Mill to Thomas Thornton, *MCW* 15:892, 893.
28. Quoted in Foreman, *World on Fire*, 461; see also Beckett, *War Correspondents*, 54.
29. Foreman, *World on Fire*, 308.
30. Leslie Butler writes that together Norton and Lowell "refurbished this venerable publication as a powerful organ of advanced Republican commentary. . . . A combination of Lowell's celebrity and Norton's editorial acumen [breathed] new life into the hallowed quarterly's old bones" (*Critical Americans*, 64).
31. *NL* 1:265–66.
32. "The Student's Repository," 558.
33. Oct. 9, 1863, A. de Vere to C. E. Norton, Charles Eliot Norton Papers, HL.
34. Oct. 9, 1863, F. Newman to E. Sargent, Antislavery Collection, BPL.
35. Cobden, "Letters," 313–14.
36. Cobden, "Letters," 314.
37. Quoted in McPherson, *Battle Cry*, 585–86.
38. McPherson, *Battle Cry*, 688.

39. Quoted in McPherson, *Battle Cry*, 688.
40. Oct. 16, 1863, *NL* 1:265.
41. Nevins, *War for the Union*, 3:155.
42. Milne, *Curtis*, 115, 118. According to David Kaser, *Harper's Weekly* was widely read by Union soldiers and a favorite "among all ranks" (*Books and Libraries*, 33), which would be of critical importance in the presidential election of 1864.
43. Cmiel, *Democratic Eloquence*, 58.
44. Quoted in Clark, *Beecher*, 157.
45. Beecher, *American Rebellion*, 8, 9.
46. Beecher, *American Rebellion*, 10, 22, 24.
47. Quoted in Nevins, *War for the Union*, 3:508.
48. "Mr. Beecher at Manchester," Oct. 17, 1863, 512.
49. "Mr. Beecher," Oct. 31, 1863, 566.
50. "Adieu to Mr. Beecher" (originally published Nov. 7, 1863). This article was reprinted in the *Living Age*, Dec. 12, 1863, 528.

Chapter 16

1. *HW* 5:18–19.
2. "Hawthorne on England," 612, 613, 615, 616.
3. Quoted in Mellow, *Nathaniel Hawthorne*, 570.
4. Mellow, *Nathaniel Hawthorne*.
5. Editor's Easy Chair, 852.
6. Drabble, *Oxford Companion*, 307.
7. "Calthrop, Samuel R. (1829–1917)," Harvard Square Library, accessed Nov. 25, 2023, https://www.harvardsquarelibrary.org/biographies/samuel-r-calthrop/.
8. *Christian Examiner*, Nov. 1863, 426.
9. Quoted in Mott, *American Magazines*, 2:160.
10. "America," Oct. 17, 1863, 510. Sir Edward Bulwer Lytton was a popular British novelist, editor, poet, and playwright. He was also a Conservative politician who had joined the corps of British literati who, with the outbreak of the war, felt free to express their latent anti-American feelings ("Sir Edward Lytton, Again," Philadelphia *City Item*, Nov. 7, 1863; Drabble, *Oxford Companion*, 77).
11. Tilton, *Amiable Autocrat*, 273. The quoted material that follows is from a printed "Private Copy" of the speech in the Oliver Wendell Holmes Papers, HL. The lecture was later published, in a somewhat toned-down form, as "Our Progressive Independence," *Atlantic Monthly*, Apr. 1864.
12. A reference to Tennyson's famous poem "The Charge of the Light Brigade" (1854), which depicted English heroism in the Crimean War.
13. "On the Weaning of America," *Daily Advertiser*. This article was reprinted in the *Living Age*, Dec. 26, 1863, 598, 599.
14. Nov. 17, 1863, *ML* 2:144.

15. Robert E. May notes, "Misinterpreting Russian purposes, northerners celebrated what seemed to them a gesture of Russian solidarity with the Union cause" (*Atlantic Rim*, 19).

16. Jones, *Union in Peril*, 86; Adams, *Great Britain*, 2:129, 163. Albert Woldman reports that the czar sent his fleet to safe harbors in America to protect them in case England went to war with Russia (*Lincoln and the Russians*, 157).

17. Adams, *Great Britain*, 2:165. Chesney's work is *Military View of Recent Campaigns in Maryland and Virginia* (London, 1863).

18. "America," Nov. 14, 1863, 630, 631.

19. "Messrs. Cobden and Bright at Rochdale," Nov. 28, 1863, 688.

20. Nov. 4, 1863, E. J. Bartlett to M. Bartlett, Edward J. Bartlett Letters, MHS.

21. "The Freedmen at Port Royal," 291, 292, 295.

22. Quoted in Kearns, *Team of Rivals*, 585.

23. White, *Eloquent President*, 232, 233, 237.

24. Wills, *Lincoln at Gettysburg*, 41–47.

25. Wills, *Lincoln at Gettysburg*, 261.

26. Cmiel, *Democratic Eloquence*, 117.

27. Ferguson, *Law and Letters*, 309.

28. Ronald White states that "at Gettysburg [Lincoln's] use of Saxon words was a foundation of his eloquence" (*Eloquent President*, 255).

29. CWL 7:23.

30. White, *Eloquent President*, 251.

31. White, *Eloquent President*, 256, 257.

32. Wills, *Lincoln at Gettysburg*, 58.

33. Quoted in Wills, *Lincoln at Gettysburg*, 38–39.

34. Quoted in Donald, *Lincoln*, 465.

35. Campbell, *English Public Opinion*, 195n3.

36. Sept. 9, 1863, LL 1:333.

37. McPherson, *Battle Cry*, 678–79.

Chapter 17

1. Emerson, *Topical Notebooks*, 1:208, 209, 184.

2. "The Negro Race in America," Jan. 1864.

3. Foner, *American Freedom*, 102.

4. Donald, *Sumner*, 2:155.

5. Donald, *Sumner*, 2:157, 158, 180, 183, 186. Eventually, Lincoln would change his mind on Black suffrage. In his "Last Public Address" (Apr. 11, 1865), he spoke about the matter as it stood in Louisiana, where a Reconstruction government was writing a new state constitution. Lincoln was disappointed that there was no provision for Black suffrage. "It is also unsatisfactory to some,"

he wrote, "that the elective franchise is not given to the colored man. I would myself prefer that it were now conferred on the very intelligent, and on those who serve our cause as soldiers" (*CWL* 8:403). Eric Foner notes that "this was a remarkable statement. No American president had publicly endorsed even limited black suffrage. At this time only six northern states allowed black men to vote" (*Fiery Trial*, 331).

    6. The Reverend Sella Martin traveled to Great Britain from Boston in 1862. His purpose was to persuade the British public to support the Union cause. He appealed especially to the working class and sought to reinforce a sense of solidarity between American slaves and British workers (Wirzbicki, *Higher Law*, 243).

    7. Adams, *Great Britain*, 2:220.

    8. Butler, *Critical Americans*, 112. Toward the end of the war, John Stuart Mill also favored Black suffrage, even without an education requirement, declaring, "At the present crisis the securing of equal rights to the negro is paramount to all other considerations respecting the suffrage." Butler, *Critical Americans*, 113.

    9. "Mr. Newman on the Slave States," Jan. 2, 1864, 11–12, 13.

    10. Jan. 16, 1864, "Slaves and Labourers," 71.

    11. Quoted in *MCW* 15:917n6.

    12. Jan. 24, 1864, *MCW* 15:917.

    13. Weinberg, *Cairnes*, 168, 169, 170.

    14. "The President's Policy," 254.

    15. Fredrickson, *Inner Civil War*, 122.

    16. Donald, *Lincoln*, 474.

    17. Quoted in O'Connor, *Civil War Boston*, 138.

    18. *EAW* 140.

    19. *EAW* 149. The Emerson family and the town of Concord were early supporters of Freedmen's Schools, and this support continued in the postwar period. Emerson's wife and daughters, as members of the Women's Anti-Slavery Society in Concord, provided clothing and other support to the freedmen at Port Royal (see Holley, "Freedmen's Children"; and Gougeon, *Virtue's Hero*, 277–78). Emerson also made a cash contribution to the enterprise, in which many of his friends were active (see von Frank, *Trials of Anthony Burns*, 372–73n19).

    20. Feb. 6, 1864, E. Peacock to C. Dall, Dall Papers, MHS.

    21. Feb. 18, 1864, T. Hughes to J. R. Lowell, James Russell Lowell Papers, HL.

    22. "The Advantages of Slavery and the Slave Trade," 221.

    23. "The Foreign Policy of England," 275, 276.

    24. Adams, *Great Britain*, 2:199.

    25. Quoted in Adams, *Great Britain*, 2:200n4.

    26. March 6, 1864, H. Bright to C. E. Norton, Charles Eliot Norton Papers, HL.

    27. William Wilberforce (1759–1833) and Thomas Buxton (1786–1845) led the movement in England to abolish slavery in the empire.

28. "Our English Letter."
29. McPherson, *Battle Cry*, 718.
30. McPherson, *Battle Cry*.
31. Records of the *New England Loyal Publication Society*, BPL.
32. Mar. 1, 1864, S. J. May to R. Webb, Antislavery Collection, BPL.
33. Adams, *Great Britain*, 2:203, 204.
34. Adams, *Great Britain*, 2:207.
35. Adams, *Great Britain*, 2:194.
36. Blackett, *Divided Hearts*, 197; Adams, *Great Britain*, 2:206, 210.
37. "The Foreign Policy of England," 483.
38. "Foreign Affairs—Europe and America," 475–76, 476, emphasis in original.
39. "Federal Warfare," Apr. 2, 1864, 404; McPherson, *Tried by War*, 85ff. and 103; Nevins, *War for the Union*, 4:10–11.
40. May 13, 1864, *AL* 2:126.
41. Apr. 12, 1864, W. W. Story to C. E. Norton, Charles Eliot Norton Papers, HL.
42. McPherson, *Battle Cry*, 706.
43. Apr. 22, 1864. Quoted in Karcher, *First Woman*, 479.
44. Quoted in Chernow, *Grant*, 373. See also McPherson, *Battle Cry*, 748ff. Andrew Ward reports that at the Battle of Fort Pillow, General Forrest's men "continued to shoot well after the Federals had thrown down their weapons and begged for mercy, and many men were killed in their hospital tents. By the next morning only about sixty-five of the garrison's three hundred blacks had survived the massacre" (*Slaves' War*, 176).
45. "The Spirit of the Campaign."
46. June 19, 1864, *AL* 2:153–54.
47. "We hold these truths to be self-evident, that all men are created equal, that they are endowed by their Creator with certain unalienable Rights, that among these are Life, Liberty and the pursuit of Happiness."
48. "Our Progressive Independence," 498, 506, 511.
49. Apr. 19, 1864, *ArL* 2:314.

Chapter 18

1. "A French Eton," part 3, *Macmillan's Magazine*, May 1864, 90.
2. "Has England an Interest in the Disruption of the American Union" was reprinted in the *Living Age*, June 11, 1864, 483–85.
3. Blackett, *Divided Hearts*, 67, 98–120.
4. Quoted in Bennett, *London Confederates*, 148.
5. Bennett, *London Confederates*, 148; Blackett, *Divided Hearts*, 141.

6. Adams, *Great Britain*, 2:194–95.
7. McPherson, *Battle Cry*, 724–26; Nevins, *War for the Union*, 4:19–23.
8. McPherson, *Battle Cry*, 732.
9. Adams, *Great Britain*, 2:226–27.
10. Quoted in Beckett, *War Correspondents*, 133.
11. Adams, *Great Britain*, 2:223.
12. For Dall and the social science movement, see Deese, "Caroline Healy Dall."
13. June 20, 1864, E. Peacock to C. Dall, Dall Papers, MHS.
14. "The Negro Found Out," June 18, 1864, 748.
15. McPherson, *Battle Cry*, 740–41, 742.
16. "The Civil War in America."
17. "Defence of Canada," 9.
18. Donald, *Lincoln*, 522, 523; McPherson, *Battle Cry*, 766–68.
19. Donald, *Lincoln*, 524.
20. *EJ* 15:446.
21. "Mr. Lincoln's Diplomacy," Aug. 6, 1864. This article was reprinted in the *Living Age*, Sept. 10, 1864, 527, 527.
22. Kirke, "Suppressed Chapter," 435.
23. Kirke, "Our Visit," 382.
24. Holzer, *Lincoln*, 509.
25. Kirke, "Suppressed Chapter," 447–48.
26. McPherson, *Battle Cry*, 768.
27. Adams, *Great Britain*, 2:218.
28. Nevins, *War for the Union*, 4:223.
29. Quoted in McPherson, *Struggle*, 280.
30. Aug. 7, 1864. Quoted in Donald, *Lincoln*, 526.
31. Donald, *Lincoln*, 527.
32. McFeely, *Frederick Douglass*, 232.
33. Aug. 23, 1864, *CWL* 7:514.
34. Quoted in Baker, *Affairs of Party*, 285.
35. Nevins, *War for the Union*, 4:99.

Chapter 19

1. Quoted in Beckett, *War Correspondents*, 147.
2. Quoted in Donald, *Lincoln*, 530.
3. McPherson, *War on the Waters*, 207–13.
4. McPherson, *Battle Cry*, 706–7.
5. Quoted in Donald, *Lincoln*, 541.
6. Sept. 25, 1864, *NL* 1:279–80.

7. Sept. 12, 1864, *CWL* 8:1, 2, emphasis in original.
8. Sept. 9, 1864, T. Hughes to W. L. Garrison, Antislavery Collection, BPL.
9. Campbell, *English Public Opinion*, 173.
10. Adams, *Great Britain*, 2:205, 206, 211.
11. "The Southern Confederation," Sept. 9, 1864.
12. "America," 382.
13. Wallace, *Goldwin Smith*, 33.
14. Wallace, *Goldwin Smith*, 36, 37.
15. Nevins, *War for the Union*, 4:225.
16. Oct. 12, 1864, Fanny Hooper to Lillian Clark, Sturgis Hooper Family Papers, MHS.
17. "Goldwin Smith," *North American Review*, Oct. 1864.
18. Neely, *Union Divided*, 87.
19. Neely, *Union Divided*, 130, 132.
20. Emerson, *Early Years*, 334–35.
21. Quoted in Donald, *Sumner*, 2:189.
22. Oates, *With Malice Toward None*, 401.
23. Quoted in Karcher, *First Woman*, 478, emphasis in original.
24. *EL* 5:387.
25. "Mr. Bright on the Presidential Election," 552, 553.
26. "The Confederate States and the Negro," 583.
27. Nov. 6, 1864, A. de Vere to C. E. Norton, Charles Eliot Norton Papers, HL.
28. Quoted in Ford, "Goldwin Smith's Visit," 9, 10.
29. Quoted in McPherson, *Tried by War*, 251.
30. Anonymous, *History of the Times*, 2:386.
31. Tennyson, *Letters*, 2:385n2.
32. *EJ* 15:433–34.
33. *EJ* 15:433–34.
34. Delivered in Boston on November 27 and reported in detail in the *Commonwealth* on December 3, 1864.
35. "Public and Private Education," in Emerson, *Uncollected Lectures*, 3, 4, 6.
36. *Atlantic Monthly*, Nov. 1864, 521.
37. Dec. 1, 1864, *MCW* 15:968–69.
38. Dec. 4, 1864, E. Peacock to C. Dall, Dall Papers, MHS.
39. Dec. 12, 1864, M. Taylor to S. May, Samuel Joseph May Papers, MHS.
40. Emerson, *Uncollected Lectures*, 40, 41.

Chapter 20

1. "Abraham Lincoln," 4.
2. Stephen, *American War*, 103.

3. Anonymous, *History of the Times*, 2:387.
4. Jan. 31, 1865. Quoted in Anonymous, *History of the Times*, 2:387.
5. Quoted in Anonymous, *History of the Times*, 2:387–88. Mackay was terminated on April 21, 1865.
6. "The United States as an Example," 249.
7. McPherson, *Battle Cry*, 828.
8. "A Few Words on Non-Intervention," *Fraser's Magazine*, Dec. 1859, 772.
9. Nov. 8, 1864. Quoted in McPherson, *Embattled Rebel*, 231.
10. Quoted in McPherson, *Battle Cry*, 835.
11. McPherson, *Battle Cry*, 836.
12. "America," *Saturday Review*, Jan. 28, 1865, 103.
13. It would be ratified on December 6.
14. McPherson, *War That Forged a Nation*, 114.
15. Foner, *American Freedom*, 95, 97.
16. Feb. 1, 1865, William Gray Brooks Diary, William Gray Brooks Family Papers, MHS.
17. Wirzbicki, *Higher Law*, 257.
18. Quoted in Goodwin, *Team of Rivals*, 681.
19. McPherson, *Battle Cry*, 829. One of these regiments was the Massachusetts 55th.
20. Bennett, *London Confederates*, 37.
21. "America," Mar. 11, 1865, 276.
22. Sebrell, *Persuading John Bull*, 192.
23. Feb. 22, 1865, F. W. Newman to E. Sargent, Antislavery Collection, BPL.
24. Feb. 22, 1865, A. de Vere to C. E. Norton, Charles Eliot Norton Papers, HL.
25. Feb. 9, 1865, *MCW* 16:992.
26. Feb. 11, 1865. Quoted in Beckett, *War Correspondents*, 164.
27. Anonymous, *History of the Times*, 2:387.
28. "America," Feb. 14, 1865, 130.
29. Heidler and Heidler, *Civil War*, 1845–46. See also Kazar, "Canadian View."
30. "The North American Federation," 159, 160. This action had unintended consequences. Robert May points out that it led to "the fusion in 1867 of four of the provinces in a Dominion of Canada, under the British North America Act, [and] constituted a vital step toward complete Canadian independence . . . [which] may have been the most tangible international repercussion of the American Civil War" (*Atlantic Rim*, 10).
31. Quoted in Sideman and Friedman, *Europe Looks*, 270.
32. Feb. 26, 1865. Chesnut, *Mary Chesnut's Civil War*, 733.
33. McPherson, *Struggle*, 236, 237.
34. James McPherson states that the Second Inaugural Address "was the shortest and most eloquent in American history" (*Tried by War*, 260).
35. Goodwin, *Team of Rivals*, 699.

36. *CWL* 8:332.
37. *CWL* 8:332.
38. *CWL* 8:332.
39. *CWL* 8:332, 333.
40. Ronald White suggests that Lincoln's emphasis on slavery in this address was a reflection of his dedication to the Thirteenth Amendment, on which he had expended so much time, energy, and political capital since his reelection. Although the measure was passed by Congress in January, it would not be ratified by the states until December. At this point, the process was ongoing (*Eloquent President*, 296, 297).
41. McPherson, *Battle Cry*, 840. David Blight notes that this gesture showed that "for the first time, [African Americans] could have a sense of belonging in the land of their birth" (*Frederick Douglass' Civil War*, 187).
42. Quoted in Oates, *With Malice Toward None*, 412.
43. Oates, *With Malice Toward None*.
44. Foner, *Fiery Trial*, 323.
45. Quoted in Beckett, *War Correspondents*, 171. The quotation is from Robert Burns's poem "A Man's a Man for A' That" (1795), which argues for the dignity of all people, regardless of rank. It was a favorite among abolitionists.
46. "America," Mar. 18, 1865, 302.
47. The Confederates abandoned Charleston on February 15, 1865.
48. Mar. 13, 1865, E. Peacock to C. Dall, Dall Papers, MHS.
49. McPherson, *Battle Cry*, 842.
50. "American Civilization," *EW* 10:408.
51. McPherson, *Battle Cry*, 846.
52. Quoted in Goodwin, *Team of Rivals*, 716.
53. Catton, "Grant and Lee," 202, 203.
54. Catton, "Grant and Lee," 203, 204.
55. Quoted in McPherson, *Battle Cry*, 849–50.
56. "America," 429.
57. "America," Apr. 22, 1865, 457, 458.
58. Apr. 17, 1865. Smith, "Letters," 116.
59. Apr. 21, 1865, R. D. Webb to C. Weston (?), Antislavery Collection, BPL.
60. Apr. 17, 1865, E. Peacock to C. Dall, Dall Papers, MHS.
61. Apr. 23, 1865. Quoted in Sebrell, *Persuading John Bull*, 196.
62. Lowell, "Scotch the Snake, or Kill It?," in *Writings*, 244.
63. Apr. 19, 1865, *EEL* 1:342.
64. Godwin, an associate of George W. Curtis, was a reformer and an early member of the New England Fourier Society (Delano, *Brook Farm*, 270–71).
65. May 15, 1865, *MCW* 16:1051–52.
66. Apr. 25, 1865, *GL* 757.

67. Apr. 28, 1865, M. Gaskell to C. E. Norton, Charles Eliot Norton Papers, HL.
68. Apr. 27, 1865, L. Peacock to C. Dall, Dall Papers, MHS.
69. Apr. 29, 1865. Quoted in Beckett, *War Correspondents*, 179–80.
70. Quoted in Anonymous, *History of the Times*, 2:389.
71. Apr. 29, 1865. Smith, "Letters," 119–20.
72. Adams, *Great Britain*, 2:257.
73. Quoted in Blackett, *Divided Hearts*, 237, 243.
74. "Reconstruction," 547, 553, 554, 555.
75. Apr. 22, 1865. Quoted in McPherson, *Struggle*, 319.
76. McPherson, *Struggle*, 319.
77. Quoted in Foner, *American Freedom*, 102.
78. Quoted in Foner, *American Freedom*, 102.
79. McPherson, *Struggle*, 320–21; Garrison Family, *William Lloyd Garrison*, 4:165n1.

Epilogue

1. Foner, *American Freedom*, 96–97.
2. McPherson, *Struggle*, 430.
3. Foner, *American Freedom*, 103.
4. Quoted in Foner, *American Freedom*, 103.
5. McPherson, *Abolitionist Legacy*, 303–9.
6. Blight, *Race and Reunion*, 257.
7. McPherson, *Struggle*, 430.
8. Menand, *Metaphysical Club*, x.
9. Butler, *Critical Americans*, 3; Karcher, *First Woman*, 561–62.
10. See Gougeon, *Virtue's Hero*, 331–32; and Gougeon, "Emerson and the Woman Question."
11. Quoted in Gougeon, *Virtue's Hero*, 332–33.
12. Quoted in Wirzbicki, *Higher Law*, 258.
13. Wirzbicki, *Higher Law*, 259.
14. Gougeon, "Legacy of Reform," 189.
15. Gougeon, "Legacy of Reform," 191.
16. Gougeon, "Legacy of Reform," 183.
17. Meyer, "Moorfield Storey"; Lewis, *W. E. B. Du Bois*, 135, 283.
18. Lewis, *W. E. B. Du Bois*, 4.
19. McPherson, *Struggle*, 431.
20. Foner, *American Freedom*, 113.
21. "The Rebellion: Its Causes and Its Consequences," July 1864, 152.

22. Adams, *Great Britain*, 2:302.

23. Quoted in Adams, *Great Britain*, 2:302.

24. Adams, *Great Britain*, 2:303. The Reform Bill of 1867 in effect doubled the electorate, enfranchising about one third of the adult male population of England and Wales (Michie, "'On Behalf,'" 133). J. W. Burrow confirms the importance of the American example in bringing about this historic development. "In the debates surrounding the 1867 Reform Act," he notes, "it was America . . . which was seen as relevant. . . . Foreseeing [that] the probable nature of democracy in Great Britain was the central issue, . . . the United States offered the most obvious indicator" (*Whigs and Liberals*, 44).

25. Quoted in Bolt, *Victorian Attitudes*, 6.

26. Apr. 10, 1866, *LL* 1:358, 361, emphasis in original. Lowell would express many of these same sentiments three years later in an essay in the *Atlantic Monthly* appropriately titled "On a Certain Condescension in Foreigners" (Jan. 1869).

Bibliography

Aaron, Daniel. *The Unwritten War: American Writers and the Civil War*. New York: Alfred A. Knopf, 1973.

Abbott, Richard H. *Cotton and Capital: Boston Businessmen and Antislavery Reform, 1854–1868*. Amherst: University of Massachusetts Press, 2009.

Adams, Charles. *Slavery, Secession, and Civil War: Views from the United Kingdom and Europe, 1856–1865*. Lanham, MD: Scarecrow, 2007.

Adams, Charles Francis. *A Cycle of Adams Letters, 1861–1865*. Edited by Worthington Chauncey Ford. 2 vols. Boston: Houghton Mifflin, 1920.

Adams, Ephraim Douglass. *Great Britain and the American Civil War*. 2 vols. New York: Russell & Russell, [1925].

Adams, Henry. *The Education of Henry Adams*. Edited by Ernest Samuels. 1918. Reprint, Boston: Houghton, Mifflin, 1973.

Adelman, Paul. *Victorian Radicalism: The Middle-Class Experience, 1830–1914*. London: Longman, 1984.

Alcott, Amos Bronson. *The Journals of Bronson Alcott*. Edited by Odell Shepherd. Boston: Little, Brown, 1938.

———. *The Letters of A. Bronson Alcott*. Edited by Richard L. Herrnstadt. Ames: Iowa State University Press, 1969.

Alcott, Louisa May. *The Selected Letters of Louisa May Alcott*. Edited by Joel Myerson, Daniel Shealy, and Madeline B. Stern. Boston: Little, Brown, 1987.

Amar, Akhil Read. *America's Constitution, A Biography*. New York: Random House, 2005.

Amestoy, Jeffrey L. *Slavish Shore: The Odyssey of Richard Henry Dana, Jr.* Cambridge, MA: Harvard University Press, 2015.

Anonymous. *The History of the Times, 1841–1884*. 2 vols. New York: Macmillan, 1939.

Arnold, Matthew. *Civilization in the United States*. 1888. Reprint, Freeport, NY: Books for Libraries Press, 1972.

———. *Democratic Education*. Edited by R. H. Super. Ann Arbor: University of Michigan Press, 1962.

———. *The Letters of Matthew Arnold.* Edited by Cecil Y. Lang. 2 vols. Charlottesville: University Press of Virginia, 1997.
Ashworth, John. *Slavery, Capitalism, and Politics in the Antebellum Republic.* Vol. 2, *The Coming of the Civil War, 1850–1861.* Cambridge: Cambridge University Press, 2007.
Austin, James C. *Fields of the Atlantic Monthly: Letters to an Editor, 1861–1870.* San Marino, CA: Huntington Library, 1953.
Baker, Jean H. *Affairs of Party: The Political Culture of Northern Democrats in the Mid-Nineteenth Century.* New York: Fordham University Press, 1998.
Barnes, James A., and Patience P. Barnes, eds. *The American Civil War through British Eyes: Dispatches from British Diplomats.* 3 vols. Kent, OH: Kent State University Press, 2003.
Beckett, Ian F. W. *The War Correspondents: The American Civil War.* London: Grange Books, 1993.
Beecher, Henry Ward. *American Rebellion: Report of the Speeches of the Rev. Henry Ward Beecher, Delivered at Public Meetings in Manchester, Glasgow, Edinburgh, Liverpool, and London; and at the Farewell Breakfasts in London, Manchester, and Liverpool.* London: Sampson Low & Son, 1864.
Bennett, John D. *The London Confederates: The Officials, Clergy, Businessmen and Journalists Who Backed the American South During the Civil War.* London: McFarland, 2007.
Beresford-Hope, Alexander. *A Popular View of the American Civil War.* 3rd ed. London: James Ridgeway, 1861.
———. *The Results of the American Disruption: The Substance of a Lecture Delivered by Request Before the Maidstone Literary & Merchants Institution, in continuation of A Popular View of the American Civil War, and England, the North and the South.* London: James Ridgway, Piccadilly, 1862.
Bergman, Peter M. *The Chronological History of the Negro in America.* New York: Harper & Row, 1969.
Bevington, Merle Mowbray. *The Saturday Review, 1855–1868: Representative Educated Opinion in Victorian England.* New York: Columbia University Press, 1941.
Biagini, Eugenio F. "Liberalism and Direct Democracy: John Stuart Mill and the Model of Ancient Athens." In *Citizenship and Community: Liberals, Radicals and Collective Identities in the British Isles, 1865–1931,* edited by Eugenio F. Biagini, 21–44. Cambridge: Cambridge University Press, 2002.
———. *Liberty, Retrenchment and Reform: Popular Liberalism in the Age of Gladstone, 1860–1880.* Cambridge: Cambridge University Press, 1992.
Bilwakesh, Nikhil. "'Their Faces Were Like So Many of the Same Sort at Home': American Responses to the Indian Rebellion of 1857." *American Periodicals* 21, no. 1 (2011): 1–23.
Black, Robert. *A Memoir of Abraham Lincoln, President Elect of the United States of America.* London: Sampson Low, Son, 1861.

Blackett, R. J. M. *Divided Hearts: Britain and the American Civil War.* Baton Rouge: Louisiana State University Press, 2001.

———. "Pressure from Without: African Americans, British Public Opinion, and Civil War Diplomacy." In May, *Atlantic Rim*, 69–100.

Blake, Lord, and Hugh Cecil, eds. *Salisbury, the Man and His Policies.* London: Constable, 1987.

Blatt, Martin H., Thomas J. Brown, and Donald Yacovone, eds. *Hope & Glory: Essays on the Legacy of the 54th Massachusetts Regiment.* Amherst: University of Massachusetts Press, 2001.

Blight, David W. *Frederick Douglass' Civil War: Keeping Faith in Jubilee.* Baton Rouge: Louisiana State University Press, 1989.

———. *Race and Reunion: The Civil War in American Memory.* Cambridge, MA: Belknap Press of Harvard University Press, 2001.

Bolt, Christine. *Victorian Attitudes to Race.* London: Routledge and Kegan Paul, 1971.

Bosco, Carla. "Harvard University and the Fugitive Slave Act." *New England Quarterly* 79, no. 2 (June 2002): 227–47.

Bowman, John S. *The Civil War Almanac.* New York: Gallery Books, 1983.

Brantlinger, Patrick. *Taming Cannibals: Race and the Victorians.* Ithaca, NY: Cornell University Press, 2011.

Bright, John. "Letters of John Bright." Edited by James Ford Rhodes. *Proceedings of the Massachusetts Historical Society* 45 (Nov. 1911): 148–58.

Brown, Lucy. *Victorian News and Newspapers.* Oxford: Clarendon Press, 1985.

Brown, Samuel Gilman. *The Works of Rufus Choate with a Memoir of His Life.* 2 vols. Boston: Little Brown, 1862.

Browning, Robert. *Browning to His American Friends: Letters Between the Brownings, the Storys and James Russell Lowell.* Edited by Gertrude Reese Hudson. New York: Barnes & Noble, 1965.

Buell, Lawrence. *Emerson.* Cambridge, MA: Belknap Press of Harvard University Press, 2003.

———. "The Literary Significance of the Unitarian Movement." In *American Unitarianism, 1805–1865*, edited by Conrad Edick Wright, 163–79. Boston: Northeastern University Press, 1989.

Bundy, Carol. *The Nature of Sacrifice: A Biography of Charles Russell Lowell, Jr., 1835–1864.* New York: Farrar, Straus and Giroux, 2005.

Burlingame, Michael. "African Americans at White House Receptions During Lincoln's Administration: Part I." *Journal of the Abraham Lincoln Association* 41, no. 2 (2022): 47–64.

Burnett, Lonnie. *Henry Hotze, Confederate Propagandist: Selected Writings on Revolution, Recognition, and Race.* Tuscaloosa: University of Alabama Press, 2008.

Burrow, J. W. *Whigs and Liberals: Continuity and Change in English Political Thought.* Oxford: Clarendon Press, 1988.

Butler, Leslie. *Critical Americans: Victorian Intellectuals and Transatlantic Liberal Reform.* Chapel Hill: University of North Carolina Press, 2007.

Campbell, Duncan Andrew. *English Public Opinion and the American Civil War.* London: Royal Historical Society, 2003.

Carroll, Francis M. "The American Civil War and British Intervention: The Threat of Anglo-American Conflict." *Canadian Journal of History* 47, no. 1 (Spring/Summer 2012): 87–116.

Cary, Edward. *George William Curtis.* Boston: Houghton, Mifflin, 1894.

Catton, Bruce. *Bruce Catton's Civil War: Three Volumes in One.* 1951–53. Reprint, New York: Fairfax Press, 1984.

———. "Grant and Lee: A Study in Contrasts." In *The American Story: The Age of Exploration to the Age of the Atom,* edited by Earl Schenck Miers, 202–5. New York: Allen and Unwin, 1957.

Chernow, Ron. *Grant.* New York: Penguin, 2017.

Chesnut, Mary. *Mary Chesnut's Civil War.* Edited by C. Vann Woodward. New Haven, CT: Yale University Press, 1981.

Clark, Clifford E., Jr. *Henry Ward Beecher, Spokesman for a Middle-Class America.* Chicago: University of Illinois Press, 1978.

Clough, Arthur Hugh. *The Correspondence of Arthur Clough.* Edited by Frederick L. Mulhauser. 2 vols. Oxford: Clarendon Press, 1957.

Cmiel, Kenneth. *Democratic Eloquence: The Fight Over Popular Speech in Nineteenth-Century America.* New York: William Morrow, 1990.

Cobden, Richard. "Letters of Richard Cobden to Charles Sumner, 1862–1865." *American Historical Review* 2 (Jan. 1897): 306–19.

Collini, Stefan. *Public Moralists: Political Thought and Intellectual Life in Great Britain.* Oxford: Clarendon Press, 1991.

Compton, John W. "The Emancipation of the American Mind: J. S. Mill on the Civil War." *Review of Politics* 70 (2008): 221–44.

Conlin, Michael F. "The Smithsonian Abolition Lecture Controversy: The Clash of Antislavery Politics with American Science in Wartime Washington." *Civil War History* 46, no. 4 (December 2000): 301–23.

Conway, Moncure. *Autobiography, Memories and Experiences.* 2 vols. Boston: Houghton, Mifflin, 1904.

———. "Thomas Carlyle." *Harper's New Monthly Magazine,* May 1881, 908–9.

Coulling, Sidney. "Matthew Arnold and the American South." In *Matthew Arnold in His Time and Ours: Centenary Essays,* edited by Clinton Machann and Forrest D. Burt, 40–56. Charlottesville: University Press of Virginia, 1988.

Cox, Samuel S. *"Puritanism in Politics": Speech of Hon. S. S. Cox, of Ohio, Democratic Union Association, January 13, 1863.* New York: Van Evrie, Horton, 1863.

Crawford, Martin. "The Anglo-American Crisis of the Early 1860's: A Framework for Revision." *South Atlantic Quarterly* 82 (1983): 406–23.

———. *The Anglo-American Crisis of the Mid-Nineteenth Century.* Athens: University of Georgia Press, 1987.

———. "Introduction." In William Howard Russell, *William Howard Russell's Civil War: Private Diaries and Letters, 1861–1862*, edited by Martin Crawford, xvii–xlviii. Athens: University of Georgia Press, 1992.
Croce, Paul. "Calming the Screaming Eagle: William James and His Circle Fight Their Civil War Battles." *New England Quarterly* 76, no. 1 (March 2003): 5–37.
Curry, Leonard P. *Blueprint for Modern America: Nonmilitary Legislation of the First Civil War Congress*. Nashville, TN: Vanderbilt University Press, 1968.
Curtis, George William. "The American Doctrine of Liberty." In *Orations and Addresses of George William Curtis*, vol. 1, edited by Charles Eliot Norton, 95–122. New York: Harper & Brothers, 1894.
Dall, Caroline Healy. *Daughter of Boston: The Extraordinary Diary of a Nineteenth-Century Woman*. Edited by Helen R. Deese. Boston: Beacon Press, 2005.
Darwin, Charles. *The Correspondence of Charles Darwin*. Edited by Frederick Burkhardt et al. 30 vols. Cambridge: Cambridge University Press, 1985–2023.
Dearinger, David Bernard, ed. *Paintings and Sculpture in the Collection of the National Academy of Design*. New York: Hudson Hills, 2004.
Deese, Helen R. "Caroline Healy Dall and the American Social Science Movement." In *Toward a Female Genealogy of Transcendentalism*, edited by Jana L. Argersinger and Phyllis Cole, 303–24. Athens: University of Georgia Press, 2014.
Delano, Sterling. *Brook Farm: The Dark Side of Utopia*. Cambridge, MA: Harvard University Press, 2004.
Desmond, Adrian, and James Moore. *Darwin's Sacred Cause: How a Hatred of Slavery Shaped Darwin's Views on Human Evolution*. Boston: Houghton Mifflin Harcourt, 2009.
Dewbury, Adam. "The American School and Scientific Racism in Early American Anthropology." *Histories of Anthropology Annual*, no. 3 (2007): 121–47.
Dickens, Charles. *American Notes for General Circulation*. 2 vols. London: Chapman and Hall, 1842.
———. *The Letters of Charles Dickens*. Edited by Graham Storey et al. 10 vols. Oxford: Clarendon Press, 1998.
Dickey, Christopher. *Our Man in Charleston: Britain's Secret Agent in the Civil War*. New York: Crown, 2015.
Dolan, Neal. *Emerson's Liberalism*. Madison: University of Wisconsin Press, 2009.
Donald, David Herbert. *Charles Sumner*. 2 vols. 1930. Reprint, New York: Da Capo, 1996.
———. *Lincoln*. New York: Simon & Schuster, 1995.
Douglass, Frederick. *Frederick Douglass: Selected Speeches and Writings*. Edited by Philip S. Foner and Yuval Taylor. Chicago: Chicago Review Press, 2000.
Dowling, Linda. *Charles Eliot Norton: The Art of Reform in Nineteenth-Century America*. Durham: University of New Hampshire Press, 2007.

Doyle, Don H. *The Cause of All Nations: An International History of the American Civil War*. New York: Basic Books, 2015.
Drabble, Margaret, and Jenny Stringer, eds. *The Concise Oxford Companion to English Literature*. Oxford: Oxford University Press, 1987.
Duberman, Martin. *James Russell Lowell*. Boston: Houghton Mifflin, 1966.
Dubrulle, Hugh. *Ambivalent Nation: How Great Britain Imagined the American Civil War*. Baton Rouge: Louisiana State University Press, 2018.
Dufour, Charles L. *Nine Men in Gray*. Lincoln: University of Nebraska Press, 1993.
Duncan, Russell. *Where Death and Glory Meet: Colonel Robert Gould Shaw and the 54th Massachusetts Infantry*. Athens: University of Georgia Press, 1999.
Dunn, Waldo Hillary. *James Anthony Froude, A Biography*. 2 vols. Oxford: Clarendon Press, 1963.
Emerson, Edward Waldo. *The Early Years of the Saturday Club, 1855–1870*. Boston: Houghton Mifflin, 1918.
Emerson, Ellen Tucker. *The Letters of Ellen Tucker Emerson*. Edited by Edith E. Gregg. 2 vols. Kent, OH: Kent State University Press, 1982.
Emerson, Ralph Waldo. *The Collected Works of Ralph Waldo Emerson*. Edited by Alfred R. Ferguson et al. 10 vols. Cambridge, MA: Harvard University Press, 1971–2013.
———. *The Complete Works of Ralph Waldo Emerson*. Edited by Edward Waldo Emerson. 12 vols. Boston: Houghton, Mifflin, 1903–4.
———. *The Early Lectures of Ralph Waldo Emerson*. Edited by Stephen E. Whicher, Robert E. Spiller, and Wallace E. Williams. 3 vols. Cambridge, MA: Harvard University Press, 1961.
———. *Emerson's Antislavery Writings*. Edited by Len Gougeon and Joel Myerson. New Haven, CT: Yale University Press, 1995.
———. *The Journals and Miscellaneous Notebooks of Ralph Waldo Emerson*. Edited by William H. Gilman et al. 16 vols. Cambridge, MA: Harvard University Press, 1960–82.
———. *The Later Lectures of Ralph Waldo Emerson: 1843–1871*. Edited by Ronald Bosco and Joel Myerson. 2 vols. Athens: University of Georgia Press, 2001.
———. *The Letters of Ralph Waldo Emerson*. Edited by Ralph L. Rusk and Eleanor M. Tilton. 10 vols. New York: Columbia University Press, 1939, 1990–95.
———. *The Topical Notebooks of Ralph Waldo Emerson*. Edited by Ralph H. Orth et al. 3 vols. Columbia: University of Missouri Press, 1990.
———. *Uncollected Lectures by Ralph Waldo Emerson*. Edited by Clarence Gohdes Jr. New York: William Edwin Rudge, 1932.
Emerson, Ralph Waldo, and Thomas Carlyle. *The Correspondence of Emerson and Carlyle*. Edited by Joseph Slater. New York: Columbia University Press, 1964.
Emerson, Ralph Waldo, and Arthur Hugh Clough. *Emerson-Clough Letters*. Edited by Howard Lowry and Ralph Rusk. 1934. Reprint, Hamden, CT: Archon Books, 1968.

Emilio, Luis F. *A Brave Black Regiment: The History of the Fifty-Fourth Regiment of Massachusetts Volunteer Infantry, 1863–1865.* 1894. Reprint, New York: De Capo Press, 1995.

Ewan, Christopher. "The Emancipation Proclamation and British Public Opinion." *Historian* 67, no. 1 (Spring 2005): 1–19.

Exman, Eugene. *The House of Harper: One Hundred and Fifty Years of Publishing.* New York: Harper & Row, 1963.

Fahs, Alice. *The Imagined Civil War: Popular Literature of the North & South, 1861–1865.* Chapel Hill: University of North Carolina Press, 2001.

Faulkner, Carla. *Lucretia Mott's Heresy: Abolition and Women's Rights in Nineteenth-Century America.* Philadelphia: University of Pennsylvania Press, 2011.

Ferguson, Niall. *Empire: The Rise and Demise of the British World and the Lessons for Global Power.* New York: Basic Books, 2002.

Ferguson, Robert A. *Law and Letters in American Culture.* Cambridge, MA: Harvard University Press, 1987.

Fergusson, Sir James. *"The Personal Observations of a Man of Intelligence": Notes of a Tour in North America in 1861.* 1861. Reprint, Lambertville, NJ: True Bill Press, 2009.

Fields, James T. *Yesterday with Authors.* Boston: James R. Osgood, 1872.

Fish, Carl Russell. "The Rise of the Common Man, 1830–1850." In *A History of American Life,* edited by Mark C. Carnes, 517–615. New York: Scribner, 1996.

Fladeland, Betty. *Men and Brothers: Anglo-American Antislavery Cooperation.* Urbana: University of Illinois Press, 1972.

———. "'Our Cause Being One and the Same': Abolitionists and Chartism." In *Slavery and British Society, 1776–1846,* edited by James Walvin, 69–99. Baton Rouge: Louisiana State University Press, 1982.

Foner, Eric. *The Fiery Trial: Abraham Lincoln and American Slavery.* New York: W. W. Norton, 2010.

———. *Free Soil, Free Labor, Free Men: The Ideology of the Republican Party Before the Civil War.* New York: Oxford University Press, 1970.

———. *Reconstruction: America's Unfinished Revolution, 1863–1877.* Updated ed. New York: Harper Perennial, 2014.

———. *The Story of American Freedom.* New York: W. W. Norton, 1998.

Foner, Philip S. *British Labor and the American Civil War.* New York: Holmes & Meier, 1981.

Forbes, John Murray. *Letters and Recollections of John Murray Forbes.* Edited by Sarah Forbes Hughes. 2 vols. Boston: Houghton, Mifflin, 1899.

Ford, Worthington C. "Goldwin Smith's Visit to the United States in 1864." *Proceedings of the Massachusetts Historical Society,* Oct. 1910, 3–13.

Foreman, Amanda. *A World on Fire: Britain's Crucial Role in the American Civil War.* New York: Random House, 2010.

Fredrickson, George M. *The Black Image in the White Mind: The Debate on Afro-American Character and Destiny, 1817-1914*. Hanover, NH: Wesleyan University Press, 1971.

———. *The Inner Civil War: Northern Intellectuals and the Crisis of the Union*. New York: Harper & Row, 1965.

Fuller, Randall. *The Book That Changed America: How Darwin's Theory of Evolution Ignited a Nation*. New York: Viking, 2017.

———. *How the Civil War Transformed American Literature*. New York: Oxford University Press, 2011.

Gallagher, Gary W. *The Union War*. Cambridge, MA: Harvard University Press, 2011.

Garrison Family. *William Lloyd Garrison, 1805-1879: The Story of His Life Told by His Children*. 4 vols. Boston: Houghton, Mifflin, 1894.

Garrison, Wendell P. "William James Stillman." *The Century* 46 (Sept. 1893): 656-59.

Gaskell, Elizabeth. *The Letters of Mrs. Gaskell*. Edited by J. A. V. Chapple and Arthur Pollard. Cambridge, MA: Harvard University Press, 1967.

Gates, Henry Louis, Jr., and David Bindman, eds. *The Image of the Black in Western Art*. Vol. 4, *From the American Revolution to World War I*. New ed. Edited by Hugh Honour. Cambridge: Belknap Press of Harvard University Press, 2012.

Gohdes, Clarence. *American Literature in Nineteenth-Century England*. Carbondale: Southern Illinois University Press, 1944.

Goodman, Susan. *Republic of Words: The Atlantic Monthly and Its Writers, 1857-1925*. Hanover, NH: University Press of New England, 2011.

Goodwin, Doris Kearns. *Team of Rivals: The Political Genius of Abraham Lincoln*. New York: Simon & Schuster, 2005.

Gougeon, Len. *Emerson & Eros: The Making of a Cultural Hero*. Albany: State University of New York Press, 2007.

———. "Emerson and Great Britain: Challenging the Limits of Liberty." In *Liberty Ltd.: Civil Rights, Civil Liberties, and Literature*, edited by Brook Thomas, vol. 22 of *REAL—Yearbook of Research in English and American Literature*, 179-213. Berlin: Gunter Narr Verlag Tubingen, 2006.

———. "Emerson and Race." In *Ralph Waldo Emerson in Context*, edited by Wesley Mott, 196-203. London: Cambridge University Press, 2013.

———. "Emerson and the Woman Question: The Evolution of His Thought." *New England Quarterly* 71, no. 4 (Dec. 1998): 570-92.

———. "Emerson, Carlyle and the Civil War." *New England Quarterly* 62, no. 3 (1989): 403-23.

———. "Emerson, Great Britain, and the International Struggle for the Rights of the Workingman." In *A Power to Translate the World: New Essays on Emerson and International Culture*, edited by Ricardo Miguel Alfonso and David LaRocca, 83-96. Lebanon, NH: Dartmouth College Press, 2015.

———. "The Legacy of Reform: Emersonian Idealism and the Civil Rights Movement." In *Emerson Bicentennial Essays*, edited by Ronald A. Bosco and Joel Myerson, 183-210. Boston: Massachusetts Historical Society, 2006.

———. *Virtue's Hero: Emerson, Antislavery, and Reform*. 1990. Reprint, Athens: University of Georgia Press, 2010.

———. "Whitman and *The Commonwealth*." *Walt Whitman Quarterly Review* 9, no. 4 (Spring 1992): 208–11.

Grant, Alfred. *The American War and the British Press*. Jefferson, NC: McFarland, 2000.

Grant, Susan-Mary. *North Over South: Northern Nationalism and American Identity in the Antebellum Era*. Lawrence: University Press of Kansas, 2000.

Gray, Asa. *The Letters of Asa Gray*. Edited by Jane Loring Gray. Boston: Houghton, Mifflin, 1894.

Guberman, J. *The Life of John Lothrop Motley*. The Hague: Martinus Nijhoff, 1973.

Gura, Philip F. *American Transcendentalism, A History*. New York: Hill and Wang, 2007.

Hale, Edward Everett. *James Russell Lowell and His Friends*. Boston: Houghton, Mifflin, 1898.

Hall, Christopher Newman. *The American War: A Lecture to Working Men, Delivered in London, October 20, 1862*. Boston: American Tract Society, 1863.

Hall, Donald. "The Victorian Connection." In *Victorian America*, edited by Daniel Walker Howe, 81–103. Philadelphia: University of Pennsylvania Press, 1976.

Hamand, Wendy. "'No Voice from England': Mrs. Stowe, Mr. Lincoln, and the British in the Civil War." *New England Quarterly* 61, no. 1 (Mar. 1988): 3–21.

Handlin, Lillian. *George Bancroft: The Intellectual as Democrat*. New York: Harper & Row, 1984.

Hanlon, Christopher. "The Transatlantic History of Civil War Literature." In Hutchinson, *History of American Civil War Literature*, 33–47.

Hartz, Louis. *The Necessity of Choice: Nineteenth-Century Political Thought*. New Brunswick, NJ: Transaction Publishers, 1990.

Harvard Memorial Biographies. Edited by Thomas Wentworth Higginson. 2 vols. Cambridge, MA: Sever and Francis, 1866.

Harvie, Christopher. *The Lights of Liberalism: University Liberals and the Challenge of Democracy, 1860–86*. London: Allen Lane, 1976.

Hawthorne, Nathaniel. *The Centenary Edition of the Works of Nathaniel Hawthorne*. Edited by William Charvat et al. 23 vols. Columbus: Ohio State University Press, 1963–75.

Heidler, David, and Jeanne Heidler, eds. *Encyclopedia of the American Civil War: A Political, Social, and Military History*. New York: W. W. Norton, 2000.

Herzberg, Max J. *The Reader's Encyclopedia of American Literature*. New York: Thomas Y. Cromwell, 1962.

Hess, Earl J. *Liberty, Virtue, and Progress: Northerners and Their War for the Union*. New York: Fordham University Press, 1997.

Higginson, Thomas Wentworth. *The Complete Civil War Journal and Selected Letters of Thomas Wentworth Higginson*. Edited by Christopher Looby. Chicago: University of Chicago Press, 2000.

———. *The Magnificent Activist: The Writings of Thomas Wentworth Higginson (1823–1911)*. Edited by Howard N. Meyer. New York: Da Capo, 2000.

Holley, I. B., Jr. "Schooling the Freedmen's Children." *New England Quarterly* 74, no. 3 (September 2001): 478–94.

Holmes, Oliver Wendell. *John Lothrop Motley, A Memoir*. Boston: Houghton, Mifflin, 1889.

———. *Life and Letters of Oliver Wendell Holmes*. Edited by John T. Morse Jr. 2 vols. Cambridge, MA: Riverside, 1896.

———. *The Writings of Oliver Wendell Holmes*. 13 vols. Cambridge, MA: Riverside, 1891.

Holzer, Harold. *Lincoln and the Power of the Press*. New York: Simon & Schuster, 2014.

Holzer, Harold, and Mark E. Neely Jr. *Mine Eyes Have Seen the Glory: The Civil War in Art*. New York: Orion, 1993.

Hopkins, A. B. *Elizabeth Gaskell, Her Life and Work*. 1952. Reprint, New York: Octagon Books, 1971.

Horton, James Oliver. "Defending the Manhood of the Race: The Crisis of Citizenship in Black Boston at Midcentury." In Blatt, Brown, and Yacovone, *Hope & Glory*, 7–20.

Houghton, Walter E. *The Wellesley Index to Victorian Periodicals, 1824–1900*. 5 vols. Toronto: University of Toronto Press, 1966.

Howe, M. A. De Wolfe. *The Atlantic Monthly and Its Makers*. Boston: Atlantic Monthly Press, 1909.

———. *The Life and Letters of George Bancroft, Two Volumes in One*. 1908. Reprint, New York: Da Capo, 1970.

Hughes, Michael F. "'The Personal Observations of a Man of Intelligence': Sir James Fergusson's Visit to North America, 1861." *Civil War History* 45, no. 3 (1999): 238–47.

Hunt, James. "Introductory Address on the Study of Anthropology." *Anthropological Review* 1 (May 1863): 1–20.

———. "On the Negro's Place in Nature." In *Memoirs Read Before the Anthropological Society of London*, vol. 1, 1863–4, 1–60. Reprinted in *The Index*, Nov. 26 and Dec. 3, 1863.

Huntington, Samuel P. *The Clash of Civilizations and the Remaking of World Order*. New York: Simon & Schuster, 2011.

Hutchinson, Coleman, ed. *A History of American Civil War Literature*. Cambridge: Cambridge University Press, 2015.

James, Henry, Jr. *William Wetmore Story and His Friend: From Letters, Diaries, and Recollections, in Two Volumes*. 1903. Reprint, New York: Grove Press, 1957.

James, Henry, Sr. *The Social Significance of Our Institutions: An Oration Delivered by Request to the Citizens of Newport, R.I.* Boston: Ticknor and Fields, 1861.

Jenkins, Brian. *Britain and the War for the Union.* 2 vols. Montreal: McGill-Queen's University Press, 1980.
Johnson, Rossiter, ed. *The Twentieth Century Biographical Dictionary of Notable Americans.* 10 vols. Boston: Biographical Society, 1904.
Jones, Howard. *Blue & Gray Diplomacy: A History of Union and Confederate Foreign Relations.* Chapel Hill: University of North Carolina Press, 2010.
———. "History and Mythology: The Crisis Over British Intervention in the Civil War." In May, *Atlantic Rim,* 29–67.
———. *Union in Peril: The Crisis Over British Intervention in the Civil War.* Lincoln: University of Nebraska Press, 1992.
Kaplan, Fred. *Dickens: A Biography.* New York: William Morrow, 1988.
Kaplan, Lawrence S. "The Brahmin as Diplomat in Nineteenth Century America: Everett, Bancroft, Motley, Lowell." *Civil War History* 19 (1973): 5–28.
Kaplan, Sidney. "The Black Soldier of the Civil War in Literature and Art." In *American Studies in Black and White, Selected Essays,* edited by Allan D. Austin, 101–23. Amherst: University of Massachusetts Press, 1991.
Karcher, Carolyn L. *The First Woman in the Republic: A Cultural Biography of Lydia Maria Child.* Durham, NC: Duke University Press, 1994.
Kaser, David. *Books and Libraries in Camp and Battle: The Civil War Experience.* Westport, CT: Greenwood Press, 1984.
Kazar, John D. "The Canadian View of the Confederate Raid on Saint Albans." *Vermont History: The Proceedings of the Vermont Historical Society,* Jan. 1965, 255–73.
Kenny, Anthony. *Arthur Hugh Clough: A Poet's Life.* New York: Bloomsbury Academic, 2005.
Kinser, Brent E. *The American Civil War in the Shaping of British Democracy.* Surrey, UK: Ashgate, 2011.
Kirke, Edmund. "Our Visit to Richmond." *Atlantic Monthly,* Sept. 1864, 372–83.
———. "A Suppressed Chapter of History." *Atlantic Monthly,* Apr. 1887, 435–48.
Klinefelter, Lee M. "Lampooned in London." *Civil War Times Illustrated* 20 (1982): 28–35.
Koch, Daniel. *Ralph Waldo Emerson in Europe: Class, Race and Revolution in the Making of an American Thinker.* New York: I. B. Tauris, 2012.
Kytle, Ethan J. *Romantic Reformers and the Antislavery Struggle in the Civil War Era.* Cambridge: Cambridge University Press, 2014.
Law, Henry William, and Irene Law. *The Book of the Beresford Hopes.* London: Heath Cranton, 1925.
Lawson, Melinda. *Patriot Fires: Forging a New American Nationalism in the Civil War North.* Lawrence: University Press of Kansas, 2002.
Leeman, William P. "George Bancroft's Civil War: Slavery, Abraham Lincoln, and the Course of History." *New England Quarterly* 81, no. 3 (Sept. 2008): 462–88.

Lewis, David Levering. *W. E. B. Du Bois: Biography of a Race, 1868–1919*. New York: Henry Holt, 1993.
Lincoln, Abraham. *The Collected Works of Abraham Lincoln*. Edited by Roy P. Basler. 10 vols. New Brunswick, NJ: Rutgers University Press, 1953.
Lindsey, David. *"Sunset" Cox, Irrepressible Democrat*. Detroit: Wayne State University Press, 1959.
Logan, Kevin J. "The Bee-Hive Newspaper and British Working Class Attitudes Toward the American Civil War." *Civil War History* 22, no. 4 (1976): 337–48.
Longfellow, Henry Wadsworth. *The Letters of Henry Wadsworth Longfellow*. Edited by Andrew Hilen. 6 vols. Cambridge, MA: Belknap Press of Harvard University Press, 1972.
Looby, Christopher. "Introduction." In *The Complete Civil War Journal and Selected Letters of Thomas Wentworth Higginson*, edited by Christopher Looby, 1–32. Chicago: University of Chicago Press, 2000.
Lorimer, Douglas A. *Colour, Class, and the Victorians: English Attitudes to the Negro in the Mid-Nineteenth Century*. New York: Holmes & Meier, 1978.
———. "The Role of Anti-Slavery Sentiment in English Reactions to the American Civil War." *Historical Journal* 19, no. 2 (June 1976): 405–20.
Lowance, Mason, ed. *A House Divided: The Antebellum Slavery Debates in America, 1776–1865*. Princeton, NJ: Princeton University Press, 2003.
Lowell, James Russell. *Democracy and Other Papers*. Boston: Houghton, Mifflin, 1898.
———. *The Letters of James Russell Lowell*. Edited by Charles Eliot Norton. 2 vols. New York: Harper & Brothers, 1894.
———. *My Study Windows*. Boston: Houghton, Mifflin, 1883.
———. *The Writings of James Russell Lowell in Prose and Poetry*. Vol. 5, *Political Essays*. Boston: Houghton, Mifflin, 1890.
Lynn, Kenneth. *William Dean Howells, An American Life*. New York: Harcourt Brace Jovanovich, 1970.
Macmillan, Alexander. *Letters of Alexander Macmillan*. Edited by George A. Macmillan. Printed for private circulation, 1908.
Mahin, Dean B. *One War at a Time: The International Dimensions of the American Civil War*. Washington, DC: Brassey's, 1999.
Maitland, Frederic William. *The Life and Letters of Leslie Stephen*. New York: G. P. Putnam's Sons, 1906.
Malachuk, Daniel. *Perfection, the State, and Victorian Liberalism*. New York: Palgrave Macmillan, 2005.
Marchand, Leslie A. *The Athenaeum: A Mirror of Victorian Culture*. 1941. Reprint, New York: Octagon Books, 1971.
Martineau, Harriet. *Harriet Martineau in the London Daily News: Selected Contributions, 1852–1866*. Edited by Elisabeth Sanders Arbuckle. New York: Garland, 1994.

———. *Harriet Martineau's Autobiography*. Edited by Maria Weston Chapman. 2 vols. Boston: James R. Osgood, 1877.

———. *Writings on Slavery and the American Civil War*. Edited by Deborah Anna Logan. DeKalb: Northern Illinois Press, 2002.

Masur, Louis P., ed. *"The Real War Will Never Get into the Books": Selections from Writers During the Civil War*. New York: Oxford University Press, 1993.

May, Robert E., ed. *The Union, the Confederacy, and the Atlantic Rim*. West Lafayette, IN: Purdue University Press, 1995.

McFarland, Philip. *Hawthorne in Concord*. New York: Grove Press, 2005.

McFeely, William S. "Foreword." In Shaw, *Blue-Eyed Child of Fortune*, xi–xix.

———. *Frederick Douglass*. New York: W. W. Norton, 1991.

McPherson, James M. *The Abolitionist Legacy: From Reconstruction to the NAACP*. Princeton, NJ: Princeton University Press, 1975.

———. *Battle Cry of Freedom: The Civil War Era*. New York: Ballantine, 1988.

———. *Drawn with the Sword: Reflections on the American Civil War*. New York: Oxford University Press, 1996.

———. *Embattled Rebel: Jefferson Davis as Commander in Chief*. New York: Penguin Press, 2014.

———. *For Cause and Comrades: Why Men Fought in the Civil War*. New York: Oxford University Press, 1997.

———. *The Negro's Civil War: How American Blacks Felt and Acted During the War for the Union*. New York: Vintage Civil War Library, 1965.

———. *The Struggle for Equality*. Princeton, NJ: Princeton University Press, 1964.

———. *Tried by War: Abraham Lincoln as Commander in Chief*. New York: Penguin, 2008.

———. *War on the Waters: The Union and Confederate Navies, 1861–1865*. Chapel Hill: University of North Carolina Press, 2012.

———. *The War That Forged a Nation: Why the Civil War Still Matters*. New York: Oxford University Press, 2015.

———. "'The Whole Family of Man': Lincoln and the Last Best Hope Abroad." In May, *Atlantic Rim*, 131–58.

Mellow, James R. *Nathaniel Hawthorne in His Times*. Boston: Houghton Mifflin, 1980.

Menand, Louis. *The Metaphysical Club: A Story of Ideas in America*. New York: Farrar, Straus and Giroux, 2001.

Meyer, Howard N. "Introduction." In Higginson, *Magnificent Activist*, 1–39.

———. "Moorfield Storey and the Fourteenth Amendment." *Crisis*, Nov. 1979, 300–301.

Michie, Michael. "'On Behalf of the Right': Archibald Alison, Political Journalism, and *Blackwood's* Conservative Response to Reform, 1830–1870." In *Print Culture and the Blackwood Tradition, 1805–1930*, edited by David Finkelstein, 119–45. Toronto: University of Toronto Press, 2006.

Mill, John Stuart. *Collected Works of John Stuart Mill*. Edited by Francis Mineka et al. 33 vols. Toronto: University of Toronto Press, 1963–91.

Milne, Gordon. *George William Curtis & the Genteel Tradition*. Bloomington: Indiana University Press, 1956.

Motley, John Lothrop. *Causes of the Civil War in America*. London: George Manwaring, 1861.

———. *The Correspondence of John Lothrop Motley*. Edited by George William Curtis. 2 vols. New York: Harper & Brothers, 1889.

Mott, Frank Luther. *American Journalism, A History: 1690–1960*. New York: Macmillan, 1962.

———. *A History of American Magazines*. 5 vols. Cambridge, MA: Harvard University Press, 1938–68.

Mott, Wesley, ed. *The American Renaissance in New England*. 3rd series. Boston: Gale Group, 2001.

———. *Biographical Dictionary of Transcendentalism*. Westport, CT: Greenwood Press, 1996.

———. *Encyclopedia of Transcendentalism*. Westport, CT: Greenwood Press, 1996.

Munson, J. E. B. "A Book Forming a Foreign Policy: *Uncle Tom* in England." *Civil War Times Illustrated*, no. 21 (September 1983): 40–43.

Murray, Nicholas. *A Life of Matthew Arnold*. New York: St. Martin's Press, 1996.

Myers, Philip E. *Caution and Cooperation: The American Civil War in British-American Relations*. Kent, OH: Kent State University Press, 2008.

Myerson, Joel. "George William Curtis." In *Dictionary of Literary Biography*, vol. 243, *The American Renaissance in New England*, edited by Joel Myerson, 30–31. Detroit: Gale Research, 1978.

Neely, Mark E., Jr. *Boundaries of American Political Culture in the Civil War Era*. Chapel Hill: University of North Carolina, 2005.

———. *The Union Divided: Party Conflict in the Civil War North*. Cambridge, MA: Harvard University Press, 2002.

Neely, Mark E., Jr., and Harold Holzer. *The Union Image: Popular Prints of the Civil War North*. Chapel Hill: University of North Carolina Press, 2000.

Nevins, Allan. *The War for the Union*. 4 vols. New York: Charles Scribner's Sons, 1959.

Norton, Charles Eliot. *Letters of Charles Eliot Norton, with Biographical Comment*. Edited by Sara Norton and M. A. DeWolfe Howe. 2 vols. Boston: Houghton Mifflin, 1913.

———. *The Soldier of the Good Cause*. Boston: American Unitarian Association, 1861.

Oates, Stephen B. *With Malice Toward None: A Life of Abraham Lincoln*. New York: Harper Perennial, 1977.

O'Connor, Peter. *American Sectionalism in the British Mind, 1832–1863*. Baton Rouge: Louisiana State University Press, 2017.

O'Connor, Thomas H. *Civil War Boston: Home Front and Battlefield*. Boston: Northeastern University Press, 1997.

Ormond, Leonée. *Alfred Tennyson: A Literary Life*. New York: St. Martin's Press, 1993.

Packer, Barbara. "Ralph Waldo Emerson." In *Columbia Literary History of the United States*, edited by Emory Elliott, 364–78. New York: Columbia University Press, 1988.

———. *The Transcendentalists*. Athens: University of Georgia Press, 2007.

Park, T. Peter. "John Stuart Mill, Thomas Carlyle, and the U.S. Civil War." *Historian* 54, no. 1 (Autumn 1991): 93–106.

Pickard, Samuel T. *The Life and Letters of John Greenleaf Whittier*. Boston: Houghton, Mifflin, 1907.

Poirier, Richard. *The Renewal of Literature: Emersonian Reflections*. New Haven, CT: Yale University Press, 1987.

Raleigh, John Henry. *Matthew Arnold and American Culture*. Berkeley: University of California Press, 1961.

Read, Donald. *Cobden and Bright: A Victorian Political Partnership*. New York: St. Martin's Press, 1968.

Redkey, Edwin S. "Brave Black Volunteers: A Profile of the Fifty-Fourth Massachusetts Regiment." In Blatt, Brown, and Yacovone, *Hope & Glory*, 21–34.

Richards, Eliza. *Battle Lines: Poetry and Mass Media in the U.S. Civil War*. Philadelphia: University of Pennsylvania Press, 2019.

Richardson, Robert. *Emerson: The Mind on Fire*. Berkeley: University of California Press, 1995.

———. *William James: In the Maelstrom of American Modernism, A Biography*. Boston: Houghton Mifflin, 2006.

Risley, Ford. *Civil War Journalism*. Denver, CO: Praeger, 2012.

Roberts, Andrew. *Salisbury: Victorian Titan*. London: Weidenfeld & Nicolson, 1999.

Robinson, William S. *Warrington Pen Portraits: A Collection of Personal and Political Reminiscences from 1848 to 1876 from the Writings of William S. Robinson*. Boston: Mrs. W. S. Robinson, 1877.

Rose, Anne C. *Victorian America and the Civil War*. New York: Cambridge University Press, 1992.

Rossi, William. "Emerson, Nature, and Natural Science." In *A Historical Guide to Ralph Waldo Emerson*, edited by Joel Myerson, 101–50. New York: Oxford University Press, 2000.

Rusk, Ralph L. *The Life of Ralph Waldo Emerson*. New York: Columbia University Press, 1949.

Ruskin, John. *The Works of John Ruskin*. Edited by Edward T. Cook and Alexander Wedderburn. 39 vols. London: George Allen, 1903–12.

Ruskin, John, and Charles Eliot Norton. *The Correspondence of John Ruskin and Charles Eliot Norton*. Edited by John Lewis Bradley and Ian Ousby. Cambridge: Cambridge University Press, 1987.

Russell, William Howard. "Recollections of the Civil War by Sir William Howard Russell, LL.D., Special Correspondent of 'The Times' (London)." Pts. 1–5. *North American Review*, February 1898, 234–49; March 1898, 362–73; April 1898, 391–502; May 1898, 618–750; June 1898, 740–50.

———. *William Howard Russell's Civil War: Private Diaries and Letters, 1861–1862*. Edited by Martin Crawford. Athens: University of Georgia Press, 1992.

Said, Edward W. *Culture and Imperialism*. New York: Vintage Books, 1993.

Sanborn, Francis B. *Recollections of Seventy Years*. 2 vols. Boston: Richard G. Badger, Gorham Press, 1909.

———. *Sixty Years of Concord, 1855–1915: Life, People, Institutions and Transcendental Philosophy in Massachusetts—with Memories of Emerson, Thoreau, Alcott, Channing and Others*. Edited by Kenneth Walter Cameron. Hartford, CT: Transcendental Books, 1976.

Scharnhorst, Gary. "From Soldier to Saint: Robert Gould Shaw and the Rhetoric of Racial Justice." *Civil War History* 34, no. 4 (1988): 308–22.

Scudder, Horace E. *James Russell Lowell, A Biography*. 2 vols. Boston: Houghton, Mifflin, 1901.

Sebrell, Thomas E., III. *Persuading John Bull: Union and Confederate Propaganda in Britain, 1860–1865*. Lanham, MD: Lexington Books, 2014.

Sedgwick, Ellery. *The Atlantic Monthly, 1857–1909: Yankee Humanism at High Tide and Ebb*. Amherst: University of Massachusetts Press, 1994.

Shapiro, Samuel. *Richard Henry Dana, Jr., 1815–1882*. East Lansing: Michigan State University Press, 1961.

Shaw, Robert Gould. *Blue-Eyed Child of Fortune: The Civil War Letters of Col. Robert Gould Shaw*. Edited by Russell Duncan. New York: Avon Books, 1992.

———. "The Letters of Robert Gould Show at the Mass. Historical Society." *Proceedings of the Massachusetts Historical Society* 102 (1991): 127–47.

Siddali, Silvana R. *From Property to Person: Slavery and the Confiscation Acts, 1861–1862*. Baton Rouge: Louisiana State University Press, 2005.

Sideman, Belle Becker, and Lillian Friedman, eds. *Europe Looks at the Civil War*. New York: Orion, 1960.

Sievens, Mary Beth, and Nina Silber. *Yankee Correspondence: Civil War Letters Between New England Soldiers and the Home Front*. Charlottesville: University Press of Virginia, 1996.

Silbey, Joel H. *A Respectable Minority: The Democratic Party in the Civil War Era, 1860–1868*. New York: W. W. Norton, 1977.

Sinha, Manisha. *The Slave's Cause: A History of Abolition*. New Haven, CT: Yale University Press, 2016.

Smith, Goldwin. "The Letters of Goldwin Smith." *Proceedings of the Massachusetts Historical Society* 49 (Oct. 1915): 106–60.

———. *Reminiscences*. Edited by Arnold Haultain. New York: Macmillan, 1910.

Smith, Jean Edward. *Grant*. New York: Simon & Schuster, 2001.

Spence, James. *The American Union: Its Effect on National Character and Policy, with an Inquiry into Secession as a Constitutional Right and the Causes of the Disruption*. London: Richard Bentley, 1861.
Stafford, John. *The Literary Criticism of "Young America": A Study in the Relationship of Politics and Literature, 1837–1850*. Berkeley: University of California Press, 1952.
Stapelton, Julia. "Introduction." In *Liberalism, Democracy, and the State in Britain: Five Essays, 1862–1891*, edited by Julia Stapelton, 7–40. Bristol, UK: Thoemmes Press, 1997.
Steele, David. *Lord Salisbury: A Political Biography*. London: University College London Press, 1999.
Stephen, Leslie. *The "Times" on the American War: A Historical Study*. 1865. Reprint, New York: William Abbatt, 1915.
Storey, Moorefield. "Harvard in the Sixties." *Harvard Graduates' Magazine* 5 (Mar. 1897): 327–38.
Story, William Wetmore. *The American Question*. London: George Manwaring, 1862.
Straka, Gerald M. "The Spirit of Carlyle in the Old South." *Historian*, no. 20 (1957): 39–57.
Sumner, Charles, *A Memorial of Abraham Lincoln, Late President of the United States*. Boston: Printed at the Order of the City Council, 1865.
———. *The Selected Letters of Charles Sumner*. Edited by Beverly Wilson Palmer. 7 vols. Boston: Northeastern University Press, 1990.
Taylor, Andrew. *Thinking America: New England Intellectuals and the Varieties of American Identity*. Durham: University of New Hampshire Press, 2010.
Tebbel, John, and Mary Ellen Zuckerman. *The Magazine in America*. New York: Oxford University Press, 1991.
Tennyson, Alfred Lord. *The Letters of Alfred Lord Tennyson*. Edited by Cecil Lang and Edgar Shammon Jr. 2 vols. Cambridge, MA: Harvard University Press, 1987.
Thomas, John L. *The Liberator: William Lloyd Garrison, A Biography*. Boston: Little, Brown, 1963.
Thrall, Miriam M. H. *Rebellious Fraser's: Nol Yorke's Magazine in the Days of Maginn, Thackeray, and Carlyle*. New York: Columbia University Press, 1934.
Tilton, Eleanor. *Amiable Autocrat: A Biography of Dr. Oliver Wendell Holmes*. New York: Henry Schuman, 1947.
Trollope, Anthony. *Four Lectures*. Edited by Morris L. Parrish. London: Constable, 1938.
———. *The Letters of Anthony Trollope*. Edited by John Hall. 2 vols. Stanford, CA: Stanford University Press, 1993.
———. *North America*. 2 vols. 1862. Reprint, New York: St. Martin's Press, 1986.
Tryon, Warren S. *Parnassus Corner: A Life of James T. Fields, Publisher to the Victorians*. Boston: Houghton Mifflin, 1963.

Turner, James. *The Liberal Education of Charles Eliot Norton*. Baltimore: Johns Hopkins University Press, 1999.

Vanderbilt, Kermit. *Charles Eliot Norton: Apostle of Culture in a Democracy*. Cambridge, MA: Belknap Press of Harvard University Press, 1959.

von Frank, Albert J. *An Emerson Chronology*. 2 vols. 2nd ed. Albuquerque, NM: Studio Non Troppo, 2016.

———. "Mrs. Brackett's Verdict: Magic and Means in Transcendental Antislavery Work." In *Transient and Permanent: The Transcendental Movement and Its Contexts*, edited by Charles Capper and Conrad Wright, 385–407. Boston: Massachusetts Historical Society, 1999.

———. *The Trials of Anthony Burns: Freedom and Slavery in Emerson's Boston*. Cambridge, MA: Harvard University Press, 1998.

Wallace, David H. *John Rogers: The People's Sculptor*. Middletown, CT: Wesleyan University Press, 1967.

Wallace, Elisabeth. *Goldwin Smith, Victorian Liberal*. Toronto: University of Toronto Press, 1957.

Waller, John O. "Charles Dickens and the American Civil War." *Studies in Philology* 57 (July 1960): 535–48.

———. "Thomas Carlyle and His Nutshell Iliad." *Bulletin of the New York Public Library* 69 (1965): 17–30.

Walls, Laura Dassow. *Emerson's Life in Science: The Culture of Truth*. Ithaca, NY: Cornell University Press, 2003.

Ward, Andrew. *The Slaves' War: The Civil War in the Words of Former Slaves*. Boston: Houghton Mifflin, 2008.

Watson, Ritchie Devon. *Normans and Saxons: Southern Race Mythology and the Intellectual History of the American Civil War*. Baton Rouge: Louisiana State University Press, 2008.

Waugh, Joan. "'It Was a Sacrifice We Owed': The Shaw Family and the Fifty-Fourth Massachusetts Regiment." In Blatt, Brown, and Yacovone, *Hope & Glory*, 52–75.

Weinberg, Adelaide. *John Elliot Cairnes and the American Civil War: A Study in Anglo-American Relations*. London: Kingswood, 1970.

White, Jonathan W. *A House Built by Slaves: African American Visitors to the White House*. New York: Rowman & Littlefield, 2022.

White, Ronald C., Jr. *The Eloquent President: A Portrait of Lincoln Through His Words*. New York: Random House, 2005.

Williams, David. *I Freed Myself: African American Self-Emancipation in the Civil War Era*. New York: Cambridge University Press, 2014.

Wills, Garry. *Lincoln at Gettysburg: The Words That Remade America*. New York: Simon & Schuster, 1992.

Wilson, Keith. "'The Beginning of the End': An Analysis of British Newspaper Coverage of Lincoln's Emancipation Proclamation." *Journalism History* 34, no. 4 (Winter 2009): 230–39.

Wineapple, Brenda. *Hawthorne: A Life*. New York: Random House, 2004.
Winger, Stewart. *Lincoln, Religion, and Romantic Cultural Politics*. Dekalb: Northern Illinois University Press, 2003.
Wirzbicki, Peter. *Fighting for the Higher Law: Black and White Transcendentalism Against Slavery*. Philadelphia: University of Pennsylvania Press, 2021.
Woldman, Albert A. *Lincoln and the Russians*. Westport, CT: Greenwood Press, 1952.
Worth, George. "*Macmillan's Magazine* and the American Civil War: A Reconsideration." *Victorian Periodical Review* 26, no. 4 (Winter 1993): 193–98.
Yacovone, Donald. *Samuel Joseph May and the Dilemma of the Liberal Persuasion, 1797–1871*. Philadelphia: Temple University Press, 1991.
Young, Robert J. C. *Colonial Desire: Hybridity in Theory, Culture and Race*. New York: Routledge, 1995.
Zakaras, Alex. *Individuality and Mass Democracy: Mill, Emerson, and the Burdens of Citizenship*. Oxford: Oxford University Press, 2009.
Zink, David D. *Leslie Stephen*. New York: Twayne, 1972.
Zukerman, Mary Ellen, and John Tebbel. *The Magazine in America*. New York: Oxford University Press, 1991.

Index

Adams, Charles Francis Jr., 75, 140, 266
Adams, Charles Francis Sr., American Minister to Great Britain, 5, 57, 78, 90, 91, 104, 110, 111, 112, 120, 130, 158, 185, 238, 256, 281
Adams, Henry, 5, 75, 110, 111, 137, 169, 177, 179, 213, 264, 349n62
Admiralty (Great Britain), 104, 296
Admiralty Law (Great Britain), 76
Agassiz, Louis, 172–73, 175, 344n54; and Saturday Club, 172
Albright, George Washington, 156, 339n22
Alcott, Bronson, 11, 17, 141, 180
Alcott, Louisa May, 348n47
American Anti-Imperialist League, 311
American Anti-Slavery Society, 11
American Bar Association, 311
American School (scientific racism), 173
Andrew, John A., Governor of Massachusetts, 38, 91–92, 93, 155, 168, 182, 183, 205, 215, 327n6, 343n17, 344n54
Anglo-African (New York), 135, 182
Anthony, Susan B., 198
Anthropological Review, 174

Anthropological Society of London, 172, 173, 174, 313
Anti-Slavery Advocate (London), 189
Army of the Potomac, 56, 67, 160, 195, 211, 212, 270, 291, 325n22
Arnold, Matthew, 7, 32, 42, 78, 157, 193, 269, 322n27; and Chartists, 12; and Emerson, 12–13, 267, 316n11
Atlantic Monthly, 2, 4, 13, 30, 38, 48, 90, 111, 121, 125, 126, 197, 205, 223, 237, 284, 321n4, 348n47, 360n26; and the South, 69; and the London *Times*, 71–72; and Emerson, 92, 150; and Darwin, 174; and African Americans, 46, 47, 182, 202–203, 323n47; and emancipation, 213; and England, 127, 219–20, 226, 241, 267, 289, 290, 348n54; and Lincoln, 274–75

Bagehot, Walter, 17, 18, 20, 26, 28
Bancroft, George, 100, 101, 206, 330n22, 331n8, 347n44
Barrett, J. R., 33, 321n32
Bates, Edward, U.S. Attorney General, 91
Bull Run, Battle of, 53–57, 61–73 passim, 325n22
Battle of Cold Harbor, 272

381

Battle of Seven Pines, 119
Battle of the Wilderness, 268, 270, 272
Beauregard, General Pierre G. T., 296
Beecher, Henry Ward, 238, 239, 262, 330n23, 352n45
Benjamin, Judah, Confederate Secretary of State, 145
Beresford-Hope, Alexander James, 20, 25, 35, 117, 139, 171, 186, 260, 271, 324n57
Bigelow, John, 186
Birmingham Daily Post (England), 70
Blackwood's Edinburgh Magazine, 48, 65, 70, 82, 83, 87, 101, 103, 144, 160, 203, 242, 324n54, 324n56
Booth, John Wilkes, 303
Border Ruffians, 13
Boston Advertiser, 39, 189
Boston Daily Evening Transcript, 166, 190
Boston Pilot, 205, 259
Boston Post, 142, 167
Boston Semi-Weekly Advertiser, 166
Boston Statesman and Weekly Post, 167, 214
Boston Weekly Transcript, 150, 169, 225, 341n18
Bourke, Robert, 64, 65, 82, 326n46, 328n44
Bragg, General Braxton, 233, 252
Brahmin, New England, 31, 168, 316n24
Bright, Henry, 62, 191, 242, 262
Bright, John, MP, 16, 55, 62, 89, 97, 105, 154, 190, 209, 211, 221, 229; and *Trent* affair, 77–78, 79
British Emancipation Society, 154
British Quarterly Review, 27, 66, 264
Brook Farm, 14, 29, 126
Brougham, Lord Henry Peter, 245, 288
Brown, Henry "Box," 175

Brown, John, 13, 33, 46, 69, 76, 167, 205
Brown, William Wells, 39
Browning, Elizabeth Barrett, 56, 136, 336n68
Browning, Robert, 56–57, 78, 81
Buchanan, James, 22, 34
Buford, Colonel John, 212
Bunch, Robert, 63–65
Bureau of Colored Troops, 200. *See also* Colored Troops
Burns, Anthony, 75, 205
Burnside, General Ambrose, 159, 160, 195, 265
Butler, General Benjamin: and contrabands, 47–48, 60
Buxton, Thomas, 262, 353n27

Cabot, James Elliot, 54
Cairnes, John Elliott, 58–59, 60, 96, 115, 126, 131, 139, 146, 154, 158, 160, 182, 187, 204, 210, 258, 259, 289, 290, 330n32
Calthrop, Reverend Samuel Robert, 243
Canada, 77, 261, 273, 297, 357n30
Carlyle, Thomas, 7, 15, 40, 96, 244; and the United States, 96, 143, 193, 194, 206–7, 221–22; 349n61; and Emerson, 207, 222, 223–24, 288, 316n6; and "Ilias (Americana) in Nuce," 221–22; and Confederacy, 222; and Lincoln, 318n55; and racism, 207, 221, 329n4; and democracy, 221
Cecil, Robert, Lord, MP, 4
Central Association for Recognition of the Confederate States, 227
Chicago Tribune, 171
Channing, William Ellery, 168
Channing, William Henry, 168, 341n14

Chartists, 5, 11, 12, 14, 314n3, 316n7
Chase, Salmon P., Secretary of the Treasury, 91
Chesney, Captain Charles, 247, 352n17
Chesnut, Mary, 68, 99, 298
Chicago Tribune, 171
Child, David, 17
Child, Lydia Maria, 2, 17, 39, 89, 103, 203, 262, 265, 284, 285, 310
Christian Examiner, 243, 323n67
Civil Rights Act, 309
Clough, Arthur Hugh, 18, 24, 28, 29
Cobb, General Howell, 294
Cobden, Richard, MP, 55, 62, 79, 105, 111, 119, 125, 144, 170, 236, 296, 317n33; and British Emancipation Society; and Emancipation Proclamation, 179; and Laird rams, 194, 198; and war with England, 296
Colored Troops, United States, 4, 161, 165, 201; 205, 237, 247, 263, 265, 266, 281, 297, 301, 302, 349n5; Massachusetts Regiments (54th & 55th). *See also* Fort Wagner, Battle of; Port Hudson, Battle of; Olustee, Florida; Petersburg, Virginia
Colyer, Vincent, 201
Commonwealth (Boston), 125, 194, 206, 207, 222, 237, 243, 262, 289, 306, 356n34; read in Great Britain, 142, 290
Confederacy, (South): and Great Britain, (England), 99, 155, 209, 239, 263, 269, 281, 288, 294, 297, 303, 319n2; British criticism of, 25-28; British support of, 28, 35, 41, 51, 57-59, 63-67, 70, 82, 83, 87, 91, 94, 125, 147, 174, 186, 209, 235, 239, 263, 269, 281; and British authors, 7, 222, 243; constitution of, 23; decline of, 125, 282, 287, 296, 301, 302, 334n20; negotiations with the North, 273, 274-75; and conscription of slaves, 224, 282, 286; and European recognition, 70, 96, 131; slavery as corner stone of, 2, 100; propaganda in Great Britain, 115-17; *see also* Hotze, Henry
Confiscation Act, 60, 61, 121, 123, 326n35
Conscription Act, 120, 215
Contraband Relief Association, 135
Courier (Boston), 69, 109, 142, 149, 167
Conway, Moncure, 54, 143, 194-95, 211, 206-207, 324n4
Copperheads, 112, 185, 211, 215, 236, 260, 262, 266, 277; allied with British conservatives, 291; and racism, 275, 284
Cox, Samuel S., 168, 191, 340n8, 340n11, 340n12; "Puritanism in Politics," 167-69
Cranch, Christopher Pearce, 29
Crittenden-Johnson Resolution, 51
Cromer, Lord (Evelyn Baring), 342n48
Crummell, Alexander, 11
Curtis, Rev. Ashley, 66
Curtis, George W., 2, 14-15, 54, 56, 89, 111, 128, 137, 160, 186, 235, 237, 242, 243, 262, 320n16; and Transcendentalism, 29, 126; and Great Britain, 40, 60, 72-73, 76, 102, 124, 232, 252; and Lincoln, 51, 103, 156, 237; and equal rights, 123-24, 255; and Saturday Club, 14, 125; and emancipation, 141, 150; and American art, 201-203. See also *Harper's (Illustrated) Weekly*; and "The American Doctrine of Liberty," 123-24

Daily Advertiser (Boston), 85, 105, 143, 190, 245, 352n13
Daily Courier (Charleston, SC), 163
Daily Covenant (Boston), 189
Daily Democratic Union (Peoria, IL), 33, 112, 321n32, 333n66
Daily News (London), 17, 52, 81, 97, 115, 151, 157, 171, 187, 235, 286
Daily Picayune (New Orleans), 68, 148
Dall, Caroline Healy, 181, 260, 271, 290, 300, 303, 305, 310, 355n12; and Transcendentalists, 180
Dana, Richard Henry Jr., 2, 13, 14, 44, 219, 317n24, 319n65; and *Trent* affair, 75, 76, 78
Darwin, Charles, 43, 78, 172, 174, 175, 342n31, 342n46
Davis, Bancroft, 44, 71–73
Davis, Jefferson, 23, 51–2, 64, 163, 176, 274, 287 ; and arming slaves, 305 ; admired by British conservatives, 52
De Mortie, Louise, 135
de Vere, Aubrey, 4, 184, 286, 296
Delane, John, 55, 72, 157, 231, 293
democracy, liberal, 1, 3–6, 8, 31, 155, 158, 232, 253, 287, 305; opposed by British conservatives, 12–13, 18, 20, 29, 35, 49–50, 64, 96, 125, 276. *See also* working class, British
Democratic Union Association, 167
Derby, Lord, leader of British Conservative party, 83, 116
Dicey, Edward, 81, 107, 113, 128, 138, 154, 207, 211, 272
Dickens, Charles, 7, 45, 78, 102, 215, 329n51
Douglass, Frederick, 61–62, 122, 135, 166, 175, 183, 189, 255, 306, 312, 315n3; and Lincoln, 259–60, 277, 280, 299–300

Douglass, Sergeant-Major Lewis (son), 204, 218
Douglass, Charles (son), 204
Du Bois, W. E. B., 311–12
Duchess of Argyll, 90, 131, 185
Dwight, John Sullivan, 30

Early, General Jubal, 276
Economist, 17, 18, 26, 28, 35, 46, 57, 95, 96, 191
Edinburgh Review, 17, 27, 81, 86, 96, 144, 147, 210, 254, 261
Edinburgh Ladies Emancipation Society, 80
Ellis, George, 71
Emancipation League, 306
Emancipation Proclamation, 2, 166, 168–69, 171, 197, 237, 248–49, 284, 340n10; and racism, 188; in Great Britain, 5, 171, 190, 239; and enlistment of Blacks, 181, 227–78
Emerson, Ralph Waldo, 3, 13, 14, 24, 58, 62, 69, 91, 109, 120, 123, 124, 132, 166, 168–69, 171, 172, 180, 183, 186, 233, 237, 248–49, 253, 254, 255, 284, 310, 312, 340n10; and emancipation, 2, 109, 149; as central figure, 91, 132; and Carlyle, 207, 222, 223–24, 321n33; and Transcendentalism, 11, 13, 19, 31, 32, 37, 168, 126, 168–69, 311, 317n45, 323n45, 330n22; and Great Britain (England), 12, 125, 133, 154, 288; and Chartists, 12, 315n3, 316n7; and Matthew Arnold, 12–13, 267, 288, 316n11; and Saturday Club, 14, 62, 80, 106, 153, 155, 160, 19; and Lincoln, 92, 131, 150, 250, 260, 273, 274, 285, 304, 318n54, 33n22; and equal rights, 37, 159, 267, 290, 341n15;

and liberalism, 289; and *Atlantic Monthly*, 13
Emerson, Edward, 284
Emerson, Ellen, 133
Evening Post (New York), 103
Evening Traveller (Boston), 39, 189
Everett, Edward, 28, 249, 251
Examiner, Christian, 243, 327n67
Examiner (London), 27, 209, 224
Examiner (Richmond), 294, 298

Farragut, Admiral David G., 110, 279, 282, 284
Fawcett, Henry, 199, 207, 215, 219, 225, 229, 234, 290
Fergusson, James, MP, 64, 65, 83, 326n46, 328n47
Fields, James T., 91, 132, 155, 166, 226, 242, 275, 344n54; editor, proprietor *Atlantic Monthly*, 127; and Saturday Club, 92; and Hawthorne, 127–28
Forbes, John Murray, 100, 106, 183, 226, 232, 329n20; and Saturday Club, 91, 161; and *New England Loyal Publication Society*, 186–87
Foreign Enlistment Act (British), 165, 185, 350n12
Forrest, General Nathan Bedford, 265, 354n44
Forster, William, MP, 32, 79, 154, 157–58, 210
Fort Donelson, 99
Fort Henry, 99
Fort Pillow Massacre, 265–66, 276, 354n44
Fort Sumter, 216, 254; and start of Civil War, 4, 25, 33, 35, 37, 38
Fort Wagner, Battle of, 216, 218, 219, 225, 237, 247, 286, 348n47
Founding Fathers, 2, 123, 213, 250

Fraser's Magazine, 4, 15, 16, 22, 47, 85, 90, 93, 96, 101, 110, 128, 151, 179, 181, 191, 192, 194, 223, 235, 355n34
free states, 18, 27, 37, 43, 60, 234, 319n65
Freedmen's Bureau, 301
Froude, James Anthony15, 90, 110
Fugitive Aid Society (Black), 135
Fugitive Slave Law, 17, 19, 23, 249, 322n12, 327n65, 330n27
Fuller, Hiram, 128, 179, 180, 335n34
Fuller, Margaret, 14, 180

Gallenga, Antonio, 251
Gandhi, Mahatma, 313
Garnet, Henry Highland, 11, 341n14
Garrison, Francis Jackson, 89
Garrison, William Lloyd, 11, 166, 205, 219, 319n63, 330n23, 339n35
Gaskell, Elizabeth, 45, 46, 135, 151, 215, 219, 304, 323n41, 332n41
Gaskell, Margaret Emily (Meta), 135–36, 151–52
Gay, Sydney Howard, 276
Gilmore, General Quincy Adams, 216
Gilmore, James, (*a.k.a.*, Edmund Kirke), 274, 275
Gladstone, William E., 133, 143, 144, 147, 148, 186, 288
Gliddon, George, 173
Godwin, Parke, 304, 358n64
Gordon, Captain Nathaniel, 100, 108
Grant, General Ulysses S., 99, 185, 200, 205, 211, 212, 252, 262, 265, 270, 272, 276, 282, 284, 287, 291, 301, 302; and Colored Troops, 349n5
Gray, Asa, 43, 78, 172, 174
Gray, Henry Peters, 201
Great Britain (England): and social hierarchy, 3, 42, 229; and global

Great Britain (England) *(continued)*
race war, 4, 68, 111, 125, 143; and imperial culture 6, 31, 203, 223, 242, 288; and white supremacy, 175, 229, 253, 256, 294, 342n48; and conservative opposition to emancipation, 14, 47, 85–87, 111, 138–39, 143, 145, 150–51, 181, 219, 224, 239, 253, 258, 271, 281–82, 285, 294–95, 329n4; and liberal support of emancipation, 60, 145, 150–51, 161, 163, 175, 187, 257, 262. *See also* Sepoys; working class, British; democracy, liberal; Confederacy; Canada

Greeley, Horace, 14, 68, 248, 262, 273; and "The Prayer of Twenty Million," 134

Gregory, William H., MP, 64–66, 82, 83, 99, 116, 130, 147, 186, 263

Halleck, General Henry, 200
Harcourt, William Vernon ("Historicus"), 155, 252
Hardee, General William J., 296
Harper's (Illustrated) Weekly, 4, 44, 51, 62, 63, 79, 103, 114, 120, 122, 125, 142, 176, 187, 190, 195, 231, 284, 295, 302, 351n42; and George W. Curtis, 14, 40, 51, 54, 60, 72–73, 89, 123, 137, 150, 201, 217, 237, 317n27; and John Stuart Mill, 95; and Black soldiers, 205–206, 265–66, 275–76; and Great Britain (England), 72–73, 232, 252, 271, 283–84, 322n16, 326n42
Harper's New Monthly Magazine, 14, 102, 125, 202, 243
Hawthorne, Nathaniel, 62, 191, 219–20, 232, 348n54; and Saturday Club, 14; and "Chiefly About War Matters," 126–28; and *Our Old Home*, 241–42
Herald (London), 116, 117
Higginson, Thomas Wentworth, 47, 189, 310, 316n22; and *Atlantic Monthly*, 13, 46, 189, 323n47; and Emerson, 46, 68, 125, 154, 323n45; and Black troops, 47, 182, 190, 289, 323n47
Holmes, Oliver Wendell, Sr., 2, 15, 30, 32, 70, 96–97, 132, 135, 154, 166, 205, 210, 216, 219, 224, 244–46, 266–67, 285; and *Atlantic Monthly*, 13; and Saturday Club, 14, and slavery, 135
Holmes, Oliver Wendell Jr., 70, 140
Hood, General John Bell, 279, 293
Hooker, Joseph "Fighting Joe," 195, 211–12
Hopkins, John Baker, 116
Houghton, Lord (Monckton Milnes), 154, 330n32
Hotze, Henry, 115–17, 145, 173–74, 177, 214, 271
Howe, Dr. Samuel Gridley, 76, 142
Howe, Estes, 76, 100
Hughes, Thomas, 57–58, 146, 154, 207, 210, 230–31, 251, 256, 260–61, 280–81, 290, 330n32
Hunt, James, 174, 175, 313, 342n40
Huntington, Samuel, 9
Huxley, Thomas, 174–75

Independent (New York), 44, 67, 203, 238
Index, 180, 214, 227, 264, 288
Indian Rebellion, 86. *See also* Sepoy Mutiny; Sepoys

Jackson, Fanny, 182
James, Henry Sr., 50, 89, 204, 217

James, Garth Wilkinson, 204
James, Robinson, 204
Jaquess, Colonel James, 274
Johnson, Andrew, 285, 292, 306, 307
Johnson, Eastman, 346n16

Keckley, Elizabeth, 135
Keyes, John S., 80
Kingsley, Rev. Charles, 7, 207, 222, 243, 244
Kirke, Edmund (*a.k.a.*, James Gilmore), 274, 275

Laird, John, 186
Laird rams (warships), 185-86, 194, 209, 213, 220-21, 241, 246, 252, 264
Langston, John Mercer, 310
Lawley, Francis, 138, 157, 235, 282, 292-93
Lawrence, Amos Abbot, 78, 142, 226, 319n65
Lee, General Robert E., 119, 139-40, 160, 165, 195, 211, 225, 252, 253, 282, 291, 301-302, 337n12; and Gettysburg, 212; and conscription of slaves, 294, 305; and surrender at Appomattox, 301
Lewis, George Cornewall, 148, 155
Liberator, 166, 200, 222, 255, 258, 280, 281
Lincoln, Abraham: and British conservatives, 20-22, 51, 71, 87, 88, 103, 128, 146, 214, 229, 251, 285, 291, 305, 318n57; and British liberals, 46, 52, 60, 82, 91, 108, 113, 143, 211, 229, 274, 280-81, 282, 304; and Northern liberals, 70, 88, 92, 93, 103, 106, 108, 127, 130, 150, 153, 155, 160-61, 250-51, 260, 280, 284, 317n27, 343n24; and *Trent* affair, 79, 80; and emancipation, 102-103, 111, 131, 134-35, 137, 159, 277, 299; and Blacks, 122, 135, 218, 228, 255, 258-59, 280, 299-301, 318n55, 333n63, 349n5; and British working class, 52, 133, 145, 158, 162-63, 176, 177, 187, 239, 281, 305, 341n21; and Northern conservatives, 169, 236, 252, 259-60, 262, 270, 284, 340n10; and "Reply to Horace Greeley"; and Gettysburg Address, 248, 25-51; and peace talks, 273-75; assassination, 303-04. *See also* Emerson, Ralph Waldo; Hawthorne, Nathaniel; Preliminary Emancipation Proclamation; Emancipation Proclamation; *Times* (London)
Lincoln's Legal Loyal League, 157
Lindsay, William, 116, 130, 186, 209, 263, 271, 281
Living Age, 8, 117
London Confederate States Aid Association, 263
London Ethnological Society, 172
London Star, 152
Longfellow, Henry Wadsworth, 2, 76, 124, 132; and *Atlantic Monthly,* 13; and Saturday Club, 44, 160, 166, 203; and Great Britain (England), 44, 85, 136; and slavery, 100, 109, 166; and Massachusetts 54th, 203
Longstreet, General James, 233
Louisville Democrat, 106
Lowell, James Russell, 2
Lyons, Richard Pemell, British Minister to the United States, 28, 77, 91, 108, 144, 154, 155, 185, 318n57, 322n19
Ludlow, John, 146

Lytton, Sir Edward Bulwer, 244, 351n10

Mackay, Charles, 138, 157, 181, 189, 234–35, 292, 293, 296–97, 357n5
Macmillan's Magazine, 57, 85, 107, 113, 129, 139, 211, 219, 221, 235, 269
Magna Carta, 3
Manchester Southern Club, 227, 263
Manchester Union and Emancipation Society, 281
Martin, Reverend Sella, 256, 353n6
Martineau, Harriet, 17, 18, 63, 67, 81, 146, 261, 254–55, 317n36, 319n63
Martineau, James, 201, 223, 345n13
Mason, James, 75, 130, 213, 263, 298, 324n55
Massachusetts 54th, 182, 189, 203, 224, 226, 237, 255
Maurice, Frederick Denison, 221–22
May, Samuel Joseph, 11, 17, 23, 32, 70, 80, 101, 209, 263, 290, 344n54
McClellan, General George B., 70, 104, 131, 284; and Antietam, 139; relieved of command, 159; nominated for president, 277; supported by British, 283
McDowell, General Irvin, 53
Meade, General George, 252; commands Union army, 212; at Gettysburg, 212, 215
Meade, John, 104, 163
Meade, Rebecca, 61, 104, 163
Milnes, Monckton (Lord Houghton), 154, 330n32
Miles, William Porcher, 63–65, 82, 83, 108
Militia Act, 121, 125
Mill, John Stuart, 5, 56, 58, 115, 138, 145, 150, 154, 170, 190, 199, 234, 289, 294, 304; "Letter of John Stuart Mill," 187; "The Contest in America," 94–95; and African Americans, 225, 258, 353n8, 96
Mobile Register, 117
monogenism, 172
Moran, Benjamin, 130
Morning Post, 116, 139
Morning Star (London), 146
Morrill Tariff, 34–35, 40, 102
Morris, Mowbray, 55, 138, 157, 235, 292, 293, 297, 305
Morris, Robert, ESQ., 39
Morton, George, 173
Morton, Governor Oliver P., 149
Motley, John Lothrop, 13, 21, 30, 52, 54, 81, 96, 100, 106, 110, 154; and Saturday Club, 15; and slavery, 32; American Minister to Austria, 15, 120 134, 135, 246, 317n28; "Causes of the American Civil War," 43, 46; and Great Britain, (England), 45–46, 90, 97, 110; and John Stuart Mill, 139, 145, 150, 170

National Academy of Design, Thirty-Eighth Annual, 201, 346n15
National Association for the Advancement of Colored People (NAACP), 311–12
National Intelligencer, 233
National Review, 43, 115
Nativist, 128
Nell, William C., 11, 135, 159, 311, 339n35
New England Fourier Society, 358n64
New England Loyal Publication Society, 135, 159, 206, 222, 232, 235, 311, 339n35
New England Workingman's Convention, 330n27

New York Herald, 261, 292, 325n22
New York Journal of Commerce, 103, 105–106
New York Tribune, 14, 103, 134, 161, 184, 194, 274
New York Weekly Caucasian, 69, 101, 188
New York World, 251
Newman, Cardinal, 194
Newman, Francis H., 194, 200, 206, 256, 296
Niagara Movement, 311
Norton, Charles Eliot, 14, 28–30, 45, 54, 56, 76, 81, 97, 103, 106, 111, 128, 237, 262, 264–65, 283, 286, 292, 296, 302, 305, 320n16, 350n30; and Emerson, 24, 124, 154, 288, 310; cultural conservative, 32; and Elizabeth Gaskell, 45, 56, 135, 151, 215, 304; and Robert Browning, 56; "Emancipation and the Constitution," 59–60, 62; "Soldier of the Good Cause," 66, 167; and John Ruskin, 55, 91, 136, 184, 192, 244; and the Saturday Club, 2, 124, 191, 280; and Lincoln, 131, 141, 153; and Union Club, 183–84; co-editor, *North American Review*, 235, 259. See also *New England Loyal Publication Society*
Nott, Josiah, 172–73

Olustee, Florida, 276, 285
Our American Cousin (play), 303
Owen, Robert Dale, 213

Palmerston, Lord
Parker Fraternity, 109, 150
Parker, Theodore, 32, 33, 56, 168; and Emerson, 321n33; and Lincoln, 330n22
Peace Democrats, 112, 142, 277

Peace Party, 153, 155, 214: and the British, 281
Peacock, Edward, 180–81, 260–61, 271, 289–90, 300, 301, 304
Pemberton, General John C., 212
Peninsula Campaign, 120, 130, 137
Petersburg, Virginia, 301, 163, 266, 276, 282
Philadelphia City Item, 103, 126–27, 332n24, 351n10
Phillips, Wendell, 168, 205, 219, 306; and Emerson, 262, 330n23; and Chartists, 315n3
Pilot (Boston), 205, 259, 260
Plunkett, Edward, 210
polygenism, 172–73
Port Hudson, Battle of, 236; as test of Colored Troops, 165, 205–206, 219, 237, 247, 285. See also Fort Wagner, Battle of; Olustee, Florida; Petersburg, Virginia
Port Royal experiment, 105–106, 248
Post (Liverpool), 190
Preliminary Emancipation Proclamation, 140–41, 152, 156, 326n35; attacked by British, 145; attacked by Northern conservatives, 149, 153
Punch, 144, 239
Putnam, Lewis, 188
Putnam, William Lowell, 70

Quarterly Review, 4, 27, 49, 55, 70, 71, 146, 191, 264, 293

racism, 6, 39, 189, 200, 224, 237, 239, 311, 342n40. See also scientific racism, white supremacy
Radical Liberals, (British), 16, 55, 317n33
Radical Republicans, 111, 155, 160, 255, 273

Remond, Charles Lenox, 122, 135
Richmond Dispatch, 104
Richmond Examiner, 294, 298
Robinson, William, 38
Robson, William, MP, 80
Rock, John, 135, 167, 295
Roebuck, John Arthur, MP, 147, 199–200, 209, 281
Rogers, John, 202, 203
Rosencrans, General William, 233
Round Hill School, 100
Ruskin, John, 7, 30, 55, 56, 90–91, 136, 184, 224, 343n28; as racist, 184; "Essays on Political Economy," 192–93; and Carlyle, 221, 222, 244, 336n68
Russell, Earl (Lord John), British Foreign Secretary, 41, 64, 104, 236, 313, 331n33; favors Confederacy, 147, 148, 322n19; and Laird rams, 231, 271
Russell, William Howard, 55, 63, 77, 110, 138, 325n22, 318n57

Said, Edward, 6, 7
Sandars, Thomas Collett, 16
Sargent, Epes, 194, 200, 206, 236, 296
Saturday Club, 2, 14, 15, 38, 50, 54, 62, 75, 80, 91, 100, 106, 111, 142, 153, 155, 160, 172, 195, 241, 255, 280, 316n22; and British, 44, 97, 132, 191; and *Trent* affair, 76; and Senator Charles Sumner, 80, 90; and Anthony Trollope, 115; and Emancipation, 131, 161, 166; and racism, 172; and William Wetmore Story, 201–202; and Massachusetts 54th, 203, 219; and Lincoln, 284; and *Atlantic Monthly*, 316n22, 321n4
Saturday Review, 8, 41, 50, 81, 90, 96, 154, 187, 190, 199, 211, 231, 244, 247, 258, 262, 273; Critical of South, 25, 26, 27, 319n2; supports Confederacy, 35, 67, 186, 234, 235, 264, 295, 322; and Lincoln, 51, 214, 300; critical of North, 67, 89, 133, 139, 238; and Confederate propaganda, 116, 117; and slavery, 171, 177, 179, 261; and racism of 203, 225, 254, 256, 272, 282, 285, 286, 293–94, 297; and Emerson, 29, 286, 320n19; and Lincoln, 51, 89, 154, 214, 300
scientific racism, 19, 116, 172, 317n44, 342n32; and American School, 173; in Great Britain, 175. *See also* racism, white supremacy
Seddon, James, 282
Sedgwick, Rep. Charles, 161
Sepoys, 4, 7, 86, 125, 143, 175, 224, 256, 286, 329n7. *See also* Indian Rebellion, Sepoy Mutiny
servile insurrection, 105, 111, 144, 145, 232
Seven Days' Battles, 119, 137
Seward, William H., Secretary of State, 65, 77, 79, 80, 120, 239, 270; and slavery, 110, 112, 108, 141; and Emerson, 91; and Emancipation Proclamation, 140; and Laird rams, 185, 229, 230
Seymour, Horatio, 143–44, 169, 236, 270, 337n36
Shaw, Francis, 126
Shaw, Robert Gould, 140; and Massachusetts 54th, 44, 182, 183, 189, 190, 204, 216–17, 219
Shaw, Sarah, 44, 56, 126, 131, 160, 182, 204, 215, 259
Sheridan, General Philip H., 262, 282, 284, 301
Sherman, General William Tecumseh, 262 276, 279, 280, 282, 284, 287, 291, 293, 295

Slidell, John, 155, 298; and *Trent* affair, 75, 76, 77, 79–80, 85, 90, 97
Smith, Goldwin, 96, 154, 267, 270, 282, 286–87, 302–303, 305, 330n32; and Blacks, 287; and antisemitism, 338n10
Somerset Club, 205
Southern Independence Association, 117, 227, 263, 269, 270, 271, 328n44
Southern Literary Messenger, 288
Spectator, 46, 48, 57, 77, 107, 147, 221, 230, 231, 235, 349n70; and Lincoln, 81, 228–29, 274, 318n57; and emancipation, 161
Spence, James, 83, 186, 219, 263, 328n51
Standard (London), 117
Stanley, Edward Lyulph, 260
Stanton, Edwin M., Secretary of War, 91, 161, 200
Stanton, Elizabeth Cady, 198
Stearns, George Luther, 306, 142
Stephen, Leslie, 207, 211, 215, 219, 225, 229, 234, 260, 313; and London *Times*, 292
Stephens, Alexander, Confederate Vice President, 1–2, 3, 23
Stevens, Thaddeus, 111
Stillman, William James, 30, 320n25
Stone, Lucy, 180
Storey, Moorfield, 311–12
Story, William Wetmore, 56–57, 78, 97, 99, 264–65; and "The American Question," 81; and Saturday Club, 81; and the Libyan Sybil, 201–202
Stowe, Harriet Beecher, 2, 68, 238; and British, 44–45; "Letter to Lord Shaftesbury," 58, 131, 262; and Emerson, 58; and the Libyan Sybil, 202

Strong, General George C., 216
Stuart, William, 144, 154
Sumner, Senator Charles, 15, 75, 76, 89, 106, 142, 148, 153, 161, 162, 168, 182, 233, 255, 311, 319n65, 341n18; and Saturday Club, 44, 62, 160; and British, 79, 179; and Lincoln, 162, 275; and Laird rams, 185, 194, 198; and John Rock, 295

Taylor, Mrs. Martin, 290
Tennyson, Alfred, Lord, 7, 40, 73, 195, 245, 345n66; and Confederacy, 288; and Emerson, 287, 288
Thackeray, William Makepeace, 7, 40, 89; and Confederacy, 243–44
Thompson, George, 256, 263
Thompson, John Reuben, 287–88
Thoreau, Henry David, 11, 14, 54, 68, 180
Times, (Chicago), 142, 251
Times (London), 5, 8, 40, 43, 231, 272; and democracy, 20; and Lincoln, 143, 153, 169, 179, 229, 251, 279, 283, 300, 304, 318n57; and the South, 22, 26, 35; supports Confederacy, 41, 157, 212, 270, 276, 296, 341n23; hostility toward North, 45, 71, 110, 147, 181, 216, 234, 287, 290, 292; and Bull Run, 56, 63; and slavery, 94, 101, 116, 170, 171, 177, 181; and racism, 6, 139, 151, 189, 203, 219, 239, 254, 258, 285–86, 300
Toussaint-Louverture, 124, 125
Transcendentalism, 11, 13, 14, 18–19, 29–38 *passim*, 46, 56, 123, 126, 168–69, 223, 310–111, 317n45, 320n19, 323n45, 324n4, 330n22, 340n12
Transcendentalists, Black, 11, 311

Trollope, Anthony, 62, 90; and Saturday Club, 115
Trowbridge, John T., 201
Truth, Sojourner, 122, 202, 280
Turner, Rev. Henry McNeal, 122
Turner, Nat, 47, 254

Union Club (Boston), 183
United States: as Model Republic, 55, 88, 128
United States Colored Troops (USCT), 4
USS Merrimack (*CSS Virginia*), 104, 105
USS Monitor, 104, 105, 245

Vallandigham, Clement, 169, 236, 237
Veronese, Paul, 184, 343n28
Vesey, Denmark, 46

Walker, Robert J., 256
War Democrats, 112, 142
Ward, Samuel G., 100, 186, 226, 232
Wasson, David, 197, 198, 345n1
Weekly Transcript (Boston), 166
Wayland, Francis, 226
Weld, Angelina Grimké, 198
Welles, Gideon, Secretary of the Navy, 91

West Indies, 3, 55, 86, 125, 147, 256
Westminster Review, 5, 151
Weston, Anne Warren, 67
Weston, Caroline, 80, 303
Whipple, Edwin Percy, 111, 224
Whittier, John Greenleaf, 2, 13, 109, 124, 244; and Saturday Club, 166
white supremacy, 3, 69, 165, 175. *See also* Great Britain (England); Confederacy
Wigham, Eliza, 80, 101
Wilberforce, William, 262, 353n27
Wilkes, Captain Charles, 75–76, 77, 97, 327n6
Women's Anti-Slavery Society, 353n19
Women's National Loyal League, 198
Woodward, George, 237
working class, American 120, 198, 330n27
working class, British, 52, 92, 145, 158, 191, 193, 223, 243, 256, 293, 304, 353n6; and emancipation, 162, 179, 236; and democracy, 12, 169–70, 253, 305; support the North, 158, 165, 172, 176, 177, 232, 238, 263, 270, 280, 303, 341n21. *See also* Abraham Lincoln

www.ingramcontent.com/pod-product-compliance
Lightning Source LLC
Chambersburg PA
CBHW020258240426
43673CB00039B/633